IMAGINING A WAY

IMAGINING A WAY

Exploring Reformed Practical Theology and Ethics

Edited by Clive Pearson

© 2017 Clive Pearson

First edition
Published by Westminster John Knox Press
Louisville, Kentucky

17 18 19 20 21 22 23 24 25 26—10 9 8 7 6 5 4 3 2 1

All rights reserved. No part of this book may be reproduced or transmitted in any form or by any means, electronic or mechanical, including photocopying, recording, or by any information storage or retrieval system, without permission in writing from the publisher. For information, address Westminster John Knox Press, 100 Witherspoon Street, Louisville, Kentucky 40202-1396. Or contact us online at www.wjkbooks.com.

Book design by Sharon Adams
Cover design by Marc Whitaker / MTWdesign.net

Library of Congress Cataloging-in-Publication Data

Names: Pearson, Clive, editor.
Title: Imagining a way : exploring reformed practical theology and ethics / Clive Pearson, editor.
Description: First edition. | Louisville, KY : Westminster John Knox Press, 2017. | Includes bibliographical references and index. |
Identifiers: LCCN 2017013698 (print) | LCCN 2017031024 (ebook) | ISBN 9781611648263 (ebk.) | ISBN 9780664262983 (pbk. : alk. paper)
Subjects: LCSH: Reformed Church—South Africa. | Reformed Church—Doctrines. | Christian ethics—South Africa. | Christian ethics—Reformed authors.
Classification: LCC BX9620 (ebook) | LCC BX9620 .I 43 2017 (print) | DDC 284/.20968—dc23
LC record available at https://lccn.loc.gov/2017013698

∞ The paper used in this publication meets the minimum requirements of the American National Standard for Information Sciences—Permanence of Paper for Printed Library Materials, ANSI Z39.48-1992.

Scripture quotations from the New Revised Standard Version of the Bible are copyright © 1989 by the Division of Christian Education of the National Council of the Churches of Christ in the U.S.A. and are used by permission.

Scripture quotations from the Revised Standard Version of the Bible are copyright © 1946, 1952, 1971, and 1973 by the Division of Christian Education of the National Council of the Churches of Christ in the U.S.A. and are used by permission.

The following chapters are published with permission:

Dirk Smit, "Could Being Reformed Have Made a Difference? On Practical Theology and Ethics in South Africa," *Essays on Being Reformed: Collected Essays 3* (Stellenbosch: African Sun MeDIA Stellenbosch, 2009), 259–74.

Piet Naudé, "The Ethical Challenge of Identity Formation and Cultural Justice in a Globalizing World," *Scriptura* 89 (2005), 536–49.

Cynthia Jarvis, "On Not Offering Psychological Banalities as God's Word: Reformed Perspectives on Pastoral Care," *The Power to Comprehend with All the Saints: The Formation and Practice of a Pastor Theologian,* ed. Wallace M. Alston and Cynthia Jarvis (Grand Rapids: Wm.B.Eerdmans Pub. Co., 2009), 255–71. Reprinted by permission of the publisher; all rights reserved.

Most Westminster John Knox Press books are available at special quantity discounts when purchased in bulk by corporations, organizations, and special-interest groups. For more information, please e-mail SpecialSales@wjkbooks.com.

Contents

Foreword   vii
   Michael Welker

Preface   ix
   William Storrar

WELCOMING

1. Imagining a Reformed Practical Theology and Ethics   3
   Clive Pearson

DEFINITIONS AND DIFFERENCES

2. Could Being Reformed Have Made A Difference? On Practical Theology and Ethics in South Africa   39
   Dirk Smit

3. Globalization and the Challenge of Cultural Justice   53
   Piet Naudé

4. Calvin's Theology: An Appraisal in Relation to the Indian Context   69
   Hmar Vanlalauva

EXEMPLARY PERSPECTIVES

5. Justice Healing   85
   Susan E. Davies

6. Beyers Naudé: Public Theologian?   99
   Denise M. Ackermann

7. Created as Neighbors: A Vision for Honoring Racial and Cultural Difference   111
   Nancy J. Ramsay

ETHICAL EXERCISES

8. The Vocation of the Reformed Ethicist in the Present South African Society — 129
   Etienne de Villiers

9. "In the Beginning . . .": Implications of the Reformed Doctrine of Creation for Social Ethics in a Global Era — 145
   Max Stackhouse

10. Christian Ethical Distinctiveness, the Common Good, and Moral Formation — 161
    Geoff Thompson

11. The Reformed Church and the Environmental Crises — 175
    Jong-Hyuk Kim

12. Reformed Resources for Practical Theology: The Christian Life and Consumer Capitalism — 191
    Cameron Murchison

13. Human Dignity and Human Cloning: Perspectives from the Reformed Tradition — 201
    Kang Phee Seng

REFORMING MINISTRIES

14. Renewal of the *Imago Dei*: Hope for the Depleted Self — 213
    Cornelius Plantinga Jr.

15. Preaching in the Age of the Holy Spirit — 223
    Jana Childers

16. The Aesthetic Profile of Reformed Liturgy — 235
    Ralph Kunz

17. On Not Offering Psychological Banalities as God's Word: A Reformed Perspective on Pastoral Care — 247
    Cynthia Jarvis

18. Temples of the Spirit: Reforming the Reformed Congregation in Europe — 261
    William Storrar

IMAGINARY ENERGIES

19. Practicing a Reformed Faith in a Land Down Under — 277
    Clive Pearson

Notes — 291

Contributors — 343

Index — 345

Foreword

In the middle of the 1990s David Willis, former Charles Hodge Professor of Systematic Theology at Princeton Theological Seminary, and I became aware of the fact that leading systematic theologians at important divinity schools of the United States expanded their ecumenical and interreligious profile by a decidedly Roman Catholic theological "vision" and/or "perspective."[1] This prompted us to ask thirty colleagues from ten different countries for their specific ideas about a future Reformed theology with an ecumenical profile.[2] The resulting publication, both in English and German, achieved a powerful resonance, yet it also generated some complaints because of the dominance of systematic theology as well as of the Anglo-American and the German-speaking parts of the world.

Around 1998 Wallace Alston, director of the Center of Theological Inquiry (CTI) in Princeton, and I pondered how these shortcomings could be compensated. We planned a series of three consultations, not only focusing on historical and systematic theological topics, but also involving biblical scholars and scholars in the areas of practical theology and ethics. Under the title *Reformed Theology: Identity and Ecumenicity* one consultation was held in Heidelberg, Germany, and two more took place in Stellenbosch, South Africa.

About eighty colleagues were involved, not only from Austria, England, Germany, Scotland, Switzerland, and the USA, but also from Africa, Australia, China, Hungary, India, Romania, and South Korea. Sadly, only two of the consultations could at that time be documented and published before Wallace Alston retired as director.[3]

It was the perseverance of the current director of the CTI, William Storrar, and of the Australian colleague Clive Pearson, visiting scholar at the CTI in 2008, that brought the work of the third consultation in this project to the fore again. Clive Pearson collected the manuscripts and encouraged the former participants to revise their original contributions "in light of the intervening years." He also wrote an encompassing introduction that reflected on the complete discourse "toward the future of Reformed theology" in the last twenty years. I am very grateful that this CTI initiative thus comes to fruition.

Michael Welker
Heidelberg, February 2017

Preface

It is highly appropriate that this volume should be published on the 500th anniversary of the Reformation in 2017. The international team of scholars who have contributed their essays in practical theology and ethics stand in a Reformed tradition that accepts the need for reform today at the bidding of the same "Christ clothed in the Scriptures" who inspired Calvin, and countless women and men before and after him.[1] It is a diverse tradition. As Calvin wrote to a congregation seeking his advice, they must not make "an idol of me, and a Jerusalem of Geneva."

Imagining a Way expresses this distinctive Reformed ethos in its multiple ways of thinking about our century's ecclesial and social challenges in very different contexts around the globe. In commending it to a wide readership in and beyond the Reformed tradition, I thank those who helped to bring these essays to birth and now to a wider public.

First, I record the authors' gratitude to Kathi Morley. With her gift for hospitality, Kathi made the international arrangements for the Stellenbosch consultation, where the essayists first presented papers.

Second, I thank my predecessor Wallace Alston for his leadership in embarking on a series of international theological consultations in the spirit of our founder James McCord's global and ecumenical vision for the work of the Center of Theological Inquiry. Wallace did so in close collaboration with Michael Welker, the distinguished theologian and pioneer in interdisciplinary and international research, who has graced this volume with his Foreword, setting *Imagining a Way* within the history of their larger project.

Third, I pay warm tribute to the book's editor, Clive Pearson, whose willingness to pick up the Stellenbosch papers and, with skill, insight, and judgment, turn them into publishable essays reflects his own scholarly vocation as a Reformed theologian. It is all the more fitting, therefore, that we have found in Westminster John Knox Press the perfect partner for his endeavor, along with the ideal collaborators in its professional staff. Clive and I record our special thanks to Robert Ratcliff, the Executive Editor at WJK, for supporting the proposal and steering it to publication.

But that is not quite the last word of appreciation.

In the Stellenbosch consultation where this volume was conceived,
two colleagues were present who are no longer with us:
Max Stackhouse from the United States
and
Russel Botman from South Africa.
Both were exemplars of the Reformed tradition
at its best on each continent.
We miss them and dedicate this volume to their memory,
and also in gratitude to
Wallace Alston and Michael Welker.

William Storrar, Director
Center of Theological Inquiry, Princeton, NJ

WELCOMING

Chapter 1

Imagining a Reformed Practical Theology and Ethics

CLIVE PEARSON

THE POSITIONING QUESTION

In some indigenous cultures it is customary to take time and set the scene through acts of greeting and recognition. The gathering begins with one of those participating surveying the space, naming the others in turn, each time saying something about the last time they met; they may make some comment about the place from which the other comes or perhaps refer to a relative or an ancestor. It is a practice that takes time because everyone in the room will do the same.

This practice of welcome is often the way of oral cultures where genealogies and family connections to one another and to various places situate you as a guests and hosts of the other. It is a way of knowing and being known. It is a way of positioning yourself and being positioned—and that, it seems, has become an important theological consideration. Writing in an editorial of *Theology Today* some years ago, Hugh Kerr referred to the importance of the "positioning question." The one he had in mind, "Where are you from?," shares much with that oral cultural practice.

Kerr observed that this seemingly casual item of small talk seldom attracts much attention or weight. It has more the feel of a chitchat conversation, and yet it has the capacity to slow us down and situate ourselves. At the most superficial level the names of the places from where we have come can seem to fall more into the realm of the accidental. It just so happens that we come from such and such a place. It was out of our personal control. Kerr's interest in this positioning question, though, digs deeper. One other way to reply is to say that we have come from our mother's bodies and, as a consequence, Kerr noted that we participate in a common humanity. Where we are from also binds us to a dependence upon others, in this instance to that "someone else [who] carried us, took care of us, and brought us to light and life." For Kerr this kind of dependence led him to reflect further upon the awareness that "only faith makes"—and that is the confession that we come from God, upon whom "we are in a position of 'absolute dependence' for our existence."

Where we are from has now become relational rather than merely spatial and temporal. How we answer this deceptively innocent question provides further insight into the unfolding of our character and identity. There is evidently much more to this simple positioning question than might be first imagined. Kerr delves a little more, knowing full well that when a theologian is asked the question "Where are you from?," it will most likely lead to others: "What is *your* theology? Where were you trained? Who is your publisher? What do *you* teach?" Those sorts of question are posed in a time of much change in theology: According to Kerr, "The history of the Christian church is a narrative of experimenting with new forms and structures." We are now "from" this particular period in history: this is our time of "during" and of our "doing," poised between yesterday and tomorrow. However we move forward, Kerr advised that this way ahead should not mean our "forgetting from where we came from." How has that past, that tradition, made us, come what may?[1]

The importance of being some "one" from some "where" is well described by *Susan E. Davies* in her essay below. Its title "Justice Healing" perhaps masks a little the personal nature of the telling story of how her identity and vocational commitments have been informed by the Reformed tradition in which she finds herself. This somewhere is a mix of places, peoples, relationships, stages of life, health, and exposures to situations in need of healing and justice—all of which have been lived out in and through various forms of ministry. Some of these ongoing formational experiences, which led Davies to becoming the kind of feminist pastoral theologian she is, have been good, yet some have been anything but good. There is here a "look[ing] back on those years" with a stark realism that nevertheless reveals "God's benevolence toward me." There indeed is a strong sense of "where" some "one" has come from, into which were inserted, no doubt, a significant number of questions to do with how, why, and when. And here that "where" embraces "three Reformed emphases—the sovereignty of God, Christian responsibility for the world, and faith as a gift of grace." Davies's writing embodies rather well a response to Kerr's positioning question, leading right back to its source in God.

ADDRESSING THE QUESTION

This brief description of Davies's rather moving essay on justice and healing leads effortlessly into yet another dimension to this practice of welcome and recognition. The presence of others is assumed. The apparent need to explain where you are from implies a degree of difference. Davies is not alone: here she finds herself in this volume in the company of a mix of friends and strangers. Some—like *Nancy J. Ramsay, Denise M. Ackermann,* and *Jana Childers*—likewise refer to certain aspects of how they were formed and from where they came. In Ramsay's case part of the purpose of such is to show how one's own formation and cultural upbringing must not be regarded as normative for all. Others writing in this volume are less ostensibly subjective. This particular cast is held together by lines of thick-and-thin trust. There is a common purpose. It takes the form of the letter of intention, which asked the writers concerned to address a particular question: Does being Reformed mean doing practical theology and ethics in a distinctive and sometimes different way? We might call this an occasional question. It is naming the reason why, and the specific occasion for which, this body of writers has been brought together. The focus for this occasion was not so much, then, on the particular instance of a practice or an ethic; rather, the interest expressed via the occasional question itself has more to do with what light the subject of each address might shine on a Reformed way of doing and behaving. The disciplinary terms, practical theology and ethics, are thus being employed in order to serve an inquiry into the nature of a Reformed identity and ethos.

There is more than an echo here of a John Leith subtitle on the Reformed imperative: *What the Church Has to Say That No One Else Can Say.*[2] This anthology is the response to the invitation. The following chapters are the product of a conference held in Stellenbosch (South Africa) in April 2004 under the auspices of the Center of Theological Inquiry, Princeton, and its then director Wallace Alston. That gathering was the third and final in a series of conferences led by Alston and Michael Welker and designed to explore aspects of being Reformed in terms of theological scholarship and ecumenicity. Like Davies, the conference contributors had all been formed and informed by the Reformed tradition. In the judgment of the present editor, their essays are of more lasting significance and worthy of publication. With the active support of William Storrar, the current director of the Center of Theological Inquiry, Clive Pearson invited all the Stellenbosch participants to revise their original conference papers in light of the intervening years. These updated essays are also one way of answering Kerr's positioning question. In the act of responding they also reveal that which they do not hold in common and which can make their authors strangers to one another.

The original Stellenbosch invitation was extremely open-ended. What has eventuated is a multifaceted collection of ways to engage with pastoral practice, selected ethical issues (economics, cloning, environment, the common good), and a concern for identity. There is no one concrete problem or issue other than the occasional question posed in the letter of invitation. Nevertheless the fact that all of those who were gathered for this task came (more or less) from the same tradition did not necessarily lend itself immediately to a common recognition of identity. The hermeneutical focus on being Reformed was filtered through differences in gender as well as those of place and culture. It was also negotiated through differences in language and intellectual infrastructure. The presenters came from very different parts of the world (the United States, Scotland, Switzerland, India, Korea, South Africa, and Australia). English is not the first language of all, though in this setting it is the functional language in which they can get by. It is evident that a number of variables play a part in any desire to build "a truly global theological network that would be as inclusive as possible." Michael Welker has noticed "vast differences in academic infrastructure, competencies, and support" from one location in the world to another.[3]

Clearly the principle of contextuality is critically important. It is evident that the way in which the Reformed tradition is apprehended and practiced in one location varies greatly. This anthology cannot but help reflect those differences by the very nature of the disciplines themselves. The intellectual pursuits of a practical theology and a Christian ethic cannot easily stand apart from local contexts so that differences of place and culture can be heightened. Kerr's positioning question comes back into focus.

The indigenous practice of greeting and recognition rarely happens in literary and academic circles. Now and then equivalents of inclusion and paying attention to who is there (and who is not present) emerge. One of the most notable examples of such would be that of Letty Russell's idea of being the church and doing theology at a "the round table." The purpose here can be partially described as seeking to encourage table talk and the sharing of perspectives. Thus the conversation makes room for the stranger and those on the margins; the metaphor is essentially one of relationships, issuing the invitation to "make connections across dividing lines of religion, culture, race, class, gender, and sexual orientation." The intention of the round table is to create "a circle of friends willing to listen and able to allow talk back to the tradition." In practice this biblical metaphor represents a sign of God's hospitality and a reminder of the already-and-not-yet nature of faith. The eschatological banquet of God's new creation for which we yearn presently lies beyond us.[4]

Now and then the practice of dialogue and exchange happens where there is a cut-and-thrust response between two or more scholars. Here one can think of the imaginary conversations that Daniel Migliore set up in the epilogues to his *Faith Seeking Understanding*. On three separate occasions Migliore hosts a discussion by several well-known theologians on areas of doctrine to do with natural theology, the resurrection, political theology, and atheism.[5] The purpose of this device is to let readers become familiar with the strengths and weaknesses of a particular interpretation of a theological point over against another way of seeing the same thing.

How the task before our writers might not be the same as other anthologies can be discerned by way of a comparison. On occasion there has been a good and significant connection made between the Reformed tradition and a particular aspect of the relevant discipline. One example of such is the collection brought together by Wallace Alston and Cynthia Jarvis on the formation and practice of a pastor-theologian. The focus here is specific. The emphasis is placed on addressing the "hiatus between mind and heart, between academic theology as an intellectual discipline and ecclesial theology as a confessional stance." *The Power to Comprehend with All the Saints* is designed to encourage and enhance the nurture and sustaining of pastor-theologian; it does so on the basis of where this happens, "the church lives," and where it does not, "the church tends to be trivialized and languishes."[6] The anthology is pervaded by a Reformed spirit and is directed unerringly to a common task—but it does not cover the wider field of either of these two disciplines.

The same could be said of *Reforming Worship*, edited by Keith Riglin, Julian Templeton, and Angela Tilby,[7] as well as Lukas Vischer's edited version of *Christian Worship in Reformed Churches*.[8] These texts are intended to reveal both the history and diversity of Reformed worship practices while seeking to discern some order. This current volume does deal with worship as well, most notably in the contributions of *Ralph Kunz* and *Jana Childers*. They both share and mediate the same kinds of interests and concerns as do volumes dedicated to worship alone.

Kunz, for instance, addresses the ever-present tension in Reformed worship surrounding ordered freedom and spontaneity. That orderliness is derived from a desire to proclaim the gospel and to do so without that kerygma being compromised by unnecessary accretions. Such freedom is not a license to do whatever one pleases but rather is bound to the need of being open to the Holy Spirit's leading. It so happens that Kunz's particular focus is on what has been transpiring over recent decades in the Swiss Federation of Protestant Churches. The presenting issue is the "proper little debate" that has emerged between those who favor a greater respect of the characteristic form and "unity" of the Reformed service and those who support a "freedom of arrangement." The former are concerned at the level of "liturgical erosion" now to be found in the Swiss Federation of Protestant Churches. Kunz is able to address this rift with the benefit of an historical perspective.

It seems as if the Swiss concern for the characteristic form is itself a relatively recent phenomenon and represents "the reform of this tradition." It is not his intention, though, to dispense with form, as might be the imagined consequence of this disclosure. Kunz looks back to the aesthetic nature, "the sparse beauty," of Zwingli's worship service in Zurich and draws upon theories of drama and theatrical aesthetics. How might these roots be "cultivated" and be helpful now? The analogy is made between a service of worship and a theater production. This claim might at first seem contentious and leads to many further questions. There is always the risk of overstaging, and there are so many paradoxes: the protagonist is God, who is "portrayable but not producible"; are the congregational members only spectators, or are they actors and participants in the service? That list of questions could be extended.

There is a considerable affinity between Kunz's desire to negotiate this tension with what Riglin and Templeton are trying to do in an English context. There is a general recognition of how it is in the very nature of a Reformed church to be always reforming—and further, in the opinion of Riglin and Templeton, that worship must be in the "vanguard of [that] reform."[9] The issue is how to maintain a delicate balance between extremes, on the one hand becoming repetitive and boring, and on the other hand making a "descent into kitsch," in the memorable words of Ernest Marvin.[10] The task is not slight. One of the core elements of Reformed worship is its reliance on Scripture: by tradition it is worship "that rests in and grows out of a deep familiarity with Scriptures"; the dilemma recognized by Tilby is that "contemporary congregations are much less familiar with Scripture than their forebears." She is convinced that the sheer range of Bible versions of varying quality have "virtually killed off the scriptural memory and cultural resonance on which our Christian formation depended."[11]

By way of comparison Childers is writing on the practice of preaching. Here Childers is well aware of how preaching and Scripture possess a priority in the tradition: preaching is of "primary importance," "near the top" of any list of hallmarks, and attracts a "symbolic importance." Childers is even willing to pluck up courage to interpret Calvin in the light of making a claim for preaching being a sacramental act.

Like Davies, Childers is personal at times in the most helpful of ways. She knows the "value of speaking from my own location." Her location has experienced a good deal of "social change." The immediate context in which Childers situates preaching is in an age of much spiritual seeking and also of a relative decline in membership of mainline denominations in the United States. It is, she argues, a time of change and, she suggests, an age of the Holy Spirit. Thus the issue at stake is partly one of whether the Reformed tradition can say something about preaching that no other tradition is likely to do. Another way of posing the same question is to ask, Can the Reformed tradition make a difference as to "how we will preach our way through the twenty-first century"? There is a clear sense in which she is embodying the tension that Kunz, Marvin, Templeton, and Riglin describe. The present is a time of "spiritual unease," searching, and empty pews. It may arguably be the age of the Holy Spirit, but the spirit is often associated with freedom and the unexpected, the surprising. What has the Reformed faith to offer in response?

Now Childers is conscious of how it is not difficult to parody the dignity of a Reformed sermon. It can be very easy to lose sight of its intent on delivering what Walter Brueggemann has described as "serious speech" to do with God and proclaim "a gospel greatly reduced."[12] Brueggemann has identified how our capacity to hear (and then act as obedient and transformed selves and communities) has been compromised through use of a selection of hermeneutical filters that operate on us in our daily living. Those filters include the way in which we are shaped by economics, technology, and science. They are part and parcel of the "Enlightenment text," against which Brueggemann places "liberating possibilities of Scripture." In his discussion of the Reformed tradition, Cornick emphasizes Brueggemann's recourse to this "rescriptive" text upon which the preacher is summoned to proclaim the alternative reality of God's kingdom. This is serious speech that plays upon the cognitive dissonance between what we experience and that "vague feeling that [life] shouldn't be like this."[13]

Childers reminds us that this dignity is designed to acknowledge the sovereignty of God and the majestic purpose of the divine activity. Far too often these days this emphasis is obscured because preaching is directed toward what the human subject might need to do—or the message becomes trivial or narcissistic. Even mere reference to God can disappear. It is not difficult to imagine why Fleur Houston then hangs her Reformed homiletics on the rather blunt question "Can a sermon be boring?"[14] The question itself is a lever for her to focus primarily on the audience receiving the preached Word. Houston is assuming the pivotal place of Scripture and the sermon in Reformed worship. The dilemma she is seeking to address is how the sermon can be faithful to the Word of God (Karl Barth) while releasing meanings that engage the imagination of new audiences (Paul Ricoeur).

Here Childers invokes Calvin, whose "model seems uncannily timely." In the face of so much trivia and narcissism, this dignity needs to be understood. It is grounded in the recognition of the majesty and sovereignty of God. It is a dignity that requires a "careful interpretation of the text," "embodied preaching," and sincerity. For this serious speech to be efficacious, there is need of the Holy Spirit. The distinctive contribution that the Reformed tradition can provide this questing and jaded age is the conviction that the Holy Spirit provides the entry point into the Word and seals its message.

The writings of both Kunz and Childers would be most appropriately housed in a collection on Reformed worship. Within that kind of setting they would contribute to a fuller critical exploration of a key concern for the Christian faith. They would also find themselves in the company of other scholars on worship who explore important themes not found in this volume. Harking back to Templeton and Riglin, their anthology also includes an extended historical account of Reformed worship as well as discussions over eucharistic understandings and lay presidency—and by extension the nature of ordained ministry—which this volume does not explore. Where the difference lies is in the company Kunz and Childers keep. Their cowriters are not confined to one area of a particular discipline. This anthology is bringing together a much looser company of interests and specialisms. The examples furnished by Kunz and Childers obviously illustrate a way into scholarly debates over liturgy and homiletics.

THE REFORMED IMAGINARY

This kind of comparison with single (sub)discipline collections masks a further distinguishing trait. The letter of invitation posed the occasional question to do with a distinctive Reformed identity and contribution. There is a dual dilemma here. The first has to do with the label "Reformed"; the second has to do with the scope and self-understanding of what constitutes a practical theology—and by extension what is its relationship to pastoral theology and ethics. From the perspective of Kerr's positioning question, the former has priority. The gathering in Stellenbosch assumed the dwelling within a common tradition or ethos.

Those most sensitive to the problems facing that tacit assumption came from South Africa. In the background was lurking the practice and legacy of apartheid. In this specific context, what did it mean to be Reformed in practice? Here we have a telling ambiguity that needs to be negotiated. It takes the form of looking for what might be distinctive in a Reformed practical theology and ethics when that same tradition can both inspire competing claims and raise the consequential stakes quite high.

Dirk Smit addresses these issues head-on. The immediate response to the organizing question is that a Reformed practical theology and ethics did indeed make a major difference to life in South Africa. The only trouble was that this difference was "disastrous." The Dutch Reformed Church was complicit in the policy and cultural acceptance of apartheid. The extent of its complicity is most vividly demonstrated by *Denise Ackermann* in her "potted biography" of Beyers Naudé. The stated intention of her argument is really to consider whether Beyers Naudé should be regarded as a public theologian. In terms of the examples John de Gruchy has presented elsewhere, the response cannot be anything other than yes,[15] but this answer is almost incidental to the drama Ackermann has related. Naudé was "God's humble servant made reluctant prophet whose role was pivotal during fraught times." His life bore witness to the cost of a Reformed practical theology lived with integrity: here his Reformed faith led him to stand in stark opposition to his own culture and church. The inevitable question arises as to how, and with what degree of coherence, can the label of Reformed be applied to other critics like Naudé and at the same time provide a canopy under which apartheid could take root and bear its fruit. That stark reality is captured by de Gruchy, who felt compelled to write of the need to free Reformed theology from alien influences and recover its liberating potential as an "alternative Calvinism."[16] Its "cry for life" needed to overcome all manner of contemporary temptations and powers, to deliver from tyranny, terror, idolatry, anarchy, and falsehood.[17] On the basis of that experience of apartheid, de Gruchy later argued that a Reformed theology must be "liberated from various captivities, not least that of the dominating social groups and ideologies, in order to be a truly liberating theology today."[18]

Now with the benefit of hindsight, Smit asks whether South Africa suffered from too much or too little Reformed theology. The present is a period of what has been called "postapartheid memory." The implications of this recent history of complicity and protest are far-reaching. Smit has indeed wondered whether it is still possible to be Reformed in his own country in view of its having "failed dismally."[19] That is the difficulty with which *Etienne de Villiers* is wrestling:

How plausible can a Reformed calling to transform society in the light of the gospel of Jesus Christ now be? The theological setting has changed radically under the new political dispensation ushered in with the collapse of the apartheid system. That vocation, de Villiers claims, is grounded in a central belief of a Reformed faith that "God the Creator and Governor is also Lord of history." It is a core theological confession that cannot be ignored, yet what it might mean now requires careful attention.

The Reformed tradition is faced with one question tumbling after another. How credible is this calling when there has been division within the Reformed churches and theologians, in the first place, as to whether apartheid can be justified? How credible is it when the system collapses and it becomes evident that the biblical and theological case for apartheid cannot be justified? Is this calling capable of being refreshed and suitably reformed under a new regime, which reflects not just the collapse of apartheid but also a modernizing process that has changed the public sphere?

Thus de Villiers has written self-consciously in the wake of the loss of that former legitimacy. It could be argued that there is no role for a Reformed faith to play in the transformation of society, at least for some years. It is certainly not as "self-evident" as it was; the "structures of credibility have been dismantled," there is "deep scepticism" about the social role of the Bible, and many members of the Reformed churches have undergone something of an "inward emigration" away from the public sphere to the private.

Yet de Villiers insists that the legitimacy of this call to transform society in the light of the gospel must be redeemed: there is still a need for a "contemporary Christian social ethics" that is "convincing" and different. Accordingly de Villiers makes a distinction between the purpose of this calling in the previous dispensation and in the new political era. The theocratic ideal upon which apartheid was based was ironically intended to "*Christianize* society." Now, de Villiers argues, is a time for a social ethics that is inclusive, recognizes the pluralist nature of society, and seeks to *humanize* society.

Hence de Villiers has answered Smit's probing question in a positive manner. For him an ethical and vocational imperative remains and overrides a problem of definition that Smit cannot ignore. That dismal failure should be set inside another recurring theme in Smit's corpus of writings: the "story of Reformed Christianity in South Africa is in fact a story of many stories."[20] Are all authentic? If so, on what basis? If not, what criteria can be invoked to discern the difference? Here the stakes are high. In less extreme situations John Leith stressed the important and difficult task of balancing gratitude with critical judgment.[21]

The way in which we define something has consequences. With reference to a particular tradition, it can mean endeavoring to stake a claim for authority and justification. The underlying assumption is that there are rival interpretations to the tradition, and the subsequent effects may be far-reaching and extend well beyond a disciplinary discussion. The nature of a living tradition of faith is that it can be both an intellectual abstraction and a way of life. Its confessional beliefs can both shape social and cultural practice and to varying degrees be realized in that practice.

One of the most telling exposures of this power of beliefs in the profession of faith is the work of Douglas John Hall, writing in the immediate wake of 9/11. In this particular instance Hall was arguing the case for taking up the "thin tradition" of a theology of the cross: he believed that theology to be more preferable in the circumstances than a more triumphalist rendering in a theology of power and glory. Hall was wanting to argue that "theology matters" and that there is a complex relationship between beliefs and deeds. The practice of faith cannot disregard theology as if it were only an intellectual abstraction. Hall observed that "the actions of believers are usually the acting out of foundational beliefs, whether in conscious or unconscious ways." One way or another, "the foundational beliefs of a religious faith will find expression . . . in the deeds and deportment of its membership."[22] For that reason there is a critical necessity for any religious tradition to possess a capacity to distinguish between "authentic and inauthentic expressions of that faith."[23]

This act of distinguishing implies an ability to define, name, and select the particular distinctives or habits of a tradition. Where there are competing claims, is it enough for either or both sides simply to invoke, in this case, the label "Reformed," as if that resolves the matter? This dilemma is one part of the series of issues that Smit is seeking to address. Were those who drew upon their Reformed faith to justify apartheid, and what is now regarded as bad practice, simply and faithfully representing the tradition in which they stood? Here Hall's wise counsel about deeds and deportment hovers a little too close for comfort. Smit is well aware of how controversial the claiming and owning of a tradition can be. So much can depend on who is telling the story and, one might add, in whose interests and for what purpose. The level of intensity surrounding competing claims can lead to the tradition itself becoming a site of struggle. That there was a strong and well-respected cadre of theologians able to draw upon the Reformed tradition in order to oppose apartheid is itself most telling.

There have been numerous attempts to define who is Reformed and why. The difficulty is reflected in David Cornick's metaphor of a "theological umbrella which lends shelter" to a diversity of individuals, confessions and churches.[24] The presence of so many variables has led to a number of introductions that have sought to identify a handful of "distinctives."[25] The problem is compounded because of "the characteristically Reformed absence of any representative voice." John Calvin is the most obvious choice but, as Smit notes while writing on the Trinity elsewhere, "not even Calvin could be regarded as speaking for the whole doctrine."[26] The 500th anniversary of his birth (2009) led to many studies and conferences dealing with Calvin[27] and his legacy to the Reformed tradition[28] and, one might add, also to modernity.[29] It is fairly common to appeal to Calvin for "roots" and "origins," but whether that claim then inspires a coherent dogmatic and practical tradition is another matter. Richard A. Muller is adamant: "The Reformed tradition is a diverse and variegated movement not suitably described as founded solely on the thought of John Calvin or as either a derivation or deviation from Calvin," as if his theology were the norm for the whole tradition.[30] Muller is writing as an historian with a specific intention of discarding the "dross" of earlier "dogmatic narratives." It is time to "deconstruct (those) master narratives" that might set Calvin against the Calvinists or interpret him as a "founder of a uniformly Calvinistic Reformed tradition" by various ways and means.[31]

The rhetoric of tradition can, of course, be ambiguous. It can so easily become a means by which a deposit of belief and expectation can become closed and staid. It loses its living voice. Leith is mindful of how a tradition can become "out of date, rigid, fixed, past-oriented." It can become a refuge for those who seek to "isolate themselves and live according to their own principles."[32] It is indeed possible for a tradition to become all played out and somehow cling to survival beyond its use-by date.

That lack of match between a received tradition and current needs can lead to what John Reader has identified in practical theology as a process of "de-traditioning" and "disimagination" or organized forgetting.[33] Faced with the effects of globalization on established practices of pastoral care, worship, and congregational life in general, Reader has made the case for a reconstruction. The world has changed, our sense of place has altered, and how we work in a global economy is no longer the same. We are faced with a rapid rise of new ethical issues presenting themselves in the field of biotechnology, for instance, for which there are no precedents.

This ambivalent sense regarding tradition surrounds the Reformed faith in some parts of the world represented at Stellenbosch. The above references to "our" and "we" need to be handled with contextual care: Hence, once again, we need Kerr's positioning question and the indigenous practice of welcome and recognition. The relevant vitality of the Reformed faith around the world is uneven. For *Clive Pearson* it is in deep trouble in his "slice of theological geography," Australia. The source of that trouble does not lie in the kinds of complexity with which Smit and de Villiers have had to wrestle in South Africa. The problem lies in how its "tradition of a robust confessional theology and practice has not been able to protect its representative churches from the general demise of the Christian faith in a skeptical democratic society." There has been an apparent dissolution of milieu. The present context is now more culturally, linguistically, and religiously diverse than ever before. It has become one of varying forms of agnosticism and apathy existing alongside a surprising resurgence of interest in a spirituality often defined in categories opposing organized religion. The history that gave place to a Reformed faith in a previous Christian landscape is giving way to the practice of "transconfessionalism" and a "competitive piety." The former strengths of a Reformed faith—its confessing nature, its reputation for thoughtfulness, its practice of justice, and the vocation and integrity of its ministry—run the risk of becoming points of vulnerability. The "Australian soul" is now more likely to privilege what feels right at the expense of what appears to be more rational and institutionally bound.

In a somewhat similar vein *William Storrar* is likewise concerned with the relative eclipse of the Reformed faith mediated through a mainline denomination. In his case the denomination is the Church of Scotland and the dilemma with which he is dealing is the empirical evidence for the rapid decline of the Reformed churches in Europe. The decline is not just in terms of numbers; it also involves sustainability of the church's institutional and bureaucratic nature and its fitness for purpose in a postmodern society.

It is evident that the issues facing the Reformed tradition in these sites are not slight. The type of pressure these representative churches are under is not likely to abate through being on the receiving end of a number of critically tested and agreed-upon Reformed distinctives or constants. Nor is any sense of obligation to Calvin or his peers from long ago likely to reverse a gathering momentum of numerical decline. There is no obvious right plan or agenda to follow. In such circumstances the desire accompanied by a sense of ecclesial responsibility to survive and maintain the structures can take priority, come what may. Without being able to vouchsafe the future, the alternative to Leith's understanding of a closed tradition might, nevertheless, furnish some perspective. Leith felt obliged to reflect on what he identified as the "traditioning of faith." The emphasis here is established in the etymological origins of the word "tradition." The Latin verb *tradere* is active and lends itself to Leith's idea of an "open tradition." There is a coming together of the actual act of "passing on" and "handing over" as well as to "what is passed on." For Leith this process of traditioning is "very human" as well as "indissolubly linked with the gospel"—Jesus Christ "is the tradition"— and is "the work of the Holy Spirit."[34]

The situation before Leith at the tail end of the twentieth century is a far cry from the prospects facing Storrar and Pearson and those for whom they write. Embedded within this recourse to an open tradition and a process of traditioning surely is "gratitude for a heritage that has shaped and nurtured" individuals and communities of faith; there is recognition that the tradition provides "resources, clues, and inspiration for life." There is also a potential freedom. There is that which is received; there is that which is handed on in and through a confessional and liberative spirit. How will that now be managed and adapted to diverse contexts in an unfolding future?

Storrar's example is full of interest inasmuch as it provides a nuanced and differentiated reading of the received tradition. There is, first, a tacit acceptance of a Reformed theology that breaks the surface in and through reference to how the Reformers had bound together theological and organizational leadership. Storrar situates this kind of innovative leadership alongside two other legacies of the Reformers: neither Luther nor Calvin set out to be prescriptive about how localized expressions of the church should necessarily be replicated elsewhere: they ascribed a priority to the worship of God in whatever endeavors were to be observed. That emphasis warrants closer scrutiny. For our period in time, Storrar is placing worship ahead of and at the foundation of any ecclesial practice of mission, pastoral care, or social justice. The reason for such lies in the nature of the asymmetrical relationship between divine agency and whatever innovative human enterprise is undertaken. The risk of a collapsed ecclesiology is thus mollified.

Storrar provides a congregational example of a church that has been able to put into practice these three principles going back to the Reformers themselves. It has managed to negotiate its way through a raft of competing models for what it means to be a church. The future sustainability and habitability of the church means taking leave of a way of being a national church that demands too much of local congregations to satisfy institutional and bureaucratic requirements. Storrar has recognized that the current mode of membership and being a church is a hybrid mix of models: the communal (and territorial), the activist (evangelical and missional), and the recreational. Each of those models has a different and discrete way of being a disciple and member. The future Reformed congregation will require theological and organizational leadership, freedom to express its way of being without undue institutional constraint, and clarity about how its life and witness are held together in worship within the walls of the church.

Storrar has thus argued the case for a level of flexibility and perhaps a certain lightness of being in this traditioning business. Faced with similarly daunting prospects, Pearson invokes Peter Matheson's understanding of the role of "iconopoiac energies" in the Reformation. This turn of phrase refers to the images, symbols, metaphors, and allegories that generated a refreshed "imaginative architecture" for societies from which an older order was passing. There is a likely association here with William Dyrness's work on visual culture and the Protestant imagination.[35] There is also a potential link to a rather select body of Reformed thinking that might then lead to the possibility of imitating Charles Taylor's work on modern social imaginaries.

The imaginary is a category taken from contemporary sociology. It has to be admitted that Taylor's primary interest here is in describing how Western culture came to be what it is. Religion transmits an ambiguous legacy and role: it clearly belongs to a more "enchanted" world. The "long road to modernity" embraces a "Great Disembedding" away from a God-given purpose for society and transcendent reference point. And yet this long road can look back to the initiative of the Reformation, which situates the individual in altogether different space. For Taylor, that which comes to constitute modernity is "an unprecedented amalgam of new practices and institutional forms, . . . new ways of living, . . . and new ways of malaise."[36] The moral order that then legitimizes these new practices, forms, and ways is a political concern for the individual, for ordinary life rather than the transcendent, for mutual benefit, security, rights, and freedom. In this terrain of modernity Taylor posits three central forms of the social imaginary: the economy, the public sphere, and "the practices and outlook of democratic self-rule."

What is perhaps of more interest for the present purpose lies not in these specifics so much as how Taylor understands the imaginary per se. The social imaginary is "something much broader and deeper than the intellectual schemes." It refers to "the ways people imagine their social existence, how they fit together with others, how things go on between them and their fellows, the expectations that are normally met, and the deeper normative notions and images that underlie these expectations."[37] The social imaginary is a set of self-understandings, background practices, and horizons of common expectations that are not always explicitly articulated; nevertheless they give a people a sense of shared group life. The social imaginary is thus "not a set of ideas; rather it is what enables, through making sense of, the practices of a society."

The difficulty in determining the distinctives of Reformed practical theology and ethics raises the question of whether the case Taylor makes for his modern social imaginaries might furnish an appropriate analogy. Leith's traditioning process presupposes lines of continuity and discontinuity with earlier representations of being Reformed. Cornick's theological umbrella creates both space and shelter for commonality and a diverse form of Reformed imaginaries. Matheson's iconopoiac energies identify metaphors and images that can then be set alongside de Gruchy's call for a "retrieval of Reformed symbols," in this case for the sake of liberation and justice. The purpose here is not to "retell the story" in the interests of "a set of theological principles or cultic acts remote from reality." The symbols after which de Gruchy aspires seek to keep alive "a dangerous memory" that is restated in "fresh and evocative terms."[38] Those symbols, those energies, are to be "embodied in the narrative of the community, the narrative etched in flesh and blood, struggle, suffering, celebration and hope."[39] Perhaps Daniel Migliore comes close to capturing the heart of a capacious imaginary through his acknowledgment of the spirit of a Reformed faith and theology. There remains a revolutionary energy, a dislike of disorder, a passion to participate in the renewal of God's world, a transforming zeal, and a willingness to be fearlessly contextual. What we have here is the spirit of a movement, a dominant tendency or character, peculiar emphases and "animating features."[40]

REPOSITIONING THE QUESTION

The pragmatic benefits of opting for a potential Reformed imaginary are severalfold. The most obvious advantage lies in the priority assigned to an ethos and a way of living; the focus does not fall on a table of more formally defined beliefs and principles. Here is not the same pressure to determine whether one style of Reformed expression of pastoral theology or ethics is more authentic than another. Scope remains for several variations of an imaginary to be at work at one and the same time, each with its own particular strengths and weaknesses. The discerning of difference becomes a bit more fluid, flexible, and relational. In some ways it depends on the company that is kept and where there are echoes of resonance and identity.

There is a tacit assumption here. Those who gathered to discuss whether there was something distinctive and different about a Reformed view brought awareness of a shared living tradition and no doubt harbored certain expectations. The present may well be a time of global flows of people and knowledge; the historic boundaries between theological traditions may now be softer and housed within an ecumenical rendering of belief and practice. Michael Welker is also surely right in his description of how "we are witnessing the slow collapse of the old and the emergence of a new world, which theology . . . has not yet fully diagnosed."[41] Reader prefers to think of a "strange, interim location." Yet there is a capacity to respond to Kerr's positioning question and perceive dimensions of personal and relational identity across subdisciplinary and cultural borders. The extent to which this affective recognition can be assumed and perhaps celebrated is readily gauged by way of a comparison made within the discursive field of a practical theology.

Now there is no need to simplify and resolve some of the tensions intrinsic to the discipline. The tracing of origins back to Schleiermacher and his division of theology into separate disciplines is well known. The subsequent need to define practical theology over and alongside pastoral theology, and perhaps ethics, has been well canvassed.[42] The argument over whether a practical theology should be primarily concerned with the ministerial functions and technical know-how of a "clerical paradigm" or something more academic, more public, is equally well rehearsed.[43] Elaine Graham, Heather Walton, and Francis Ward have helpfully described how the practice of theological reflection has evolved through six stages in history, thus situating us in time.[44] There is no need to doubt the credentials of several fine anthologies: the most notable would include that edited by Dorothy Bass and Craig Dykstra.[45] There is no need to prove that the discipline is "properly theology."[46] There is no need for a detour.

The comparison can be made with the intention of a recent anthology edited by Claire Wolfteich.[47] None of the writers in this Stellenbosch volume would expect to find themselves in Wolfteich's company. The reason lies in the particular tradition she represents. Wolfteich is willing to concede that the discipline of a practical theology is largely Protestant.[48] She is self-consciously writing as a Roman Catholic: the contents about "shared work of intellect, spirit and imagination" are divided into three parts. The first may be seen simply as an invitation to consider the discipline. Here the emphasis falls upon the historical and the conceptual framing of a Catholic perspective. It is designed at one level to "help readers gain an initial understanding of key terms and issues."[49] There is the standard provision of a definition: "practical theology" entails critical thinking about what we do and how we live out our faith: it engages in the "study of practices, contexts, cultures and communities in dialogue with faith traditions and informed by the best human knowledge available."[50] The purpose of this first section is also designed in such a way that the reader might become familiar with what Wolfteich discerns to be "the emergence of a distinctively Catholic practical theological synthesis": that synthesis embraces spirituality and the prophetic work for justice and aesthetics.[51] The second section is devoted to the "concrete practices of faith" by way of a "range of disciplinary pathways." It sets out to explore the Catholic tradition in terms of a "dynamic practice of handing on the faith." The particular issues through which a theory is worked out have to do with a mix of ritual, popular religious practices, and the prophetic character of missiology. Here we have certain themes that are not peculiar to the Catholic tradition but that one might expect to find in an invitation into its concrete practice: the Eucharist, spiritual direction, and family life. The self-reflexive nature of this invitation is further expressed through a concern for the "ebonization" of the American Catholic church and for youth ministry with Latino/a. The third and final section is centered on teaching and research.

There is a deep sense of purpose behind the way in which Wolfteich has named her anthology in terms of its being an "invitation." The intention is to encourage further the development of Catholic "voices and visions." Wolfteich is mindful of how the discipline "historically has been seen as a largely Protestant guild."[52] This collection of essays is destined to "fill a void and provide a stimulus to research and graduate theological and ministry programmes."[53]

Wolfteich's invitational approach excludes those who dwell within a Reformed imaginary. It is like a *via negativa* though the exclusion zone is not confined to them. It is arguably the case, of course, that being Catholic is more transparent than being Reformed: through papal encyclicals like *Laudato Si'* there are official positions with regard to beliefs and moral codes. The Reformed imaginary cannot lay claim to such authorities, but its proposed rhetoric of spirit, ethos, and animating features is consistent with Wolfteich's voices and visions. Through that practice of welcome and response to Kerr's positioning question, it becomes possible to hear how, why, to what extent, and for what purpose those present stand inside a common living legacy. The core imaginary lies behind both the summons and the desire to be present. It permeates the spirit of the subsequent discussion.

IMAGINING A WAY

That reference to a living legacy is taken from Smit. It was made in response to Calvin's influence upon the Reformed faith and its ethics. Smit is most aware of differing interpretations of Calvin's own understanding of a particular theological doctrine and how that understanding might be converted into practice. For the sake of clarifying what it means to be Reformed, he suggests that it would be "helpful to remind ourselves of some very general and well-known characteristics of Calvin's own vision." What Smit reckons as beyond dispute is Calvin's conviction that theology is concerned with the realities of everyday living. It is a *theologia practica*. It is pastoral and practical rather than speculative or scholastic in intention. If this is the case, then the Reformed imaginary will need to play itself out in the issues presenting themselves in the contemporary period.

It now is an invidious task to nominate which issues those might be. Reader has presupposed that this "strange interim location" will naturally give rise to some "emerging themes."[54] In terms of ethical considerations, the present is bearing witness to a raft of issues for which there is no long-established precedent. How will Kerr's positioning question and this talk of a Reformed imaginary handle matters arising out of biotechnology and robotics, for instance, not to mention the prospect of paradigmatic shifts brought about by an increasing recognition of this Anthropocene epoch and whatever might be the longer-term consequences of the Pluto flyby into the beyond?

Even those seemingly routine matters of Reformed practice, like preaching and pastoral care, are being subjected to great pressure merely by the present being a time of intensifying globalization. The sense of place and belonging is altering away from the more stable congregational pattern in which Reformed confession and practice arose. Reader argues that globalization is like an empire that forms an enclosure around us, leaving us at the mercy of its "full spectrum dominance." The (Western) world is now "a place of blurred boundaries where the new and the old, the global and the national, exist alongside each other: they permeate, enhance, transform and colour each other."[55] Reader is relentless: the discipline of a practical theology finds itself inhabited by too many "zombie categories." These are the living-dead practices and conceptual frameworks, which Reader argues "have served us well for many years and continue to haunt our thoughts and analyses, even though they are embedded in a world that is passing before our eyes."[56]

There is not too difficult a risk hidden within this setting. The most obvious has to do with the fear of becoming anachronistic and the flight to being relevant. Sometime ago now, Leith warned the Reformed faith of this ambivalent myth of relevance: "We are in danger of being relevant, without a message."[57] At the time Leith was writing about what he perceived to be a decline in preaching and was conscious of theology as the only skill the preacher has, or for that matter the church, that is not found with greater excellence somewhere else, in particular the skill to interpret and apply the Word of God in serious teaching and pastoral care.[58]

What is evident in the work of the contributors to this volume is a deep awareness of a changing world and the pressures that are brought to bear on a Reformed ethics and a practical theology. It manifests itself in a willingness to name that shifting context while delving deeply into the Reformed imaginary for the sake of retrieving core ideas, symbols, and practices. How those iconopoiac energies then manifest themselves in specific practical themes and issues becomes the critical feature of the response made to the occasional question that brought this particular group of scholars together in the first place: Does being Reformed mean doing practical theology and ethics in a distinctive and sometimes different way?

Following are eight categories of particulars: the praxis of care; race; other faiths; social and cultural justice; the common good; climate change and the Anthropocene epoch; economics; genetic engineering, cloning, the post(trans)human.

1. THE PRAXIS OF CARE

That desire to be true to the principles of a Reformed faith is made plain by *Cynthia Jarvis* in her determination not to offer psychological banalities for the Word of God in the delivery of pastoral care. There are, of course, all manner of issues and situations in which a Reformed reading of pastoral care and the cure of souls might be applied—and perhaps make a difference. The particular point of entry into this field that Jarvis makes is through examples taken from care of the dying. It is a context now full of expert medical care and professional technique. It has become a scene in which those called to an ordained ministry can be very unsure of both their role and their identity. Often psychological banalities constitute the words addressed to a patient who did not really want to be asked how he was feeling, managing, and whether he wished to talk about what was happening. Jarvis makes a quiet aside to the reader consistent with Leith's warning: "Either we come to bear witness to a word not our own or we might as well not come at all."

The difference a Reformed understanding of pastoral care might assume is set initially over and against a professional model of counseling, CPE training, and technique. Jarvis takes a step back from verbatims and current practice and delves further into the Reformed tradition. She draws out a distinction between "how we are saved" and "who saves us." Jarvis is able to receive wisdom from the past in order to configure for the present. The intention is to show how pastoral ministry is not about our own gifts, our own psychological capacities, nor what we can do for ourselves. That is the risk the contemporary world puts before us. Jarvis seeks to show that pastoral ministry is designed to place the individual and congregation into the presence of God. The salvific work belongs to God and not us. The pastoral care enabled by the Reformed ministry sets the cure of souls inside a practice of ministry that includes preaching, thus in a sense placing people inside the narrative of God's purposes.

This emphasis Jarvis places upon a theological rendering of pastoral ministry complements the way in which *Cornelius Plantinga* follows through with the practical implications of doctrine. The biblical idea for which he has a concern is the image of God and, more specifically, its place in the redemptive work of God. The pastoral dilemma he addresses has to do with how the renewal of the image of God might be a source of hope for the depleted self. This self is the self that already feels itself to be "half dead" or emptied. It is the self for which life's circumstances have led to a sense of having "too little self."

This coming together of the image of God and the self is rather timely in Western cultures. For them the present is a theological setting where common reference to the self often attracts the qualifying categories of self-development, self-assertion, self-esteem, self-worth, and self-fulfillment. Plantinga's pastoral interest lies in the shadow side of this contemporary phenomenon made available through Donald Capps's work on the depleted self and the prevalence of shame over guilt. That practical intention is made possible through his reading of the biblical tradition of the image of God through a theological lens of both creation and redemption. It means that Plantinga can situate being made in the image of God alongside the renewal of that image in and through Christ. The pastoral task now becomes one of how this self should be seen in the light of a relationship of dying and rising with Christ. On what basis can these depleted selves be invited to take up their cross in a spirit of self-denial? Is this not simply an improper request?

Through this coupling together of creation and redemption, Plantinga distances himself from the various attempts made to define the image of God. What capacities, what set of attributes, what lines of relationship are privileged? These issues have been subject to change from one period to another. In relatively recent times, being made in the image of God has been used to support various forms of human rights and the gracious bestowal of a dignity that does not depend upon the accidents of birth, race, and status. John Kilner has rightly observed that this is indeed a powerful image, bringing power to liberate and demean.[59] Plantinga is nevertheless reluctant to press the image of God "into too narrow a mold." There is no expressed intention to discern how humankind "resembles" God. Plantinga is content with acknowledging that the image of God is a "rich multifaceted reality." The "often cryptic appearance of the phrase" in the Bible possesses the capacity to "epitomize the human relation to God.

Plantinga's desire to address the issue of the depleted self is just as important as his proffered response. In so many ways what constitutes personhood, individuality, and sociality are pressing questions for a globalized world caught up in so much digital and biotechnological change. Kerr's positioning question *Where are you from?* could equally easily take the form of *When?* or *What time are you from?* For the sake of its own plausibility a Reformed imaginary needs to be able to engage with critical contemporary matters as they arise. The depleted self is one such presenting dilemma and can serve as an entry point into a much larger debate surrounding the efficacy of a theological anthropology that is Reformed in character. Through his attention to redemption in tandem with creation, Plantinga is able to make a case for "reposing" and "resting" in God's grace. That otherwise overly daunting call to self-denial and imaging Christ lies beyond the person whose sense of self has been so compromised.

2. RACE

The image of God has been invoked by writers like James Evans Jr. in seeking to address racism.[60] The tendency has been to focus upon race and culture being constituent elements of being human and thus being "made" in the image of

God. In a manner of speaking, belonging to a particular race becomes an inalienable gift of creation. Our race as much as our culture is part of our answer to the question Where do you come from? From the theological case made by Evans on behalf of black African Americans, it is evident that the denial and abuse of race represent sin. For those gathered in Stellenbosch, the necessity of coming to terms with apartheid was matched elsewhere with what is really an inner theological imperative for the Reformed tradition to deal with racism in general. It is a worldwide problem and manifests itself in many forms. Its overt expression is found in the foundational sins of colonizing settler societies and policies of ethnic cleansing, racial profiling of offenders, the shooting of unarmed citizens (too often, it seems, by police), and the rhetoric of fear and hard-line responses to those seeking asylum. In these patterns of racism, hatred and discrimination are quite obvious. Such overt racism contrasts with the hidden biases of *aversive* racism, critique of which lies at the heart of *Nancy Ramsay's* vision for honoring cultural and racial differences while dealing with racism as sin.

In this instance Ramsay is writing as a self-confessed Reformed pastoral theologian. Her particular interest here is in paying attention to "the systemic and structural dynamics that shape and distort the context of care." She is seeking to participate in the process of reclaiming the "theological integrity" and "theological intentionality" of the discipline within the interdisciplinary "web of care." The specific themes she draws upon are housed within a theocentric center of professing the sovereignty of God. Its broad shape embraces Reformed perspectives on being made in the image of God, with due weight being given to original, actual, and social sin; then she presents a vocation of loving the neighbor.

Ramsay shares de Villiers's commitment to a Reformed emphasis on the transforming of culture. That transformation is to be understood in terms of responding to God's redeeming love. For Ramsay the presenting issue is the discrepancy that exists between "a biblical vision of life together" and the various ways in which "racism continues in our daily lives." The critical step for Ramsay is her mode of definition: racism is not simply a matter that is external to us personally or an issue of personal prejudice. Rather, racism is "an interlocking system of advantage (as well as disadvantage) based on race." It leads rather easily into a process of "internalizing a privileged identity" and "a learned indifference to the fact of racial discrimination." Ramsay concludes that such "internalized privilege" is "even more insidious than overt racism." It is aversive racism.

That term was first used by Joel Kovel in his psychohistory of white racism.[61] It was then developed into a more comprehensive theory by John Dovidio and Samuel Gaertner. In their seminal work on *Prejudice, Discrimination, and Racism*,[62] they worked their way toward a definition of aversive racism as "a form of prejudice characterizing the thoughts, feelings, and behaviors of the majority of well-intentioned and ostensibly nonprejudiced" citizens. Dovidio and Gaertner had thus accepted the relative decline of overt racism in the wake of civil rights legislation; they argued that racial prejudice has "given way to near universal endorsement of the principles of racial equality as a core cultural value."[63] Racial biases are now "less blatant than in the past." Dovidio and Gaertner have, nevertheless, also recognized a more subtle and indirect form of prejudice among those who are willing to accept egalitarian standards.

The effects of these forms of bias and prejudice are potentially visible in evidence of persistent racial disparities, such as in a range of health indices including infant mortality rates.[64] They are also likely to be found at work in the decision-making and social interactions of various institutions, such as the legal profession and education. In a somewhat similar vein Ramsay herself has written on how "white allies" should seek to address hidden discrimination based on race in the formation and practice of a faculty of theology.[65] These forms of prejudice can also be manifested in what Derald Wing Sue has described as "the microaggressions of everyday life."[66]

For Dovidio and Gaertner these indices and practices are symptoms. They are the consequence of "inadvertent" and "subtle biases," the origins of which are to be found in the unconscious mind. They described their aversive theory as an "unconscious type of racial bias."[67] There is thus a contradiction between "having egalitarian conscious or explicit attitudes but negative unconscious, or implicit, racial attitudes."[68] This work on aversive racism is effectively seeking to delve into the psychology of diversity and give an account of how stereotypes, caricatures, and an implicit racism form "outside of awareness."[69]

Dovidio and Gaertner probed into this otherwise unacknowledged, indirect, hidden form of discrimination by means of various methodologies and experimental paradigms that measure and assess implicit attitudes.[70] The way in which this unconscious practice operates has been further described by Mahzarin Banaji and Anthony Greenwald. Their book *Blindspot: Hidden Biases of Good People* is a psychological inquiry into how and what we see. There are ingrained habits of thought and "mindbugs" that lead to errors in how even the "good person" perceives, reasons, remembers, and make decisions.[71] Then it becomes relatively easy for these unconscious inferences and hidden biases to be framed in "shades of truth," "truthiness," and "stereotypes": we become unaware of how we become *homo categoricus* with regard the Other. Ramsay's use of experimental social psychology tests in the field of employment reveals the same.

Dovidio and Gaertner have subsequently strived to develop models and strategies which might reduce intergroup bias. This kind of social psychology works toward a common motivational identity for in-groups and out-groups in order to reduce bias and the distorting effects of categorization. Christena Cleveland has drawn upon this work of Dovidio and Gaertner for a theological purpose. Her work on *Disunity in Christ* is designed to expose and overcome "the hidden forces that keep us apart."[72] It is clearly a form of racism that needs to be contested practically because it is "pervasive" and "persists because it remains largely unrecognized and thus unaddressed."[73] This evident form of good intentions and hidden bias lies behind the kind of outrage and frustration felt by Jennifer Harvey. Writing for justice-minded white Christians, she argues the case for moving away from a reconciliation paradigm to one that is based on confession and reparation.[74]

It is arguably the case that Davies as well as Ramsay are both dealing with aversive racism. Ramsay also tells of her experience of growing up and gradually becoming aware of a problematic white history and a condescending practice of pity and charity. Ramsay reflects on how seemingly good people become "embedded in a sinful practice" and how that practice is transmitted across generations. There is a hidden effect to aversive racism: the wound that is inflicted upon the disadvantaged race returns and places in peril the soul of the ones who have reaped the benefits of such. For a frame of reference with which to engage this form of racism, Ramsay relies upon a Reformed theocentric ethic and piety. It is shaped by a due recognition of the sovereignty of God, the reality of sin, the gift of the *imago Dei*, and the vocational call to the love of neighbor.

3. OTHER FAITHS

It is evident that a Reformed faith must come to terms with its capacity for becoming complicit in apartheid, aversive racism, and subsequent variations of such. The present period is one of globalization and increasing interconnectedness across cultures, ethnicities, faiths, and worldviews. The category of the Other, with a perceived sense of difference, exists alongside and in some degree of tension with the "huge homogenization process" that *Piet Naudé* attributes to globalization. That otherness manifests itself in diverse forms with which a Reformed imaginary must necessarily engage. The radical urgency of responding to escalating numbers of refugees and asylum seekers displaced by civil war and terror insurgencies is a case in point. Fleur Houston has captured here the category of otherness through the biblical themes of stranger, exile, and hospitality. The imperative for providing protection is set within a mimetic rendering of Scripture that reflects the compassionate possibility of these themes. Writing out of an English Reformed background, Houston significantly invokes the practice of a duly constructed ethical imagination between "the world as it is and the world as it ought to be."[75] That language of ethical imagination is especially apposite for our purposes. It evokes the capacity of images, symbols, stories, and themes embedded in a tradition to address contemporary issues afresh and offer an alternative perspective to "the posturing of politicians and the ideological arguments that are so often a feature of national discourse."[76]

It is not difficult to see how the plight of the Other expressed through the pressure to seek asylum is likely to foreground cultural and religious difference. The clash of otherness can so easily morph into various forms of fear, a concern for social cohesion, and outbursts of popular prejudice surrounding policies to do with borders, security, and citizenship. Susanna Snyder refers to the "new racism" that can accompany the fear of migrants who come from former colonies and were somehow deemed to be inferior as well as the fear of those who threaten a Judeo-Christian civilization.[77] The Stellenbosch conference did not directly address such issues, which would now demand attention. It touched rather too lightly on the way in which differing faiths relate to one another around the Reformed world. The occasional question that led to these addresses could perhaps now be reframed in order to ask, Does being Reformed mean relating to other faiths in a distinctive and sometimes different way?

The way in which that revised question might be answered is likely to be informed by the time and place in which it is posed. The Reformed faith shares a Christian heritage that extends from demonizing the Other through evangelism and mission to various models of interfaith dialogue and concern for the common good. It can matter whether the question is posed in contemporary Europe, where those other faiths are likely to be in a minority and confront a widespread mix of agnosticism and indifference: Linda Woodhead has observed that dialogue is often then conducted in the abstract, with little concession being made to the inequality of power and a lack of what might be called a level playing field.[78] The situation is in reverse in Asia, where the Christian faith is in the minority. It has often been associated with colonialism, trade, and a missional imperative. Certainly here is an ambiguous legacy for a postcolonial world. In what ways can the Christian faith be expressed in and through Asian symbols and modes of knowing that may be in some degree of tension with Western missionary practice? How plausible and attractive is a Christian faith that in the past has often been associated with privilege and makes exclusivist revelatory claims in a context of multiscriptural religiosity? This list of questions could easily be extended.[79] Where investigation of a Reformed understanding of practical theology and ethics might sit with regard to the religious Other or indigenous custom calls for a volume in its own right. The shift of Christianity's "center of gravity" away from its historic centers in Europe and North America to the global South demands such.[80]

In the present volume this very large field of inquiry is covered by what amounts to a case study. The matter of whether or not the Reformed faith makes a difference was tackled by *Hmar Vanlalauva* through a reading of Calvin in "the pluralistic Indian context." There is a need to be more specific and once again consider Kerr's positioning question. Vanlalauva's particular interpretation of Calvin is informed by the legacy of the Presbyterian mission to his homeland of Mizoram, India. Relatively recent work has been done on a Mizo contextual theology, seeking to make use of indigenous beliefs and spirituality.[81] That is not Vanlalauva's concern here. He is writing self-consciously in the wake of the radical transformation wrought by "mission and missionaries coming to our local land who were all rooted in the Calvinistic faith and tradition" within the "short span of 50/80 years." When writing later on this legacy, Vanlalauva identified the following areas where the coming of a Reformed mission made a clear difference: the rejection and removal of animistic practices, improvement in the status and role of women, abolition of slavery, establishing primary education, developing a written form of language through the translation of the Bible and

Christian hymns, the practice of medicine, an emphasis on the virtue of work, and a ban on excessive drinking.[82]

The present task before him is more daunting. Vanlalauva sets out to provide an "appraisal" of how distinctive key features of Calvin's theology may relate to the pluralist context of religions in India. The focus of attention is on the "contemporary" context rather than on earlier missionary periods through which Calvin's theology effectively became "part of the Christian faith and tradition in India." Vanlalauva is faced with a complex hermeneutic. The presenting issue is how to negotiate adverse criticism suggesting that Calvin's theology is likely to encourage an exclusivist understanding of the Christian faith, which is out of kilter with the pluralism to be found in India.

What Vanlalauva (and any other Reformed apologist in India) is dealing with here is the shadow side of making a difference and bequeathing a legacy. The issue that can nag away at any form of self-confidence is whether the Christian faith is bound to do "interpretive violence" to the cultural traditions of India (in this case). Ankur Barua asks whether the Christian worldview cannot but help demonstrate religious aggression and situates this question alongside the received understanding of Hindu tolerance. The underlying assumption is that Christianity is authoritarian and dogmatic and "breeds intolerance." The comparison can be made with Hinduism, which "represents a universalistic religion which breathes the air of open-minded tolerance."[83] Barua's argument examines Hindu responses to standard inclusivist Christian typologies of other faiths[84] and much more closely scrutinizes its claim to tolerance.[85]

The first step in Vanlalauva's response is simple enough. Calvin's theology needs to be understood in terms of the time and place in which it was generated. It is directed toward a particular sociology, and that theological setting was not one of having to respond to multiple other faiths that bore little or no resemblance to a Christian structure of belief and practice. Vanlalauva recognizes that Calvin needed to respond to "the demand of his age." The second step is the selection of doctrines that might illustrate the benefits or otherwise of Calvin's theology in this very different context. Vanlalauva opts for the knowledge and sovereignty of God. Both of these areas of belief are likely to be to the fore in an ongoing Reformed imaginary. But, as Vanlalauva shows, these "two important issues," which are "central to Calvin's theology," carry a high risk. The first problem lies in the distinction made between a knowledge of God that is natural and one that is mediated through Christ and is attested to through the primacy of Scripture and the interior witness of the Holy Spirit: "In the eyes of a number of Indian Christian theologians, Calvin's view of the knowledge of God appears to have lost its relevance." The second problem lies in the way in which the sovereignty and providence of God become vehicles for a theory of predestination that seemingly limits the grace of God and human freedom and responsibility.

Vanlalauva is in no doubts as to the benefits of the Reformed mission to the indigenous Mizo people. In terms of a hermeneutic retrieval of Calvin in much-changed circumstances, he is a sympathetic critic. The Indian context exposes some "weaknesses" in Calvin's theology that are either then modified or justified for the sake of that theological setting. Vanlalauva follows the way of those Indian theologians who are inclined to opt for a cosmic Christ or discern the presence of Christ in other faiths. The manner in which Calvin arrives at his understanding of predestination is explained in terms of the exigencies of the complex social, political, and economic pressures of the time. Vanlalauva is really exploring the Reformed legacy through a reading of Calvin in the presence of the Indian religious "main line." How a Reformed imaginary might play a future role in the practical theology and ethics of the Indian subcontinent may well be rather different from this tradition's historic centers. In the meantime Vanlalauva believes that the mainline religious traditions will find in Calvin a "good partner."

4. SOCIAL AND CULTURAL JUSTICE

The way in which a Reformed imaginary will need to engage with other faiths is a rather complex business. There are multiple settings in which this imperative will occur. Vanlalauva has demonstrated how a Reformed faith should address both its legacy in an indigenous mission field and its potential role among the company of theologians addressing the religious plurality in India. Barua refers to the encounter between the Indic and Abrahamic faiths, which operate from very different philosophical and metaphysical assumptions. In this kind of setting the Reformed imaginary comes in the form of what Hindu critics describe as a "foreign religion." From a Western experience, Barua's encounter no longer needs to happen "overseas." The global flows of people in recent times has led to culturally and religiously diverse neighborhoods throughout Europe, North America, Australia, and New Zealand. Some time ago, Diana Eck wrote of how a "Christian country," the United States, had become the "world's most religiously diverse nation."[86] This coming into the everyday experience of each other invariably raises matters to do with integration, assimilation, and the rhetoric of unity and diversity.

The presence of so much difference within particular nations has led to an increasing concern for whether or not a liberal multicultural society can actually deliver social justice.[87] The issue is no longer simply one of whether special rights for disadvantaged cultural groups or programs of affirmative action are justified. From the perspective of political philosophy, David Millar is addressing a different kind of question: "Does the very idea of social justice still make sense when societies become multicultural?"[88] The question is deceptively simple. For Millar the critical issue is not a case of society becoming socially just "through the distribution of resources according to valid principles of justice." The issue is whether or not there is reasonable agreement among the members of a culturally diverse society as to what those principles are. The moment a culture becomes more varied in its composition, the less "bounded" it becomes. In a variation on this theme, Naudé seeks a particular form of cultural and aesthetic justice based on identity. The need for such is established through effects of globalization.

The tendency is for the emphasis to fall upon the "mass," the worldwide, co-opting, and assimilating power of the seemingly universal. It can become ideological, requiring the Other to become like us. The irony of this irrepressible pressure is how it also marks out difference. Naudé has rightly identified how globalization is not simply about a free market and a digitally interconnected world: it is also a cultural force that has a profound effect upon "personal and national identities, social cohesion, and human coherence." What Naudé shows concern for is the prospect for cultural justice and the process through which personal identity is formed. The rise of globalization as a cultural force threatens the way of life of many peoples: it possesses the power to undermine patterns of cultural justice that are embedded in local cultures and through "what people take for granted." It can readily create the illusion that globalization's values are the only values now worth having. The aesthetic values of a culture as found in its national symbols of identity run the heightened risk of being taken away.

This way of thinking and behaving can easily become a contemporary equivalent of a survival of the fittest. The ethical dilemma Naudé has identified is one of what then ensues from such asymmetric power. The loss of what can be taken for granted is a burden unequally shared, deepening personal and communal "subjugation and humiliation." In the face of this threat of sameness, Naudé is defending the "right to be different" and "the right to [a] life unself-consciously" lived. Those most at risk are being asked to make the most far-reaching shifts for the sake of development and participation in this transnational power.

The cosmology lying behind globalization and its effect on cultural and personal stories sits uneasily with a Reformed imaginary. During the apartheid regime, Naudé wrote a number of essays about a Reformed perspective on apartheid, essays frequently cited by others. Yet on globalization's influence, there is no overt discussion on how a Reformed ethic might make a difference. Its presence is hidden away in a "few [concluding] biblical perspectives" surrounding "the challenge of who is Lord" and a reading of "the household of God in which difference is welcome."

5. THE COMMON GOOD

The emphasis on the future, on what might be, is more overtly opened up by *Max Stackhouse*. The emergence of a whole raft of new ethical issues surrounding sexual orientation, cloning, and ecology has Stackhouse posing a penetrating series of questions. Those issues lie at the intersection of evolution and theology. What should be a Reformed understanding of the doctrine of creation? It is evident that the human subject now has the capacity to alter what formerly appeared to be pregiven patterns of life. On what basis, then, do we seek to preserve some aspects of creation and yet alter others?

Stackhouse's interest lies in what he deems to be prior questions. Is there a "right knowable order of things in the biophysical universe"? Is there an "ethical connection to creation"? For the success of his argument, Stackhouse assumes an open rather than closed system of nature. There is an apologetic side to his thinking as he seeks to express a doctrine of creation where nature and what exists are open to the transcendent. Stackhouse is writing while fully aware that this Reformed tradition, and what it might want to say on these matters, now finds itself within a mix of global and local cultures; it would be easy to say that a Reformed view might simply be an act of special pleading in a forum of voices that include the secular public, tribal religious practices, and other major religions. In this increasingly complex setting, Stackhouse argues for a plausible form of public theology established in the idea of common grace.

Geoff Thompson presses harder. The Reformed traditions of common grace and civil responsibility lie in the background. The dilemma resides in a wrestling of what constitutes the basis on which a Christian social ethic might participate in the quest for the common good. It is not self-evident. The very idea of the common good can harbor significant injustices, "hidden prejudices and unacknowledged strategies of exclusiveness"; there is the core issue of whether a distinctive tradition can contribute to that which is common: Will it be accepted in the public forum? Will it be true to the actual tradition it is representing? There is also the ever-present risk of the church's sectarian withdrawal from the world into a position of ecclesial isolationism. Regarding that risk, Thompson is clear: he has no desire to establish a Christian commitment to the common good in theories of natural law or orders of creation. Nor should such activity beyond "the walls of the church" be seen as "an additional practice that the church might take up once it has been morally formed." Thompson makes the case, rather, that the church must engage with issues beyond its own walls as a consequence of its own formation as a Christian community. That word "formation" is critical since it assumes a process. The means by which socially involved Christian communities are formed is initiated not through the mere "replication of all of [the New Testament's] specific beliefs and practices; rather, a Christian social ethic is "initiated by hearing and responding to the proclamation of Jesus' life, death and resurrection." Thompson draws upon the work of Richard Hays in order to promote a moral vision that is grounded in three foci in the specific sequence of community, cross, and new creation. This is a community that seeks to "embody an alternative order" and be a "sign of God's redemptive purposes for the world." It acts out of an understanding of the cross that calls those with power and privilege to account. It recognizes the eschatological framework and prospect of a new creation, though we live in this time and place.

6. CLIMATE CHANGE AND THE ANTHROPOCENE

Stackhouse made reference to some specific issues that must be addressed in the wake of a Reformed commitment to a doctrine of creation. One of those has to do with the care of the environment. With the passage of time, that ecological concern has increasingly become more concentrated upon climate change and the common good. Writing in the *International Journal of Public Theology*, Clive Pearson has argued that the present time is a kairos moment for theology: our capacity to read "the signs of the times" (an interesting hermeneutical problem in its own right)[89] cannot but identify climate change as one of those "occasional issues" with which theology must engage and do so for the sake of the public good.[90]

It is arguably true that the problem has deepened with the advent of the Anthropocene epoch. It does not necessarily matter whether the relevant working group of the International Commission on Stratigraphy wishes to recommend the planting of a golden spike to determine whether we are now living in a new geologic epoch rather than the Holocene period. Clive Hamilton, Christophe Bonneuil and François Gemenne have identified how the Anthropocene has become an umbrella term that also covers Earth systems sciences and the social sciences. The critical assumption upon which the Anthropocene is based is the claim that there has been a "step-change" in the relationship between humanity and nature. The human species has become a "geologic agent" and has profoundly affected the interconnected Earth systems of climate, oceans, air, biological life, rocks, and atmospheric chemistry.[91] The haunting question has become whether or not, through human agency, we have already sealed the likely requiem for our species.[92] From a theological perspective the matter becomes one of endings and how we live justly in an interim period.[93]

The term "climate change" is a vexed label; it can easily lend itself to talk of what is described as a "(super)wicked problem"[94] and become a politicized naming in which great stakes are at work. How to encompass this transdisciplinary problem within an adequate conceptual framework is a widely recognized dilemma.[95] It could indeed be one of those umbrella terms that Ernst Conradie wrestled with in dealing with the problem of relating the universal to the particular (and vice versa) in the discussion about climate change and the common good.[96] Mike Hulme has declared that the term "climate change" should be seen more as an umbrella term that gives shelter to a number of discrete problems: global warming, rising sea level, loss of biodiversity, and population growth.[97]

For a Reformed faith one of the key questions must be, How are the doctrines of creation and salvation to be related to one another?[98] The threat of climate change and ecological deterioration necessarily puts pressure on how we understand the purpose of creation in the light of the sovereignty and redemptive grace of God.[99] The issue is not one of what we can do "to save the earth"; nor is it a case of hoping for an intervention of God in order to do the equivalent of a reset of creation.

Jong-Huk Kim is not dealing with climate change per se. He seeks to situate threats to "the delicate balance of the ecosystem" inside a Reformed "faith and lifestyle." The environmental crises he identifies are not merely crises of the environment. They are "deeply rooted in the fallen race and creation," which stand in need of reconciliation and a new way of living. Without using the language of

God's economy, Kim nevertheless invokes a Trinitarian view of the redemptive work of a sovereign and gracious God, to whom all gratitude is due.

7. ECONOMICS

This debate on caring for creation is being played out in a global context of many competing pressures. For some time Sallie McFague has drawn a contrast between a market-driven economic framing of the world and an ecological-economic framing of the world.[100] These two world views are deemed to be dramatically different in terms of their underlying values. They are the "mirror opposites of each other."[101] McFague argues that market capitalism is motivated by self-interest. It is a "type of economics that allocates scarce resources . . . on the basis of an individual's successful competition for them."[102] It does not necessarily consider the needs of the planet or all of the planet's inhabitants.[103] The contrast McFague makes is with the ecological-economic model, which "recognizes that we are both greedy and needy, even more so."[104] The axiom upon which it is built is the awareness that we require an economic agenda not focused upon individual selves. Our well-being is "seen as interrelated and interdependent with the well-being of all other living things and earth processes."[105]

Of particular significance for effecting a bridge with Kim's concerns and those of *Cameron Murchison* is McFague's more recent writing on consumption and the practice of restraint.[106] Murchison's intention is to examine the relationship between a Reformed theology and the capitalist economic order. That is not, of course, McFague's particular aim. She is seeking to respond to an "economic and environmental breakdown of more serious proportions than any generation of human beings before us."[107] Murchison's focus lies on a Reformed practical theology by which we might live in cultures that are embedded in consumerism. McFague's horizon is a planetary agenda. It is now time to put in place a "communal spirituality" that takes seriously the questions, Where are we? and, How might we live well in a context where there are "too many human beings using too much energy and taking up too much space on the planet?"[108] McFague proposes a countercultural kenotic, self-emptying, way of life rather than one that aspires to self-fulfillment on the basis of consumption.[109]

Murchison is effectively dealing with the legacy of Max Weber's *Protestant Ethic and the Spirit of Capitalism*.[110] The Weberian thesis assumed that "certain attitudes and habits engendered by Calvinism contributed to the development of capitalism." For his review of the theory, Murchison relies upon a rereading of Calvin himself and the distinction between production and consumption. The underlying assumption is that Calvin's emphasis on industry and frugality naturally led to capital accumulation, which would then provide the "launching pad for capitalist production." Murchison takes issue with potential consequences arising out of this implicit practical theology. The core question becomes, What, then, is the purpose of wealth? Is it, for example, to promote individual well-being and perhaps the pursuit of luxury and abundance? Writing in *The Oxford Handbook of Christianity and Economics*, Stackhouse asks, "Whence came the impulse to buy all the stuff produced?" And again, by way of comment, How did this "productive system" break free from "its earlier doctrinal underpinnings"? What influences were at work that "led not only to shopping for goods as a kind of entertainment connected to self-image, but [also] made religious 'shopping' for feel-good experiences an evangelical event"?[111] Welcome to the branding of cultures immersed in and dedicated to "affluenza."[112]

Murchison stays with Calvin and, in particular, with Calvin's own theological understanding of creation and calling. Individuals are directed to give their energies to work: that is their calling. The focus is on frugality and temperance in economic matters. What is left over is not meant for luxury, but for "relieving the needs" of others in the church community. Calvin always alludes to the communal framework for faithful Christian living. The purpose is fellowship, not the acquisition of wealth. On the other hand, there is a later "supplementary Protestant work ethic" that enabled the creation of "the longings that would undergird consumption."[113] In a rather strange way some of the impulses released within this Protestant ethic prepared a way for "the pleasures of . . . modern consumer hedonism."[114]

Murchison is distancing Calvin from a full capitalism in favor of a nuanced embrace. The dilemma that this implicit Reformed practice now needs to negotiate is the sheer level of change and difference between our world and that of the early Christians. Here then is a variation on the theme of consumption and the accompanying "moral paralysis" with which McFague deals. The alternative theory with which Murchison contends is John Schneider's argument on behalf of "luxuriating wantonly in abundance." This theory looks upon the present as providing a new species of acquisition that can liberate other human beings. Capitalism creates wealth that did not exist before and can initiate an improved lifestyle for many who otherwise would be left in poverty. Murchison is thus faced with the case that Schneider makes for acquisition and its enjoyment becoming desirable goals. This way of thinking is, of course, the "polar opposite" to McFague's emphasis on kenosis. Murchison is equally mindful of how this emphasis on creating wealth ignores costs other than economic. Writing self-consciously from within the Reformed tradition, Murchison invokes Calvin's understanding of reciprocity in matters of wealth.

8. GENETIC ENGINEERING, CLONING, THE POST(TRANS)HUMAN

Schneider was nevertheless accurate in one of his predisposing claims: the period in which we live is qualitatively different from the world of the early Christians. Nowhere is that more evident than in the field of theological ethics. The present is bearing witness to a remarkable range of fresh questions for which there are no direct precedents. The dawning of the Anthropocene epoch and its ecological challenges are matched by those arising out of genetic research, the emergence of artificial intelligence, and even the possibility of extraterrestrial life captured in the whimsical query about whether Pope Francis would baptize such aliens.[115] For Brent Waters the convergence of biotechnology, nanotechnology, robotics, and medicine ushers in a "brave new world" and the prospect of being posthuman.[116] The more recent discussions have raised the bar further to consider the relationship of theology to transhumanism, or *h+*.[117] What is the likely end of an ever-increasing array of "improvements" made possible by cell regeneration and "implantable devices that interact directly with the brain"? It is no wonder that *Kang Phee Seng* has likened the twenty-first century to "another planet" in comparison with the preceding centuries.

Kang's particular interest lies in the intersection between genetic engineering and a Christian theological ethic. This field is intrinsically complex due to a number of factors. The most obvious lies in the very nature of faith and how it makes up its moral mind. Here the dilemma immediately presents itself. On what basis can a Reformed or even a Christian position be put when there is no obvious link back from stem-cell research, for instance, to Scripture and the way in which it bears witness to the Christ event? The absence of such should come as no surprise. Neil Messer has rightly drawn attention to how there are multiple issues that modernity simply assumes but that biblical writers could not possibly foresee.[118] The hermeneutical problem is only sharpened the more we follow in the wake of Rachel Muers and consider what might constitute a theological ethics for coming generations.[119] In the circumstances it is valid to ask how a Christian ethic can be constructed on the basis of Scripture as a key source.

That line of inquiry likewise begs the question, What makes a Christian ethic Christian? Victor Lee Austin has identified several qualifying quests regarding method, authority, and definition as characteristic of any ethic that bears the name Christian or theological.[120] It is not work that can be ignored in the public spaces in which a Christian ethic must necessarily play itself out in practice. For the present purpose it is sufficient simply to recognize that this quandary exists; now is also not the time to make a detour into differing types of Christian ethics. The prior task is to acknowledge that the raft of dilemmas emerging out of biotechnological research and application are not peculiar to the Christian faith or any one of its constituent traditions.

The field is full of questions for which there are no precedents. Some of those have to do with levels of risk and for whose benefit and at what cost a genetic decision is made. It is not difficult to identify particular kinds of risk, like the practice of eugenics with a racist intent or perhaps in the service of more gifted children. The complexity is compounded because it is possible to identify what might be designated as a therapeutic benefit over and against a designer lifestyle option. Therese Lysaught observes how images of children suffering from a genetic disorder understandably become "icons of biotech research." The advances in biotechnology repeatedly put before us a highly contested "ethical dilemma," which is often then reduced to silence before the face of such a child.[121] Messer observes that it is also easy to list the apparent benefits for infertile couples, those who suffer from genetic disease, and those who are in need of an organ or tissue.[122]

These kinds of dilemmas can put pressure upon a further point of tension brought about by the sheer speed of discovery and the opening up of new possibilities. The implicit or explicit acceptance of some forms of genetic research and engineering can quickly lead to the possibility of one process paving the way for the acceptance of another, or indeed a way of changing the very nature of the moral framework within which the biotechnological possibilities arise.

The subject of this research and practice must eventually lead to the question What does it mean to be human? This type of question can be posed in a number of ways. It is present in the debate over the status of the embryo and its relationship to human life as well as the fate of surplus embryos. Would the one who is cloned be any less a human?[123] Lysaught wonders what it would be like to know you are an "imitation" or a replacement for a dead sibling?[124] Does not a child have a right to their own genetic identity? The discussion over what it means to be human is not just one of function and the possible commodification of human life. It is also an ontological question. The standard questions over what constitutes personhood, personal identity, and individuality have now become sharpened. What role does our genetic blueprint play alongside the equally important determinative factors of environment and experience? The technical advances necessarily lead to questions over the relationship between being human and the body. Can we photocopy or Xerox the soul?

The public context in which the Reformed imaginary must engage these debates can be highly emotive. The technology of genetic reproduction is not infrequently likened to playing God. For that to be plausible requires a loss of theological transcendence. For Kang, that balance is furnished through his drawing upon Reformed and ecumenical understandings of the Trinity and the incarnation. The ethical position he adopts is premised on a desire not to let human procreation be transformed into a "mere biological operation." The ease with which that can happen is through seemingly innocent shifts in language. Procreation becomes reproduction; babies are made rather than begotten. This latter distinction is taken from the work of Oliver O'Donovan. The act of begetting preserves the delicate balance of a child truly coming from us yet being different. It is a "chanced combination" rather than one which is manipulated and controlled. Kang's Reformed imaginary is applied for the sake of preserving that covenantal sense of a child being a "gift" given and received regardless of certain genetic qualities sought for and attained. The way in which the sovereignty of the triune God is invoked allows the prospect of a relationship between equals, between parent and child, rather than one of client and commodity.

AN AMBIVALENT VALUING

The invoking of an imaginary is a form of traditioning. The imaginary draws upon the past for the sake of establishing a principled framework; it does so also in order to understand and interpret the present for the sake of the future. It is likely that the themes and issues that a Reformed ethic and pastoral practice will need to engage in that future will stretch the ecclesial tradition. How plausible and attractive will a Reformed imaginary be for generations whose identity, sense of intimacy, and imagination are shaped by a network of apps[125] is a moot question. One thing that can be said is that the Reformed faith does offer a well-developed repository of theological beliefs and biblical ideas for attending to the tasks of a practical pastoral care as well as responding to life in the Anthropocene and biotechnological era.

To varying degrees the writers in this volume have positioned themselves inside a Reformed tradition and ethos. There has been a shared assumption of how a Reformed faith is called to participate in the transforming of an unjust world as well as to nurture the private faith and well-being of the individual. It is a self-critical appropriation of this tradition, however. The personal stories told by Davies, Ramsay, and Ackermann especially have testified to an ambivalent valuing of the Reformed legacy. There is a recognition of how its conversion into practice can mask blind spots that play themselves out in the denial of what a Reformed agenda would actually prize. The South African experience of apartheid serves as a stark warning. And yet, even at such times, there is scope and an inner impulse within the ethos that can furnish a refreshed and redemptive direction. This ambivalent experience is revelatory. It demonstrates that a Reformed expression of faith presupposes both a hermeneutic of suspicion as well as one of a retrieval of hope and charity.

The imaginary that has emerged with the way ahead in mind has prized the sovereignty of the triune God, a deeply realistic awareness of sin, a costly love of neighbor, and a central role assigned to Scripture. It is an imaginary that aspires after a common good and a civil society yet also is mindful of a deep disorder in human life, a disorder requiring the grace of God.

DEFINITIONS AND DIFFERENCES

Chapter 2

Could Being Reformed Have Made a Difference?

On Practical Theology and Ethics in South Africa[1]

DIRK SMIT

Does being Reformed mean doing practical theology and ethics in a distinctive and sometimes different way?
—Wallace M. Alston, letter of invitation to the conference sourcing *Imagining a Way*

My struggle has especially been against the [Dutch Reformed Church] as volkskerk which threatened the identity of the church as the church of Christ. I thought that the best way to change this was simply by doing good Reformed theology.
—Willie Jonker[2]

IN A SOMETIMES DIFFERENT WAY?

Does being Reformed mean doing practical theology and ethics in a distinctive and sometimes different way? This is the question put to this conference in the letter of invitation. For South African Reformed Christians and theologians, this is indeed a critical question. It is such not in the sense of an inquiry whether we should do practical theology and ethics in ways that are distinct from the work of scholars from other Christian traditions and communities; rather, it is in the sense of an inquiry whether we should not have done our own theology differently in the past, and whether we should not be doing it differently in the present. Is there not something involved in being Reformed that challenges the ways in which we have been doing, and perhaps still are doing, practical theology and ethics? If we had been more Reformed in our theology and ethics, would that not have been better for the church in South African society? Should we not, as Reformed theologians, have done our work in a different way?

Many people have little doubt that this is indeed the case. This is precisely the claim of John de Gruchy's well-known Warfield lectures, *Liberating Reformed Theology.* It is already hidden in his deliberately ambiguous title. He claims that Reformed theology is a liberating theology, but what we need is again to liberate this liberating theology from what it has become, from what it has been made, also, although certainly not only, in South Africa. The problem in South Africa, argues de Gruchy, in contradicting the widespread wisdom of popular opinion, has not been too much but too little Calvinism, not the presence but rather the absence of truly Reformed theology. If we had done our practical theology and ethics in a different way, in a more Reformed way, things would have been radically different. His whole work, then, becomes a sustained effort of critical retrieval, suspicious and creative reclaiming, and self-critical engagement with the Reformed tradition itself, appealing to its liberating moments and trajectories, and unmasking and criticizing oppressive moments and trajectories.[3]

It is also the claim of a very important essay by Willie Jonker, the retired systematic theologian of the Stellenbosch Faculty of Theology. He was invited to reflect critically on the *kragvelde,* the powerful influences determining the way of the (white) Dutch Reformed Church. He argues that three such forces historically characterized the Dutch Reformed Church: its close association with the Afrikaner people, its Reformed heritage, and a pietistic form of spirituality, mainly resulting from the influence of Scottish ministers in the nineteenth century. Jonker shows that the Dutch Reformed Church tried to uphold the confessional heritage but in reality combined it with support for the Afrikaner people and eventually its policy of apartheid. Since the fall of apartheid, the Dutch Reformed Church faces serious challenges from the side of the pietistic spirituality in its midst. According to Jonker, the Dutch Reformed Church has sadly never been Reformed enough, and it still faces the same temptation.[4]

Over the past years, the same claim has also been made by many well-known Reformed South African scholars—including Jaap Durand and David Bosch, Takatso Mofokeng and Lekula Ntoane, Allan Boesak, Christiaan Loff and Hannes Adonis, Coenie Burger, Russel Botman and Piet Naudé—from different churches, different generations, and different phases of the struggle against apartheid.[5] They all share the same conviction. A church is not necessarily Reformed because it has "Reformed" in its name. Practical theology and ethics are not Reformed simply because they are done by theologians who belong to Reformed churches. Even deliberate claims to be "Reformed" offer no guarantee thereof. It is necessary to keep asking the critical normative question: Should "being Reformed" not imply a distinctive way of doing theology and therefore sometimes a different way from what we are actually doing?

The answer to this question is notoriously difficult and extremely controversial. Who could determine what being Reformed would mean? Claiming and owning the tradition is precisely part of the problem. Like all living traditions, being Reformed is "a historically extended, socially embodied argument, precisely in part about the goods which constitute the tradition," in the well-known words of Alasdair Macintyre.[6] In South Africa this has been particularly and painfully true. The story of Reformed theology in South Africa was integrally woven into the story of society at large, which itself was a story of division, exclusion, separateness, and conflict, a story of worlds apart. The story of our Reformed theology is a story of many stories, depending on who is telling the story.[7]

During the struggle against apartheid, the Bible was sometimes called "a site of struggle." It meant that the interpretation of the Bible was controversial yet also of crucial importance. It made a difference to whom the authority belonged to determine the reading of the Bible, and the same was true of being Reformed.[8] To claim that being Reformed means something distinctive and could or should have made a difference to our practical theology and ethics— that is already deeply controversial. Therefore, before we reflect briefly on the question, perhaps it could be helpful to remind ourselves of some very general and well-known characteristics of Calvin's own vision and of his own kind of theology.

ON CALVIN'S THEOLOGIA PRACTICA

Looking to Calvin in search of what being Reformed means is, of course, already controversial.[9] Even if that would be acceptable, however, Calvin scholarship is itself a site of struggle.[10] These struggles become particularly fierce when the focus is not merely historical, reconstructing what Richard Muller calls the "unaccommodated Calvin," but when it is also to find some vision or orientation in Calvin's life and work: they have been fierce now for several centuries, as in South African circles.[11] Whose Calvin? Whose Reformed theology? That is already the question. Through the lenses of which tradition of interpretation should one read Calvin? In the case of South Africa there are several candidates, ranging from Kuyper's version to Barth's, each with its own controversial local *Wirkungsgeschichte*, or history of effects.[12]

Yet, in spite of these controversies, it would be difficult for anyone to deny that Calvin's theology was practical. It was not so in the contemporary sense of an academic subdiscipline within the theological curriculum, but in the general sense of *theologia practica*, as it was indeed known during his life and times. For Calvin, theology was not speculative, merely theoretical, merely intellectual. He was very much aware of the practical purposes of theology, and for him this commitment was of extreme importance. For Calvin, doing theology was all about practice, about life, piety, obedience, discipleship, and renewal.

Almost everyone, irrespective of their tradition of Calvin-interpretation, seems to agree with this broad but crucially important consensus. Calvin's *Institutes* should be read as a "handbook of piety," explains Lewis Battles: it is "spiritual biography in a systematic form," "paving the road" for readers—who are members of the congregation and students of theology—to read the Scriptures in the same "personal, experiential way."[13] The *Institutes* is an *Erbauungsbuch*, a book intended for edification, instruction, spiritual formation, claims Paul Böttger.[14] Calvin's theology is all about the renewal of the mind, says Ellen Charry, who uses that claim as the key to unlock the practical, pastoral purpose of all theology.[15] "Calvin regarded theology as a practical science designed for the edification of the church," according to John Leith.[16] Calvin's theology is intended toward the glorification of God, toward worship, prayer, and spirituality. It is intended toward reformation, toward renewal of believers, of church, and of society. It is, therefore, deeply historical, not timeless; it is rhetorical, very intentionally and deliberately, consciously and carefully addressed to specific audiences and readers, in order to persuade and move them toward concrete decisions, actions, and policies. That intention has been convincingly demonstrated by many, including Serene Jones in her study of *Calvin's Rhetoric of Piety*.[17] In short, his theology has a pastoral purpose, a political purpose, a teaching purpose, a catechetic purpose, an edifying purpose: the seemingly diverse claims in recent Calvin scholarship somehow all complement one another. Calvin was deeply committed to a *theologia practica*, in spite of the "deceptively orderly and seemingly dispassionate pages."[18]

For the Reformed tradition and community, for the Reformed vision and faith, for doing Reformed theology, and for being Reformed, this style is indeed characteristic and distinctive. But why was this the case? Why was Calvin so deeply convinced of the practical purpose of theology, and why was this so remarkable? For him, the goal (*finis*) of life, the very purpose of being human, was to know God—as in the opening question and answer of the Geneva Catechism (1542). This concept, Calvin's notion of knowledge (*cognitio*), argues Hans-Joachim Kraus, is so "fundamental and essential" to Calvin and belonged to the "newness of concepts," "even to a modern language" introduced by Calvin. For him, "knowledge of God is not a theory but a praxis: the praxis of trust and obedience, the praxis of life under God and his will." So it is essentially called in the *Institutes*: "All right knowledge of God is born of obedience" (*Institutes* 1.6.2). . . . Just as the knowledge of God is praxis, so also is theology . . . praxis, because, according to Calvin, it stands in a threefold definition: when it is executed correctly, it works *aedificatio* (the establishment of the community and the life of the Christian), bears *fructio* (fruit), and is characterized by *utilitas* (usefulness)."[19]

Once again, there are many ways to understand and appropriate the content of Calvin's practical knowledge of God. Calvin scholarship again faces serious internal divisions, yet again it is also possible to claim a rather broad consensus. This knowledge is Trinitarian; it is knowledge in Jesus Christ, knowledge of the Father through the power of God's Spirit; it is knowledge of the Living God, and it is intended to become visible, to become concrete, to be practiced in the real world. It is indeed a life-changing knowledge.[20]

ON CALVIN AND THE CHRISTIAN LIFE

It is for this reason that the Christian life occupies such a central role in Calvin's thought and work.[21] Again, this is characteristic and distinctive of the Reformed vision, as can easily be demonstrated by many developments and disputes. The Christian life, discipleship, sanctification, the third use of the law, a life of grace and gratitude, the covenant, vocation, ethics; organizing the church according to Scripture; transforming society, politics, economic life, culture, education, science, yes, history and the world, according to Scripture; a life of confessing the faith in the face of challenges and crises, temptations and threats, including moral and ethical challenges and temptations; longing for justice, dreaming of freedom, praying for peace; living before the face of God, being united with Jesus Christ, being renewed by the power of the Spirit; daily dying and being raised again—all this belongs to being Reformed, this is distinctive of the Reformed faith,[22] following Calvin's own conviction that *non enim linguae est doctrina, sed vitae* (doctrine is not an affair of the tongue, but of life; *Institutes* 3.6.4).[23]

What, then, is the Christian life, according to Calvin? When the renowned Reformed scholar John Leith finally published his 1948 Yale dissertation in 1989 as *John Calvin's Doctrine of the Christian Life*, his supervisor, Albert Outler, summarized the answer when he wrote: "The heart of the matter for Calvin was the *sola Gloria Dei*. This was echoed in his oft-repeated motto, 'We are God's; . . . to Him, therefore, let us live and die'" (*Institutes* 3.7.1).[24]

We know to whom we belong. This is our deepest comfort. We do not belong to ourselves. We belong to Jesus Christ, with body and soul, in life and death, and hidden in this wonderful comfort of God's promises is the claim of God on our whole lives. This is indeed the heart of Calvin's views on the Christian life, and the heart of the Reformed tradition's sense of identity and calling. The evidence is there in a series of confessions, including the Heidelberg Catechism (1563), Barmen Declaration (1934), Belhar Confession (written 1982, adopted 1986), the Brief Statement of Faith of the Presbyterian Church (U.S.A.) (1983), the *processus confessionis* (from 1997 onward) of the World Alliance of Reformed Churches, and others, yet also in many documents, liturgies, events, figures, theological and popular works, and historical developments.[25]

In Calvin's vision the Christian life deals with real people, with the real church, and with the real world. It may sound almost commonsensical and trivial, but it is of crucial importance for understanding the distinctiveness of being Reformed, and appreciating this more fully could perhaps have helped us to do our practical theology and ethics in sometimes different ways.

Calvin was interested in *real people*, in the concrete implications of our belonging to the living God and his Christ for our everyday lives. For him, knowledge of God and knowledge of ourselves go hand in hand: they mutually inform one another. He was deeply concerned with human nature, with human relationships, with the hidden sinfulness and idolatries of hearts and their everyday consequences in our daily activities. He was addressing issues related to our *vivificatio* and our *mortificatio*, how we continuously become alive in Christ and through the Holy Spirit.[26] He was aware that grace calls forth gratitude, acts, indeed lives of newness, justice, fairness, compassion, freedom, equity. This is why he is often described as a true *pastor*, concerned with real people and their real experiences.

Calvin was also interested in the *real church*, in the concrete implications of our belonging to the living God and his Christ for the real, visible, worshiping, organized church. Particularly since his return from Strasbourg to Geneva, he realized that the confession of the church should be practically embodied by and in the church—in and around the renewal of worship, in and through the organization of the congregation, in and through the order and discipline, the ministries and the structures of the church, in the search for practicing in the visible church the unity, the holiness, the catholicity, and the apostolicity of the invisible church we confess and believe. Like few others in history, he made his concrete, practical reflections on the real church an integral part of his theology, in the practical ecclesiology of the *Institutes*, book 4. For him, *ecclesia reformata semper reformanda* means exactly what it says: a Reformed church should be continuously reforming, according to the Word of God. Unlike many of his contemporaries, he did not think that the order, the structure, the ministries, the services, the (lack of) unity of the real church could be left to whichever social and political powers and ideas of the day to determine how the real church should be and should live. This is why he became such an influential *reformer of the church* and why his thought became such a major international legacy.

Calvin was also interested in the *real world*, in society, in the city-state of Geneva, and in its politics and legal system, its culture and economic life, its educational system, its health system, its human and inhuman qualities, its social achievements, challenges, and failures. His theology was framed by politics. "That God may rule among the nations—is this not the central theme of Calvin's theology?" asks Battles. "This explains the 'political frame' of the *Institutes*: it begins with the letter to the French king, Francis I, and ends with the famous chapter on political government. Calvin's theology lives in the real world and squarely faces it."[27] His reformation was intended to be world-transformative.[28] For him, the whole of creation, including nature and history, was the theater of God's glory, where we should live thankfully before the face of God, to whom we all belong. This is why he is known as a *social humanist* and why his impact on our modern world—on democratic politics, on civil society, on free-market economy, on social care, on public education, on science and scholarship, yes, on today's complex processes of globalization—can be both highly praised and furiously criticized, but hardly denied.[29]

In his *Calvin, Geneva, and the Reformation*, Calvin-scholar Ronald S. Wallace, who also wrote on *Calvin's Doctrine of the Christian Life*, therefore rightly summarizes this broad consensus when he describes Calvin as "social reformer, churchman, pastor, and theologian." He was a theologian precisely in that he was a pastor, a renewer of the church, and a social reformer; he was a theologian precisely because he was interested in the continuous renewal of real people, of the real church, of the real world.[30]

The polemical nature of all three of these aspects of Calvin's theology is obvious. It is indeed possible, and often popular, to do Christian theology in ways that are not concerned with the renewal of the lives of real people, with the continuous reformation of the real church, and with the transformation of the real world, all according to the Word of the Living God. For the Reformed tradition and community, these forms of doing theology should be seen as forms of temptation, in whichever new historical situations they may present themselves.

This emphasis on the transformation of real people, the real church, and the real world remained characteristic of the Reformed vision—but what does "real" really mean, when used in this way? John Leith's essay on "Calvin's theological realism and the lasting influence of his theology" may be helpful. He describes Calvin's realism as the capacity to see things as they really are and to speak about them simply, concretely, and clearly;[31] even so, the expression "as they (really) are" is ambiguous. It refers, one could probably say, to the way things are and the way they could be, as well as to the way they are for us and the way they are for the Living God and his Christ. In Calvin's epistemology, we learn to see and know ourselves, the church, and the world in the mirror, which is Jesus Christ, as we look into the face of the Living God. Faith, for Calvin, is never to stop thinking about what we see in this mirror: faith is "contemplating the face of God" (*Institutes* 1.1.2).

This form of realism, therefore, calls for a double hermeneutic. It must involve seeing, reading, interpreting, understanding both the real content of the Scriptures *and* the real conditions of our own lives, of the church, and of the world. It is not surprising, therefore, that all the Reformed theologians who are known for their own forms of realistic theology—albeit in their own particular ways, including Abraham Kuyper *and* Karl Barth, Reinhold Niebuhr *and* H. Richard Niebuhr, A. A. van Ruler, T. F. Torrance—were very much aware of this double hermeneutic, this simultaneous seeing of the Scripture and everyday reality.[32] The same is true in Michael Welker's "biblical-realistic theology," and in South Africa in John de Gruchy's "seeing things differently."[33] It is only this "realistic double vision" that makes it possible to distinguish between destructive and creative powers, between structures and developments, between life-destroying and life-sustaining potentialities;[34] it is this double vision that makes it possible to live a life of discernment.

In the subdisciplines of practical theology and ethics, this double vision, this challenge to do realistic theology, seeing things—ourselves, the church, the world—"as they really are," would lead to serious difficulties, to perennial tensions and continuing controversies, about method and content, about theory and practice. It did so in South African Reformed circles.

BEING REFORMED AND PRACTICAL THEOLOGY IN SOUTH AFRICA

Calvin's world no longer exists. We live in a radically different reality. It is no longer possible to return to sixteenth-century Geneva. Every attempt to do that, to accommodate Calvin to our present needs and purposes, must fail and will in effect betray his own historical, contextual, and rhetorical theology and legacy. Doing his form of *theologia practica* has become impossible. Between us lies the advent of modernity and also the impact of the Enlightenment on theology. One major effect was the gradual division of *theologia* into diverse subdisciplines, each struggling to establish itself as academic disciplines in the context of modern universities, with its own subject matter and methodology. It is indeed against this background that we now consider the question, Can being Reformed make a difference in the way we do practical theology and ethics?

In 1991 the South African Council of Human Science Research, in their well-known series on methodology in scholarly disciplines, published research by Coenie Burger on the state of practical theology in South Africa.[35] The investigation was done in the late 1980s, a time of crisis in church and society. Together with Hennie Pieterse, the respected practical theologian from the University of South Africa, Burger first presented a survey of practical theology in Germany, the Netherlands, and the United States of America. The reasoning behind this line of approach was that developments in these three countries had the strongest influence on local scholarship in the discipline at the time. Against this background, Burger carefully inquired into how almost all the practitioners in university departments and seminaries, across the whole country, responded to the major issues and questions related to their work. His findings are still very instructive with regard to our question.

More than half of the people were from the Reformed-Presbyterian-Congregational tradition. Did being Reformed offer them anything distinctive, and did it make any difference to what they were doing? The answers were confusing and self-contradicting.

Only a small minority claimed very explicitly that they were Reformed. The majority were reluctant to acknowledge their confessional heritage. However, when asked which definitions of practical theology they preferred, the majority chose definitions that probably sounded Reformed to them. Their responses to other answers, however, belied this claim. In practice they were not doing what their own definitions said.

The definition that most of them preferred was from Willie Jonker's inaugural lecture "Theologie en praktijk," where he emphasizes four aspects of the practical theological task: (1) It deals with the services of the church itself (not merely with training ministers). (2) It is fully theological (not merely methodological). (3) It studies the Scriptures with a view to be in the service of the church (not merely developing theories for the practice of the church). (4) It involves serious study (*een degelijke kennisname*) of the concrete human beings to whom the services of the church are directed (therefore never ignoring and neglecting the church's responsibility to study seriously the real, historical, contextual, contemporary world).[36] In short, two aspects of the practical theological task are seen to be crucially important at the same time: "a radical theological orientation" (studying the Word, in the service of the church) *and* therefore precisely studying humanity, communication, life.[37]

The Reformed respondents to Burger's questions preferred this definition but seemingly affirmed only the aspect of studying the Word of God, effectively ignoring all three other aspects.

First, they did see their work as primarily training ministers for the official ministry in the church, thereby uncritically and simply continuing existing practices and views of the minister. Burger was very critical in his comments. With McCann and Strain, he regarded this tendency as a dangerous temptation for practical theology not to keep enough critical distance from the existing ministries and practices of institutionalized churches. He agreed with Jonker that "a radical theological orientation" is necessary for the discipline, and also with Rudolf Bohren that "the best preparation for practical theology is a solid knowledge of the whole of theology."[38]

Second, however, almost without exception these practical theologians acknowledged that they hardly ever read any theology, and certainly not systematic theology. They did not in any way consider that necessary for the practical theology they were doing; they were not aware of general developments in theology. Burger concluded that there was hardly any correlation between their confessional theological heritage and the presuppositions actually at work in what they were doing (*die respondente se effektiewe uitgangspunte*). It is possible to speak of "theological inconsistency and even schizophrenia," Burger wrote with surprise.[39]

Third, they also ignored the importance of understanding the historical context, the reality in which they lived, the society at large. Burger's comments are critically important. The second dangerous temptation, he said (in addition to a lack of theological orientation and critical distance), is irrelevance, because of a failure to see the needs of human beings and of society; it is a failure "to see the world with the discerning and sensitive eyes of the Lord." In practical theological circles in South Africa at the time, he observed a need for "real contextuality."

For Burger, however, such discernment is not necessarily the result of what is often called empirical or phenomenological theology, based primarily on quantitative surveys and the results from questionnaires and interviews. True discernment calls for something deeper, something that can easily elude both practical theology and the church, particularly in times of crisis. With some understatement, Burger wrote:

> A time of crisis, like we experience in South Africa today, does not necessarily improve the church's judgement of what is happening and what is at stake. It can happen very easily in such a situation that the church is so afraid of the real, deeper questions of the time and that the church feels so

unprepared and unable to face these real questions that it becomes the easy way out simply to continue with traditional ministerial practices.

It is not easy to discern, in times of crisis, what the real questions of the historical situation are and where the deepest need is. To know where and how the church should fulfil its calling of healing in such a situation is even more difficult.

In South Africa, however, practical theology can simply not escape in-depth discussions concerning the social and political situation. Any form of ministry and service that does not take the social and political situation of South Africa into account, and seek to respond in responsible ways, should be seriously questioned.

This again underlines the folly of thinking that a church or that practical theologians on their own, without conversation and consultation with others, can determine what the real problems and needs are in any given situation.[40]

Burger wrote these comments during the time of crisis in South African society. It is immediately clear that his own pleas (for more theology and better understanding of the context), like Jonker's views much earlier (for more theology and better understanding of human beings), both reflect the "double vision" of being Reformed, seeing the real world through the lenses of the true Word. Both were obviously concerned for practical theology to be more distinctly Reformed and to be done in different ways.

ON BEING REFORMED AND ETHICS IN SOUTH AFRICA

What has been the case with ethics? Again, could being Reformed have made a difference?

South African scholarship has already offered several recent-history overviews of the subdiscipline of theological ethics: there have been books, volumes of journals, literature surveys, and several careful interpretations and critiques, in papers and articles, among others by Etienne de Villiers, Piet Naudé, and Nico Koopman.[41] The question of whether being Reformed could have made a difference has never been the direct focus of these studies; nevertheless, it is still possible to infer from their work at least four perspectives of interest.

First, with regard to the recent history of South Africa, it would be difficult and even problematic to consider the ethical work done in scholarly circles in isolation from the moral discourses and ethical controversies occurring in church and society. In particular, de Villiers and Koopman have repeatedly used James Gustafson's description of four different types of moral discourse—prophetic, narrative, technical, and policy—to demonstrate convincingly that the most important ethical work in South Africa was not done in academic circles but in the lively, everyday confrontations in church and public life.[42] The *moral discourses* that really made a difference in South Africa were the slogans, visions, declarations, public accusations and appeals, speeches and cries of prophets and protesters; the parents' and preachers' stories of human experiences, sufferings, aspirations, fears, memories, undergirded by stories of faith, hope, and love from the Bible; and the speeches, explanations, motivations, ideological language, programs, and practical decisions of policymakers, politicians, and people in positions of power.

Compared with this, the discourses of scholarly ethics—of graduate teaching and postgraduate work, of publications, journals, books, and academic conferences—were largely irrelevant, if not absent and silent. Serious ethics, at least in the recent past in South Africa, was not done in academic circles, but as part and parcel of the everyday activities of church and public life. The more interesting question is, therefore, whether it could have made a difference if all these everyday moral discourses would have been more Reformed?

Second, regarding these complex moral discourses in church and society, both de Villiers and Naudé point to the fact that a certain kind of Reformed morality and ethics did indeed play a dominant role. Thus de Villiers repeatedly refers to "the conservative Reformed morality" that dominated public life in South Africa. He attributes this cultural practice to the "theocracy temptation" to which the Afrikaans Reformed Churches succumbed. Naudé refers to an "Afrikaner civil religion, formed and sustained by both Scottish evangelicalism and Kuyperian Neo-Calvinism," which was not paying enough attention to "Karl Barth's criticism of religion and natural theology," he claims.

Here we face de Gruchy's and Tanker's comments again. Was the dominant morality in South Africa indeed Reformed and therefore too Reformed? Or was it Reformed only in name, but not really Reformed, not Reformed enough? Naudé quotes Jonker with approval: "My struggle has especially been against the DRC as *volkskerk* which, according to me, threatened the identity of the church as the church of Christ. I thought that the best way to change this was simply by doing good Reformed theology."[43]

There is no doubt how Jonker, de Gruchy, Naudé, Boesak, Botman, and many others would answer our question Could being Reformed have made a difference? Yet that raises another serious question: What *is* "good Reformed theology"?

Third, regarding the nature of scholarly ethics specifically in (white) Dutch Reformed circles during these years, Naudé makes interesting observations about its awareness of context and contextuality. For many years in South Africa, he says, those doing Dutch Reformed Church ethics, an integral part of Dutch Reformed Church theology, were not really aware of being part of Africa, theologizing on African soil, and having to face African issues and problems. He refers to Jonker's warning that many of them had not even been aware that their theology (and ethics) was oriented toward Europe: they believed that they were simply doing "theology."[44]

One could probably argue that this lack of contextual awareness in the Dutch Reformed Church showed a serious lack of being Reformed, at least in Calvin's sense, and that to a large extent it was caused by the lack of church unity in the

Dutch Reformed Church family and the deliberate and almost sectarian absence of the Dutch Reformed Church from ecumenical church circles in South Africa at the time. And that absence also showed a serious lack of being Reformed according to Calvin's vision. The lack of church unity led to the lack of contextual awareness.

During the first years of the dramatic transformations in South African society, Naudé continues, scholarly ethics in (white) Dutch Reformed circles did become more contextually aware. However, its ethicists were now more particularly aware of the impact of (Western) secularization, rather than being more aware of being part of African life and realities. The long list of ethical questions and issues that he finds in Dutch Reformed Church scholarly publications of the time certainly confirms this observation. The focus, at least during the first years of transformation, is still more on Western developments and issues than on everyday South African realities and challenges. Again, it remains a serious question whether such work is being truly Reformed?

Fourth, regarding scholarly ethicists in South Africa, Naudé also points out that it would be unfair to consider their work in isolation from the work in other theological subdisciplines. Even regarding moral issues and questions, practitioners of all theological fields carry a shared responsibility. He demonstrates, for example, how influential biblical scholarship is within the South African context, because of the powerful influence of the Bible as the book of the church. In South Africa, interpretation matters, in David Tracy's famous phrase, which makes biblical scholarship a practice with enormous power and therefore responsibility.[45] At least within South Africa the question of what might be the distinctive Reformed perspectives should properly be addressed to the whole of theological activity, not merely to scholarly ethics.

SO, COULD BEING REFORMED MAKE A DIFFERENCE?

It is clear that the question in the letter of invitation, from a South African perspective, implies a variety of other critical questions.

First, do we care enough about *real people*? During the apartheid years, could it have made a difference if practical theology and ethics in South Africa would have been more sensitive to the real needs of real people, as Calvin had been? And can it make a difference today? In their edited volume *Liberating Faith Practices: Feminist Practical Theologies in Context*, Denise Ackermann and Riet Bons-Storm claim that practical theology is probably the theological discipline least influenced by feminist voices. When practical theologians say people, they (mostly) mean males, whether male clergy or other male persons. Therefore Bons-Storm, from the Reformed tradition in the Netherlands, argues for a feminist practical theology sensitive to particularity, to difference, and especially to excluded, marginalized concrete Others, the "little ones." "My colleagues speak about 'people.' This denies the fact that there are no 'people.' There are only women and men in their different situations, and in their different positions of power and powerlessness in society and the churches," she writes. In similar vein Ackermann argues for a feminist theology of praxis for healing and suggests communal lament as vital to healing in the South African society.[46] Would not such a theology of praxis—caring for real, concrete, marginalized people, and searching for grace and forgiveness, for justice and reconciliation, for fellowship and healing amid suffering and injustice—have been more faithful to Calvin's own deeply pastoral intuition and theology and thus to being truly Reformed?

Second, do we care enough about the *real church?* Could it have made a difference if practical theology and ethics in South Africa would have been more committed to the unity and therefore the radical renewal of the real church, like Calvin, instead of working, for example, primarily within a clerical paradigm or a fundamentally empirical approach toward congregational studies? Instead, practical theology and ethics were simply strengthening the status quo, lacking the ability to discern, the spiritual sensitivity that can see differently, that can recognize the deep need for fundamental renewal and reformation, according to God's Word. Could we have cared more for the service of the church, in Jonker's words, the witness and integrity of the church, for the living unity, the real reconciliation and the caring justice to which the church is called? Would it not have been different if more practical theologians in South Africa had showed the *fyngevoeligheid*, the spiritual sensitivity and discernment, for what really matters in the church of the triune God—the sensitivity that practical theologians in the tradition of Jonker, Firet, Heitink, Burger, and Louw all take as its primary task?[47] Would it not be different now? And, is not the first task of theological ethics the responsibility to look in the right direction, to see and accept the real challenges, the real threats to the Christian life—as de Gruchy, de Villiers, and Mouton have argued?[48]

Third, do we care enough about *our context*, our society, our world? Could it have made a difference if practical theology and ethics in South Africa would have been more responsive to the real challenges of their real sociohistorical context, as Calvin was? And would our work—our priorities, our research, our teaching—perhaps be different today? Or is being Reformed no longer possible, given the complexities of the modern world, with globalization, economic injustice, ecological destruction, and greed?[49] Have Reformed theologians indeed lost their nerve, as Michael Welker seems to suggest, and retreated into self-secularization?[50]

Fourth, is our theology in general *theological* enough? Is it not unfair toward practical theologians and ethicists to ask them how being Reformed could affect their work, when their work is precisely being done in institutional separation from other theological disciplines? Could it have made a difference if Calvin's sense that the whole of theology is practical could have been retained? Is this still possible, to regain some form of meaningful unity in the practice of theology, between what has developed into often completely separate disciplines? Does being Reformed not fundamentally challenge the way in which each theological subdiscipline, including practical theology and ethics, continuously attempts to establish itself as a separate scholarly enterprise, with its own distinct method and field? In two earlier conferences, systematic theologians and biblical scholars have already considered whether being Reformed makes a difference to their work: But is the ultimate challenge not to have representatives of all these disciplines together in order to consider these questions?

And finally, is our theology *Reformed* enough? Could it have made a difference if we had retained Calvin's sense of how the whole of theology is about the honor of God and therefore about the Christian life? What if we really lived like people who do not belong to ourselves? Is it (still) possible for practical theology and ethics to take their respective points of departure in a deep commitment to the *vivificatio* and the *mortificatio* of the gospel of Jesus Christ, in a deep commitment to continuous renewal and reformation according to God's Word, and therefore in a deep commitment to the confessional tradition, including a willingness to confess again, whenever necessary? Or is all of this excluded by the scholarly canons of modernist academic activities and its claims of objectivity and neutrality? But then, do we really agree on what being Reformed means? Where do we find the Reformed tradition? Who speaks on its behalf? This will probably be an underlying theme in all discussions of Reformed identity, and South Africa's recent past offers a helpful illustration of its difficulty. It will continue doing so because here being Reformed seemingly did make a major and disastrous difference: some feel there was far too much Reformed theology, and some feel it was far too little.

Chapter 3

Globalization and the Challenge of Cultural Justice

PIET NAUDÉ

In a recent essay "Globalisierung in wissenschaftlich-theologischer Sicht,"[1] Michael Welker gives an interesting shorthand description of globalization:

> Globalisierung heist: Entwicklung eines immer staerker verdichtenden Netzwerks von Verbindungen und Interdependenzen zwischen Menschen und Kulturen. In diesem Prozess können stärker die Spannungen, Konflikte und Zusammenstösse zwischen den Kulturen, zwischen politisch-ökonomischsen Interessen und den Rechts- und Wertsystemen hervorgehoben werden.[2]
>
> Globalization can be described as follows: The development of an increasingly close network of connections and interdependences among peoples and cultures. In this process the tensions, conflicts, and clashes between the cultures, between political-economic interests and the legal and value systems can emerge stronger.

Welker then explains how the ecumenical church and academic theology participate in and contribute to the closer interconnection of the world, but he warns that we should maintain "eine gesunde Skepsis gegenüber allgemeinen Bildern der Globalisierung [a healthy skepticism toward general pictures of globalization]."[3] The reason for this skepticism is that the ideal of closer connections and communication in the world usually does not materialize in practice:

> Das Bild vom "global village," von der Welt als Dorf, in der alle mit allen harmonisch kommunizieren, . . . verfehlt aber völlig die heute möglichen Realisierungschancen in wirklicher Raumzeit.[4]
> The presentation of a global village, of the world as village, in which everyone communicates harmoniously with everyone, . . . however, completely lacks the opportunities to be realized today in actual space and time.

Welker builds this sober conclusion on concrete experiences in building a truly global theological network that would be as inclusive as possible but which time and again stumbles, due to vast differences in academic infrastructure, competencies, and support in various parts of the world.

Based on the updated and detailed overview of ecumenical literature regarding globalization by Konrad Raiser and others,[5] it is clear that the predominant focus is the ethical and theological challenges related to the impact of a global neoliberal market economy and its concomitant "*ökologische Brutalismus* [ecological brutalism]." A prime example is the Accra Confession,[6] which depicts the current global system as an evil empire that destroys both the lives of people and the earth.

An emerging theme, and the focus of this chapter,[7] is the issue of globalization as a powerful *cultural force*, shaping personal and national identities, social cohesion and human coherence "at the intersection of trans-national forces, cross-cutting the local and the global."[8] Welker's description[9] of globalization specifically mentions cultural networks and tensions among cultures and how Bedford-Strohm reminds us that "auch kulturelle Prozessen unter dem Stichwort 'Globalisierung' in den Blick genommen [werden muss] [cultural processes should also be viewed under the catchword 'globalization']."[10] The economic face of globalization calls forth issues related to distributive and ecological justice; also, the cultural-technological face calls forth issues related to cultural and aesthetic justice, including values that shape identity formation.[11]

GLOBALIZATION AS CULTURAL FORCE OF IDENTITY TRANSFORMATION

There are as many definitions of culture[12] as there are social scientists. For the sake of our discussion here, two notions of culture will be put forward. The first is by Clifford Geertz, who espouses a semiotic view based on his interpretation that the "[hu]man is an animal suspended in webs of significance . . . spun [by the self, and] I take culture to be those webs." Culture is, therefore, an "interworked system of construable symbols" in which social events can be intelligibly described.[13] Through their interrelation these symbols form a cultural map within which people negotiate their identities. In a later publication on social cohesion, Chirevo Kwenda takes a shorter route and sees culture merely as "our way of life" and "what people take for granted." In other words, "It is that comfort zone within, and out of which, we think, act and speak. If it is our 'mother culture,' we do all these things without having to be self-conscious about what we are doing."[14]

Both culture and identity are fluid and hybrid notions. On an individual level, we live in overlapping social territories and migrate among different social roles constructed on the basis of who we are and who we are becoming. On a group or national level, this is equally true: cultures and identities are constantly negotiated between "what is taken for granted": between what is an assumed network of significance and a changing environment that might seek to disarrange our symbolic cultural maps.

In an ideal world, such identity negotiations may occur peacefully, in symmetrical powers, and over an extended period, so that natural assimilation and hybridization enrich this "meeting of cultures" and evolving of identities. But we have ample examples in history and the contemporary world that such processes often derail. "We know that for these four words, 'our way of life,' people are often prepared to kill or be killed. In such instances, it becomes clear that there is a very small step from 'a way of life' to life itself. Thus, a threat to a people's culture tends to be perceived and experienced as a personal threat."[15]

The dichotomies represented by Jewish versus Palestinian, Hutsi versus Tutsi, Catholic versus Protestant, Serbian versus Croatian, America versus Islamic fundamentalists—all these are the violent results of derailed identity negotiation coupled with cultural acts of threats and resistance. There are also less violent yet intense processes of interchange by Nigerians in France, Turks in Germany, Mozambiqueans in South Africa, Aborigines in Australia, and Hispanics and Chinese in America (and the list can go on and on).

These regional cultural negotiations are both intensified and mondialized (from French *le monde*, "the world") by the Janus face of cultural globalization. Like all globalization processes, this one is equally ambiguous[16] and even contradictory: *The globalization of culture is one hand of a huge homogenization process, while at the same time fostering a celebration of cultural difference and fragmentation.*

Related to the latter, one may point to the hybridization of culture as "a global phenomenon that happens locally" through interesting cultural mixes of music, art, literature, and architecture. For example, the postcolonial discourse on creolization, ambivalence, and multiple identities is a way of writing back in response to a hegemonic global culture[17] and is related to a process of identity transformation.

But the romantic idea of multiculturalism is betrayed by a globalizing process that creates a mirage of differentiation but in fact is an encompassing force toward *Vereinheitlichung* (unification/standardization).[18] In this earlier work, Raiser points out three central challenges for the ecumenical church in the twenty-first century: a life-centered vision (*lebenszentrierte Vision*) to replace a destructive anthropocentrism, the acknowledgment of plurality, and facing the inner contradictions of globalization. He verbalizes one of these contradictions as the simultaneous process of "Vereinheitlichung von Lebensstilen und kulturellen Formen [unification of lifestyles and cultural forms]" and the "Anstrengungen [strains]" caused by a defense of "einheimische Kulturen, religiöse Traditionen [und] ethnische und rassische Identitäten [indigenous cultures, religious traditions, [and] ethnic and racial identities]."[19]

Globalization slowly moves toward a depersonalized mass society typified by "mass communications, mass consumption, homogeneity of patterns of life, mass culture."[20] The process is driven by megacultural firms "based on the commodification of Anglophone culture with the aid of the electronic highway."[21] Writing from an African perspective, Samuel Kobia depicts the situation of this continent as being subject to both economic and cultural colonialization, subject to the cultural hegemony carried by modern Western capitalism.[22] Here the economic, technological, and cultural intersect in a deadly asymmetrical negotiation: "You can survive, even thrive, among us, if you become like us; you can keep your life, if you give up your identity." With reference to Claude Lévi-Strauss, "We can say that exclusion by assimilation rests on a deal: we will refrain from vomiting you out (anthropoemic strategy) if you let us swallow you up (anthropophagic strategy)."[23]

Seen in this way, globalization acquires an ideological nature as *la pensée unique,* aspiring to be the only valid view, "imposing itself as the paradigm to which all other cultures should be adjusted."[24] Where previous forms of cultural subjugation were spatially confined and time-bound, the commercial homogeneity of a consumerist culture expands itself with the aid of the newest and fastest technological communication (itself an ambiguous blessing in the twenty-first century!).

THE ETHICAL ISSUES

"What are the ethical issues?" one might ask. In the ebb and flow of history, many cultures and civilizations have come and gone. Globalization is just a new and more potent cultural force that speeds up this process of assimilation, subjugation, and eventual extinction. The museumization of "indigenous" cultures of yesteryear is but the same as fossils and mummies kept for the (possible?) attention and curiosity of future generations.

It is not that simple, though. Enough work has been done on the ethical issues related to the casino economy[25] of digital capitalism. Here I wish to argue the case for *cultural justice* and outline the ethical issues in the following two broad themes: first, the moral significance of cosmological stories in shaping identity and values; second, the unequal burden of suspending or surrendering "what is taken for granted."

Cosmological Stories and Narrative Moral Identity

Let us accept with Peter Berger,[26] Ninian Smart,[27] and David Tracy[28] that the role of religion is to construct a comprehensive view of the world by framing parts of reality in the context of that which transcends reality (i.e., ultimate reality). Let us accept with Larry Rasmussen that "we are incorrigibly storytellers"[29] and concur with Thomas Berry that religious cosmologies are designed to answer identity questions like, Who am I? Who are we? Where are we going? "For peoples, generally, their story of the universe and the human role in the universe is their primary source of intelligibility and value."[30]

On these assumptions one could argue that globalization in its cultural garb usurps and misplaces the role of religion by constituting its own cosmological narrative. We have here, writes Welker,[31] a clash of value systems where justice, compassion, and care for the weak are endangered by an Olympic or Nietzschean ethos. At stake is not merely the physics of our information age but its metaphysics, "its significance to individual and social morality, . . . and its consequences for the formation, maintenance, and alteration of personal identity."[32] Homogenization takes on the proportions of an autonomous force governing the lives of individuals and communities.[33]

To a certain extent globalization as encompassing cosmology reflects the moral tendencies of both modernity and postmodernity. According to Zygmunt Bauman, globalization—as autonomous force against which a person apparently can do nothing but to be swept along—does "shift moral responsibilities away from the moral self, either toward a socially constructed and managed supra-individual agency, or through floating responsibility inside a bureaucratic 'rule of nobody.'"[34] But like postmodernity, globalization creates a climate of evasion of moral responsibilities by rendering relationships "fragmentary" and "discontinuous" (or even "virtual"), resulting in disengagement and commitment-avoidance.[35]

We have learned from various forms of narrative ethics (from H. Richard Niebuhr to Stanley Hauerwas): *Agere sequiter esse* (what we do is a result of who we are). And who we are is determined by the narrative communities in which we are formed. From a moral perspective "it is possible to argue that the real challenges embedded in globalisation concern not so much what we *do*, but who we *are*, who we are becoming."[36] The mass culture of a globalizing world is a powerful narrative agent that contributes significantly to moral formation. Its values become *the* values, the way things *are*, the way *everybody* acts.

This analysis might provide some clue to a vexing question: Why do societies in rapid transition (e.g., from so-called non-Western cultures such as Islamic, African, or Eastern European to cultures being Westernized) so often exhibit a partial or total value collapse? The answer might be that societies in transition undergo a collective identity crisis as they move from the known to the not-yet. It is because they cannot yet adequately answer the question, Who are we? that they are unable to exercise responsible and virtuous options.[37] In a situation of transition a "contraction of time" appears that instinctively cuts off the past (nobody wants to return to an oppressive past) but cannot yet conceptualize the future ("a journey into unchartered territory without safety equipment").[38] In this way life is a continual "collapsed present," driven by emotional, physical, and economic survival in which clear moral ideals and ethical visions are difficult to uphold.

Into this situation of confusion and anomie,[39] where people find themselves "in between stories"[40] and in a situation of *Heimatlosigkeit*,[41] the globalized consumer culture steps to provide a viable alternative: "the only answer," *the* moral story. It works so well because consumerism ("We want more for less!")[42] exactly sustains itself by creating constantly changing demands that have to be satisfied instantly, thereby creating an ever-shifting "hedonistic presence," closed to both the past and the future.

The notion that what Africa (or Eastern Europe or Latin America or Iraq and Afghanistan) need is more development aid and physical infrastructure, however important, is fatally flawed and may in practice result in the intensification of resistance and loss of hope in "democracy." What needs to be restored and cultivated is a culturally mediated reconstruction of the self in a personal and collective sense. In political terms, the African Renaissance, for example, is as much about economic development as it is about a postcolonial restoration of cultural pride and selfhood "to counter the excesses of European modes of being-in-the-world."[43]

The crucial insight, missed by most development agencies, is that restoration of being not only precedes economic restoration but, at least in an African situation, is *the precondition* for economic survival. Being precedes bread.[44] Why? Because in a situation of scarce resources, you need a view of identity that resists economic greed and self-referential individualism. What is required is a notion of identity as *identity-in-community, which underpins redistribution patterns that in turn guarantee physical and economic survival.*

We need the survival of (the) community instead of the survival of the fittest. But then we need a cosmological story and other local narratives to sustain exactly such communities in which moral formation can take shape. If not, globalization in the name of "development aid" will do the job for itself.

Perhaps the following case study, reconstructed from actual events, conveys this journey of identity and life "in between stories" in a way that arguments are unable to do:

> My brother Sipho and I grew up in a rural village in the Limpopo province of South Africa. My father was a farm laborer and my mother a domestic worker. They were both functionally illiterate, but had a keen sense that the education of their children was of paramount importance. By the time we reached high school age, the whole extended family contributed to send the two of us (one year apart) to a former model C school in Pretoria. After matriculation we both attended university—again with the material and emotional support of the family. This support was not so much contractual as a familial, moral issue. It was a form of "donation" that everybody

tacitly knew would one day return, though in no exact manner as in written contracts, to assist parents in their old age and make the same possible for other siblings after us.

The eventual graduation festivals were huge family affairs, with praise singers, pap, and slaughtering of goats.

We both were excited to land our first jobs, I with my degree in humanities in the academic administration of the university in Port Elizabeth, and Sipho with his B Commerce degree at an international consulting firm in Johannesburg. We never openly spoke of it, but took it for granted that we send a monthly amount "back home" and visit at least once a year.

After about eighteen months Sipho's contributions dried up. The next year he did not return for his annual visit. What is more—when my grandfather passed away, he did not attend the funeral. I took the courage to talk this over with him and soon realized that he had embraced the yuppie lifestyle of Egoli, the City of Gold: designer clothes (from Carducci to Billabong and Man about Town), a red BMW 318i, and a townhouse in Fourways.

He now traverses a different world. He has embraced different values. We feel not so much a sense of betrayal as of sadness to have lost him. He has become a different person. Yet in the eyes of most, he is a highly successful person, a sign that the new South Africa is really opening opportunities to create a new black middle class. And I am not sure that he would ever want to return to our village. Due to its location in the mountains, it is called Tshilapfene, "the place of the baboons."

Surrendering What Is Taken for Granted

In a perceptive essay referred to several times above, the historian of religion Chirevo Kwenda explains the notion of cultural (in)justice as follows:

> Where people live by what they naturally take for granted, or where the details of everyday life coincide with what is taken for granted, we can say there is cultural justice—at least in this limited sense of freedom from constant self-consciousness about every little thing. Cultural injustice occurs when some people are forced, by coercion or persuasion, to submit to the burdensome condition of suspending—or more permanently surrendering—what they naturally take for granted, and then begin to depend on what someone else takes for granted. The reality is that substitution of what is taken for granted is seldom adequate. This means that, in reality, the subjugated person has no linguistic or cultural "default drive," that critical minimum of ways, customs, manners, gestures and postures that facilitate uninhibited, unself-conscious action.[45]

The injustice lies in the unequal burden and stress of constant self-consciousness that millions of people carry on behalf of others without gaining recognition or respect. In fact, they are objects of further subjugation and humiliation, varying from physical violence to subtle body language that clearly communicate that you are stupid and do not know "the ways things are done or said here."

On a regional and national level, these forms of exclusions (Miroslav Volf reminds us) range from domination and indifference to abandonment and ultimately elimination. From the "inside" this exclusion results from being "uncomfortable with anything that blurs accepted boundaries, disturbs our identities, and disarranges our symbolic cultural maps."[46]

The "fall of the Berlin wall" or "end of the apartheid regime" are designations of many societies that moved from oppressive political systems to greater civil liberties after 1989. Sometimes underestimated are the massive identity renegotiation processes in the postliberation period, often leading to an upsurge in ethnic violence and loss of social stability. As we saw in the previous section, questions of culture and life-in-community then arise with great urgency: it takes tremendous courage and political wisdom to (for the first time?) assert "what we take for granted" and to act unself-consciously after decades of identity-suspension and identity-suppression.

Shortly after the first democratic elections in South Africa that ended forty-six years of minority rule, the African theologian Tinyiko Sam Maluleke made the following incisive observation:

> Issues of culture are again acquiring a new form of prominence in various spheres of South African society. *It is as if we can, at last, speak truly and honestly, about our culture.* This is due to the widespread feeling that now, more than at any other time, *we can be subjects of our own cultural destiny.* . . . The reconstruction of structures and physical development alone will not quench our *cultural and spiritual thirst.* On the contrary, the heavy emphasis on the material and the structural may simply result in the intensification of black frustration. We do not just need jobs and houses, *we must recover our own selves.*[47]

The struggle against apartheid, communism, imperialism, or Americanism forced and still force a kind of uniformity of resistance, aimed at *the right to be "the same."* But the postliberation struggle aims at a restored subjectivity and agency with *the right to be different.* In the ethical terms of this section, this is *the right to live unself-consciously.* Three years later Miroslav Volf echoed this from a different perspective:

> In recent decades the *issue of identity* has risen to the forefront of discussions in social philosophy. If the liberation movements of the sixties were all about equality—above all gender equality and race equality—major concerns in the nineties seem to be about identity—about the *recognition of distinct identities* of persons who differ in gender, skin color, or culture.[48]

Let us make this argument about culture and distinct identities more concrete. I found it quite remarkable to see how much emphasis is placed on *language* in the process of identity renegotiation.

On a first level, language itself plays this exclusivist role. To this I will turn in the next paragraph. On a second level, a "language of exclusion" is created by naming or labeling the Other in a manner that takes the Other outside "the class of objects of potential moral responsibility."[49] This does not only justify exclusion but also in fact necessitates it. "The rhetoric of the other's inhumanity *obliges* the self to practice inhumanity."[50] Like supporters of the linguistic turn, one could state that exclusion is equally language-sated. Words do kill.

But in a more subtle way, language itself, as in "mother tongue" and "foreign" language, plays an exclusionary role. In a remarkable essay, "Aria: A Memoir of a Bilingual Childhood,"[51] Richard Rodriguez recounts how he grew up at Sacramento, California, living in a Mexican immigrant home in a predominantly white suburb. During his first few years in school, he struggled with English but then managed to move between the language of the public (English) and the private language of the home (Spanish). "Like others who feel the pain of public alienation, we transformed the knowledge of our public separateness into a consoling reminder of our intimacy."[52]

He eloquently spells out life in two linguistic and social worlds:

> But then there was Spanish: *Español*, the language rarely heard away from house, the language which seemed to me therefore a private language, my family's language. To hear its sounds was to feel myself specially recognized as one of the family, apart from *los otros* (the others). A simple remark, an inconsequential comment, could convey that assurance. My parents would say something to me, and I would feel embraced by the sounds of their words. Those sounds said: I am speaking with ease in Spanish. . . . I recognize you as somebody special, close, like no one outside. You belong with us. In the family, Ricardo.[53]

But this juxtaposition of a double identity was shattered by a simple request from the teachers (nuns at the Catholic school) that, in order to improve their academic performance, English should be spoken at home. This led to an ambivalent outcome: a growing confidence in public, but a devastating silence at home:

> There was a new silence at home. As we children learned more and more English, we shared fewer and fewer words with our parents. Sentences needed to be spoken slowly. . . . Often the parent wouldn't understand. The child would need to repeat himself. Still the parent misunderstood. The young voice, frustrated, would end up saying, "Never mind"—the subject was closed. Dinners would be noisy with the clinking of knives and forks against dishes. My mother would smile softly between her remarks; my father, at the other end of the table, would chew and chew his food while he stared over the heads of his children.

What followed was first a "disconcerting confusion."[54] Then, as fluency in Spanish faded fast, a feeling of guilt arose over the betrayal of immediate family and visitors from Mexico.[55] Thereafter followed an understanding that the linguistic change was a social transaction, where the intimacy at home was traded for the gain of fluency and acceptance in the public language. "I moved easily at last, a citizen in a crowded city of words."[56] But the ambiguities remain. This is evident from the end of the essay, where Rodriguez describes the funeral of his grandmother:

> When I went up to look at my grandmother, I saw her through the haze of a veil draped over the open lid of the casket. Her face looked calm—but distant and unyielding to love. It was not the face I remembered seeing most often. It was the face she made in public when a clerk at Safeway asked her some question and I would need to respond. It was her public face that the mortician had designed with his dubious art.[57]

It was, in the terms set out above, the burdensome face of someone who constantly had to surrender what is taken for granted. You can keep your life if you give up your identity. You can keep your culture as long as you hold its values and customs, its "things taken for granted," with diffidence. This cultural diffidence is a disposition that causes people either to be ashamed of their own culture or to simply ignore it as irrelevant in the modern world.[58]

These powerful images from a single life and immigrant family form a metaphor, a simile, a parable of national and transnational processes of cultural injustice. In *The Political Economy of Transition*, Tony Addy and Jiri Silny reflect on the changes that occurred in the ten years of 1989-99 in Central and Eastern Europe. They make the interesting observation that the "market Bolsheviks" (economic advisers who advocated the move to a full market economy in one jump) not only harbored a blind faith in policy prescriptions from "the West" to be applied unaltered to "the East," but also showed "little respect for indigenous knowledge and practice."[59] The rapid privatization of former industries was carried out "in a way which did not respect positive cultural and ethical values within the region. Under conditions of globalisation, the process tended to block creative responses."[60]

In a bizarre example of exclusion by elimination, the application of rigid market rules meant the literal closure of what Addy and Silny call "cultural industries": "For example, rich traditions of film-making were lost and historic theatres, orchestras and other artistic companies were decimated. It would take a great deal of time and money to rebuild such industries and cultural assets."[61]

Would it therefore be justified to include *aesthetic justice*[62] as an integral part of cultural justice? I think so, because the symbols of national identity (statutes, flags, books, artifacts, photographs, histories, and language) are normally the first spoils of war. The subjugation of the Other is completed with the removal or destruction of identity-confirming symbols. And in the context of globalization, this war is mostly fought without military armors, in a faceless silence, and in the name of advancement and consumerism.

GLOBALIZATION AND CULTURAL JUSTICE: A FEW BIBLICAL PERSPECTIVES

I have argued that globalization as a cultural force poses two ethical challenges: First, the challenge of a competing cosmological story with its effect on identity and value formation. Second, the challenge of cultural justice with its effect on community-in-diversity and the freedom of an unself-conscious life. A full biblical-ethical response is not possible in the confines of this essay. What follow are a few suggestions drawn from select passages that may provide some direction to these challenges.

Globalization: the Challenge of Who Is Lord

By constituting a cosmological narrative and providing *the* alternative normative "story," globalization enters the age-old realm of the battle of the gods; the battle for ultimate loyalty; for the ultimate frame of reference from which to interpret the self and life-in-community.

It is common knowledge that the period reflected in New Testament writings was dominated by two forces:[63] the residual influence of Hellenistic culture and Roman political rule since the occupation of Palestine in 63 BCE and its incorporation into the province of Syria. I only pursue the issue of Roman political authority here.

Although Roman rule allowed relative local religious freedom to occupied territories, its growing usurpation of religious power (in a time that has not yet seen the modernist division of life into spheres) brought local Christian communities into growing conflict with the Roman state. There is no room here for an extensive treatment of a complex[64] topic. For the sake of my overall argument, I refer to three New Testament passages to illustrate what became a battle for ultimate loyalty and for the guiding orientation point in constructing a moral identity and community.

First, in Mark 12:13–17 the sensitive question of imperial tax is of great religious significance. The denarius (for which Jesus asks) clearly supported the emperor's apotheosis: the laurel wreath symbolized divinity, reinforced by the inscription "Emperor Tiberius, venerated son of the venerated God" and "high priest." The pericope reaches its climax in what can be read as an ironic parallelism or perhaps even as an antithesis: "Render to Caesar the things that are Caesar's, and to God the things that are God's" (12:17 RSV). In so saying, Jesus does not contest the legitimacy of the state, nor does he denigrate what belongs to Caesar. But, in a time of the total interpenetration of politics and religion, this saying "effectively secularizes civil authority and removes it from the realm of ideology."[65]

Second, the well-known (and often misused)[66] Pauline passage in Romans 13:1–7 forms part of the paraenetical section that is introduced in 12:1–2. The former could be read as the public practice of love, a theme followed through from 12:21 to 13:11–14. The significance of this passage for my argument here does not lie in a (futile?) reconstruction of a "doctrine of the state" but the clarity and apparent ease with which Paul shifts the origin of state power from the gods (however perceived) to the Christian God. "There is no power [*exousia*] that is not from God [*hypo Theou*]" in 13:1 (cf. CJB) can therefore be construed as implicit critique of a self-divinized authority that later required the confession that Caesar is lord.

Third, by the time the Apocalypse was written, specifically Revelation 13, the emperor cult had been established and was vigorously enforced as state religion.[67] Here the Roman Empire (by now established as *imperium* in the technical sense of the word, with a uniform supervisory authority over the whole Mediterranean) is described as the incarnation of Satan's power upon earth and as a caricature of Christ. The issue at stake is ultimate loyalty, the battle of the gods, because the state demands what is appropriate to God and to Christ alone. "In making these demands, the state is from the devil. It is not satanic because it is imperfect, but because it is totalitarian. It does not have too little authority, but too much, authority over 'every tribe and people and tongue and nation' (13:7 [RSV]). It is demonic in its *totalitarian deification*."[68]

The political impotence of early Christian communities made only passive resistance possible. But the simple confession of Christ's lordship was, especially in the Eastern regions of the empire, in fact a public, active political act since from a Roman perspective it represents both "atheism" and anarchy. In the face of martyrdom, the faith communities are reminded that God has set a limit to the rule of the dragon ("forty-two months," 13:5), that they are blessed if they "die in the Lord" (14:13) since their names are entered "in the book of life" (13:8).

Although there were varied responses in the New Testament to the growing totalitarianism of an encompassing global empire, there is enough textual evidence to state at least the following: as moral communities,[69] the early Christians were confronted with the question of what will serve as ultimate reference point, as principle in the narrative, symbolic arrangement of the Christian life. They simply chose the person of Jesus, confessed as *kyrios*, and derived direction from their memories of him, against the deified, global power of the day.

The conclusion is clear: Insofar and where globalization assumes the character of a religion, it needs to be resisted, confronted, and where possible transformed with a Christ-centered ethics. The implication for the people of God is a renewed vision of Christ's lordship as constitutive for their very existence as a community, and as their identity-confirming narrative in times of change and transition. Where loyalties shift to other gods, where the cosmic preeminence of Christ is compromised,[70] or where the "gospel of Jesus Christ" is no longer faithfully transmitted in word, liturgy, and (especially) a life *coram Dei*, identity and moral orientation are lost. Into this vacuum so-called "global values" step as alternative moral and identity-forming story.

Welker is right to warn against reducing the biblical traditions about money and God to a simple dichotomy of "God versus Mammon."[71] There is no way that moral formation, which hopefully leads to real action,[72] can take place in a vacuum of "anti-ökonomischen Manichaismus" or by a simple-minded "ökonomisches Analphabetismus." Jesus's own ministry and the life of the early church testify to discipleship in the realities of that time, challenging the then-dominant political, social, and ethical paradigms while living in the world.

This brings us to the ecclesiological challenge of cultural justice in the world today.

Globalization: A Challenge to Households of Life-in-Communion

Challenged by the processes of globalization, a very important reinterpretation of *oikoumenē* (the whole inhabited earth) and *oikodomē* (upbuilding community) occurred in ecumenical circles. This came about as the former ethical concerns of Life and Work (ethics) and ecclesial concerns of Faith and Order (church unity) converged in a number of studies[73] emphasizing that the core challenge of globalization is the nature of the household or households we create and belong to. And in this regard, the churches "als zentrale Akteure einer weltweiten Zivilgesellschaft [as central actors of a worldwide civil society]" play an important role.[74] Whereas the first ethical challenge above relates to the sovereignty of God (and concomitant moral claim of God on our lives through Christ), the second relates to the type of communities we build amid the claim that we now live in a "global village."[75] This is expressed in no uncertain terms by the Johannesburg delegation (see endnote 25 above):

> Moral issues, formerly seen as having to do mainly with personal conduct within stable orders of value, have now become radicalized. They now have to do with life, or the death, of human beings and of the created order in which we live. *Before we can even speak of a 21st century "global civilization" life together on this planet will need shared visions and institutional expressions for which we have few really relevant precedents.* As Christians we speak of an *oikoumenē*, or inclusive horizon of human belonging, offered by God in Jesus Christ to the human race. Following the scriptures we call this a "household of life," a "heavenly city" where justice, peace and care for creation's integrity prevail.[76]

This moves the focus to ecclesiology: The challenge is for the church to be one such "precedent" or "institutional expression" of a life-centered spirituality and ethics[77] and of a moral community known for true *koinōnia*. Yet in the light of cultural injustice and burden of unself-conscious living, how could the church be such a moral community? The answer is deceptively simple: by following Christ.

> As the early hymn recounts, Christ did not cling to his nature of being God and did not grasp on to his equality with God, but was humbled in self-donation, even to the death on the cross (Phil 2:5–8). Those who are in Christ consider whatever was to their profit as a loss (Phil 3:7); they are new creations (2 Cor 5:17); they have been crucified with Christ and no longer live, but Christ lives in them (Gal 2:20).

Christians no longer take their natural identity dead-seriously but find their new consciousness in Christ and his self-donation; only thus does a community of (cultural) justice become a possibility. Not without reason, the Pentecost as birth of the church is described in the book of Acts as an event in which the well-mannered Spirit, in search of cultural justice, enabled a speaking in the diverse known languages of those gathered in Jerusalem!

For our purpose here, let us examine the view expressed in Galatians 3:26–29. In the context of the argument that faith in Christ liberates from the curse of the law, the writer nevertheless accentuates the permanence of the promise to Abraham, fulfilled in Christ.[78] Through faith Jews and Gentiles are now sons and daughters of God. Through baptism all have been clothed with Christ. Therefore "there is neither Jew nor Greek, there is neither slave nor free, there is neither male nor female, for you are all one in Christ Jesus. And if you belong to Christ, then you are Abraham's offspring [*sperma*], heirs according to promise" (RSV).

This "egalitarian" view of the religious community corresponds in a contradictory manner to Jewish formulas in which the threefold distinction is upheld by men who thank God for not being a Gentile, slave, or woman. This is not so much rooted in "discrimination" as understood today, as in the disqualification from religious privileges that were open to free Jewish males. Whether this passage is a remnant of Thales (sixth century BCE),[79] derives from fanatical circles, or is a fragment of an early baptismal formula, it remains a powerful witness to a community that enables what was described as "cultural justice" above: *This community both transcends cultural, economic, and gender identities and simultaneously affirms these identities in a manner that enhances unity and avoids the isms of ideology and exclusion.*

That this had tremendous social implications at the time is evident from New Testament witnesses to the struggle with regard to circumcision for Gentile converts (Gal. 2; Acts 15), the contradictory position of women in the early church (Acts 2; 1 Cor. 11), and the status of slaves after their conversion (e.g., Onesimus in Phlm. 16). It certainly has and wherever realized will have tremendous social significance as "precedent" community in a global world today.[80]

We can therefore conclude that, theologically speaking, cultural justice is not so much the result of reclaiming minority or indigenous rights as it is the vision of a Christlike household "where fully realized human identities and values, far from being forgotten, meet in search of graciously shared abundance of life. This household welcomes all the different human cultures, identities, and interests, including our own."[81]

This is the vision of the African-rooted Belhar Confession,[82] borne in a situation of radical cultural injustice, under conditions of pluralism gone wrong, and in the face of a suppressive and homogenizing sociopolitical system. Following the teaching of the Heidelberg Catechism about the communion of saints, Belhar believes that, due to Christ's reconciliation, "the variety of spiritual gifts, opportunities, backgrounds, convictions, as well as the variety of language and culture, are opportunities to reciprocal service and enrichment in the one visible people of God."

I close with two magnificent biblical passages where the idea of the household of God extends beyond the people of God and the church to all of creation. Here we reach a confluence of various forms of justice: economic, cultural, and ecological. These passages confirm the "usefulness" of the Scriptures to address the issue of cultural justice in a globalized world:

Under severe depressive spiritual conditions, about forty years before the fall of Samaria, proto-Isaiah sees the vision of the peaceable kingdom. Divisions and life-threatening enmities based on natural identities (wolf-lamb; leopard-goat; calf-lion) are overcome through a radical transformation of those very identities (lions eat straw and children put hands in the viper's nest). "They will not hurt or destroy, . . . for the earth will be full of the knowledge of the Lord as the waters cover the sea" (Isa. 11:6–9 RSV).

Under conditions of persecution and a seemingly hopeless situation for the second-generation Christians, the apostle John sees the vision of a truly global community (truly global and truly in communion) before the throne of God: "After this I looked, and there before me was a great multitude that no one could count, from every nation, from all tribes and peoples and languages, standing before the throne and in front of the Lamb, . . . and the one who is seated on the throne will spread his tent over them. Never again will they hunger, never again will they thirst" (Rev. 7:9, 15–16, alt.).

While we live under the ambiguities of a globalizing world that is marveling at its opportunities but at the same time despairing at the consequences, we nurture these visions as narratives of a radically other world made possible by the knowledge of the Lord.

Chapter 4

Calvin's Theology
An Appraisal in Relation to the Indian Context

HMAR VANLALAUVA

John Calvin is acknowledged to be the most influential Protestant reformer and thinker after Martin Luther. He is also regarded as one of the most important interpreters of Protestant Christianity. His writings, particularly the *Institutes of the Christian Religion*, are of great theological significance. Without doubt, Calvin has contributed immensely toward the growth and development of Protestant theology. His influence has been so widespread that not only the Reformed/Presbyterian Churches but almost all the Protestant ecclesial and theological traditions have been influenced by his thought in one way or the other.

Calvin's theology is part of the Christian faith and tradition in India. Through the Protestant missionaries working in different parts of India, Christianity made an inroad into India and thus has constituted a part of our inherited faith and tradition. However, in the Indian multireligious context, the inherited Christian traditions have lost much of their relevance. At the same time, in the changing context of today, there is a genuine concern to reflect creatively and critically upon our inherited faith and tradition. Since many of the Indian Christians have been nurtured in the Calvinistic faith and tradition, it is important and necessary to study Calvin's theology both creatively and critically in relation to the questions that arise out of his own historical context as well as in relation to the Indian context. The churches across the world having historical links with the Calvinistic tradition have recently celebrated Calvin's birth five hundred years ago (in 1509). It thus is appropriate to have a study of Calvin's theology at this juncture.

In this chapter we have selected two important issues, the knowledge of God and the sovereignty of God, which are central to Calvin's theology and, on the basis of these two issues, we shall study Calvin's theology in relation to the Indian context.

THE KNOWLEDGE OF GOD

The knowledge of God is one of the most fundamental concerns of Calvin's theology.[1] In his writings, the knowledge of God is stated in relation to the needs and challenges of sixteenth-century Europe. As Dowey has pointed out,[2] the doctrine of the knowledge of God is formulated on the basis of the biblical witness and in light of the ecclesial tradition, especially over against what he considered to be distortion of truth, as represented on the one hand by the papal authority and on the other hand by the authority given to subjective interpretations offered by the spiritualists and the radicals.

Calvin therefore vigorously affirmed the authority of the Bible for the authentic knowledge of God. Whether one looks at Calvin's doctrine of the knowledge of God in terms of a basic, constitutive theme or as a central perspective, it is clear that the knowledge of God is crucial for understanding Calvin's doctrine of God in particular and for understanding his whole theology in general. Such being the case, the knowledge of God is taken here as one of the key points for our study of Calvin's theology.

In Calvin's thought the knowledge of God is understood as the knowledge of God's will or promises to the human being and the world. As T. A. Noble has pointed out,[3] to know God in Calvin's thought is to know God personally in the living encounter of faith and to respond with praise and gratitude. As we have indicated earlier, the knowledge of God in Calvin's thought is not merely intellectual. Nor is it a conclusion on the basis of strict argumentation. Rather, it is an existential and practical knowledge of God. For Calvin, the knowledge of God is not passive or static. It is rather active or dynamic. It carries with it a right relationship between God, humans, and the world. A man or woman who truly knows God does so in reverence and fear, responding to God's will with praise and gratitude.[4]

How do we know God, and in what ways can human beings come to possess the knowledge of God? This is the main concern of Calvin's doctrine of the knowledge of God. In Calvin's thought, God is infinite and incomprehensible. Human beings cannot know God unless God reveals himself. The only possible way of knowing God lies with the revelation of God himself. God reveals himself, and in his revelation God accommodates himself to the human capacity. In what follows, we highlight some important concerns that underlie Calvin's thought.

First, in Calvin's thought there is a possibility for human beings to know God through his revelation in nature. God, the Creator, made himself known through his creation. Though God is infinite and invisible, the finite human being can see God's majesty in creation and even in the constitution of human beings. Here it is important to notice that the human being is created in God's image. As the bearer of the image of God, humans can reflect the glory of God as in a mirror. According to Calvin's thought, in all human beings the *sensus divinitatis* and *conscientia* are implanted, through which the revelation of God occurs, even in the innermost being of humans. Calvin emphatically asserts that the knowledge of God is made available for all. *Sensus divinitatis* and *conscientia* are present in every tribe or people, however civilized or uncivilized they may be. If Adam had not fallen, then human beings, irrespective of color and creed, could have possessed a true knowledge of God.[5]

Second, while the knowledge of God is universal and all human beings have the privilege of knowing God, in Calvin's thought, the fall makes a difference. It completely seals off the way for human beings truly to know God. For Calvin, as a result of the fall, the image of God in human beings is effaced. *Sensus divinitatis*, *conscientia*, and all other human faculties are corrupted. The human being is totally depraved in all spheres of life. Though God's revelation in nature is genuine and true, the fallen human being can in no way possess a true knowledge of God.[6] In Calvin's thought, however, individual human beings still retain the *sensus divinitatis* and *conscientia*, no matter how corrupt they are. It therefore is impossible to hide oneself from God's presence, however much one dislikes it. For Calvin, the impious themselves know the fact that some awareness of God's presence is ever alive in all human beings. Nonetheless, Calvin made it clear that the possession of the *sensus divinitatis* and *conscientia* carries no spiritual advantage. On the contrary, it finally leads to idolatry because of the fall.[7]

Third, after taking into account the human situation as mentioned above, Calvin speaks of God's revelation in the Christ event, to which the Bible bears witness. This is, according to Calvin, the only possible way for human beings truly to know God. Though God's revelation in nature is genuine, the true knowledge of God can be attained by fallen human beings only when they are encountered by the redemptive love of God manifested in the Christ event. In Calvin's thought, whereas God's revelation in nature is a manifestation of God's hand and feet, revelation in the Christ event is the manifestation of God's heart.[8] This is what the Bible bears witness to. Through the works of the Holy Spirit, the Bible serves as the means through which the fallen human being can come to know God. Since this is the case, the Bible occupies a unique place in Calvin's thought. Through that text, God accommodates himself to the capacity of human beings.

For Calvin, the Bible carries more weight than tradition. It does not depend on the church's authority but on the internal testimony of the Holy Spirit. The

Bible is, from the beginning, accompanied and used by the Holy Spirit with respect to the knowledge of God. As we have indicated earlier, it cannot be separated from the work of the Holy Spirit.

Through the Bible the Holy Spirit helps and enables human beings to know God. Such being the case, the Bible is indispensible in bearing witness to God's revelation in the Christ event and in being used by the Holy Spirit to bring to us the true knowledge of God.[9]

Fourth, the Holy Spirit plays a key role in bringing the knowledge of God. Calvin strongly asserts that the Bible, consisting of the Old Testament and New Testament, receives its true meaning and goal only through the work of the Holy Spirit.[10] The work of the Holy Spirit is indispensable not only in communicating God's revelation in the Christ event to the writers of the Bible, but also for believers to appropriate God's redemptive love manifested in the Christ event. The significance of the Holy Spirit in the knowledge of God is clearly reflected in Calvin's definition of faith. For Calvin, faith is "a firm and sure knowledge of the divine favor toward us, founded on the truth of a free promise in Christ, and revealed to our minds, and sealed on our hearts by the Holy Spirit."[11] Here Calvin speaks of the knowledge of God within the Trinitarian framework. Jesus Christ, in whose life and work God reveals himself, is God the Son, the Second Person of the Godhead; also, the Holy Spirit, who communicates that revelation and enables believers to appropriate God's redemptive love, is no other than the Third Person of the Godhead.

Calvin's understanding of the knowledge of God mentioned above was developed not in a pluralistic context like India but in the sixteenth-century European Christian context. As indicated earlier, Calvin spoke of the knowledge of God not to justify the claim of Christians over against the other faiths but to make a distinction between the true knowledge of God and the false or corrupted knowledge in the European Christian context of the sixteenth century. As Cornelis van der Kooi has put it, Calvin's doctrine of the knowledge of God "stands in contrast with the ignorance and impiety that dominated the Church of the sixteenth century and manifested itself in doctrines and practices that ultimately were nothing less than idolatry."[12] For Calvin, the church of the sixteenth century had departed from Christ and the Scripture. At the same time, the spiritualists or radicals also departed from the Scripture. Calvin's doctrine of the knowledge of God was worked out in this context. Such being the case, Calvin's view could lead to misunderstanding unless the context out of which it was developed is taken seriously.

It may be true to say that Calvin's doctrine of the knowledge of God has strong biblical support. His assertion of the finality of God's revelation in the Christ event is biblically sound. Even his view of God's revelation in nature is in agreement with the main thrust of the biblical teaching. It is also true to say that Calvin's understanding of the knowledge of God is in line with the Christian tradition. His view of the centrality of the Scripture in the knowledge of

God has a strong support in the patristic writings. Though the role of human reason is given a bigger role in patristic thought, the Scripture still occupies a central place. At the same time the finality of the Christ event is clearly affirmed, and it is accorded a unique place in the knowledge of God. Augustine asserts that, because of the total human blindness, no one can come to God except through God's redemptive love manifested in the Christ event.[13] Calvin's understanding of the knowledge of God is also in full agreement with that of the other Protestant Reformers. Luther asserts that, though the natural revelation is open to all, sufficient truth for the human being is revealed only in the Christ event. He is quite convinced that God comes to us and meets us in Christ alone.[14]

While Calvin's doctrine of the knowledge of God is in basic agreement with the patristic thought as well as the thought of the other Protestant Reformers, it goes against the scholastic thought, which stresses the positive role of natural revelation in the knowledge of God. In the scholastic thought, which dominated the Roman Catholic view of the sixteenth century, it was widely held that God could be known by human reason through created things. Contrary to Calvin's view, the knowledge of God became theoretical and intellectual. The Holy Spirit and the Bible bear witness to God's revelation in the Christ event and play a key role in Calvin's doctrine of the knowledge of God; but in the scholastic tradition, human reason and the authority of the church are pivotal. Thus Calvin's doctrine of the knowledge of God may be considered as an improvement over the scholastic tradition.

Calvin's view of the knowledge of God is also opposed to the view of the spiritualists or radicals who reject the authority of the Scripture in preference to the inner experience of the Holy Spirit. Against the spiritualists, Calvin strongly asserted that the knowledge of God remains tied to the Bible, which bears witness to the Christ event. The Bible and the Holy Spirit are inseparable. It is through the Bible that the Holy Spirit advances the true knowledge of God to the believers.

Whereas Calvin's doctrine of the knowledge of God (mentioned above) has influenced Protestant Christian thought for a number of years, it has received a negative treatment in the hands of theologians of our day.[15] In the contemporary theological thought, there is also a strong emphasis on human reason and experience. The biblical revelation no longer enjoys supremacy in the contemporary theological thought in general. However, while the contemporary theological thought has tended to go against Calvin's thought, the mainline Protestant churches and a number of influential theologians, including Karl Barth, still vigorously maintain a position similar to Calvin's doctrine of the knowledge of God.

What is the importance of Calvin's doctrine of God in the Indian context, and to what extent could it be helpful in understanding the Reality? First, it must be pointed out that with regard to the primacy of God's revelation, Calvin's view is in agreement, to some extent, with the mainline Indian religious traditions. If we carefully study the mainline Indian religious traditions, we cannot deny that all of them accord a unique place to the revelation of God in the knowledge of God. They claim to have in the Scriptures the revealed truth. In the mainline Hindu tradition, the revealed truth in the Scriptures is what was heard by the *rishis* and the testimonies of those who experienced God. In Islamic tradition, the revealed truth in the Qur'an is the speech of God to Prophet Muhammad. It is God's command and God's will toward humankind. Since the Scriptures bear divine revelation, both in the Hindu and the Islamic traditions, the Scriptures also constitute the primary source of the knowledge of God. They are all given authority in the matter of faith and practice.

With regard to the content of the knowledge of God, what is found in the Hindu and the Islamic traditions is also similar, to some extent, to what is found in the Bible. As in the case of Calvin's thought, both in the Hindu and the Islamic traditions, there is great emphasis upon the transcendental aspect of God. Even though Nirguna Brahman is thought to be passive and attributeless in the Advaitic tradition, yet in the theistic tradition, Brahman is known as an active and living God. He is known as the creator, preserver, and supreme ruler of the whole universe. He is all-powerful, all-knowing, loving, compassionate, and merciful. That God is also known as the God of Grace.

Like Calvin, the Indian religious traditions, excepting Advaita and Neo-Hinduism, give importance to the mediated or indirect knowledge of God.[16] It is accepted that the true knowledge of God is acquired through mediation. Since the distinction between God and human beings is upheld in all the mainline Indian traditions except in the Advaita, it is inevitable to stress the importance of the mediated knowledge of God.

Calvin's view of God's revelation in nature is found relevant in the pre-Christian Mizo context. Despite their "ignorance and dullness," the Mizos in the pre-Christian era claimed to have possessed some knowledge about God. However, in line with Calvin's view, the pre-Christian Mizos are thought to have obtained not much benefit from this knowledge about God. Despite their knowledge about God, they were in full bondage to the fear of the evil spirits.

While mentioning the points of agreement between Calvin's thought and the mainline Indian religious traditions, there appears to be a significant difference between the two, so far as the knowledge of God is concerned. What makes the most significant difference between the two is God's revelation in the Christ event. As we know, in the mainline Indian religious traditions, there is no explicit recognition of God's revelation in the Christ event. Calvin vigorously asserted the finality of God's revelation in the Christ event. Apart from this, there can be no possibility for human beings truly to know God. He was also quite firm in maintaining the view that we can come to know God only through the Scripture, which bears witness to the Christ event. As mentioned elsewhere, "Scripture alone" is the principle that influenced Calvin's thought. Without referring to the context in which he worked out his doctrine of the knowledge of

God, Calvin's thought can be interpreted in an exclusive manner. His assertion of the finality of Christ as well as of the primacy of the Bible may also be taken as the ground for rejecting all the claims of other faiths.

If we look at the contemporary theological debate, what would soon draw our attention is an increasing recognition of the presence of Christ not only in other faiths but also in secular traditions. In this new theological situation, the exclusive attitude to other faiths is no longer tolerated, and the traditional claim for the superiority of the biblical revelation draws severe criticism. In the Indian Christology represented by S. J. Samartha and Raimondo Panikkar, limiting Christ to Jesus of Nazareth is inadmissible.[17] In the contemporary Indian theological thought, in which there is an awareness of religious plurality, Calvin's doctrine of the knowledge of God, which has been often quoted to support the exclusivistic attitude to other faiths, found a formidable challenge. In the eyes of a number of contemporary Indian Christian theologians, Calvin's view of the knowledge of God appears to have lost its relevance. Is there any other way of understanding Calvin's doctrine of the knowledge of God?

As we have indicated earlier, Calvin did not work out his doctrine of the knowledge of God in a religiously pluralistic context like India. When formulating his doctrine, the issue was not justification of the Christian belief over against other faiths like Islam and Hinduism. On the contrary, the point at issue was the distinction between the true knowledge grounded in God's redemptive love manifested in the Christ event, to which the Bible bears witness, and the false knowledge based on human reason and the church's authority.

Such being the case, it is important to recognize that there may be room to make Calvin's doctrine of the knowledge of God relevant and meaningful in the Indian context. With this end in view, two suggestions are put forward: First, it is necessary to spell out the crucial aspect of Calvin's understanding of God's revelation in the Christ event. Considering his christological viewpoint, the self-giving love of God must be stressed as the most crucial point in the Christ event. In this regard, Calvin's thought has to be reinterpreted in the light of the Bible witness and the global Christian understanding.

Second, following the *extra-Calvinisticum*,[18] there is sufficient room to reinterpret Calvin's doctrine of God in the Indian context in a more meaningful way. What is an important issue in India is the presence of Christ in other faiths. On this matter, the *extra-Calvinisticum* can help us see that in Calvin's thought the knowledge of God in and through the Christ event is not confined to, but at the same time cannot be separated from, the particular historical event. Therefore God's self-giving love, or saving knowledge of God, is supremely and normatively manifested in and through Christ; although that saving knowledge is not separable from the historical Christ event, it is at the same time not confined to the historical knowledge and acknowledgment of the event. This enables us to understand Calvin's doctrine of the knowledge of God better and to relate it to the contemporary Indian context in a more meaningful way.

THE SOVEREIGNTY OF GOD

Calvin's view of God's sovereignty is an important issue selected as another point for our study of Calvin's theology. The idea of God's sovereignty occupies a central place in Calvin's thought.[19] For him, the doctrine of the providence of God and of predestination are clear witnesses to the sovereignty of God. God's sovereignty is understood as the absolute authority and lordship in human affairs as well as in the universe. It is God's personal governance of the world and may also be understood in simple terms: the whole of creation is subject to God's decree and sovereign control.

Calvin's doctrine of providence clearly portrays the sovereignty of God. For Calvin, God unceasingly rules by his providence in pursuance of his own will and purpose. He acts in all things. God is ever present in the world. He constantly directs and preserves all creatures. All events are governed by his secret will. God regulates individual events, and they all proceed from his plan. Nothing happens by accident. Not even a leaf or sparrow falls without his command. He gives life to his creatures and makes use of these creatures to accomplish and realize his will. Even the devil is in God's control. God's will is the highest cause. Calvin's doctrine of providence affirms God's permanent and universal activity in the world. In all his providential activities, God is absolutely sovereign. Nothing happens by chance.[20]

In Calvin's doctrine of predestination we have seen the pointed expression of the sovereignty of God. By his eternal decree God has predestined some to eternal life and some to eternal death. Both election and reprobation proceed from the free and sovereign will of God. Though the gospel is freely offered to all humankind, all those who encounter the gospel do not respond positively. In Calvin's thought, the reason lies with the predestination of God. Our salvation does not depend on our decision but wholly on God's grace.

In Calvin's thought, God's sovereignty, as expressed in the doctrine of predestination, contains a soteriological aspect.[21] It is a means of appreciating the wonder of redeeming grace. Calvin uses the doctrine to illuminate the fact that we are freely saved by faith in Christ through God's grace. It is an affirmation that God's grace is quite sufficient for human salvation. At the time of the Reformation, Protestant Christians had to stop seeking assurance from their work or ecclesial authority. But many were tempted to doubt their salvation, and they were soon compelled to seek assurance in the wrong way. In this context, Calvin's doctrine of predestination was found to be an indispensable aid to assurance. It serves as an affirmation of their faith as well as the ground of their assurance of salvation.[22] Thus Calvin's doctrine of God's sovereignty as expressed in the form of predestination plays an important soteriological role. This was quite relevant and helpful in the context of Protestant Christians who were looking for their faith assurance.

In Calvin's time, his fellow Protestant Christians suffered greatly because of their Protestant faith. Calvin was deeply aware of their situation. Out of his concern to help and comfort those suffering Christians, Calvin was compelled to stress God's sovereignty. For him, God's sovereignty, as expressed in terms of providential activities, is the source of comfort and strength. That sovereignty assured all the suffering Protestant Christians that history rests in God's hands: in the end God's will endures, and nothing can separate them from the love of God in Jesus Christ.[23] So, from such an historical point of view, Calvin's view of God's sovereignty is relevant and quite meaningful.

While Calvin's doctrine of God's sovereignty serves a useful purpose, we cannot deny that it has limitations and weaknesses. It is considered to have the features of a tyrant, without any quality of love. It is also thought to negate human responsibility and then to make God the author of sin. Hence a number of critics of Calvin's thought have held a different theological view of anthropology. Following Augustine, Calvin takes seriously the fallen human condition. Those who do not share Augustine's view of anthropology tend to oppose Calvin's doctrine of God's sovereignty. Many of his opponents who mercilessly attacked Calvin, like Pighus, did so from the standpoint of Pelagius, the main opponent of Augustine.

Calvin's view of God's sovereignty is the demand of his age. Several factors influenced Calvin's view of God's sovereignty, such as the papal claim to supreme authority in the matter of faith and practice, the rise of a new monarchy on the European political scene, emergence of new economic power, the growing influence of the new philosophies that advocate human freedom, and the increasing secularism. In one way or the other, all these factors influenced Calvin's view of God's sovereignty. Like many of his contemporary thinkers, Calvin recognized that the above forces challenge the doctrine of the sovereignty of God. In the face of this challenge, Calvin developed his doctrine of God's sovereignty. In the other historical contexts, in which many of the factors that influenced Calvin's thought are absent, Calvin's view of the sovereignty of God may not be equally relevant.

Calvin's view of the sovereignty of God is severely criticized for its emphasis on the will of God. Here it must be mentioned that there is nothing wrong in stressing the will of God and its related idea, God's power. This is the central idea of the Bible. In laying emphasis upon this central idea of the Bible, Calvin is doing justice to the biblical faith. However, Calvin appears to have gone wrong in laying such an emphasis upon God's will at the cost of God's love, assigning a subordinate place to the latter.[24] In Calvin's thought, God's sovereignty is not without God's love, but God's love is subordinated to God's will or power. It is not God's grace that has chosen us but God's will. This is the point at which Calvin's doctrine of sovereignty is found to be weak. In the past, when the point is stressed by the Calvinists, it has provoked strong protests, notably the Arminian protest in Holland.

While it may be true to say that Calvin has gone wrong in giving God's love a subordinate role, it is wrong to say that Calvin's doctrine of God's sovereignty is without any quality of love. God's love is the main component of

God's sovereignty. Calvin teaches predestination in order to show that God's election is the sole ground of human salvation. This is, in Calvin's thought, a manifestation of God's love. God's preservation of creation as well as his control of the devil also indicates that God is loving, kind, and merciful.[25] Since this is the case, we see that in Calvin's thought, God's sovereignty and God's love are inextricably bound.

Calvin's view of God's sovereignty is often considered to have negated human responsibility. Since Calvin has stressed God's absolute freedom and human inability, God's sovereignty must have appeared to have negated human responsibility. For this reason, Calvin's doctrine of God is found to be incompatible with contemporary thinking. At this stage, it is important to notice that as created beings endowed with God's image, human beings are free to exercise their free will within the sphere of God's sovereignty. Even after the fall, for Calvin, the fallen human being is still allowed to exercise limited freedom: therefore, when doing evil, the human being is still responsible.[26] As far as the cause of reprobation is concerned, in Calvin's thought, not God but the human being is held responsible.

Thus, in Calvin's view of God's sovereignty there is room for human responsibility. Here it should also be noted that in Calvin's thought, God is the one who frees the fallen human being from bondage to sin. We can have freedom to do God's work in the world only because of his saving action.[27] However, for Calvin, no human being possesses total or absolute freedom. It is only God who enjoys total, absolute, and unlimited freedom.

As pointed out earlier, Calvin claims that his doctrine of providence as well as his doctrine of predestination is based on Scripture. Yet in some areas he appears to have crossed the limits. For example, Adam's fall is willed by God, and some are predestined to eternal damnation.[28] Calvin claims that his doctrine is in line not only with the teaching of the Bible but also with the Christian tradition. He is right to some extent, insofar as almost all the aspects of his view relating to the sovereignty of God can be found in the writings of the patristic and the scholastic theologians.

In patristic thought, God is almighty, Lord, creator, upholder, and ruler of the world. He is the preserver and redeemer of the world.[29] Origen taught that the world is guided by God's providence. It has its origin in God, and all things in heaven and earth are governed by divine power.[30] Over against the doctrine of fate and chance, Augustine stressed that all things are preserved and governed by the sovereign, wise, and beneficent will of God.[31] Hence the patristic thought endorses Calvin's doctrine of God's sovereignty. What underlines patristic thought and Calvin's theology are the freedom and absolute independence of God.

Predestination occupies a prominent place in the patristic thought. Some of the patristic theologians, including Athanasius and Chrysostom, maintained the idea of predestination with reference to the person and work of Christ. In Augustine's thought, predestination is firmly grounded. It is a positive doctrine of grace in which God chose some for eternal life and left the others. It is a doctrine that emphasizes the sufficiency of God's grace for human salvation.[32] In Calvin's doctrine of predestination, one can easily notice the presence of this soteriological aspect. This is a clear indication of the relation between Calvin's doctrine of God's sovereignty and the patristic thought.

In the scholastic writings, Calvin's doctrine of God's sovereignty has also a strong support. For Thomas Aquinas, God has taken care of the world and human beings just as parents take care of their children. For him, God is the one who sustains the universe and preserves creatures mediately and immediately. Each and every creature depends on God, and without God none can exist even for a moment.[33] Duns Scotus and William of Ockham emphasized God's absolute will. In their thought, God is absolute sovereign power. In Calvin's doctrine of sovereignty, the influence of Duns Scotus and Ockham is clearly discernible. Because of their influence, Calvin's doctrine of God's sovereignty appears to have been rooted much deeper in God's will and power than in God's love.

While Calvin's view of God's sovereignty is basically in agreement with both the patristic and scholastic traditions, there are certain aspects in which Calvin's view of sovereignty may be distinguished. In the patristic and scholastic traditions, divine foreknowledge was introduced to explain the problem associated with the doctrine of predestination.[34] On the basis of the divine foreknowledge of the future condition of the individuals, some are elected and some are rejected. For Calvin, this view implies the subordination of God's will to the human condition. This is unacceptable for him. Calvin was also not in agreement with scholastic idea of divine permission of evil. While scholastic thought accommodates the ideas of divine permission of evil in making God free from evil, Calvin asserted that everything that happens depends upon God's will. Even the fall of human beings is ordained by God.[35] This is clearly a point of divergence between Calvin on the one hand and the patristic and scholastic thoughts on the other.

In the above two areas where Calvin was in disagreement with patristic and scholastic thoughts, Calvin's God appears to be dreadful. As mentioned before, this is the point where Calvin's doctrine of the sovereignty of God draws criticism. It may be considered as its weakest point. At this point, Calvin was not in agreement with the other Reformers. Even Karl Barth, who is in line with Calvin in maintaining God's sovereignty, criticized him at this point, saying that Calvin tore God and Jesus Christ asunder.[36] However, this assertion of God's sovereignty should not be isolated from his thought about the whole character of God. In his view of God's sovereignty, Calvin did not go against the patristic and scholastic thoughts. His main concern was to defend the idea that human salvation depends not on human merit but purely on God's grace.[37]

Today, Calvin's view of God's sovereignty is criticized and challenged from various quarters.[38] It is considered to be hierarchical, oppressive, and dualistic. It is also considered to have encouraged a sense of distance between God and the world. It is seen to attend only to the human dimension of the world. It is also thought to have supported domination of the world.[39] These views necessitate the rediscovery of the relevance of Calvin's doctrine of God for our context today.

If we look carefully at Calvin's view of God's providence, we will see that the transcendence and the immanence of God meet in the history and experience of human beings. The supreme ruler is taking care not only of human beings but also all creatures, including the minutest part of creation. In Calvin's thought, God's sovereignty is opposing exploitation and domination. No one can deny the sociopolitical concern of Calvin's understanding of God's sovereignty. Truly speaking, Calvin's God is the God of the poor and the suffering men and women. His theology was formulated in the context of suffering. His doctrine of God's sovereignty is meant for the persecuted and the oppressed. In his *Institutes* his address to King Francis I contains the following statement:

> We, indeed, are perfectly conscious how poor and abject we are.... We are (if you will) the mere dregs and off-scouring of the world, or worse.... Some of us are in bonds, some beaten with rods, some made a gazing stock, some prescribed, some most cruelly tortured, some obliged to flee; we are all pressed with traits, loaded with dire excretions, lacerated by slanders and treated with greatest indignity.[40]

In view of this suffering and oppressed context, Calvin emphatically asserted God's sovereignty, saying that our doctrine of God must stand above all the glory and power of the world.[41] He also wrote that the oppressors would not go unpunished for "God hears the cries and groaning of those who cannot bear injustice."[42] It is doubtful that many of the contemporary theologians have enough courage to take the side of the poor and suffering as Calvin did. In Calvin's thought God is the defender of the poor.[43]

What is the importance of Calvin's doctrine of the sovereignty of God in the Indian context? It may be true to say that Calvin's view of God's sovereignty has some relevance to the Indian context. As we have seen, the idea of God's sovereignty is present, in some sense, in all the mainline Indian religious traditions. God is known as omnipotent, omniscient, and transcendent. In the Hindu tradition, especially in the theistic line, there is a strong assertion that God is the supreme ruler of all. A reference can be made to Madhva's concept of God as Svatantra and his view of the sovereignty of God. The personal supreme God is the one who causes, preserves, and controls the universe and all human beings.[44] In short, the idea of God's sovereignty is affirmed in the Hindu tradition.

The idea of God's sovereignty may be said to be the core of the Islamic faith. As found in the Qur'an, out of ninety-nine names attributed to God, thirty-six names are used to describe God's sovereignty. Among the Muslims, the commonest idea is that God is the sovereign king who rules over all.[45] As he is the sovereign Lord, all should be obedient to his will. Thus the idea of God's sovereignty is clearly and strongly affirmed in the Islamic tradition.

In the tribal religious tradition, as found in the pre-Christian Mizo strand, the high god and the spirits are considered to be superior to the human world. The high god known as *Pathian* is thought to be all-powerful and all-knowing.[46] However, in their fear of evil spirits, which badly dehumanized them, the high god, or Pathian, was hardly invoked. When Calvin's idea of God's sovereignty was made known to them by the Calvinistic missionaries, the fear of evil spirits was overcome, and all the Mizo tribes have become liberated to a great extent not only from the oppressive spirits but also from various dehumanizing forces.

The importance of Calvin's idea of God's sovereignty can be seen not only in the missiological context, but also in the sociopolitical and economic context of India. Today our country is passing through a difficult time. As we know, despite the national government coming into power after independence, in various places we see domination over the weaker sections of the society by the powerful. With the rise of the new economic power, economic exploitation has increased, and this has led to the increase of poverty in the Indian society. Everywhere there is discrimination based on caste, sex, religions, ethnicity. At the same time, religious fundamentalism and communalism are surging their heads. Truly speaking, everywhere in India there is a manifestation of human depravity. This is the problem Calvin had in mind when he developed his idea of God's sovereignty. In Calvin's thought, God is the sovereign Lord, the sovereign Lord of justice and love. Whatever is in conflict with God's holy will is to be transformed and corrected. It therefore is important to rediscover the value of God's sovereignty in the Indian context.

While stressing the importance of Calvin's idea of God's sovereignty, one should be conscious of its limitations and weaknesses. India is a caste-ridden society in which a deterministic idea in the form of karma is strongly embedded. For this reason, when making use of Calvin's thought, it should not be allowed to strengthen the oppressive system operating in Indian society.

CONCLUSION

In the light of our study of Calvin's teachings, no one can deny that Calvin's theology has a number of weaknesses and limitations. Like other Christian theologies, it is a human construction in a particular historical context. Its nature and characteristics are conditioned by its own historical context. As mentioned earlier, one of its weaknesses lies in its overemphasis upon God's sovereign will at the cost of God's love. Almost all the criticisms and attacks leveled against Calvin's theology are related to this point. Calvin did accept that God's love is the basic tenet of the Christian faith; but because of certain historical factors, he could not but stress God's will much more than God's love. His doctrine of the knowledge of God, particularly his emphasis on the finality of Christ, should also be recognized as another weak point. In a pluralistic religious context like

India, his understanding of the finality of Christ needs some modification along the lines suggested above.

Despite its weaknesses and limitations, Calvin's theology may still be found relevant in the Indian context. As indicated earlier, it is in basic agreement with the concept of God found in some significant areas of India's mainline religious traditions. In short, the Indian religious traditions that have a deep interest in the concept and reality of God have a good partner in Calvin. Today in India, where evil and destructive forces are so active, we need to be encouraged by Calvin's confidence in the power and love of God. Truly speaking, God's sovereignty is not just a matter of the past but also a reality of the present and the future. What the poor, the oppressed, and the marginalized need most is the God of power and love, on whom Calvin firmly put his faith and confidence throughout his life.

EXEMPLARY PERSPECTIVES

Chapter 5

Justice Healing

SUSAN E. DAVIES

INTRODUCTION

Three major Reformed emphases—the sovereignty of God, Christian responsibility for the world, and faith as a gift of grace—have significantly shaped the way I have conceived and effected my vocational commitments. I will preface my remarks on those themes with a brief discussion of pastoral theology, reporting my primary commitment to healing and justice as a feminist pastoral theologian. After developing the three Reformed emphases, I will conclude with suggestions for the justice healing of the Reformed tradition.

PASTORAL THEOLOGY

Pastoral theology is the branch of Christian theology that attends to the lived experiences of the Christian community in its various contexts, reflecting on the church's embodiment of God's healing power in this wounded world. In this personal reflection I think back on my own experiences of the church's embodiment of God's justice and healing power. Pastoral theology is historically tied to ethics because it reflects upon and engages the practices of Christian individuals and communities. It is sometimes seen as a mediator between systematic, biblical, historical, or moral theology on the one hand, and the concrete experience of particular congregations/churches in specific contexts on the other hand. Pastoral theology regularly enacts the hermeneutical circle of action, reflection upon the action and the tradition, theorizing, and returning to action. In turn, I will reflect on the actions in which I and others have engaged in light of the Reformed tradition, offer theory, and propose action for the church and for pastoral theologians and ethicists as part of the church.

Over the generations pastoral theology has had several foci. The work of ordained ministry has been and remains an important component, as does the "cure of souls," whether through a sacramental system, through the diligent application of discipline by the minister and/or elders, or through application of psychologically honed pastoral skills. Increasingly, pastoral theology understands itself as that branch of theology "commissioned to enable the community of faith to practice what it preaches."[1] I will offer some suggestions for the community of faith, which it might practice and which might even change what it preaches.

HEALING, SALVATION, AND JUSTICE

As groundwork for this consideration of pastoral theology, I draw our attention to the linguistic and theological connections between salvation and healing. Since in Christ, God was reconciling the world to Godself, the core of the pastoral theology I propose is healing and justice.

Healing, deliverance, and salvation are the root meanings of σώζω (*sōzō*) and its derivatives, including σωτηρία (*sōtēria*), which are used in a variety of ways in both Testaments. In Second Isaiah and Paul, the emphasis is on God's eschatological salvation of the world, whereas in the Psalms and the Synoptics the usual meanings are more immediate healing and deliverance. At the core of all usages, however, is "the idea of the preserving or restoring of the integrity of a person or thing or a functional nexus, however constituted."[2] Salvation and healing are inherently linked in Scripture and in this pastoral theology.

An example of the use of σώζω and its derivatives for healing and salvation is found in the familiar pericope of the two nameless women, one dying as she begins adult life, and the other suffering the entire length of the girl's life from the devastating flow of the same blood that makes the girl a woman. Each of them is restored to life in community, each of them is saved, healed, made whole by the power that comes forth from Jesus the Nazarene[3] (see Mark 5:21–43, esp. vv. 23, 28, 34).

"Justice healing" is the central metaphor for the way I have conceived and effected my vocational commitments. By that phrase I mean the church's active participation in God's ongoing work of justice and wholeness for all of earth's communities. My own experience of salvation has been a progressive healing of body and spirit through solidarity and alliance with those on the margins of church and society. At the core of the human situation and the divine drama of salvation are human brokenness and sin, from which we long to be healed, and from which we have indeed been proleptically healed in Christ. Our responsibility as the church, and particularly as pastoral ethicists and theologians, is to do the justice that brings the healing. Justice, God's justice for the world, for the marginalized and oppressed, is God's healing of the world through the power of the Holy Spirit. In the words of Isaiah 58:6–7 (NRSV),

> Is not this the fast that I choose:
> > to loose the bonds of injustice,
> > to undo the thongs of the yoke,
> to let the oppressed go free,
> > and to break every yoke?
> Is it not to share your bread with the hungry,
> > and bring the homeless poor into your house;
> when you see the naked, to cover them,
> > and not to hide yourself from your own kin?

You will hear me speak with some passion of the necessity for justice. The purpose of justice is healing and wholeness for all God's creation. At the core of my pastoral theology is a passion for the healing that justice brings, healing of the individual, the Christian community and its theologies, the peoples of the world, and the earth itself.

The Sovereignty of God

God's sovereignty as seen in the Calvinist polemic against idolatry is well summarized in John Leith's words: "Reformed theology has resisted every effort to get control of God, to fasten the infinite and indeterminate God to the finite and the determinate, whether it be images, or the bread and wine of the sacraments, or the structures of the church."[4]

At its most basic, this doctrine of God's sovereignty has relativized the claims of all human relationships and institutions. It has made clear that if we put our trust in anyone or anything—whether the Bible; our parents; our nation; our pastor; our significant other; our racial, ethnic, gender, or class identity; our income; our social, caste, or academic standing; our family or tribal connections—anything or anyone other than God, our trust is doomed to betrayal.

Pushed further, even trust in our particular Reformed version of God, our carefully developed theologies, and our cherished ecclesiologies and liturgies—these too come under the warning involved in the sovereignty of God.[5] The best we can do as human beings, in the face of God's self-revelation in Christ, is to respond in our limited speech, our creative genius, and our rational thought. We may never presume we have fully grasped and expressed the reality of the sovereign God.

Michael Weinrich connects the Reformed understanding of the sovereignty of God with *ecclesia reformata semper reformanda*. He goes on to say,

> The church is to remember that it does not live out of itself and can only be the living church if it shapes its existence and perspective as a response to the continually new address by God that it hears. . . . The church is not the earthly agent of God but . . . [God's] worldly witness (Acts 1:8). The Protestant church is a worldly church in that it knows that it does not possess God's Word, does not manage it, and does not distribute it more or less generously. The church itself has to hear the Word continually anew, always has to seek it anew like manna in the desert.[6]

The church must itself be healed as it hears the Word continually anew.

Language

As a white North American feminist pastoral theologian in the Reformed tradition, I regard all human structures as temporary, flawed, and changeable, in need of healing justice. This conviction has led me to a variety of commitments. First, human languages are human constructions, shaped over millennia in multitudes of cultures to express human ideas, experiences, and needs. We have created visual languages, spoken and then written languages, musical languages, signed languages, architectural languages, and theological languages. Each of us uses one or more of them with varying degrees of skill, and as everyone here knows, words and thoughts do not easily transpose themselves from one language to another. Two years ago I left an exhibit of Impressionist paintings and photographs, wondering how I might write light. I have heard light expressed musically and have seen it rendered visually. But I had no idea then or now about how to write light.

All human languages are human creations and thus fall under the warning inherent in the doctrine of the sovereignty of God: We cannot put our trust in human language. When we do so, we attempt to put limits on the limitless.[7] The debate that has consumed large parts of the European and North American churches about the appropriate language for the Trinity is an example. Is "God the Father" a human metaphor, or is it language that is inherently constitutive of the revealed nature of God? It is certainly language derived from human biology, not amoebic biology, and thus presumes that human reproduction can legitimately be written into the ultimate reality of the universe. Obviously, I disagree. I would argue that, based precisely on the limited nature of all human constructions, we tread on fearfully heretical ground when we try to claim divine absoluteness for any human expression.[8] Who is restored to, or excluded from, life in the Christian community by the languages we use? How are all of us saved, healed, and made whole by the power of Christ in our language?

Social Structures

Another area that comes under this same stricture is that of the social and political structures that pretend to be God-given. The sovereignty of God leads me to teach in distinctive ways and about particular subjects. If God is the absolute relativizer of all human constructions, then when I teach, no single position is taken as absolute, and no one group or person, particularly the professor in the classroom or the culture, is taken as the ultimate norm. And any social structures that presume a divinely given hierarchy of genders, individuals, races, sexualities, or ethnicities must be challenged, in the name of God's justice healing.[9]

Thus I taught a course on Gender, Race, and Class as part of the theological curriculum because those social structures are so all pervading and often invisible that they seem to be built into God's purposes for humanity. Revealing their origins in the variety of our cultures, and pulling back the curtain on the sources of their power in our lives, is both unsettling and freeing for students studying for the ministry. Our responsibility as Reformed pastoral theologians and ethicists is to strip away the pseudo-divine power of these human social constructions and thus to refuse to be trapped by the cultures in which we live. We must ask, again, who is restored to life in community? Who is excluded by our cultural accommodation?

Nationalism

The sovereignty of God requires that, wherever possible, I challenge the too-frequent conflation of God with country, ethnic society, or religious group. As a citizen of the United States, I have listened, watched, and objected in many practical ways to the use of Christian symbols and language as justification for the actions of the current and former United States administrations. A recent administration in Washington was one of the most dangerous we have known, both for its domestic policies and for its arrogant and illegal doctrine of preemptive war in the name of national security. But most important, from a Reformed perspective, it adopted Christian language for these policies and identified the righteousness of the "Christian" God with the identity and safety of the United States. The sovereignty of God makes clear that neither the nation-state nor any civil subdivision has a right to claim ultimate loyalty, whether in Mother Russia, the United States, or South Africa.[10] And again, as Reformed pastoral theologians and ethicists, we are responsible for exposing the idolatries that infect our societies.

Christian Responsibility for the World

The second Reformed theological position I consider here is Christian responsibility for establishing God's rule in the world.

Personal Responsibility

I was raised in white liberal upper middle-class Congregationalism in the U.S. Midwest. Because of my class and racialized status, I believed that "our people" were those who could make changes in society, and I understood from the church that it was my responsibility to do so.[11] We were taught a form of noblesse oblige rather than alliance building or justice making. It was our responsibility, as the good people, the clean people, the nice people, the white people, to help others who were "less fortunate" than ourselves.

Here we see the arrogance of the distorted doctrine of election as it continues to affect Reformed churches in the United States. (Indeed, white racism is partially rooted in this corruption of predestination and election.) Such language and posturing are built on the presumption that God has graciously given "us" deserved food, clothing, housing, and social status because we worked so hard to earn them, while continuing to deny that our "good fortune" is built directly on the bloody suffering of millions in our nation and around the world. One could easily draw connections here with South African politics and "informal settlements."

As part of this social-class responsibility, during my junior year in high school I went on what was called the Southern Tour, sponsored by our state Congregational Christian Conference. We visited black colleges and churches founded during and after the Civil War by the American Missionary Association. After the ten-day tour, I wrote a paper in which I denounced the whites-only real estate covenant of an adjacent residential neighborhood and presented it to the state conference. (Mind, I didn't notice that the covenant also excluded Jews.) Of course, I did not try to take any public action to change the covenant, because taking action to change structures from which I benefited was not part of noblesse oblige. Rather, it was a form of what was called liberal guilt.

What was clear to me, however, was that as a Christian of the Reformed tradition, I was responsible in the face of God for at least identifying, if not changing, social structures that oppressed and dehumanized others, to say nothing of myself. Since those early days, I have understood myself to be part of the community Jane Dempsey Douglas describes:

> Faith, hope, and love draw Christians out into society to be agents of renewal for the whole human community, because the church is the outpost of the reign of God, already at work in our world. Our standard for all real community is taken from the biblical visions of the reign of God: a new community in the Holy Spirit, a reign of love, justice, and peace, where all human barriers fall.[12]

In the intervening years, I have been involved in a variety of church and nonchurch organizations that have worked to change legal and social structures that oppress those on the economic, political, and social margins. In the more radical groups, I have often been one of the few who were church-identified and have not infrequently found both suspicion and surprise when I voiced a theologically based commitment to freedom and justice. This is particularly true in nonchurch feminist organizations, for whom the church in all its forms is experienced alternatively as irrelevant, totally committed to retaining current misogynist teachings and practices, and/or personally abusive and destructive. These are important places to carry out the church's "evangelical mission of salvation for the whole of humankind."[13]

Responsibility to Community

As a feminist pastoral theologian, I share with the Circle of Concerned African Women Theologians the necessity for "doing theology in community."[14] I am particularly concerned about communities of accountability, that is, those communities to whom each person understands oneself to be accountable for ministries of speaking, writing, action, and faith.

Whether I am writing a sermon, an article, a lecture, or a book, I am doing so in dialogue with a great cloud of witnesses. That certainly is true for all of us in whatever part of the human community we reside. We cannot do other than use the languages, images, experiences, and knowledges that have shaped us, which we in turn have both chosen and shaped. At the same time, our dialogue partners are crucial and must be thoughtfully chosen so as to foster justice healing.

My first dialogue partners were in the liberal white tradition of my home church in the Midwest. They were almost all male, white, and North American or European. The same can be said of my college experience, although most of my instructors were white women. It was not until seminary in the late 1960s, when for the first time I began to discover the intellectual and social history of the black church in the United States, James Cone's Black theology, and my first inklings of Asian and white South African theologies.

The 1970s and early '80s burst with the excitement of new theologies: liberation theologies from Central and South America, white feminist theologies, womanist, *mujerista*, and lesbian and gay theologies. They challenged most of what I had learned in the first two rounds of seminary and required me to listen carefully to those whose experience was very different from my own. It took many years and much debate to convince me that my white United States' world and middle-class assumptions were too narrow, too clouded, and too destructive. All too often we white professional women followed in the footsteps of our white male forebears and contemporaries, presuming that our experience and our perspectives were universal, and thus that we could speak in the name of all women. In 1979 Audre Lorde famously called us on our class arrogance, universalizing, and white racism.[15]

Parish Ministry

In the late 1960s and '70s, I was in parish ministry, first on the staff of an evangelical Presbyterian church in revolutionary Berkeley, then as assistant minister in white upper-middle-class commuter Connecticut, and finally as pastor in a small coastal congregation in Down East Maine.

During the years as pastor of that last white Congregational church, sermons were my major writing. As I wrote, I held in mind three or four very different members of the congregation, asking myself whether what I was preparing to say might open the door to God's grace-filled, justice-healing presence for those persons. They were my primary dialogue partners.

But I had a larger community of accountability, even though they were not present in the congregation. I was accountable to the white and Native American women and children in Maine who were trapped on back dirt roads in trailers, with no floor, no phone, no transportation, and alcoholic and abusive husbands. I was accountable to the African American women and men whose appearance in the homes of my parishioners was as victims, criminals, athletes, comedians, or entertainers on their TVs. I was accountable to the lesbian women and gay men who lived in the community and were members of the church but whose identity could not be named. I was accountable to the Jews for whom what I called the Old Testament was for them the Law and the Prophets, the gift of God to the people of Israel. I was accountable to Asian and Native and Hispanic Americans, whose history in the United States was either simply not present to the people in Hancock or else was so severely distorted that they were portrayed as mere caricatures rather than living people.

Whatever I said in my sermons, newsletter articles, and public and private conversations had in some way either to include the truth of this larger community, as I understood that truth, or at least not contribute to their demeaning or caricature.

One might reasonably point out that the community of accountability here is significantly larger than the church, let alone the members of the World Alliance of Reformed Churches. And that would be quite correct. It is precisely as a Reformed Christian that I am accountable to God for the well-being, the justice healing, the reconciliation of the world to God and to itself. The church needs to be what Letty Russell describes as a "community of faith and struggle working to anticipate God's New Creation by becoming partners with those who are at the margins of church and society."[16] As pastoral theologians and ethicists, such partnership, such alliance, is part of our responsibility.

Seminary Faculty Member

When I joined the faculty at Bangor in the early 1980s, my community of accountability widened immensely, in large part because of the explosion of formerly silenced voices around the world in the 1980s and '90s. When I taught Feminist Theologies and Ethics, the bibliography was longer than the syllabus, and I was responsible for exposing students to a global community of women in dialogue with the Scriptures, their cultures, their experiences, their theological heritages, and with other women from every continent. When I taught Feminist Theologies and Ministry, I asked how the issues facing women in African churches may resonate with, differ from, or instruct white women and men in northern New England who intend to serve a variety of denominations. How are aboriginal and Maori women responding to their own situations, and how can the ministry we engage in Maine be in solidarity with them? How can white women and men in Maine build alliances with the Somalis recently arrived, and with the First Nations peoples on whose land we live? What happens to a woman of Franco-American heritage from a low-income family in a white middle-class feminist classroom? Is she silenced, made to feel ashamed of her background? (The answer to that was, in part, yes.)[17]

Is it important that Maine students hear Musa Dube's passionate presentation to African church leaders about their responsibility to develop both a new theology and a new practice in the face of the devastation of HIV/AIDS?[18] Should they be studying Delores Williams's *Sisters in the Wilderness*[19] or Emilie Townes's *A Troubling in My Soul*?[20]

Of course they should, precisely because of the Reformed tradition's understanding of the church's responsibility for the world, and because, in Deborah Mullen's words, "By our baptism we become participants with Jesus in God's amazing love and radical plan to redeem and transform the earth. By our baptism we take on the burden and the blessings of being the body of Christ in the world."[21]

Dr. Isabel Phiri, now Secretary of the Circle of Concerned African Women Theologians, a Presbyterian whose voice is missed at this Conference, rightly points to the founding of The Institute of African Women in Religion and Culture as a significant factor in the raising up and voicing of women's theological work in community.[22] Dr. Nyambura Njoroge speaks of African women theologians "emerging within this generation of theologians who emphasize 'doing' rather than 'thinking' theology, have attempted to be at the heart of where theology is being created, in the womb of the community of faith, to academically articulate what is being produced."[23]

In so doing, Reformed women contribute to the working out of God's purposes in human history. God calls the church to be the instrument of God's purposes—not simply the salvation of individuals, but "also the establishment of a holy community and the glorification of . . . [God's] name through all the earth."[24] As Elsie McKee states, Calvin "drove himself to teach and shape the whole community in the patterns of life that would nourish its relationship with God and reflect its confession, and he did this most prominently by public and corporate means."[25]

FAITH AS GRACED GIFT

The third and final area of Reformed theology that has been deeply operative in my life involves faith as a gift that must be understood and lived.

Horace Bushnell was a nineteenth-century white Congregational pastor whose book *Christian Nurture* shook the foundations of then-current theology and practice regarding the spiritual life and salvation of children.[26] In the face of the dominant mode, which expected children to reach a crisis in which they were convicted of their sinfulness before they could receive the grace of God, Bushnell argued that children should be raised in the church so that they never know they are not Christians.

Faith as Gift

I grew up in the 1940s and '50s at Bushnell Congregational Church in Detroit, Michigan, and indeed I never knew that I was not beloved of God. In later years I struggled to respond when people asked me when I had accepted Christ or when I was saved. I wish I had known then that wonderful quip about being saved on a Friday in Jerusalem (thus through the cross and dying of Jesus), although now I would change it to a Sunday in Jerusalem (and thus through the rising to new life).

Indeed, although I did not know the words then, I would have, and do, echo Calvin's classic definition of grace: "a firm and certain knowledge of God's benevolence toward us, founded upon the truth of the freely given promise in Christ, both revealed to our minds and sealed upon our hearts through the Holy Spirit."[27] Donald McKim's exposition of Calvin's definition describes the gift of faith I have received:

- The Christian who is united with Christ by faith has a faith that is comprehensive in scope.
- Faith is *knowledge*—its content is "God's benevolence."
- Faith is *assured knowledge*, "firm and certain," enough for us to trust God fully.
- Faith is *personal knowledge* of "God's benevolence toward us." It is not just intellectual but is also a matter of the heart.
- Faith is a *gift*. God's goodwill is "freely given" and reaches to us in Christ, even before we are aware of it.
- Faith is a *relationship*. Faith is "revealed to our minds and sealed upon our hearts." The whole person receives God's promise in Christ in personal terms and receives the person of Jesus Christ as Lord and Savior.[28]

This faith has allowed me to explore freely a wide variety of understandings of God within and beyond the Christian faith, to raise fundamental questions about atonement theories and Christian symbolism, and to engage across religious barriers. I have been able to do so precisely because my faith and trust are in God rather than in the strength of my faith.

Although I was relatively privileged by race and class, family alcoholism and incest shaped my childhood and youth. The church, though a wonderfully welcoming place, was nevertheless also the scene of inappropriate sexual approach by a pastor. Neither my home nor my church was a safe place for me, nor were they locations that nurtured a young woman's independent voice. In both places the church's active participation in God's ongoing work of justice and wholeness was at best hamstrung by the behavior of its members and ministers.

What is remarkable, as I look back on those years, is that my own conviction of God's benevolence toward me never wavered. In later years, as my marriage was dissolving around me, a friend asked me why I was still alive. I responded by saying I knew that the power at the center of the universe was "for" me—not only me, of course, and not "against" others, but that God was there, supporting and loving me. Would that all of our churches, broken earthen vessels though they are, could provide such a grounded faith "sealed upon our hearts through the Holy Spirit."

D. W. Waander's observation about Calvin's attitude toward the doctrine of election has indeed worked itself through my life, thanks to Horace Bushnell's controversial reworking of Christian nurture. Waanders says, "[Calvin] saw the doctrine of election as a comfort for Christians, removing the struggle to earn salvation through good works. He also sought to shift the Christian's focus from subjective, inward searching or pulse-taking to a more objective faith in Christ, i.e., a trust in divinity rather than in oneself."[29]

My surgery for a brain aneurysm has provided a remarkable immersion in the loving, justice-healing, compassionate, strong, and beautiful presence of God. It was the first time I had faced a life-threatening medical situation and thus the first time I had been the focus of such broad and intense prayer from every corner of the earth and its many religious traditions. I could feel the prayers in my body as well as in my spirit, and thus I was graced with extraordinary experiences of the beauty and wonder of God. Faith is indeed a gift, and I am deeply grateful.

Faith Seeking Understanding

Faith as a gift that requires understanding began to take shape for me in confirmation class. From that year forward I have yearned to understand the history, theology, and practices of what I now know as the Reformed tradition. My eighth grade "discovery" of the Congregational connection to the Puritans gave me the historic grounding I had been missing as a white-bred Protestant. Realizing that my religious forebears had struggled and died for their faith in England, Europe, and New England was an important support for my adolescent romanticism.[30] And it gave me the beginnings of the courage to speak the truth as I saw it—hence the paper on the whites-only real estate covenant.

My college Biblical History major began to open wide the doors of understanding. I vividly remember accosting my state conference youth minister in the Detroit airport at Christmas during my sophomore year. I raged at him for not telling me that people had actually written the Bible, when he had known, he had *known* about J, E, D, and P all along, and he hadn't told me or any of us.

Faith seeking understanding has led me through four rounds of theological education at different schools, in the end giving me three degrees. It continues to move me into reading theology and biblical interpretation from every part of the globe, and to such globe-trotting as this conference. I come here to learn from your words and your persons, to clean some of the accumulated white western dirt from my lenses, although I deeply regret the absence of black African women to help me wash my glasses. Ours is a communal faith, shaped distinctively by the contexts in which the church lives, in both time and space. The Reformed tradition was shaped in the cauldron of sixteenth-century Europe and continues to be re-formed by its multiplicity of locations and languages. Here I stand, still trying to understand and follow the ways God is leading us toward justice healing for the world.

HEALING THE REFORMED TRADITION

The Reformed tradition has both fomented revolution á la Müntzer, Luther, Calvin, Zwingli, and Anne Hutchinson, and it has erected such obscene structures as apartheid and American slavery. The ties between Reformed theology and capitalism are well established, so that we have a particular responsibility for the monstrously bloated and greedy corporate globalization that is destroying lives and cultures in the United States as well as in other countries. The spreading revelations of clergy abuse and molestation in every country and church are not peculiar to our tradition, but they are certainly part of our responsibility.

My high school experience of clergy sexual misconduct was not reported to the church, nor even to my mother. I am sure that my youth minister had received no instruction in seminary on power issues involved in his behavior, let alone the corruption of the parishioner's relationship with God. We would not now be talking about such matters in the theological curriculum and the church if it were not for the work of Marie Fortune and many others who labored on the margins for years before being taken seriously.[31] The clergy assault I experienced, and much more vicious violations, continue to be part of the culture of many of our congregations and among far too many of our clergy. It is essential that we listen to, take seriously, and act upon the testimony of the women and men in our churches who have been abused in the name of God. As pastoral theologians, we must name these violations, give appropriate resources to our churches, and provide thorough instruction for our students about the theological and human consequences of such obscenities.

The Reformed tradition has much blood and agony on its hands, including the theological travesties of apartheid and Manifest Destiny, with its attendant dehumanization and destruction of indigenous peoples throughout the Americas. Many of our churches still refuse to ordain women or work actively for women's safety and well-being in the face of AIDS as well as oppressive cultural traditions. Many in our tradition continue to condemn gay, lesbian, transgendered, and bisexual people.[32]

The tradition that nurtured me also needs healing. In order to be faithful as pastoral theologians and ethicists, we need to be broken open by the voices and theological insights of those on the margins of our churches and our societies. God's sovereignty must be transformed by the vulnerable God of liberation theologies. Our Christian responsibility for the world must be transformed into solidarity with those on the edges. Our faith seeking understanding must be transformed into new vitality by the lives and voices of women and other marginalized groups. We must, with Johanna van Wijk-Bos, "identify with those members of a deprived group who suffer most, and . . . [learn] to recognize the necessity of systemic change. . . . To bring about that change, there must be people who act in alliance with the powerless."[33]

Our Reformed tradition is inclined to the sins of pride and arrogance, of certainty that we are the saved, the righteous, and that those unlike us or who disagree with us theologically are surely among the condemned sinners in the hands of an angry God. Our heritage of engagement with the world, our deep awareness of God's sovereignty, and our insistence that faith is itself a gift— these will not continue to bear fruit unless we carefully heed and allow ourselves to be changed by those who challenge our pride. And here we return full circle to the limitless love of God, for the power of justice healing and of salvation lies not in our hands nor in our minds. Rather, it is in the hands of the One who brings the future toward us on the winds of the Spirit.

CONCLUSION

I close with the words of my friend, a white North American feminist theologian and ethicist, Elly Haney, who was an organic intellectual. Her words about justice healing would well be my own.

> The theology and ethics I have developed have been born out of my own struggles with oppression and unearned privilege, my love of God and commitment to justice, the incredibly rich voices of people engaged in similar struggles, and the ache and anger in my heart at the beauty and desecration of this earth and its inhabitants. I do not have much confidence that significant global change will occur without an intervening major catastrophe. I do know that we have to continue. I do know that we must live not only in resistance to the status quo, but also in anticipation of new creation.[34]

Chapter 6

Beyers Naudé: Public Theologian?

DENISE M. ACKERMANN

THE MAN AND HIS CONTEXT

"There is a fascination about individuals who pit themselves against the might of a state, particularly when this involves a spiritual rebellion against their own community, with all the ostracism and pain that this brings," writes Peter Randall in an essay on the life and work of Beyers Naudé.[1] Such individuals crop up in the histories of different societies. South Africa has been blessed to have individuals who, for a just cause, have pitted themselves against the might of the state: women such as Emma Mashinini, Albertina Sisulu, Helen Joseph, and Mama Zihlangu; and men such as Steve Biko, Walter Sisulu, Nelson Mandela, and Desmond Tutu. What sets Beyers Naudé apart is the fact that he was compelled to take up a stance against his very own cultural and religious community and to pay the particular price that such action demands.

Who was Beyers Naudé? Born on May 10, 1915, in a parsonage of the Dutch Reformed Church (DRC), from an impeccable Afrikaner Calvinist background, Beyers Naudé was named after General Beyers, a staunch Afrikaner nationalist who headed a rebellion against South Africa's participation in the First World War. His childhood and youth were typical of most patriotic and religious

Afrikaners of that time. Not surprisingly, he decided to enter the ministry and went off to study at the University of Stellenbosch.[2] His leadership gifts were recognized when he was elected *primarius* of his residence and president of the student's representative council. Interestingly, signs of a rebellious streak emerged when he, together with several other students, started an anonymous campus newspaper called *Pro Veritate* (devoted to liberty and truth!), which raised controversy during its short life on the campus. After completing his theological studies, he became a minister in the Dutch Reformed Church in 1939. In 1940 he was also formally and ritually inducted under oath of secrecy into membership of the *Afrikaner Broederbond*.[3] This secret society was committed to Afrikaner domination of institutions of power in South Africa: the government, the economy, education, social institutions, and the church.

Beyers Naudé served as a minister to six congregations in various parts of South Africa. In 1953 he undertook a study tour of North America and Europe that further broadened his experience and his understanding of societies different from his own.[4] In 1958 he was elected to the moderature of the Transvaal Synod of the Dutch Reformed Church, an influential position, which signaled that he was being prepared for higher office. One result of his new position was that he came into contact with younger and more skeptical Dutch Reformed Church dominees who were questioning the application of the Group Areas Act and the exclusionary race classification of the black and colored community.[5] Tensions had begun to surface within the Dutch Reformed Church. A series of informal meetings took place in the homes of disaffected members in an attempt to deal with the deplorable ignorance of white Dutch Reformed Church members on the implications of segregated structures in church and community.

An event then occurred that was to change the course of history in South Africa. On March 21, 1960, a crowd of black people protested peacefully against the pass laws outside the police station at Sharpeville, an African township near Vereeniging. Police opened fire: sixty-nine protestors were killed and hundreds others wounded. According to Peter Walshe, this incident signaled the culmination of a decade of "sporadic black passive resistance."[6] Roman Catholic Archbishop Denis Hurley, commenting on the effect of Sharpeville on Beyers Naudé, writes: "Out of that tragedy God spoke to Beyers Naudé."[7] A state of emergency followed Sharpeville: the African National Congress and the Pan-Africanist Congress were banned; the already-draconian security apparatus was tightened; capital flowed out of the country, the economy slumped, and Verwoerd withdrew South Africa from the British Commonwealth. Tensions between English-speaking multiracial churches and the state increased.[8] "Afrikanerdom was rocked to the foundations by the Sharpeville massacre. How could a policy designed to reduce friction lead to such violence?" commented Johan Kinghorn.[9]

The second crucial event in the life of Beyers Naudé was the Cottesloe Consultation in December 1960. The initial move for this consultation came from Anglican Archbishop Joost de Blank, with the support of the World Council of Churches (WCC) and its member churches in South Africa, which included the Cape Dutch Reformed Church, the Transvaal Dutch Reformed Church, and the Nederduitsch Hervormde Kerk (NHK). Eighty representatives from the South African churches and six World Council of Churches' representatives met on December 7–14, 1960. From later accounts it is clear that many of the participants were deeply affected by their experience of this international, ecumenical, and interracial gathering. It was Beyers Naudé's first experience of true ecumenism.[10]

Cottesloe, a symbolic watershed in the life of Beyers Naudé, caused one "of the most acrimonious debates in the history of Afrikanerdom between 1950 and 1980."[11] Although its findings were modest, Cottesloe did go to the heart of the policy of apartheid, and its resolutions were in direct conflict with Prime Minister H. F. Verwoerd's policy of total territorial separation.

Most important, the Cottesloe resolutions recognized all racial groups as "indigenous" and as citizens of South Africa and demanded equal rights for all to participate in the life of the country and to share in the responsibilities, rewards, and privileges of citizenship. It asserted that there were no scriptural grounds for the prohibition of mixed marriages; it acknowledged that wages received by the "nonwhite" majority were below subsistence level and affirmed that the right to own land "wherever he is domiciled, and to participate in the government of his country, is part of the dignity of the adult man [sic]."[12]

Beyers Naudé tried to explain these findings to his people. A storm broke over his head. To Verwoerd and his followers, Cottesloe meant treason in Afrikaner ranks. The Prime Minister called on the churches to rid themselves of their betrayers, and they did. Severely reprimanded, the Dutch Reformed Church delegates were stripped of their synodical duties, and opposition to government policies in the Dutch Reformed Churches was stifled. As debate closed down in the Afrikaner establishment, it was kept alive by small groups within the Dutch Reformed Church, often in home-based Bible study groups. As a result of this crackdown, a monthly Christian journal (once again called *Pro Veritate*) appeared in May 1962, edited by Beyers Naudé and overseen by an ecumenical, multiracial board. During this period Beyers Naudé became convinced that effective change could only take place outside the official framework of the mainline churches. According to John de Gruchy, "The idea of forming a confessing church in South Africa, similar to that born during the struggle in Nazi Germany, had long been debated in South Africa. It had inspired Beyers Naudé to launch the Christian Institute."[13] This ecumenical and interracial body came into being in 1963, with Beyers Naudé as its director.

The next two years were times of turmoil and personal conflict for Beyers Naudé. Here was a leading candidate for moderator of the General Synod of the Dutch Reformed Church and a true Afrikaner taking a stand that was extremely threatening to the foundations of Afrikaner civil religion. In 1963 he was elected as moderator of the Southern Transvaal Synod of the Dutch Reformed Church. "This despite Cottesloe, despite *Pro Veritate*, despite his resignation from the Afrikaanse Broederbond: Could he have made a mistake after all; was the church in fact ready for change? Or was it a strategy to tempt him into compromise; was it pressure to bring him back into line?" asked Randall.[14] He was soon to know. Virulent attacks on the Christian Institute (CI) and on his person increased, and finally he was faced with an ultimatum. He was called to resign from *Pro Veritate* and had to choose between the Christian Institute and his position as a minister of the Dutch Reformed Church. He chose the Christian Institute.[15] After serving six different congregations over his twenty-three years as a minister of the Dutch Reformed Church, Beyers Naudé preached his last sermon to a packed church at Aasvoëlkop, Johannesburg, on September 22, 1963. Then, in a gesture symbolizing the stripping of his status, he took off his robe before a silent congregation, some of whom were weeping.[16]

I have devoted time to recounting certain events in the life of Beyers Naudé in order to illustrate the changes that occurred in his life. I came to know him in 1971 through my membership in the Christian Institute and gratefully acknowledge the life-changing role he played in my life as I struggled to live my faith in apartheid times. In the Christian Institute, I met an eclectic group of Christians, some of whom were members of the Black Consciousness Movement (BCM), who spoke about liberation and black theology, poetry, and drama, and who openly envisaged a future in which black people would exercise political power. Those were heady days. Not surprisingly, they came to an end abruptly when the Christian Institute was banned in October 1977. The above few sentences do not communicate the excitement and the dangers of those times. The Christian Institute's Cape Town offices were twice set alight; shots were fired at the home of Theo Kotze, its director in the Western Cape and a leading light in the antiapartheid struggle, who eventually went into exile. Beyers Naudé's passport was confiscated; ties between the Reformed churches in the Netherlands and those in South Africa were broken, and the Soweto riots of 1976 shocked the world. In 1976 the security police continued their harassment of the Christian Institute, regularly searching its offices, while political rhetoric against the Christian Institute heated up.

In 1977 Steve Biko, the first president of the South African Students Organization and a leading black consciousness leader who was closely involved with the Christian Institute, was murdered in detention. Shortly thereafter the Christian Institute—together with seventeen other organizations, mainly black consciousness groups—was declared an unlawful organization: its offices were closed down, and all its documents were confiscated. This event also signaled the end of *Pro Veritate*. At the age of sixty-two, Beyers Naudé was subjected to a banning order that restricted him to his home; cut him off from attending meetings of any kind, whether social, political or religious; did not allow him to speak in public; and made it unlawful to quote him. Commenting on this kind of punishment, Peter Randall writes:

> Banning causes a profoundly damaging loss of spontaneity in one's human relationships. There is the risk of developing a permanent attitude of

distrust towards new contacts—and even some old contacts—and a general feeling of suspicion: could they possibly be agents of the system? . . . The loss of spontaneity in terms of Christian fellowship must have hit the Naudés particularly hard. Expressions of fellowship, for a banned person, are limited to meeting with one other at a time; for a couple or a family there is not legal opportunity to experience anything of the fullness of Christian community.[17]

Public Christian witness became a forbidden activity. This was a period of intense frustration and very hard on Beyers Naudé, his wife, Ilse, and his family. Originally banned for five years, his banning order was later extended for a further three years and then, to his surprise, lifted after a total of seven years on September 26, 1984. Barely a month later he was approached by the leaders of the South African Council of Churches (SACC) to succeed Desmond Tutu, who had just been appointed bishop of Johannesburg. He accepted reluctantly. "I was white, for many years I belonged to a church that defended apartheid on biblical grounds, I was already sixty-nine, and after seven years of banning, . . . I had not had much contact with what was happening in my country and particularly in the black churches. . . . Moreover I was very hesitant to stand in Desmond Tutu's shoes."[18] However, he accepted the position and served as secretary of the SACC from 1985 to 1988.

During that time and thereafter, Beyers Naudé continued to speak, teach, and preach about the need for confession, reconciliation, and unity among the churches. He pleaded ceaselessly for the Dutch Reformed Church to become one united church. Ecumenism, economic justice, love, and the value of the human person were his abiding themes. He led protest marches and visited sites of struggle, suffering, and conflict. I have an abiding memory of him at the funerals of young black activists—often the only white face.

This biographical sketch does not do justice to a man whose integrity and personal charm, courage and honesty, and prophetic humility above all set him apart from his contemporaries. The moving homage that the South African nation paid to "*Oom Bey*"[19] after his death (on Sept. 7, 2004) speaks volumes for the high regard in which he was held. After these glimpses into his life, I shall now try to assess Beyers Naudé as a public theologian.

ON BEING A PUBLIC THEOLOGIAN

In South Africa the explicit use of the term "public theology" is fairly recent. This does not mean that public theology was not practiced in a variety of ways, particularly in opposition to apartheid. According to Nico Koopman, public theology is found in publications, seminars, conferences, public declarations; civil protests such as marches, hunger strikes, and memoranda to the government; welfare programs and the quest for economic and political justice; and even in an official confession (Belhar Confession, 1982, 1986).[20]

There are different understandings of what is meant by public theology. For some it is the need to explain, justify, and defend theological claims in a public way and to seek at least a degree of consensus and universality, as represented by David Tracy's critical correlation approach. David Hollenbach describes public theology simply as "the effort to discover and communicate the socially significant meaning of Christian symbols and tradition," which serves the church as well as society. He continues: "Public theology wants to bring the wisdom of the Christian tradition into public conversation to contribute to the well-being of society."[21] Martin Marty believes that "purely private faith is incomplete. . . ."[22] Last, Robert Simons explains, "When theology is described as public, the meaning of 'public' is that such theology is accessible to intelligent, reasonable, and responsible members of a society, despite otherwise crucial differences in their beliefs and practices."[23] I accept that public theology as *public practical theology* not only affirms the public character of all theology but also points to the fact that theology lives in the tension between theory and praxis, between what we believe and what we do about what we believe. Public practical theology that is done in service of God's reign comes out of a critical consciousness informed by social analysis, a concern for justice, the creative use of human imagination, and the willingness to risk actions that express our hope for a better world.[24] All these understandings of public theology assume that the church is sensitive to the public order that surrounds it and with which it desires to be in communication.

In the light of these understandings, we ask, Can we call Beyers Naudé a public theologian? If so, what kind of public theologian was he? Before tackling this question, I refer to Ronald Thiemann's paper "The Public Theologian as Connected Critic," delivered in Prague in June 2003. I was struck by his caution that the churches' contributions to the *res publica* need "a clear and authentic understanding of their status as public theological institutions" and his description of their roles as that of "connected critics." Connected criticism, according to Thiemann, "oscillates between the poles of critique and connection, solitude and solidarity, alienation and authority. Connected critics are those who are fully engaged in the very enterprise they criticize, yet alienated by the deceits and shortcomings of their own community."[25] Thiemann's understanding of a "connected critic" is my entry point for trying to answer the question posed above. I shall, with reference to Thiemann's description of the connected critic and to my own understanding of public practical theology, explore whether Beyers Naudé can be called a public theologian.

BEYERS NAUDÉ, A CONNECTED CRITIC

Critique and Connection

In the early part of his life, Beyers Naudé was not critical of his context and background. Describing this background, he told Dorothee Sölle, in a published conversation, that he came "from a very conservative, deeply religious Afrikaaner [sic] home. . . . [My] whole background is one of a deeply religious, strongly nationalist Afrikaaner tradition."[26] His rise in the hierarchy of the Dutch Reformed Church, his membership in the *Broederbond*, his professional path as a minister—all would not have been possible if he had been a critical member of his community. It demanded loyalty, which he described as follows: "In the Afrikaner society there is such a deep sense of loyalty. . . . Loyalty to your people, loyalty to your country, loyalty and patriotism have in a certain sense become deeply religious values. . . . Anybody who is seen to be disloyal to his nation, to his people, is not only deemed to be a traitor, but in the deeper sense of the word, he is [also] seen as betraying God."[27] He understood this loyalty (and subsequently its traps), and he never lost his deep connection with his own people.

Despite remaining an Afrikaner in body, mind, and soul, Beyers Naudé became a fearless critic of his people's adherence to apartheid policies, precisely because he cared for them and remained deeply connected to them. His coming to critical awareness was a process, as described above. Critical awareness was quite naturally followed by the need for change-making actions. Critique and the active seeking of change do not sit comfortably in a society that demands loyalty and balks at change. Beyers Naudé knew what it was like to be torn between loyalties to one's family, friends, church, and people on the one hand, and the injustice and suffering caused to the majority of South Africans on the other hand. Talking to Dorothee Sölle about forced removals, he said, "And, you know, I must feel the agony of this, especially because I know that the people who are in control and in power doing this, these are my people. I cannot deny that I am an Afrikaner. I don't want to deny it. How can I? I am nothing else but an Afrikaner, and yet in that sense I don't see myself to be there."[28]

The establishment of the Christian Institute under his leadership was a major turning point in Beyers Naudé's life. Writing about its establishment, he stated that the Christian Institute was an organization born in the church and that it wanted to work in the church, not in a competitive manner but supportively.[29] Remaining connected to the church was a primary consideration throughout his life. But the church is more than the white Dutch Reformed Church. The separation of the white Dutch Reformed Church from the black family of Dutch Reformed churches was intolerable for Beyers Naudé. "No one who loves the church as the Body of Christ can ever be happy about this state of affairs," he wrote.[30] He saw his church undergoing a "purposeful and fear-ridden process of isolation."[31] Through his work in the Christian Institute, Beyers Naudé developed a profoundly ecumenical understanding of the church while at the same time remaining a faithful member of the Dutch Reformed family of churches. His understanding of the church was inclusive:

> If we mean by church mainly the institution, the structure, the visible, traditional symbols, then I believe that the church, in that sense, will experience one crisis after another, until it comes to the recognition, understanding that the church in the real sense of the word, is where the people

of God are, where life is being discovered again, the true meaning of love, of human community, of mutual concern for one another, of caring for people, of seeking true meaningful relationship, understanding between people, not only between Christians, but [also] between all people.[32]

Beyers Naudé's commitment to ecumenism is clear from a statement he made before the Schlebusch Commission set up in February 1972 to investigate certain organizations, including the Christian Institute. He described the Christian Institute as follows:

> The Christian Institute is an organization of individual Christians from all churches in South Africa, with four main aims and objectives. In the first place, to give a more visible expression to the biblical truth of the unity of all Christians, all believers. In the second place, to relate the truth of the Gospel more immediately to the questions of our daily existence and to make its meaning more clear to its members and to all who wish to know it. In the third place, to act as a group of Christians who wish to help bring about reconciliation between the widely divergent, divided and conflicting groups of Christians of different Churches and colours in our country. And in the fourth place, to offer the services of our members to any Church or group of Churches who wish to make use of them to give a better expression of the Kingdom of God in South Africa.[33]

Once he had committed himself to the Christian Institute, which in his words "seeks deep and radical change, in repentance and faith, obedience to the will of God and the transformation of society in his name,"[34] his critical voice became clear and unambiguous. He described the Christian Institute as "a fellowship of Christians who seek individually and together to be used by God to give practical expression to a growing desire for fellowship and understanding between Christians in our country."[35] Writing in *Pro Veritate*, he said that the Christian Institute was convinced "that bringing every facet of life into obedience to Christ means rejecting the heresies of racism, apartheid and 'Christian nationalism.'"[36]

Clearly he had set himself on a collision course with his own people and their policies. In 1976 he wrote: "Majority rule will be coming to South Africa in the next decade . . . [because] the culture of any community cannot be secured by entrenching itself in isolation or by ensuring its future existence through selfish legislation, but only through the inner vitality of its culture, its moral values and its willingness to serve its fellow men. And this is the challenge that every minority group in South Africa has to face today."[37] These, and many similar views expressed in *Pro Veritate*, resonated with black Christians as they suffered discrimination and alienation from white Christians who supported traditional Dutch Reformed Church views on apartheid. They felt connected to the Christian Institute and its mouthpiece and saw them as beacons of hope in dark times. In 1971 an unidentified black man in Soweto wrote: "Every night I hurry into my room where I light my candle and take *Pro Veritate* from under my mattress to read. Then my heart is full of hope and I thank Christ. Then I can go to sleep."[38]

Solitude and Solidarity

In his autobiography, Beyers Naudé's chapter on his banning is called "Sewe maer jare" (seven lean years). Faced with being cut off from all his previous activities and interests, he recounts how he was faced with three options: First, he could devote himself to further theological study and learn a black language. Second, he could write a book about the questions and problems that had brought him to this place. Third, he could leave South Africa so as to further the cause of the Christian Institute in exile. He wrestled with these options, but when his wife, Ilse, said: "If you feel that it is your duty to go, do so, but do not expect me to follow you," he dropped the third option. Instead, he decided to expand his contact with members of the Black Consciousness Movement and to find ways of helping those who were opposing apartheid.[39]

This was not an easy decision. Describing his experience of being banned, he tells Dorothee Sölle: "The moment they succeed in making you a nonperson, whatever you say, therefore, loses significance and loses meaning, and therefore in that sense they invalidate what you are saying, and . . . remove the danger that the ideas and thoughts that you present could therefore have some impact."[40] Beyers Naudé knew a kind of solitude, albeit an enforced solitude that he later described as the most enriching time of his life. In his enforced solitude he found solidarity.

> They came to our front door, one by one, day after day, black but also white, young but also old, from early in the morning to well after dark and sometimes deep into the night. And as I began to discover how little I really knew about what lived deep in the hearts of the majority of our population, I began to realize that I must use my banning to listen and to learn. Thus seven years of listening and learning followed, and the seven leanest years of my life became the seven richest years of my life.[41]

He became involved in the illegal activities of the African National Congress (ANC) as he supported young activists intent on joining the military wing of the African National Congress. He records that he always asked each one of them the same question: Are you sure that you have no other option? He assisted in disseminating African National Congress literature and with small sums of money helped some young people who went into exile or crossed the borders, seeking military training. Most of all he built up relationships of trust with members of the Black Consciousness Movement as well as with members of the liberation movements and came to make their cause his own.

Alienation and Authority

Beyers Naudé attests to the blessings of his seven years of banning. It was not primarily an experience of alienation. This does not mean that he did not experience alienation, particularly from his own people. His persecution by the state and his increased support for the liberation movements alienated him more and more from his own people. His support of the World Council of Churchs' Programme to Combat Racism was greeted with shock and horror by his own community when, in 1970, the WCC granted R143,000 for nonmilitary purposes to the liberation movements in South Africa. His support for this grant had consequences that he described in an article as "The Parting of the Ways." "Die tyd vir vroom woorde is verby [the time for pious words is past]," he wrote in *Pro Veritate*.[42] In his view South Africa was now separating itself from the world community by further enforcing racist rule. This was also a testing time for white people who had to face the rightness of the black cause and black majority rule. Finally, it was a decisive time for the Dutch Reformed Church, which had to decide whether to continue to support apartheid or to work for a new South Africa.[43]

As he inveighed against the apartheid state, as his alienation from his own people grew, his moral authority and stature grew. Though crying from the wilderness, his voice gave hope to the millions who saw in him a man of prophetic courage and deep and abiding moral values precisely because he had dared to confront his own community. In an article titled "The South Africa I Want," Beyers Naudé wrote that he did not want authoritarian rule or a political ideology based on a system of separate advantages for whites and control of people's movements. He wanted the permanency of all South Africans to be recognized, freedom for all, black political representation, the pass laws repealed, and free compulsory education for all South Africans.

Whatever it is that confers moral authority on a human being who is willing to suffer for their beliefs, who identifies with the suffering of others in visible and practical ways, who is prepared to face alienation from their own community, and who is quite clearly a person whose actions and thoughts are undergirded by profound faith, Beyers Naudé possessed it. Above all he was a person of extraordinary humility. He had an almost childlike acceptance of and belief in the ultimate goodness of humanity. Self-effacing, open, and always hopeful, Beyers Naudé gained a moral stature rare in these times or any times.

WAS BEYERS NAUDÉ A PUBLIC THEOLOGIAN?

Ron Thiemann's categories for evaluating a "connected critic" are not divorced from my understanding of a public theologian. Thiemann writes: "Connected critics are those who are *fully engaged* in the very enterprise they criticize, yet alienated by the deceits and shortcomings of their own community" (emphasis added).[44] For "fully engaged" I read "praxis," action, or "the doing of the word." In the paper I gave at Prague in June 2003, I concluded that public practical theology was theology involved in praxis for the reign of God. "Public practical theology takes praxis, the 'doing of the word,' as the measure by which its integrity and its authority will be judged in the public square."[45]

Can Beyers Naudé therefore be called a public theologian? This question has no straightforward answer because the very term "public theology" is complex, contested, often vague and ambiguous. Hence my question mark in the title of this essay. There appears to be no single normative way of doing public theology, and the very word "public" can have a variety of meanings. Dirk Smit has pointed out that there are at least six different stories to relate on the origins and development of public theology.[46] Is the very nature of all theological discourse not public in some sense or other? What is the difference between a feminist, liberation, or contextual theologian and a public theologian?

As the questions multiply, and if public theology is in its broadest sense concerned with the common struggle for justice and the general welfare of people and their quality of life in a society, Beyers Naudé was a public theologian. If public theology is concerned with the public witness of the gospel and the church's need to be involved in works of justice and care in society, Beyers Naudé was a public theologian. If he is assessed in terms of Thiemann's concept of a "connected critic," he was a public theologian throughout the latter part of his life. Beyers Naudé remained deeply committed to the church while critical of all actions that did not speak of justice and care for dignity and worth of all people.

His life and his work met the criteria of a public theologian who, in Hollenbach's words, with passion and courage wanted to "bring the wisdom of the Christian tradition into public conversation to contribute to the well-being of society." Beyers Naudé was without doubt "fully engaged" in actions that express the values of the reign of God: justice, love, freedom, peace, wholeness, and the flourishing of righteousness. He was primarily driven by his desire to be obedient to where his God was leading him. In a sense he could do no other. His life was quite simply an active living out of his faith in a highly charged public arena at a particular time in South African history.[47]

However, despite such assessments, I doubt that Beyers Naudé would have referred to himself as a public theologian. In my view he would probably have rejected all labels and simply called himself a servant of Christ, called to witness to the demands of the gospel. Obedience to Beyers Naudé's understanding of the teachings of Christ—motivated by reverence for the humanity of God and the ethical demands of living in faith, hope, and grace—was central to our conversations and his embrace of those painful times in his life. Conversations with him were characterized by his unfailing kindness and remarkable humility. I have always thought of Beyers Naudé as God's humble servant and a reluctant prophet, whose role was pivotal during fraught times in my country's history.

In his farewell sermon to the Aasvoëlkop congregation in 1963, he chose Acts 5:29 as his text: "We must obey God rather than men" (RSV). After a straightforward exegesis of the text, Beyers Naudé turned his attention to the difficult question: In situations of conflict, how do we know that we are, in fact, obeying God rather than "man"? Through our conscience? How do we know that our conscience is right? He talked about his own struggle to find reasons to cut his ties with *Pro Veritate* and the Christian Institute, something required by the

Southern Transvaal Synod of the Dutch Reformed Church if he wanted to keep his status as a minister in his church.

"But time and time again, at times with great agonizing, fear, and resistance in my heart, the Lord brought me back to this part of Scripture, as if he wanted to say: Whatever this text may mean to others, this is my answer to you: Obey God rather than man."[48] He then explained that the choice went deeper than his concern for his pastoral work, the church, *Pro Veritate*, or the Christian Institute. "It is a choice between religious conviction and submission to ecclesiastical authority. By obeying the latter unconditionally I would save face but lose my soul."[49] Next he addressed his congregation and his church and then concluded with these words:

> If the NG Kerk does not understand and exercise more deeply this obedience demanded by God, then we will suffer endless loss and sorrow. . . . If our Church continues with this deliberate and fear-inspired process of isolation, with its tragic withdrawal from the Holy Catholic Church in South Africa, in Africa, we will spiritually wither and die. . . . Oh, my Church, I call this morning in all sincerity from my soul—awake before it is too late. Stand up and give the hand of Christian brotherhood to all who sincerely stretch out their hand to you. There is still time, but the time is short, very short.[50]

His plea was not heeded. His words were indeed prophetic. Today the white Dutch Reformed Church is still struggling to come to terms with its history, with its separation from its "sister" churches, and thus with the experience of being truly ecumenical.

Duncan Forrester writes: "Truth is not something to be comprehended, controlled, used or appropriated. It is rather to be indwelt, lived out in action and witnessed to. And that is what Christian public theology is about today."[51] Beyers Naudé lived his faith with consistency, courage, and hope. His witness was that of a man of God who devoted himself to the cause of human dignity and justice in South Africa through very demanding times. He was a prophet outside the walls of the church who loved the church to the end and is assured of an honored place in the painful story of South Africa's transition to democracy.

Chapter 7

Created as Neighbors
A Vision for Honoring Racial and Cultural Difference

NANCY J. RAMSAY

PREFACE

As a Reformed pastoral theologian, my method is shaped by Seward Hiltner's conviction that pastoral theology is a constructive theological endeavor arising from engagement in ministries of care. Unlike Hiltner, but like many contemporary pastoral theologians in the United States and other parts of the world, my focus for considering ministries of care locates particular needs within an ecological contextual frame that is highly systemic. There are occasions, such as here, where my theological engagement begins not with a particular moment of offering care but with attention to the systemic and structural dynamics that shape and distort the context for care. I use a praxis methodology in which I presume that theological understanding arises not only from reflection on the historical Christian biblical and theological tradition but also through practices of care such as love, forgiveness, compassion, and advocacy. I am informed especially by liberation and process theologies.

Since the mid-1970s in the United States, pastoral theology and pastoral care have been in the process of reclaiming their theological integrity yielded up in the third quarter of the twentieth century due to an uncritical embrace of popularized psychology. This recovery of theological intentionality has been particularly apparent since the 1980s. While psychology continues to be a valued partner in the interdisciplinary enterprise of pastoral theology, critical theories of culture, systems theory, economics, and other social sciences also inform contemporary pastoral theology and care. In the past fifteen years the horizons of pastoral theology have widened to engage public policy and systemic issues that impinge on the needs of particular persons and families, issues such as children and poverty, intimate violence, and racism. This more ecological focus frames pastoral responses within a web of care.

This chapter is a revised version of the Edwards Lecture delivered at Louisville Presbyterian Theological Seminary in February 2004 and demonstrates pastoral theology as public theology. It also discloses my own formation as a Reformed pastoral theologian through my interpretation of several theological themes: a theocentric ethic; humanity's creation in God's image; original, actual, and social sin; and neighbor love as human vocation. Methodologically, the reciprocity of critique between theological and social science sources also demonstrates a Reformed commitment to discerning the distortions of sin in church as well as in culture, with the wider goal of enlarging God's love in the world.

The Brief Statement of Faith—Presbyterian Church (U.S.A.) begins (borrowing from the Heidelberg Catechism), "In life and in death we belong to God." It is that assertion of God's sovereignty that establishes the frame of this essay, in which I draw on Scripture and theology to critique culture and church and to frame a vision for life in community that presumes the centrality of love as the intention of God as creator. This theocentric ethic shapes Reformed piety as actively engaged in transforming culture so that it better reflects God's redeeming love.[1] Indeed, the vision for care in this essay is a compassionate resistance to forces that deform and destroy human life.[2]

Alongside this theocentric frame, the relational interpretation of creation in God's image is clearly indebted to Reformed perspectives that locate the *imago Dei* in our relationality as it reflects God's love.[3] For Reformed Christians, relationship is the essence and vocation of human beings. Neighbor love then emerges as the central ethical foundation for life in community and our vocational goal.

Sin seems to be what Reformed Christians know most about. Here I draw on several Reformed insights about sin as the universal condition of human experience. Racism is not merely a sociological, economic, or political disorder. It is sin. As such, it reflects a Reformed understanding of original sin as the inescapable, pervasive disordering of human life, in which all participate equally. As such, original sin contributes to the actual and social dimensions of sin by distorting our capacity to choose the good in church and culture. Since humankind's creation in God's image is disclosed through love of God and neighbor, sin is the refusal to be in relation.[4] It is the lie that rationalizes the commodification or dehumanization of another.

INTRODUCTION

Most of us have complicated feelings about race and the fact of racism in our culture and our life together in congregations. There is major work yet to do in this nation's and our local communities' efforts to deconstruct the injustice of racism at personal and structural levels. For every hopeful indicator such as congregational partnerships or increasing numbers of persons of color in positions of leadership, including the U.S. presidency, there are also reminders of how entrenched racist patterns remain in areas such as our legal, economic, housing, educational, and ecclesial systems. Even our language trips us up. That phrase "persons of color" could reinforce the problematic idea that white racial identity is normative. It is similar to the phrase "racial ethnic minorities," which implies that European Americans have no racial and ethnic identity and hides the fact that in terms of the world's population, whites are a minority. Our language about race is far from precise.

The fact that the sin of racism continues to plague us contrasts sharply with two powerful images about life together that shape the imaginations of Christians: humanity's creation in God's image and neighbor love. Scripture is filled with reminders that creation in God's image is fulfilled in relationships of compassion, mutual love, and respect. For Christians, to be is to be with. In the story we often call the Good Samaritan, the love of God and neighbor are presumed by all as a summary of the law and the vocation to which we are called. In the face of questions that might limit the meaning of neighbor, Jesus made the radical point that there is no room for barriers of race, class, culture, or nationality in this vision for love. Yet Christian tradition is itself complicit in the patterns of racism that divide us in church and culture.

Against this backdrop of such a compelling biblical vision for life together shaped by love that refuses dehumanizing barriers such as race and class, I offer a brief analysis of how it is that racism continues in our daily lives, especially in the lives of European American Christians who do not intend to practice racism. I also share a brief history of how it is that the idea of race and the reality of racism took shape literally at the origins of the colonies in what is now the United States. Finally, I return again to the resources of Christian tradition to suggest ways to confront the sin of racism and practice love more proactively across lines of race and cultural difference.

PRESENT CONTEXT

In the fall of 2002 a report was released describing a joint study conducted by Massachusetts Institute of Technology and the University of Chicago to measure racism in employment.[5] The researchers developed comparable fictitious résumés using typically European American names and typically African American names. The résumés were developed for a wide range of positions from upper management to service-sector positions in Boston and Chicago. They found that despite equal preparedness, the European American résumés received responses 50 percent more often. They then increased the level of preparedness and sent the résumés again. Increasing skills did not increase responses to the African American files but did improve responses to those of the fictitious European Americans. The blatant discrimination is all the more interesting since before the study the personnel officers assured the researchers that the African American applications would receive preferential treatment.

This description of the outcome is not news to African Americans and other persons of color, but it probably surprises many of us of European heritage. Given a climate in which many businesses are seeking to have a more racially diverse workforce and to demonstrate AAEEO guidelines,[6] such consistent discrimination suggests some level of unconscious privileging of identities more familiar to the personnel managers. This discrimination was constant across all types of business, including government agencies supposedly held to a higher standard of inclusion. The claim of preferential treatment by which many vilify Affirmative Action is undercut by such a study: it is clear that preferential treatment is in place for European Americans. Affirmative Action for those marginalized by the dominance of European Americans is an effort to correct an uneven "playing field." It is safe to assume that a number of these personnel officers are Christians who would quickly protest that they are not racists. Indeed, they would likely be startled by the pattern of discrimination. What might be going on?

One way to understand our predicament is to go back to definitions because how we define problems shapes our strategies for responding to them. Presently two difficulties exist in the way many European Americans define racism. Some define racism as a problem that is external to us personally. Others define it as existing simply as personal prejudice. Reducing racism to personal prejudice means that racism is only associated with blatant discrimination like that associated with the Ku Klux Klan. Persons who do not actively discriminate will report that they are not prejudiced because they have no awareness of larger systemic dimensions of racial dominance. Many European Americans do add a more systemic analysis, but we still define racism as a system of disadvantage based on race. That is, we know there are problems in employment, education, and the legal system, for example. However, this definition locates the problem at a safe distance from ourselves. As a system of disadvantage, racism remains an external barrier we can help other persons overcome, but we do not need to inspect our own behavior.

Something quite different happens if we define racism as "an interlocking system of advantage (as well as disadvantage) based on race."[7] Such a definition discloses the way privileged status operates interdependently at personal, group, institutional, and cultural/symbolic levels to assure and reproduce better opportunities for most European Americans. In the employment study I just described, the fictitious European American applicant will be perceived by European American personnel officers as someone more like themselves, who will fit into the unspoken ethos of the dominant culture at their business; they will be those whose self-understanding is shaped by a similar group identity through schools, churches, and media; and whose institutional experiences have taught them similar ways of thinking and speaking and a worldview that unconsciously describes their experience as normative. Privilege of this sort typically functions outside the awareness of the one who enjoys its benefits. It is just the way things are. But regardless of our awareness of it, privilege reproduces both its benefits and the losses that occur: it excludes those who do not look like neighbors.

Racism arises and endures through a process of internalizing a privileged identity and behavior. White children do not get up in the morning and decide to be racists. Usually they learn racism by watching adults, by going to school and to church, by making sense of the images in various media and the dominance those images indicate and reproduce. Some children, of course, will be actively taught to hate and fear. But most of us Christian European Americans would say we were not actively taught to be a racist. Rather, like all the most important norms, we learned the unspoken rules. This more covert form of racism is called aversive racism. It is internalized privilege that is oblivious to the consequences for those it excludes; but however civil it is, I regard it as even more insidious than overt racism.

Consider, for example, the conversations that parents of children of color must have with their children about how to be safe in a culture dominated by European Americans, about where not to go, how to respond to police, how to respond in stores if followed as potential shoplifters. Imagine helping your child prepare to succeed in a culture where the playing field is uneven and sometimes more like a minefield. Such parents can discern their children's many gifts and readiness to love and contribute to the community, but they also know the lie of meritocracy in this country, which promises everyone an equal chance to succeed.

Aversive racism exists through a learned indifference to the fact of racial discrimination. Being oblivious to racist actions allows European Americans to avoid dealing with guilt or the accountability that is required if we acknowledge the privileges provided by racism as a system of advantage. For example, in my family I never received explicit instruction about race. While I did overhear an occasional racist joke, I saw my parents interact with African Americans in cordial and respectful ways. But my social, ecclesial, and educational experience was entirely with persons who looked like me. I could perceive the economic realities of racial oppression before I had conceptual tools to understand them. As a young Christian girl, I was learning to imagine a definition of neighbors in a two-tiered sense: at one level I could see the practice of charity, no doubt often experienced as condescension; at another level I saw mutual care and respect and an easy reciprocity. This two-tiered version, of course, is not the definition Jesus had in mind. I am also aware that growing up, throughout my entire education, I was always taught by whites. The curricula in public schools and seminary and graduate school in the 1970s and early '80s always privileged Western or northern European thought, even when other points of view were shared. Somehow while growing up, I never worried about what I was missing or how different my worldview would be if my education had placed the wisdom of my northern European heritage alongside the often more ancient wisdom of other racial and cultural heritages. My educational and social experience means that I came to imagine my experience as normative. For me, redefining racism as a system of advantage based on race has meant decentering this Eurocentric worldview so that it is no longer normative. Now I have the more challenging task of understanding and engaging the critiques of other perspectives without privileging the plausibility of my own "first language." This autobiographical review illustrates how aversive racism is subtly internalized to reproduce the biases it carries.

Unfortunately, aversive racism has a more sinister side. I remember, for example, an experience in a course on sexuality and pastoral practice when I had made a presentation on patriarchy and a white male student said, "I see what you mean about patriarchy, but frankly it works for me, and I doubt I'll change." My experience suggests that his candor about a system of privilege is rare, but his sentiments, sadly, are not.

Aversive racism simply puts a veneer of "niceness" over very real economic, political, social, educational, and legal discrimination and oppression. It allows me to engage in the sin of racism without feeling guilty. Wendy Farley suggests that we European Americans gradually deepen our participation in this sin as we learn ways to rationalize indifference to persons who do not look like us. It begins as young children observe the implicit and important rules for being white in this culture. It begins by learning the lie—the code, if you will—on which racism relies. As a code of behavior and norms, racism differentiates among those whom God intends to be neighbors. In this way, as Farley explains, our experience of learning racism is like the fall, when sin finds its way into human experience through "a willingness to be beguiled by evil."[8] Born into a culture and church already thoroughly racist in its practices of privilege and exclusion, I needed no explicit instruction to be inducted into this lie. The ordinary attention of any child is sufficient either to begin the process of learning a worldview based on a privileged identity or internalizing one based on a stigmatized identity. But once beyond preschool age, the process becomes more explicit. Now that the code is transmitted, the child (such as I) has learned the rationalizations of meritocracy, suggesting that persons who have less either have not worked hard enough or do not wish to succeed. In other words, they have chosen their situation rather than experiencing discrimination from persons who look like me. Such rationalizations allow callousness to form so that this break in empathy can be tolerated. In other words we have to learn not to respond with the mutuality of care and regard that describes neighbors. These rationalizations lead European American children like me unconsciously toward a two-tiered definition channeling care more toward pity and patronizing charity. Gradually, as children become more critically aware, our education is increasingly shaped by such forces as institutions, media, and language. This concretizes into a sort of bondage, the falsehood inherent in racism—a two-tiered definition of neighbor.

In bondage I, for example, had learned that economic discrimination was real in a way that disproved part of the message of meritocracy, but by defining racism as a system of disadvantage based on race, I could buffer myself from a sense of personal accountability. As Stephen Ray suggests, in his book *Do No Harm*, the language we use to describe social sin can itself become part of the problem.[9] He is exactly right: my language obscured how I was part of the problem. My imagination itself was corrupted by the codes of whiteness I learned as true and later chose not to critique more fully. Bondage corrupts by mystifying the way sin arises and endures so that it blunts our ability or readiness to confront sin.

The notion of original sin is helpful to us. It describes a milieu of deception that inducts persons, largely unwittingly, into patterns of dehumanized and dehumanizing behavior. If bondage were the last word, racism would be a tragic feature of human life that dehumanizes those it privileges as well as those they oppress—something we may despair of changing. But racism is not merely tragic. Sin is not reduced to bondage. It is not finally about fate. Sin is an ethical category. It requires that I acknowledge how I use or abuse my own freedom to act differently. Sin raises the fact of accountability and the reality of guilt. My freedom to "see" racism may have been reduced by the corruption of my imagination and understanding, but I did not lose my ability to think critically or to engage new experiences and voices. There were times when I assented to the lies into which I was unwittingly inducted. I am complicit in this sin. My fingerprints are on my guilt. But this affirmation of accountability also carries the possibility of different choices, repentance, and transformation toward recovering the true meaning and experience of neighbor.

HISTORICAL CONTEXT

The lie of racism as bondage to a two-tiered definition of neighbor continues in the United States, in part through ignorance about race as a social construction and through ignorance about the historical origins of racism in the colonies. It is helpful briefly to review the concept of race and the origins of racism in this country. By describing race as a social construction, I mean to convey several things. Race varies in definition and significance across periods of history and in different cultures. Our society is one of the most racialized in the world. Racial difference represents the tiniest fraction of our DNA. Over many centuries persons have variously speculated on what racial difference means while always constructing a definition to serve the interests of their own racial identity.

The terms many European Americans use to describe racial groups obscure at least as much as they disclose. For example, Latino or Hispanic is, in fact, a cultural marker not a racial one. It describes persons who share the cultural ties of the Spanish language while including several different racial and national identities. The term Asian American may be convenient for Euro-Americans, but it includes about twenty-eight ethnic groups with widely diverse linguistic, historical, geographical, religious, and cultural experiences. In Asian countries, many would find that our clustering of these different groups is nonsense. The term white only defines in the negative. It functions simply to separate the dominant group from other racial and cultural identities. In fact, in the United States some Caucasian peoples such as the Irish, Greek, and Eastern Europeans were considered black once they immigrated here, but over time, if they were willing to yield some of their distinctive ethnic practices, they could become white. The term European American obscures diverse ethnic, religious, and historical differences. The wages for the privileges of whiteness included ethnic rootlessness for many. In short, despite our pretense of precision in our language about race, it has always been a slippery term that describes at least as much about economic differentiation in this country's history. Race really serves to mark inclusion in the interlocking system of advantage I have been describing.

While recorded history includes a variety of explanations about race, at about the time European powers were beginning to explore, exploit, and colonize, they needed to define racial difference in a way that would allow brutality toward others and subsequently the enslavement of some without guilt. I will necessarily abbreviate a painful and fascinating series of rationalizations detailed in a brief history of the origins of racism in the United States in Ronald Takaki's book *A Different Mirror: A Multicultural History of the United States*.[10] Takaki describes how by the sixteenth century, white was synonymous with Christian and civilized. Initially, race did not necessarily refer to color. When the British brutalized the Irish, they described them as a lesser race that nonetheless could be rehabilitated. But shortly after their conquest of Ireland, they encountered Native Americans on the shores of America, and also they were sorting out how to consider the status of Africans though their darker skin meant Christian Europeans more readily assigned to them a dangerous association with the devil.

Shakespeare's play *The Tempest* gives us a window into the social process the English were going through to determine how to differentiate among peoples and to set racial boundaries. Their ideologies about such differences had much to do with their economic and colonial aspirations. The English understood the play to be set in the New World and could recognize in Caliban their challenge to understand and try to civilize the heathens who at least were less developed if not also different in kind. Such persons had not yet tamed their passions so as to be ruled by reason. In the play we see how Caliban, on the one hand, seems able to be initiated into culture; yet on the other hand, he is also racialized as dangerous, a demon. In the colonies this ambivalence also emerges. In New England the Puritans' sense of religious mission and the scarce arable land lead to a racialization of Indian savagery that could justify genocide, such as not experienced in the colony of Virginia.

In Virginia, however, Africans were useful for farming, and that led to a fairly rapid process of constructing a racial justification for slavery within less than a century. The first record of Africans arriving in Virginia was in 1619, where about twenty Africans joined a large number of northern Europeans as indentured servants along with some Native Americans as well. While they may have had suspicions about each other, they shared a very difficult life of heavy labor and no comforts. In about twenty-five years, slavery was beginning to emerge as the period of indenture for Africans stretched out. Takaki indicates that by 1669, fifty years after arriving, Africans were defined as property.[11] Slavery already existed in other parts of the new world.

Initially the Virginia settlers constructed racial difference by religion, so the boundary was between Christians and heathens. When Africans started converting to Christianity, bondage was not altered because racial difference then became a matter of black and white. But the economically elite in Virginia realized both the political danger of allowing poor whites to recognize their shared economic interest with Africans and the economic benefits of having slaves rather than temporary white workers, so the rich planters legislated a hierarchical construction of race in the colony of Virginia. In 1670 legislation was passed that began a process of giving small privileges to poor Whites while taking away rights from the Africans. In 1790 Congress took its first action on citizenship by limiting naturalized citizenship to whites. That law stayed in effect until 1952, despite some adjustments being made in the intervening years.[12]

White racial identity, however, proved quite fluid. Immigrants on whom the country would depend for development were received differently. The Africans and Asians established what some observers call "the mudsill."[13] Others, from southern and eastern Europe, found an ambiguous status depending on their willingness to become white and American. One historian, John Dollard, described immigrant working-class Caucasian persons as "our temporary Negroes," while another described them as not-yet-white ethnics.[14]

The end of the nineteenth and the early part of the twentieth century was a period marked by racial unrest. Jim Crow laws were severe and lynchings were commonplace. There were 2,500 lynchings between 1896 and 1900 alone. The Depression made racism and ethnic prejudice much worse. Eugenics and its veneer of science absolutized racist assumptions by the early 1920s. The census form from each decade is a window into these increasingly specific demarcations about gradations of privilege while also illustrating our pretense of precision about race. In 1930, for example, the form differentiated immigrant white, "native whites," and "native whites" born of "native white parentage."[15] Fighting a war against fascism helped calm the fears requiring these distinctions. On the other hand, internment camps became a reality. Following World War II the pervasive patterns of racism in business and education and every level of government meant that the GI Bill of Rights decisively privileged European American male veterans, and subsequently their children, while only a very small percentage of African American veterans could claim their benefits. Some observers nevertheless suggest that the GI Bill may be the most significant Affirmative Action in United States' history. The Civil Rights Movement, and the subsequent Civil Rights legislation, made important contributions, but racial violence is still at very significant levels, with post-9/11 fears again raising matters of boundaries and racism. Theologian Fumitaka Matsuoka summarizes this problematic history by observing, "We live in a culture from whose inception racial discrimination has been a regulative force for maintaining stability and growth and for maximizing the dominant group's cultural values."[16] Certainly the linkage of racism and class interests underscores the sin of turning a person into a commodity by defining their value to the dominant culture economically. The dehumanization at the root of racism leads us to search for the resources in Christian tradition, to help us confront and resist racism.

THEOLOGICAL PROPOSALS

Earlier I observed that two central affirmations in Christian faith are helpful for our response: humanity's creation in God's image and neighbor love. As you can imagine, these positive claims for life together also lead to talking about sin as an important insight into what goes wrong among us. Some theologians describe the sin of racism as a lie into which European Americans are inducted even before we have words for our experience. Gradually the deception of the myth of meritocracy and learned callousness toward the lie of the dehumanized Other corrupts our hearts and imaginations and seem to imprison us. We become unaware of the enormous deception that this assumption of racialized privilege is and what it prevents us from seeing.

I find it helpful to describe this deception with the image of Afghan women in burkas, through which a small grid of cloth allows them to see. However, they know there is a much larger world they do not see because of their clothing. Many European Americans have no idea how racial privilege narrows our understanding and perception. Racism in the United States may help us understand the idea of original sin; it may do so because it has so thoroughly insinuated itself into the fabric of this country from the very beginning that I cannot name an aspect of our life together that is not tainted by racism. Being affected by it is unavoidable. However, as corrupting as it is for our hearts and minds, racism is not our fate. Its continuation relies on the choices of those it privileges. Those of us who are European Americans can choose to interrupt racism. We can choose love over fear and confront the corrupting lies on which racism rests.

This corruption of our imaginations and perception of the racialized Other thickens the distance between us with fear, which eclipses the love that creation in God's image intends. Instead, those subjected to racial subordination, and especially those forcibly brought to the colonies, experience an "erasure of identity," what King describes as "nobodiness" in contrast to the "somebodiness" presumed by creation in God's image and required between neighbors.[17]

If love is the meaning of creation in God's image, and the vocation to which God calls us, then sin is the refusal to "realize love in life."[18] It is the refusal of relation, even though we are created as selves-in-relation. Christians have long acknowledged that "to be" is "to be with." Racism dehumanizes all of us. It is more apparent how internalized stigma and resisting a nobody status deplete persons of hope and rob the future of generations. Consider the children, especially of marginalized groups in some inner city areas, who say they do not anticipate reaching twenty-five years of age. It is less apparent to many European Americans how the sin of racism endangers us, in part because we learn to understand racism as something for which we are not personally accountable, and we learn not to notice the privileges that establish and reproduce racism. However, as Wendell Berry has written in reflecting on his family's history as slave owners, racism is a deep and complex wound:

> I have been unwilling until now to open in myself what I have known all along to be a wound, a historical wound, prepared centuries ago to come alive in me at my birth like a hereditary disease, and to be augmented and deepened by my life. If I had thought it was only the black people who have suffered from the years of slavery and racism, then I could have dealt fully with the matter long ago: I could have filled myself with pity for them, and would no doubt have enjoyed it a great deal and thought highly of myself. But I am sure it is not so simple as that. If white people have suffered less obviously from racism than black people, they have nevertheless suffered greatly; the cost has been greater perhaps than we can yet know. If the white man has inflicted the wound of racism upon black men, the cost has been that he would receive the mirror image of that wound into himself. As the master, or as a member of the dominant race, he has felt little compulsion to acknowledge it or speak of it; the more painful it has grown the more deeply he has hidden it within himself. But the wound is there, and it is a profound disorder, as great a damage in his mind as it is in his society. This wound is in me, as complex and deep in my flesh as blood and nerves. I have borne it all my life, with varying degrees of consciousness, but always carefully, always with the most delicate consideration for the pain I would feel if I were somehow forced to acknowledge it. But now I am increasingly aware of the opposite compulsion. I want to know, as fully and exactly as I can, what the wound is and how much I am suffering from it. And I want to be cured; I want to be free of the wound myself, and I do not want to pass it on to my children.[19]

Berry's description of the effects of racism is instructive. We may more readily realize that dehumanizing another has serious consequences but, by avoiding acknowledging our own complicity in racism, European Americans may rarely acknowledge the peril of our racist behavior for our own souls. In Ezekiel the prophet describes redemption as receiving a new heart of flesh rather than stone (36:26). As selves-in-relation, to participate in dehumanizing another is actually to turn our own hearts into stone. For European Americans a preliminary step toward neighbor love must involve acknowledging our complicity in reproducing racism and exploring how our own hearts and minds are corrupted by this sin: perhaps then, as Berry suggests, we will be ready to seek forgiveness and begin to pursue the practice of love that honors each neighbor.

In his now classic book *The Spirit and the Forms of Love*, Daniel Day Williams offers us good advice for the practice of love that has communion in freedom as its goal. Several of the categories he describes as necessary for authentic love seem quite relevant for the practice of neighbor love in the context of racism:[20]

1. A first step seems simple enough though racial stereotypes make it more difficult: it is recognizing that the other is real, a distinct person apart from our projections of our own needs or stereotypical expectations. To understand this requires honestly attending to this other nondefensively.

2. He also reminds us that love does not exist abstractly. To love is to act and be acted upon. Love necessarily will include suffering because being in relationship includes becoming vulnerable to the other. Once we allow love to decenter us from a self-absorbed focus, we become open not only to the joys of the reciprocity of care; we also know the sorrows of the other as our own.

3. Love, in fact, brings direction and purpose to our lives because loving shapes our future actions and commitments. The hopes and needs of the other inform our actions and future decisions. In other words, the one whom we love changes us. We cannot love across racial barriers and remain aloof from the struggle for justice.

Let us consider these several aspects of love in relation to the well-known story in Luke's Gospel of the Samaritan, the Levite, the priest, and the man left half dead by robbers. In his sermon on this passage, Martin Luther King Jr.[21] observes that Jesus turned abstract questioning about identifying a neighbor, intended to narrow the parameters of obligation, into describing the practice of love. Certainly it was a love that did not recognize the barriers of race, nationality, or class. In his sermon King suggests that fear likely prevented the priest and Levite from stopping. It was a dangerous situation. He suspects that each asked himself, "What will happen to me if I stop to help this man?" King suggests that the Samaritan asked a different question: "What will happen to this man if I do not stop to help him?" The Samaritan recognized a shared humanity that transcended the differences plaguing their relationship in daily life. For the Samaritan the man left by the robbers was a real human being. He chose to respond as a neighbor who freely entered into a caring relationship in a way that then widened his own vulnerability to the danger and suffering of the man. His own situation was altered as he delayed his journey in order to tend to the stranger's wounds and share from his own resources for the man's care. He obligated himself further when he offered the innkeeper money to cover further expenses, if necessary, until he could return. In the context of our reflection on racism, I think this Samaritan was not only aware that the man would have died if he did not stop. I think he also understood what Wendell Berry described, that failing to stop would have imperiled his own soul, his own humanity. It is that awareness that fuels Berry's urgency for honesty about racism. Berry rightly recognized that, as one created in God's image, it is his own humanity that is on the line if he now fails to confront racism. It may have corrupted his heart and imagination before he could defend against it, but now, having seen it for what it is, he is obligated to enlarge love rather than refuse its possibilities.

Creation in God's image describes neighbor love as our vocation. To "be" is actively to become a neighbor to all whom God loves. Deconstructing the sin of racism begins in relationships between neighbors, in the biblical sense of the word. For those whose humanity has known the stigma of nobodiness and whose daily life is scarred by exploitation, fear, and the material consequences of oppression, the choice to risk neighbor love is a sign of remarkable grace and determined hope. For those whose humanity has been corrupted by unearned privileges disguised as their right and whose well-being is marked by fear of the dangerous Other, the choice to love as neighbor begins with repentance, truth-telling, and listening that shatters the pretense of racial superiority. It means learning to widen the sphere of neighbor and learning to practice love as mutual regard, where everyone is an insider in the sphere of God's love.

PRACTICES

In my own journey and in teaching about racism, I have discovered that it is particularly helpful for European Americans to read or experience the stories of other European Americans who are proactively confronting racism. Examples of such are the memoir of Lois Stalvey, *The Education of a WASP*,[22] or Catherine Fosl's biography of Anne Braden, *Subversive Southerner*.[23] In the story of Stalvey, we find the choices of a white housewife in Omaha who encounters new information about racial discrimination and chooses not to look away. As she finds more and more truth about the reality of racism in schools and housing and employment, she is blessed with African Americans who are willing yet again to extend themselves to a white woman, and she responds to their neighbor love in kind. I ask my students of all races to read this story because we find in it that confronting racism is not rocket science. Neither is it impossible. Rather, Stalvey's journey required the courage to choose truth over denial and the embrace of freedom rather than the fearful, confined vision of unacknowledged privilege (like the burka image I mentioned earlier). She and her family were blessed with a widening circle of African American friends who accepted them as neighbors. I do think her story, and that of any antiracism activist, is a reminder that the vocation of love is a journey to be undertaken with neighbors. The lure of rationalizations and the painful consequences of naming privilege as well as the hard work of discerning what is true and just in complex situations— all these argue against isolated efforts.

Another resource for Christians lies in the stories of congregations who have defied the pull toward homogeneity and are deliberately living into the pluralism within their membership and in their surrounding context. It helps those of us who often worship in largely segregated communities of faith to have models for practices that may help us better embody God's vision for congregations as diverse communities of neighbors. In their book *We Are the Church Together*,[24] Charles Foster and Theodore Brelsford describe their experience of studying the congregations and describe practices that seemed to enlarge their capacities to transcend racial and cultural barriers to neighbor love.

One of their first insights was the importance for congregations to make a commitment to inclusion as more than tolerance or assimilation. This commitment set them on a journey in which each member was forced to discover how their practices of faith and beliefs were shaped by their particular experience. They learned that their own experience was important but could not be presumed as the norm for others. Lots of respectful negotiation is needed to develop a truly inclusive community, where each is valued. They exchanged the myth of a melting pot in which our differences blend into some homogenous whole, for the better metaphor of a mosaic. Celebrating differences helped them value the commonalities of their shared faith. For those in the dominant culture, this required vigilance against reproducing familiar patterns and much greater tolerance for an often messy ambiguity as genuinely new practices that were inclusive emerged.

The authors describe a need to acknowledge that pluralism is the context and not the problem for congregational life. This means a conscious commitment for persons truly to learn about how their racial and cultural identity have shaped them and the significance of their neighbor's different experience. Racial and cultural self-awareness as a necessary first step for genuine appreciation of the Other is an important practice for a successful multicultural community. Racial identity development theory as described in Beverly Tatum's book *"Why Are All the Black Kids Sitting Together in the Cafeteria?" And Other Conversations about Race*[25] is a good resource for racial self- and Other-understanding. In multicultural congregations education and governance have to include ongoing attention to how being this multicultural family is different than in the more homogenous or segregated settings outside the congregation. Breaking down the "walls of hostility" requires work inside the congregation as well as outside. Developing practices that enlarge neighbor love requires time and energy and patience. But along with that investment comes a richness absent in homogenous settings. Christmas celebrations widen to include Kwanzaa and the Feast of the Virgin of Guadalupe. Potlucks become adventures in tastes and customs. Worship where everyone is an insider includes a growing sense of anticipation for the unexpected possibilities that collaboration and generosity of spirit bring.

Particularly significant are the theological gains and spiritual richness that come through, trusting the empowered participation of persons who in their shared life together begin to discover a vision of that eschatological banquet when the rainbow of God's creative love is present at the table. Multiplicity gradually becomes a primary lens for experiencing God's presence. Congregants who persevere in the ambiguity and careful negotiation and liturgical practices foreign to their experience actually begin to perceive differently and find their imaginations and understanding of what it means to be the church transformed in subtle or more dramatic ways. Daniel Day Williams was right: whom we love as neighbors changes us. Joining our lives with neighbors of different races changes what we hope for.

CONCLUSION

I remind you of a familiar story told in Acts 10, the story of Peter and Cornelius. Each was known as a righteous man and highly esteemed in their respective communities. The Spirit called each of them to step across a racial barrier into a future fraught with danger for each man; and yet, trusting that this was the future into which God called them, each obeyed. They bore witness to God's love that would not be confined to the stereotypes of the day, and the church has never been the same. Now is also a time when God's Spirit is calling us to step out of our comfort range and across racial barriers into a future we do not know except that it belongs to God, who is faithful. Neighbor love changes those who risk it.

With God's help, we will never be the same, and our love will make a difference.

ETHICAL EXERCISES

Chapter 8

The Vocation of Reformed Ethicist in the Present South African Society

ETIENNE DE VILLIERS

INTRODUCTION

The conviction that Christians are called by God to contribute to the transformation of society is central to the Reformed tradition.[1] This conviction is based on a belief that is equally central to the Reformed tradition: God the Creator and Governor is also Lord of history. He is working out his divine purposes in human history and calls his people to be instruments in the fulfillment of his purposes. His purposes entail not only the salvation of souls, but also the establishment of a holy community and the glorification of his name through all the world.[2] In a world marked by sin, the Christian calling to serve these purposes of God inevitably implies the calling to work for the transformation of the world and, more particularly, society.

This conviction has profound implications for understanding the vocation of Reformed ethicists. As the right actions of Christians, including their right actions in society, form the subject matter of the ethicists' academic studies, they cannot escape the conclusion that an important part of the vocation of ethicists is to help fellow Christians to contribute to the transformation of society. More particularly, it is part of the ethicists' vocation to indicate to their fellow Christians what the practical implications of the gospel of Christ for the transformation of society are. Such an indication is only of real help if it is not abstract and general, but concrete and directed to the particular context and society in which they are living.

In this essay I explore the vocation of Reformed ethicists in the present South African society and, more in particular, the implications of the Reformed conviction that we are called by God to contribute to the transformation of society in implementing the ethicists' vocation. The reason is that this central conviction of Reformed faith has, within a very short time span, lost its previous legitimacy, even for Reformed Christians in our society. In my opinion restoring the legitimacy of this conviction is one of the most important challenges the Reformed ethicists face in the execution of their vocation in the present South Africa. This challenge would only be met if the conviction is given a satisfactory and convincing content, based on at least the following: an adequate, contemporary Christian social ethics, a strong Christian consensus on what a good society in the South African context entails, and the effective translation and promulgation of this Christian vision of the good society in the broader South African society. Before turning to an explication of the vocation of the Reformed ethicist in this regard, some of the factors contributing to the loss of the named conviction's legitimacy in our society are discussed. For it is only on the basis of an adequate analysis of the factors contributing to this loss that a satisfactory account of the vocation of the Reformed ethicist in the South African society can be given.[3]

THE TRANSFORMATION APPROACH'S LOSS OF LEGITIMACY

In the previous political dispensation, Reformed churches and theologians in South Africa differed strongly on many issues, except on one thing: Christians have God's calling to transform society in the light of the gospel of Christ. Ironically, the disputes they had with one another were mostly related to different interpretations of what this conviction implied in the South African context.

The three Afrikaans Reformed churches took their point of departure in the theocratic ideal expressed, among others, in section 36 of the Confessio Belgica. According to this theocratic ideal, the state is an institution of God that has to serve him by protecting the true Christian religion against false religion, by listening to the voice of the church, and by striving to serve Christian values in its policies and actions.[4] As a result of the exceptionally close relationship between the Afrikaans Reformed churches and the Nationalist government, the theocratic ideal did not remain a pipe dream.[5] The government shared the conviction that South Africa was a Christian country and even gave expression to it in the 1983 constitution.[6] For the most part it accommodated the wishes of the Afrikaans Reformed churches to introduce legislation regulating public morality—for example, on abortion, censorship, gambling, and trading on Sundays—that reflected their conservative moral views.

Theologians and historians differ on whether the Afrikaans Reformed churches played a decisive role in formulating and instigating the apartheid policy of the Nationalist government or only supported it once it was formulated and implemented. It cannot be denied, however, that the theological justification of apartheid by these churches was directly linked to their allegiance to the theocratic ideal. In a 1955 report on "The Scriptural Basis for the Apartheid of Races," approved by the Dutch Reformed Church, any attempt to justify the apartheid policy solely on practical political grounds—such as the need to preserve Western civilization or Christianity in Southern Africa—was rejected. Views and policies on racial relationships had to be based solely on God's revealed Word as the final measure. Therefore, the report set out to demonstrate that the apartheid policy was indeed, in its view, based on what the Bible prescribed.[7]

Reformed churches and theologians who opposed apartheid and were involved in the struggle against the apartheid regime were just as convinced that the Bible condemned apartheid and that they were called by God to struggle for a new and liberated South Africa. An example is ABRECSA (Alliance of Black Reformed Christians in Southern Africa), founded in 1981. ABRECSA rejected what it considered the wrong interpretation of the Reformed tradition of the Afrikaans Reformed churches, and it strived to work out the implications of what they saw as the correct interpretation. They affirmed that in the Reformation tradition (1) the Word of God is the supreme authority; (2) Jesus Christ is the Lord of the whole of life; (3) Christians bear responsibility for the world in its totality; (4) obedience to earthly authority is only obedience in God; (5) unity of the church must be visible.[8] On the basis of this affirmation, they set out to actively oppose apartheid and the theological justification of it by the Afrikaans Reformed churches. Their opposition to apartheid prepared the way for the Declaration on Racism that the General Council of the World Alliance of Reformed Churches adopted in Ottawa in August 1982 and in which Dr. Allan Boesak, chair of ABRECSA, played a prominent part. It declared "that apartheid is a sin and that the moral and theological justification for it is a travesty of the gospel, a betrayal of the Reformed tradition, and a heresy."

With the dawn of the new political dispensation in South Africa in 1994, everything changed. Within a short time span, it became apparent that the conviction that Christians have a calling to transform society in accordance with the gospel has almost completely lost the self-evident nature it had for Reformed Christians in the previous political dispensation.

In my opinion three major factors have contributed to this development.

Disillusionment with the "Biblical" Basis of Apartheid

Theologians, ministers, and members of the Afrikaans Reformed churches, who were initially convinced that the Bible prescribed or at least supported apartheid, eventually had to admit that they were mistaken. In the case of many of them, it resulted in a deep-seated skepticism about any attempt to transform society in the light of the biblical message.

Transformation Loses Credibility

In the Afrikaans Reformed churches, the credibility structures undergirding the transformation approach in the previous political dispensation fell apart in a rather dramatic and even traumatic way. The old constitution that gave political legitimacy to the efforts to ensure that Christian values were recognized in government policies was abolished. The loss of political power of the National Party meant that these churches lost the sympathetic ear of politicians sharing the same theocratic vision. They also lost their position of privileged access to the state-owned radio and television and the printed media. All of this amounted to a severe loss of social status and public influence. Many members of the Afrikaans Reformed churches experienced a traumatic power loss of both the political party they supported and the churches to which they belonged. Adding to this experience was the fact that primarily Afrikaner people experienced the brunt of accusations in the Truth and Reconciliation Commission, much retrenchment and unemployment as a result of the implementation of affirmative action in the civil service, and the threat of expropriation as a result of the new government's land reform program. All that led, among other things, to what Jürgen Moltmann called the "inward emigration" of a considerable many members of the Afrikaans churches.[9] Many of them have completely dissociated themselves from what happens in the public sphere and have withdrawn to their own private sphere of purely personal relationships, interests, and religious experiences.[10] They do not have any desire that their churches should even try to exert a public influence.

As in the case of Germany after unification, South African churches, church leaders, and theologians who actively supported the liberation struggle found that appreciation for the role they played in the apartheid era did not translate in the new South Africa into privileged public roles. It is true that quite a number of church leaders and theologians, including a number with a Reformed background, were awarded with political posts for their contribution and as politicians have continued to play influential public roles. The experience of those who remained church leaders and theologians was rather one of a severe loss of public influence. Their loss of public influence was, partly and ironically, the result of the success of the liberation struggle. In the new South Africa it was no longer necessary for churches and church leaders to fill the political vacuum that was left with the banning of liberation organizations and the imprisonment of their leaders and to play a vicarious political leadership role. The leaders of the ANC (African National Congress) and the PAC (Pan Africanist Congress) who were released from prison and returned from exile after 1990 took over the political leadership role and expected the churches not to interfere with politics.

The Modernization of Social Structures

After the dawn of the new political dispensation, the one factor that perhaps more than any other contributed to the Reformed tradition's transformation approach losing legitimacy was the introduction of a new liberal constitution. The new liberal constitution, for the first time in South African history, clearly insists on the separation of religion and state. This makes it difficult, if not impossible, for the government to implement the distinctive views of a particular religious group, let alone the distinctive views of a particular religious denomination within that religious group. It is clear that the separation of religion and state in the new South Africa has, up till now, caused considerable confusion and uncertainty among churches that were used to direct involvement in public matters. In the present political dispensation, the state is seen as a purely human institution that must obey the will of the majority, not favor any particular religion, promote a set of common human values expressed in the bill of rights, and ensure religious freedom to all religious institutions.[11] Apparently the view that society should be transformed in accordance with the Christian gospel is discredited by the new liberal constitution as politically illegitimate.

The separation of religion and state is but one example of the entrenchment of pluralism in the present South Africa. Already in the previous political dispensation, the influence of modernization could not be completely abated. Especially in the 1980s it became clear that not only politics, but also other social systems like economics, science, and the arts, increasingly asserted their independence from religion and moral systems other than the liberal. With the dawn of the new South Africa, the demise of the theocratic worldview of the Reformed tradition and the introduction of a liberal constitution allowed modernization processes, including pluralism, to proceed seemingly unabatedly. The autonomy of the different social systems, even of a social system such as education that was previously strongly based on Christian religious values, has been increasingly acknowledged. The concomitant result was the increasing loss of legitimacy of the traditional Reformed conviction that all spheres of life should be brought to obey the law of God.

On a personal level the increasing influence of *individualism* can be noticed in the South African society. Also among members of the Reformed churches, cultural globalization—the increasing influence on local culture of factors originating in other parts of the world[12]—has, among other things, led to the spread of both *utilitarian individualism*, which entails the devotion to the calculating pursuit of one's own material interest, and *expressive individualism*, which stresses the freedom to express oneself, against all constraints and conventions.[13]

The result of the dismantling of credibility structures and increasing modernization is that the transformation approach has not only lost much of its legitimacy in broader society, but also for many members of the Reformed churches. One even notices within the South African Reformed churches the increasing adherence to two other traditional approaches that stand in opposition to the transformation approach of the Reformed tradition: the two-kingdom approach of Lutheranism, which accepts that principles other than biblical apply to politics and economics; and the sectarian approach, which sees society as evil and hostile and denies the social-ethical responsibility of Christians.

RECONSTRUCTING THE TRANSFORMATION APPROACH

What implications does the transformation approach's loss of legitimacy have for the vocation of Reformed ethicists in the present South African society? Should they abolish the effort to develop a distinctively Christian social ethics that strives to contribute to the transformation of the South African society and concentrate academic efforts on the development of a purely personal or intrachurch Christian ethics? Or should they rather, in order to ensure the continuing social relevance of the church in South Africa, develop a Christian rationale for promoting the implementation of liberal values, as Peter Beyer suggests?[14]

In my opinion there is no need to abolish the transformation approach of the Reformed tradition. However, this approach has to be reformed in turn. We need to take leave of what I call the exclusive version of the transformation approach that was often dominant in the past. And we must develop a more inclusive version that critically takes account of modernizing processes happening in the world and in South Africa in particular. In my opinion the development of such a contemporary, inclusive version entails at least the following tasks for the Reformed ethicist in the South African context:

The Development of an Adequate, Contemporary Christian Social Ethics

A Christian social ethics based on the exclusive transformation approach strives to Christianize society. It is exclusive in more than one way:

- It strives to Christianize society by expecting the explicit recognition of Christ's lordship in all social spheres, yet on the basis of a particular Christian confession, usually the Reformed confession.
- It regards the moral values of the Bible as the sole and final measure for policy formation and action in all social spheres.

As long as all members of society profess the Reformed faith and agree on the implications of recognizing the lordship of Christ for the different social spheres, the Christianizing of society need not be problematic. It becomes problematic when differences on the implications of the recognition of Christ's lordship surface among Reformed Christians. It becomes more problematic when Christians from other confessions have to accept the Reformed interpretation of what the Christianizing of society entails. And it becomes highly problematic when the recognition of Christ's lordship is expected from non-Christians. As soon as a society is characterized by a plurality of Christian social visions and confessions, plus other religious and nonreligious worldviews, a particular Reformed strategy for Christianizing society can only be realized by authoritarian enforcement and by disregarding individuals' freedom of conscience.

As a result of these problems experienced with Christianizing society as goal of the transformation approach, Reformed theologians influenced by Karl Barth have proposed that the goal should rather be to humanize society.[15] The humanizing of society is a goal with which non-Christians can also identify. Yet as Barth demonstrated in *Christengemeinde and Bürgergemeinde*, the humanizing of society does not necessarily mean the acceptance of a universally recognized set of criteria. Christians can still develop their own criteria for the humanizing of society. The only problem with humanizing as goal of the transformation of society is that it is not comprehensive enough. It reflects an anthropocentric bias and does not include the enhancement of the well-being of other living creatures. The Reformed ethicist therefore needs to be on the lookout for a more suitable and inclusive goal for transforming society. The optimal protection and enhancement of all life on earth or the flourishing of all God's creatures are formulations of a more inclusive goal that may be worthwhile to explore.

In his famous essay *Politik als Beruf* (*Politics as a Vocation*), published in 1919, Max Weber convincingly took to task those Christians who regard their own interpretation of the moral message of the Bible as the sole and final measure of political policies and actions.[16] In this book he specifically criticized Christian pacifist politicians who campaigned against the use of any violence by the state on the basis of their understanding of the Sermon on the Mount. He depicted them as proponents of an ethics of conviction (*Gesinnungsethik*). According to Weber, it is typical of proponents of such an ethics to apply their religiously inspired moral convictions in an abstract and absolute way without taking into account the specific nature of politics, the particular role and responsibility that they as politicians have, and the disastrous consequences that a decision to ban the use of violence by the police and the military could have. They are only interested in obeying what they believe the will of God is, and they are quite happy to leave the responsibility for the consequences of their decisions to the almighty God, who in his providence determines the outcome of events in accordance with his will.

In opposition to the ethics of conviction, Weber proposed an ethics of responsibility (*Verantwortungsethik*). In contrast to politicians who adhere to an ethics of conviction, politicians who adhere to an ethics of responsibility would be willing to

- take full personal responsibility for deciding on the right political actions;
- take seriously the specific nature of politics as a separate life sphere, with its own principles and demands (including what Weber calls *die Sache* of politics: the maintenance of order);

- take seriously their particular role responsibility as politicians to do what is needed to maintain order—and not only what they regard as their moral responsibility; and
- seriously consider the consequences their political decisions could have on the political power play before taking and implementing such decisions.

In my opinion Weber has convincingly demonstrated that ethics, and that includes Christian ethics, is not a simple matter of mechanically applying only moral principles in particular circumstances. It is a much more complicated matter in which, before making a decision on the right action, a particular person or group of persons need to take responsibility for thoroughly analyzing the concrete situation and deliberating the possible consequences of different options for action, yet also for weighing different value systems in play. It is especially important not only to consider moral values based on the Bible but also not to ignore the functional values valid in the different social systems (e.g., in economy: efficiency and productivity) and the cultural values of a particular people (e.g., the *ubuntu* [humanity toward others] values of African people).

What I suggest is that the adequate, contemporary Christian social ethics, which we as Reformed ethicists need in the South African society, cannot but be an ethics of responsibility.[17] It is only when Christian social ethics is conceived as an ethics of responsibility that justice can be done to both the Christian moral tradition and the achievements of modernization, including the development of modern societies into relatively independent social systems. Only then can Christian social ethics take adequate account of the different cultures of the peoples of South Africa.

This is not to deny that certain aspects of Weber's view on the ethics of responsibility are problematic. Weber uses the image of polytheism to describe the different value systems the ethics of responsibility has to take account of. This image, however, suggests that no one system of moral values has a priority over the other value systems but has to compete on an equal footing with these other value systems for recognition. From a Christian perspective the central moral values that we believe are an expression of the moral will of God do have some priority. It is true that this priority is not absolute, in the sense that moral values always completely replace functional values that seem to be in tension with it. This was, unfortunately, the way in which the priority of moral values was for a long period understood in the history of the Christian church. For more than a millennium the biblical prohibition against usury (Deut. 23:19), for example, was used to condemn all imposition of interest, even after it became clear that the imposition of interest is an economically desirable practice. We should rather acknowledge that functional and cultural values are, for the most part, not in opposition to moral values but are valid in their own right and stand with them in a complementary relationship. The challenge that we are faced with in a Christian ethics of responsibility is to facilitate between the moral, functional, and cultural value systems in such a way that they are all accommodated optimally.[18]

This is not to deny that functional and cultural values can sometimes be in strong opposition to moral values that are central to Christians. For example, this happens when functional values that are valid in a particular social sphere start to play an imperialistic role in other social systems. A valid economic value like competition can cause havoc if it becomes dominant in the family. For this reason William Schweiker is of the opinion that the role of moral and religious values over against other values is primarily a limiting one: to prevent them from claiming validity outside their sphere of competence.[19] Schweiker seems to imply that the difference between moral and other values lies in the fact that moral values have transsystemic validity, while other values only have intrasystemic validity. If he is right, the transsystemic nature of moral values may be one way of conceiving their priority with regard to other values. Their priority comes into play not only when functional and cultural values overstep the limits of their sphere of competency, but also when perverted versions of them become prevalent within social systems. For example, even in business the dog-eats-dog interpretation of competition is never acceptable from a Christian moral perspective. In other words, the priority of moral values consists, at least partly, in the fact that they play an indispensable limiting role with regard to other values, both on the borders of social systems and within them.

Christian Consensus on What the Good Society in South Africa Entails

Christians cannot effectively contribute to the transformation of the South African society if they are not strongly motivated to do so or have disparate visions on the good South African society. In my opinion it is part of the vocation of Christian ethicists in South Africa to help provide Christians with a strong motivation to contribute constructively to the transformation of the South African society and to work toward achieving a strong consensus on what a good society in South Africa entails. These two tasks, of course, go hand in hand. Christians will only be motivated to work for the transformation of society if they are inspired by a common Christian vision of the good South African society.

The crucial question is How can such a common Christian vision be achieved? It is not only undesirable, but also impossible in the present South African society, to impose a particular Christian social vision in an authoritarian way on other Christians and non-Christians as it was often done in the past. The only way is to strive to achieve a strong Christian consensus through intense yet open dialogue. Christian ethicists need to stimulate the debate on the good South African society in the media, their church denomination, and especially in ecumenical organizations. In my opinion they also need to propagate the idea that covenants should be concluded between church members on a denominational level and between church denominations on an ecumenical level, on the basis of agreements that have been reached. On this need I agree with the Swiss theologian Johannes Fischer: the threat that moral dissensus in modern societies poses to the normative status of morality can only be overcome by exercising the meta-responsibility to conclude covenants on the basis of moral consensus that has been reached through dialogue.[20] For Christians this includes the responsibility to contribute to the conclusion of moral covenants both within the Christian community and in society at large.

We can distinguish different levels in the debate on a good South African society on which Christians should strive to reach a strong consensus:

Level 1: Identifying and defining major issues and challenges in South African society. A shared Christian vision of a good society in South Africa can only be formulated if Christians agree on what the major issues and challenges in our society are. At the South African Christian Leadership Assembly (SACLA) held in Pretoria on July 7–12, 2003, delegates from a representative number of churches in South Africa came a long way in agreeing on what the major issues are. They identified seven so-called "giants" that need to be killed in a sustained national process of action and advocacy, through Christians in the church and broader society: crime, poverty, unemployment, racism, gender/sexual discrimination, the family in crisis, and HIV/AIDS. The challenge that lies ahead of churches is to also reach consensus on which manifestations of these issues have priority and on what their causes are. It would, for example, not help if churches agree that poverty is a major issue, but some of them find the increase in poverty among white people the most pressing, while others are of the opinion that the major issue is with poverty among black people in the rural areas. It would also be of no avail if some churches refuse to take apartheid's contribution to poverty into account, while others insist on doing so.

Level 2: Ascertaining levels of accepting a normative biblical basis for developing a Christian vision of a good South African society. To reach sufficient consensus among Christians in this regard is quite challenging: they often interpret the Bible differently as a result of the different theological traditions in which they stand. On one extreme of the spectrum of views on the use of the Bible in Christian ethics is the fundamentalist view that the normative character of the Bible is only recognized by accepting that all biblical guidelines are still valid today. On the other extreme is the relativist view that biblical guidelines have no contemporary validity since they are culturally determined. One of the biggest present challenges that Reformed ethicists face is to convince fellow Christians to abandon these all-or-nothing approaches. On the one hand we have to admit that many of the specific biblical guidelines cannot be directly applied to contemporary societies (such as the prohibition of usury in Deut. 23:19 and guidelines regarding the jubilee year in Lev. 25), or are just not acceptable anymore (e.g., guidelines regarding the death penalty in the Old Testament and the submissive conduct expected of women in Israel and the early church). We also have to admit that not all the normative elements needed for constructing a Christian vision of a good contemporary society can be found in the Bible.

On the other hand, we can profess that the Bible still provides basic moral orientation to contemporary Christians.[21] Certain moral principles in the Bible—such as the love commandment, the Ten Commandments, and justice (including the obligation to provide special care to the weak in society)—form such an integral part of the faith community's basic identity. They must as such be taken as foundational in formulating a Christian social vision. The Old Testament vision of God's kingdom of peace (*shalom*) and the New Testament vision of the new earth and the new heaven can provide inspiration and stir the moral imagination. Normative analogies can be drawn between the church's new life in Christ as sketched in the New Testament (such as the realization of visible unity, joining all natural and cultural differences into life-giving richness; and real reconciliation, overcoming deep divisions and structures of alienation) and the new society that we Christians should strive for in South Africa.[22] And even culturally determined biblical guidelines not directly applicable anymore can serve as normative paradigms because they are expressions of more general moral intentions that are still applicable today. An example appears in the jubilee guidelines of the Old Testament that played an important role in the debates around the turn of the millennium on canceling the debts of the poorest developing countries. Although they are not applicable anymore in their specific formulation, the expressed normative intention of care for those who are entangled in debt is just as valid today.

Level 3: Formulating a Christian vision of a good South African society. On the basis of insight into the major issues in the South African society and the relevant normative elements in the Bible, positive content must finally be given to the Christian vision of a good South African society. The idea is not to formulate a comprehensive program, complete with policy and strategy recommendations, but rather to provide an integrated and inspiring model of the values that should guide us in the public sphere and to project the desirable end states in South African society for which we should strive. This is a complex and creative exercise that cannot be undertaken by Christian ethicists alone. The reason is that insights from academic disciplines other than theology must be incorporated. Planners need to engage also with visions of the ideal South African society developed in social spheres other than the religious, such as the economy and politics (e.g., the Reconstruction and Development Programme of the ANC). Justice should be done not only to biblical moral values, but also to values and goals recognized in these other social spheres. All of this can only be done responsibly if representatives from other academic disciplines and other social spheres are involved. Reformed ethicists, however, have a special responsibility to instigate such an interdisciplinary initiative. They also have the responsibility to see to it that the results of the initiative are as widely disseminated as possible, to facilitate the optimal consensus on a Christian vision of a good South African society. Consensus formation can be enhanced even more if the institutional backing of recognized ecumenical organizations can be obtained.

Translating and Promulgating a Christian Vision for South African Society

The crucial question with regard to the effective promulgation of the Christian vision of a good South African society is this: Should it be promulgated in the broader South African society in its distinctively Christian form, or is some translation of it needed to ensure its wider acceptance? In his book *Waakzaam en nuchter: Over Christelijke ethiek in een democratie* (Vigilant and level-headed: On Christian ethics in a democracy), the Dutch Reformed theologian Gerrit de Kruijf argues that a democracy is irresponsible if it tries to operate with a distinctively Christian vision. The Barthian approach of prophetic Christian witness in public on political and economic matters is, in his opinion, not appropriate in contemporary liberal democracies.[23] He does not deny that there may come a moment when faith in Christ cannot tolerate certain developments within a particular liberal democratic state and that faithfulness to Christ and political disobedience may coincide. Such a *status confessionis* is, however, something extraordinary.[24] In normal circumstances the witness or prophetic approach is incompatible with a liberal democracy because it insists that the Christian view should be the basis of policy and legislation and that other views need not be taken into account. In addition, it is not a constructive approach because the church knows in advance that its prophetic Christian witness cannot be accepted in plural democracies as the basis for policy and legislation. If churches and individual Christians want to responsibly contribute to consensus and policy formation, they should not make pronouncements on societal issues on the basis of their own "thick," or strong, Christian morality but do so rather on the basis of the "thin" cultural values shared by all in plural societies.[25]

The social scientist Peter Beyer has a rather similar view in this regard. He is of the opinion that the predominance of globalization as the contemporary outcome of the process of modernization does not necessarily mean that the public role of religion has been played out. The reason for this is that global instrumental systems—such as the capitalist economic, sovereign state, scientific, health, and educational systems—are *totalizing* in the sense that they are applicable to anything in their environment but not *all-encompassing* because there is much that they exclude.[26] Among these are the meaning and thematizing of the social whole, the "private sphere" or "life world" and many problematic effects of their operation. This is where religion, as the one mode of communication that is in principle both totalizing and encompassing, can and does play an important role. It can and does serve as a kind of system specialization that deals with what, from the perspective of the dominant functional systems, are residual matters. Religion's role in this regard is typically antisystemic in the sense that religious adherents, leaders, and professionals tend to see their communication as essential because it addresses the problems that the dominant systems either leave out or create without solving. "Antisystemic" may mean against the dominant structures and values of emerging global society, as is clearly the case with some contemporary forms of fundamentalist religion. The antisystemic role of religion can, however, also be prosystemic in the sense that liberal moral values like equality and freedom, which Beyer claims are inherent in the social systems of modernity, are taken as the point of departure in criticizing the negative effects of these systems, as is the case in liberal Christianity (e.g., the WCC).

Both de Kruijf and Beyer affirm that the church can and should play a constructive role in public debates on social issues. They seem to imply that this can only be done if the church is willing to suspend its own distinctive Christian morality and base its public contribution to a debate on the good society entirely on common values. Probably de Kruijf and Beyer would argue that the church should not have any problems with such a view because there is a great deal of overlapping between Christian and cultural values. This may to some extent be the case in Western societies. In the case of many non-Western societies, and even liberal Western societies, it has lessened over the last century. As Robert Bellah and his coauthors in *Habits of the Heart* have demonstrated with regard to the American society, the enormous historical influence of biblically inspired Christian values on the moral consensus in that society is being strongly undermined by the utilitarian individualism enhanced by the dominating economic system of capitalism.[27] One suspects that the same undermining processes are taking place in societies in the previously Christian Europe.

I am personally of the opinion that de Kruijf's and Beyer's views are, in the case of the South African society, only valid with regard to certain aspects of the participation of the church in public debate. Thus de Kruijf is right in saying that Christians can hardly expect legislation in liberal democracies to be based on strong Christian values. Legislation on abortion, for example, has to allow different-minded groups and individuals to act in accordance with their own consciences. Christians can, however, strive to shift the moral consensus in society to bring it more in harmony with Christian moral values and in this way indirectly influence legislation. They can do it by using arguments for their views that can also be accepted by non-Christians. In a society like South Africa, it can also be done by giving adequate publicity to official church views on societal issues. The majority of South Africans are Christian and are therefore perfectly able to understand typical Christian arguments.

We also have to take into account that the South African society is and has always been a strongly religious society. In a 1995 World Values Study, 81 percent of South African respondents reported that they considered themselves to be religious, with 98 percent of those surveyed stating that they believed in God and 70.7 percent rating God's importance to them as 10 on a scale of 1 to 10 (where 10 = "very important").[28] The different religions share the view that religions should be allowed to play a public role in society on a fair basis. In the South African constitution, recognition was given to this shared conviction in

Section 15, which stipulates that religious observances are allowed in state institutions on a fair basis. The separation between religion and state in the South African democracy is therefore not such a hard one. Some room is given for religions to play a public role and exert a public influence.

Something else that we have to take account of is that public discourse on moral issues and the good society is not only about government policies and legislation. It is, inter alia, also about the way business is conducted by private companies, new technologies are developed by scientists and companies, and new trends appear in structuring intimate relationships. Many of these moral issues are discussed in the media. Journalists and the public expect churches and theologians to have their own distinctively Christian views on these issues. In fact, that is often the main reason why they are consulted by the media. Christians also become involved in the discussion of ethical issues in their workplace. To the extent that businesses are owned by Christians or are managed by them or exclusively serve Christians, they also have the opportunity to take a Christian stance on moral issues. It is, however, true that increasingly people from different religious and cultural backgrounds can be found in the South African workplace. Even there it becomes increasingly necessary to use ethical arguments non-Christians can agree with and to seek moral consensus among people with different views of life.

Reformed ethicists in South Africa also have to take into account that our society is African. Still only a minority of the population are predominantly Western orientated, with predominantly individualist values and attitudes. The majority of the African population still adheres to values and display attitudes that are, to a lesser or greater extent, communal in nature. It may be that we, in the end, have to conclude that the strong privatization of religion, and even the sharp differentiation of social systems that are typical of Western societies, do not apply to the same extent to our new democracy. The work of some social scientists points in this direction. Although José Casanova accepts the differentiation of social systems in Western societies as valid, he argues that the privatization of religion is a historical option, but not a necessary one. It was the authoritarian role of religion in Europe that facilitated the privatization of religion. The exclusive limitation of religion to the private domain of life did not necessarily flow from the factors that gave rise to secularization. The public role of religion may therefore, in his view, be compatible with democratic institutions, and religion could still play an important role in civil society by humanizing the rational systems of modernity.[29]

In discussing Casanova's views, Abdulkader Tayob, a lecturer in religious studies at the University of Cape Town, argues that not only the privatization of religion yet also the differentiation typical of Western societies have no counterpart in postcolonial societies in Africa. The reason is that Casanova's prime factors of differentiation—religious reformation, state formation, capitalism, and scientific developments—are either absent or distorted in these societies. The lack of differentiation does not, however, translate in religion playing a transforming role in postcolonial African states. The opposite is rather the case. Unlike Europe, where debates have raged within religious traditions about the transformation of society, critical debates are almost nonexistent. Religions in postindependent societies seem happy to demand a fair share of the state's support and resources in exchange for loyalty.[30] In other words, although the weaker privatization of religion and the weaker differentiation of social systems in African societies seem to provide the churches more scope to contribute to the transformation of society, it can also be a hindrance to such a contribution when it leads to cozy relationships between churches and governments based on mutual interests.

CONCLUSION

In this essay I have tried to draw out the implications of the Reformed conviction that Christians are called by God to contribute to the transformation of society for the vocation of Reformed ethicist in the present South African society. This conviction was taken for granted by Reformed Christians in the previous political dispensation but has lost much of its legitimacy since the advent of the new liberal democracy in 1994. In my opinion its legitimacy can only be restored by reconstructing or reforming the traditional transformation approach and by developing a more inclusive version that suits the contemporary context. One may say that contributing to the development and the implementation of an inclusive transformation approach is the most important part of the vocation of Reformed ethicist in the present South African society. It entails contributing to the development of an adequate contemporary Christian social ethics, the formulation of a Christian vision of a good society in South Africa based on a strong Christian consensus, and the effective translation and promulgation of this Christian vision in broader society. All this poses a most formidable task for Reformed ethicists. Fortunately, however, they are not alone in this task. They share this task with many others in the church of Christ: among others are fellow theologians, social scientists, politicians, and businesspeople. If God wills, they can together play an important role in the transformation of the South African community toward a better society.

Chapter 9

"In the Beginning..."
Implications of the Reformed Doctrine of Creation for Social Ethics in a Global Era

MAX STACKHOUSE

Perhaps no doctrine is so disputed in the Reformed tradition as to its implications for social ethics and practical theology as the doctrine of creation. I refer, of course, not only to the century-long debates about the implications of evolution for cosmology, biology, anthropology, and epistemology; I also have in mind the longer theological debates about the "covenant of works," "natural theology," "natural law," and "orders of creation" in relation to theologies of history and salvation. The issues behind these debates can be formulated in terms of several questions:

1. Is there any transcendental meaning or divine intent behind and thus in some sense built into existence?
2. Is there any constant pattern, law, or form by which existence is shaped and life is to be lived?
3. Is there any normative knowledge that humans can derive from considering the nature of things as they are?

Recent intense ethical debates related to these issues have been generated by new questions about homosexuality, cloning, and ecology. Such issues raise the question of how much we can or should attempt to intervene in altering what appear to be pregiven patterns and take responsibility for managing life by social engineering, genetic engineering, or geoengineering, recognizing that many dimensions of creation have already been altered over the centuries.[1]

But I do not intend to plunge us into these debates. I want to ask, as it were, the previous questions. What must humanity have as capacities or abilities to address these questions? And how should we view creation so that we feel dutybound to protect parts of it and simultaneously free to think about altering other parts of it? What, in other words, is presupposed in thinking about such issues and in trying to discern how we should live with regard to them? At the outset, I think that we have to ask whether there is anything like a knowable right order of things in the biophysical universe, and whether there is anything ethical connected to creation. If so, how is it related to disputed concepts such as "orders of creation," "common grace," "the nature of nature," "natural law," the "natural knowledge of God," "the cultural mandate," and of course their relation to concepts of sin and fall? Indeed, it is the question of whether Christians, who speak much about justification and redemption in Jesus Christ, and are given an ethic of love and sanctification, can also speak compellingly of how it is that we can speak of justice in a way that can make sense to all humans. Is there any *logos* in creation that all can know?

I raise this cluster of issues here for three reasons: First, as founder of the Kuyper Center for Public Theology at Princeton Theological Seminary, where Abraham Kuyper gave his famous *Lectures on Calvinism*, I can hardly avoid thinking of these questions here in South Africa, where Kuyperian influences were, by all reports, influential at least in the past, yet often, I have been led to believe, in distorted forms. I may find my views of this part of the Reformed tradition corrected by raising the questions here; and it is quite possible that Kuyper looks different from the North than from the South, and from the left side of the Atlantic compared to the right side. Second, it could be that taking up these questions here, with fear and trembling on my part, might prompt a dialogue that could evoke a healing recovery of (may I say it?) truth and reconciliation between parts of the Reformed family, the ethical heartland of Protestantism, especially with regard to social ethics. I will expand briefly on this reason before raising a third.

I will not extensively take up the issue of race relations in our two countries, for we all know that it is a persistent problem that we are seeking to address after very difficult and problematic histories. I will, however, call attention to David Bosch's magnificent essay comparing the history of Calvinistic thinking and its sociopolitical influence in America and in South Africa on this point. He convincingly argues, contrary to many external impressions, that, although Kuyper was a man of his times who held that each people has a distinctive group consciousness and that different peoples are at different stages of social development, he was so driven by a zeal to reinvigorate Calvinism that he thought could and should overcome racial differences. Bosch quotes Kuyper's remarks from his Princeton *Lectures on Calvinism*. Kuyper wrote:

> In the commingling of blood [was] the physical basis of all higher human development.... Groups which by commingling have crossed their traits with those of other tribes... have attained a higher perfection.... The history of our race does not aim at the improvement of any single tribe, but at the development of [hu]mankind taken as a whole.... Now in fact history shows that the nations among whom Calvinism flourished most widely exhibited in every way this same mingling of races.[2]

Bosch goes on to show, however, how the doctrine of election as influenced by a "Romantic nationalism" was disseminated by "young Afrikaners who had studied in Germany in the 1930s." After the ties between Holland and the South African *volkskerk* were essentially broken, these young pastors did, however, draw from aspects of re-Reformed pietism to generate ideas of "separate development." Such non-Kuyperian views have to be seen as matters of social history, missionary strategy, and cultural formation more than of his doctrine. Is there any point where it can be easily said that Kuyper's theory of "sphere sovereignty" is the source of a doctrine of race as a fixed "order of creation"? I doubt it. In fact, that doctrine appeared among "White Christian" racists in America who had no discernible contact with Kuyperian thought.

I raise these opening two questions and touch on this issue not only here, but now also for several reasons. South Africa and the United States are, as only a few other countries in the world are, multiethnic and multicultural: we are forced by our circumstances to try to live with these differences as we simultaneously affirm a common humanity. Since we have come to acknowledge this socially and politically more fully only in the last few generations, we now have to ask, What is divinely given in regard to differences and similarity? What can we identify as necessarily constant? And what can and should be altered? These issues are central not only to our concrete social and cultural histories; they are also global in scope, for in certain limited ways we are emblems of the larger world situation, as it is emerging. Postmodern advocates have recognized that the premature universalistic pretensions of some modernist thinkers and movements have been shattered; their arguments have given considerable comfort to those who want to return to premodern worldviews, which they assert but no longer attempt to justify since all possibilities of a rational defense of any perspective is thought to be shattered as well. Fewer have recognized that an alternative postmodernism is emerging in the form of a much more cosmopolitan development, prompted by an increasingly globalized civil society, one unlike that nation-state of modernity and without a comprehending political order. That, I think, is why the United States, as the last remaining superpower, and historically anticolonial and anti-imperialist in its self-understanding, is today tempted to a neoimperialism. What will become of that is still to be seen, but the larger picture involves the prospect of a new comprehending civilization, with greater pluralism and diversity than we believed possible.[3] With these matters in mind, I offer the third reason for raising the question of a creational order. I think that on the whole the classical Reformed tradition, in accord with the larger Catholic and ecumenically engaged evangelical traditions, has a higher regard for the creational structures than the more radically christocentric accent of Karl Barth or the exodus-focused accent of most liberation theologies. Neither of these highly influential theological orientations have dealt extensively with efforts to find common theological bases for ethics in complex societies, with no comprehending political order. They are modern in their focus on nations, insofar as they have a developed social theory.

Incidentally, we should not, as many do, hold the view that globalization is essentially the spread of free-market capitalism as if this were some autonomous force homogenizing all cultures and leading us toward a new class war by impoverishing some and enriching others. Nothing quite so simplistic as that is happening, although many have inherited Marxian glasses, which see everything in terms of the polarization of the classes. In fact, different forms of capitalism are emerging in different parts of the world and creating new middle classes precisely as various traditional, feudal, nationalist, and socialist economies fail, and as cultures that support the older patterns of life are threatened or find ways of selectively integrating aspects of global developments into their own religious, intellectual, and cultural frames of reference.[4] Still, it is true that most societies are struggling to cope with a great series of challenges: the explosion of technology, the expansion of higher education with its emphasis on the sciences, the spread of communications, the availability and speed of transportation, the growth of international law, and the emergence of common moral standards (Human Rights, the Nobel Peace Prize exemplars of public virtue, concern about world ecology). Even the legacy of several world wars created the bases for international military cooperation (NATO, UN Peacekeeping Forces, regional pacts, temporary alliances for "humanitarian intervention"), and the uneasy coalitions that resist nuclear expansion and resist terrorism. We are also bound together by the frightful spread of deadly communicable diseases that respect no social or political borders. These several developments have generated a context that increasingly comprehends every other contextual reality and thought, evoking the resurgence of the great world religions, which have long given shape to large-scale, enduring civilizations. These now increasingly absorb primal and local religions and cultures into larger frames of reference and produce new interactions that allow and even demand wider access to resources, markets, capital, and new ranges of labor.

The result, not the cause, of these developments is an economic revolution that makes all traditional and state-planned modes of production and distribution obsolete, and the great world religions will need to generate a social ethic that will assist the society in integrating into a more comprehending worldview. Viewed this way, the modernization and rationalization of the increasingly global economy in its highly differentiated modes of operation is as much, if not more, the product rather than the source of the process of globalization. In consequence the whole world is being woven into a new multiethnic, multicultural interdependent society, including South Africa, North America, and other regions to which we are ever more closely tied.

Now we must discover whether there are any universalistic principles or purposes to guide our increasingly common life while leaving space for our cultural particularities. Ironically, the very forces that cracked open the Eurocentric claims to dominance and universality and plunged us into the diversity and fragmentation of postmodernity are now forcing us again to inquire into the possibilities of a common normativity, one that is not unilaterally imposed but universally disclosed and/or discoverable. If one becomes identified, it will constitute an alternative postmodernity, global in implication.

The Kuyperian project was concerned about such matters. We are therefore now forced to face the world's religions and cultures in new ways. And in these issues, we surely must ask what Reformed theology has to offer in this task. I propose that it has a public theology to offer, one that cannot only address public social issues in a vastly expanded common life that includes those who are not a part of the faith, but can also do so in a way that can be understood and debated by a public where not all are believers; where some are believers in alternative frames of reference, religious or philosophical; and where some are convinced that all worldview debates are dubious, ideological, contextual, or personal. I do not see this as hiding our particular and confessional beliefs when we turn to public discourse, nor is it possible or proper to attempt to impose one tradition on the whole of the emerging global civil society. Rather, it is an attempt to self-critically examine the deepest convictions we have and compare and contrast them with other great traditions, to test them to see what sorts of things are or could be of more universal importance. These issues are crucial in many places today since those who are addressing the institutional questions are increasingly antitheological in presupposition, although the moral assumptions that formed the institutions they endorse were shaped by theology and probably cannot be sustained without it.[5]

"FOR GOD SO LOVED THE WORLD . . ."

One thing our Christian theology could offer to this situation is our vision of salvation. Christians believe, as I understand our common heritage, that the God who created the universe has a purpose in mind for humans and for our world in general, an end to which we may all be brought. The end of salvation was made clear to us in Jesus Christ, although it could be, for inscrutable reasons, that some may be doomed. We do not know who is elected to salvation, whether all or some, and we do not know when it will be, for no one knows the time; but believers live by the kind of faith given in the grace that confers authentic hope, knowing only that the end, in the form of the coming kingdom of God, has been inaugurated in time by the life, death, and resurrection of Christ, although the world has not yet been brought to the culmination of that process. We say confidently that the kingdom is working within and among us, but we cannot say "Lo, here" or "Lo, there" with complete confidence. Only God can bring that final end to completion: to put it another way, that final end will be brought to us, since its consummation is on the far side of an apocalyptic break in time and space. That break keeps us ever realistic about the inevitable realities of disruptions in history and about death as our earthly destiny. Beyond these matters, we cannot "know" much about the shape of things on the far side of life, and we distrust those who say they know much. We can only poetically speculate about the new Jerusalem, and we can rejoice that this image portrays, beyond the break, a joyful complex civilization to which all the nations bring their gifts, where all join in choruses of praise, and where the flowing waters of life, nourishing plentiful food to eat, and many herbs of healing are not in the primitive state of primal innocence but in the midst of a city that has foundations, whose builder and maker is God, ruled by the One who was slain out of love for us. This means that we direct our lives toward actions, institutions, and states of affairs that beckon the *novum* of a new future to come, crying *Maranatha*, but knowing that we cannot attain it by our efforts.

Still, movement toward that prospect shapes the fact that, as agents of the sovereign God who offered that promise, we give our best efforts to our tasks in this world. And the great Reformed doctrine of predestination means that there is nothing we can do that would decide whether we would be a part of that ultimate state of affairs or not. We are therefore freed by that doctrine to do what we can do in this life, using the capabilities, gifts, and talents we have been given to seek to improve in this life what can be improved.

We suspect, moreover, that such eschatological images actually point toward an end for humanity that differs from other great and grand religions and philosophies. Quite practically, this means that we do not form the teleologies of our ethics by thinking about returning to a community of spirits of the elders, as is the custom in many primal religions—and held by some heterodox Christian movements, such as the Mormons, who develop elaborate genealogies and baptize the ancestors retroactively (a teaching that makes the Latter-day Saints attractive to some cultural traditions). Nor do we think that the final state of affairs is having an inner piece of the divine Oversoul within us, sadly separated from the cosmic spirit, but capable of being cultivated by the observance of dharmic law and disciplined spiritual consciousness to attain a reunification with it, as dominant Hindu teachings have it. Nor do we think that it is the bliss of detached emptiness, of no-thing-ness, found in the Nirvana of Buddha consciousness; nor the return to the primitive paradise, as Islam often portrays it.[6] Nor do we say, with the secular religion of Marxism, that we can attain full equality in a perfect classless society by acting politically according to the scientific laws of history's dialectics; nor, with Darwin, that it is all for the spreading of our genes in the blind forces of a struggle for survival that ends in entropy.

In his own striking way and with practical social implications, Kuyper offered an interpretation of Christian eschatology's importance in contrast with alternative views, as in his widely known political address "Maranatha." He declared:

> The *destination* of a journey always determines the *road* you have to take. If for you and me that destination is wrapped up in the final catastrophe which is scheduled to occur when Jesus returns to this earth, the cry of *Maranatha* is the crossroads where our road and that of our opponents diverge. To them the return of the Lord is an illusion hardly worth the laughter of ridicule; to us it is the glorious end of history. . . . To us . . . it is the decisive fact of the future by which not only our *spiritual* life but also our *political* course of conduct is utterly controlled.[7]

Kuyper is aware that the data of the ultimate future is not in and that the Christian hope has to be understood as something not obvious to all. Indeed, he goes on to show that the nontheological parties—the Conservatives, who want to perpetuate forever the traditions that they have built up over time; the Liberals, who want to maximize freedom from all traditions in all things; the Revolutionaries, who want humanity to make its own ultimate future by radical action; and the Socialists, who plan an industrialized, egalitarian aggregation of citizens mechanically connected to each other by their common membership in a classless state—all these parties have a particular way of defining the ultimate good that will get us to this or that notion of the ideal state. Kuyper knew that each one of these views seeks to dethrone God and to establish a society created in their own image, that they would never make it, that their efforts are likely to make things worse, and that in any case their efforts will be judged from a more profound eschatological perspective. With Kuyper, all Christians know that no nation and no party is so ultimately important as to deserve ultimate loyalty and so ultimately capable as to deliver the common good. They are not inclusive enough to ever be really common, never good enough to perfect themselves.[8]

In other words, Christians can address practical issues by focusing on salvation; but it will mean a parting of ways from nonbelieving neighbors. In fact, there are moments when Kuyper sounds as if he holds that Christians must separate themselves from nonbelievers on this basis. In that same address, for instance, he continues:

> Only one thing the cry of *Maranatha* has irrevocably instilled in you: you may not accede to their counsel. You may not join them or connive with them. Nor may you abandon the country to them. Rather, all those who love Christ and await his return from heaven must heartily unite with all sincere believers in the land to resist their philosophy and to rescue the country from their pernicious influence.[9]

And yet he also knew that believers cannot withdraw into their enclaves of piety and abandon the public domain. The Kuyperian slogan "In isolation lies our strength" was intended to mean a certain internal clarification of difference from the surrounding world, yet for the sake of clarifying the mission to and for it, not the defensive withdrawal into enclaves of pious tribalism, as it apparently became in South Africa, or ethnoconfessional communitarianism, as it too often became in the United States. The withdrawal was to clarify the ultimate ends of existence so that believers could reengage the world with the courage and conviction to confront the forces that sought to use power to shape a society without God. Kuyper believed, as I read him, that a good public theology can render a nonutopian and ethically framed worldview and thereby help build an interim polity before there is the realization of any final vision. A good public theology can identify the locus of historical realities where more justice could be done, more wisdom obtained, more freedom realized, and the "principled Pluralism" of a viable civil society more fully actuated.

Elsewhere Kuyper writes:

> We regard as incontrovertible the assertion that the laws governing life reveal themselves spontaneously in life. In the very process of painting and sketching and performing and sculpting[,] our artists discovered the laws for the artistic enterprise. And it enters no one's mind to consult the Bible or ecclesiastical authorities when it comes to learning what the purpose of art is. (We are not talking here about judging the moral character of art objects.) The same is true of the laws which govern our thinking, the laws which govern commerce, and the laws which govern industry. We learn to know the laws of thought by thinking. By doing business we discover the art of commerce. Industry blazes its own path. The same is true for political life. To deny this truth is to fall short of respect for the Creator.[10]

In other words, he knows not only that eschatologically the faiths differ and that a major line of demarcation can be drawn between those who are believers in one eschatological vision as compared to those who believe in another, but he also knows that a commonality can be found among those who do not hold to the Christian ultimate vision, between them and Christians. An eschatological view may be the most ultimate frame of reference for ethics, but most ethical, social, political, and practical issues are penultimate, and on this front much of the most honored theology, today and in certain historic periods, has been less articulate. Kuyper climaxed his point by an appeal to the Creator.

"GOD CREATED"

With these considerations in mind, prompted by being here in South Africa in a globalizing era, I propose that fundamental practical and socioethical issues, as well as a whole raft of related theoretical questions, are implied by the claim that "the LORD made heaven and earth, the sea, and all that in them is" (Exod. 20:11 KJV). It is a stupendous claim, in many ways shared by Jews, Muslims, theistic Hindus, Confucians earnest about the mandates of heaven, and various primal religions. It entails the claim also that this first gift of grace, existence, represents the divine desire to extend something that reflects the glory of the Creator not only into time, space, and life, but also particularly to humanity. Humans, all these traditions believe while articulating it in divergent ways, are made in the divine image and thus have reason (the capacity to discover the intelligible in all the realms of creation), freedom (the capacity to choose and exercise resolve since there is a certain nondeterminacy in creation), and passion (the capacity to feel and to develop affections that bind us to others and to creation itself). These appear in a material and historical realm that derives from a purely spiritual and eternal realm of the Creator.

With claims such as this in mind, we can ask whether, from a "creational" viewpoint, with its inevitable overtones of something like the "spontaneous" recognition of what Kuyper and other Reformed theologians called "common grace" or "general revelation," there is a basis for discovering together something of the substance of justice. That prospect appears in rich and complex forms of "natural law" thought in ancient philosophical traditions, East and West, in classic Catholic and Reformation theologies, and today in expansive parts of the evangelical traditions.[11] In each instance it requires rational communication and mutual understanding, the exercise of persistent will, and the formation of bonds of affection with those who have other views of salvation and different visions of the ultimate human ends. If that is so, it can surely also be done with fellow humans beyond the Christian family of faiths.

I am well aware of many contemporary thinkers' deep suspicion of "natural law" and of anything seeming to affirm "natural theology," and the contextual reasons for that suspicion are also well known, although I agree with those who hold that the famous attack by Barth on the Brunnerian contributions to modern theology is too harsh and not fully faithful to Calvin and other major Reformed voices, to the wider reach of the Christian tradition, or to the deeper reaches of the common human experience.[12] It would have been faithful if ideas of common grace and natural theology were proposed in a way that tried to offer methods leading to salvation; but none of the Christian traditions, and most of the world religions, seek to do so. They instead are properly to be seen as a kind of *preparatio evangelicum* by Christians, an interim set of resources for developing and preserving a *jus gentium* for the common life in which the ongoing preaching, teaching, and debating of the many theological possibilities can continue. After all, every theology is a humanly constructed proposal to the church and to humanity. It is a canvas and a palette with which many paintings can be made. It is not a finished picture. But in the making of every picture, certain common patterns of artwork can be discovered, as Kuyper pointed out. Each is an interpretation of a number of elemental themes that believers hold to have been revealed, and these elements can be and have been arranged in a variety of ways, as theologians variously select and prioritize the elemental themes. They do so while identifying the critical issues that need to be represented to and for people's lives in the community of faith and in the wider civilization.

Moreover, Barth's radically eschatological and christocentric theology and liberation theology's salvific programmatics have helped save the church from being swallowed into racist (in neopagan Europe) or classist (in neofeudal and colonialized Latin America) or both (in South Africa and in the American south) exploitations enforced by governments that claimed to be legitimated by the natural order of things. However, neither one of these two powerful twentieth-century theological movements generated the social forces that overthrew the tyrannical regimes, nor have they yet proved themselves able to form dynamic churches, to construct a viable civil society, or to engender new economic systems once those regimes are removed. On the contrary, while focusing on this first great manifestation of God's grace, creation, especially in its relationship to its constituent elements of the biophysical ecology—the "cultural mandate," *the imago Dei*, and dual sexuality,[13] which are shared by all branches of humanity—some commonalities can be found by a modified re-Reformed point of view that can aid the development of a public theology for the increasingly pluralistic societies that anticipate and prepare the way for a new global civilization.

Perhaps it need not even be said, but one other theological option needs to be set aside if we are to see creation as a common theological resource for practical theology and ethics. We need not, indeed dare not, have a literalistic view of creationism when we approach these questions: those who do hold such a view have all too often discredited an ongoing and finally necessary reception of elemental creational themes. But if we view the mythic narratives of Genesis as a highly symbolic set of complex pointers toward how life and history work, they reveal certain decisive realities in, with, and by which humanity lives in time and space. Indeed, we can find insights of great significance and even of universal and perennial importance.[14] When we say, for example, that "God created . . . ," we are not only speaking of the fact that we dwell in a biosphere, a primal structure of an ecological order from which life was called into being and in which we live and move and have our being, but we are speaking of it as "creation" and not merely as "nature." And there is a world of difference between the two.[15] This protological claim about the meaning-laden, spiritual-laden, and ethical-laden origins of life provides a hypothetical account of whence comes existence and all its multiple powers and potentialities by proposing that before anything else was, God was; that it could not continue to be if God were not; that when everything is gone, God will still be; and that all that exists is, in its fundamental being, seen by God as phenomenologically and morally worth our regard: it is "good."

Then, at the highpoint of the creation process, humanity—male and female—is created, like all plants and animals able to participate in the creation of new life physically, but unlike any one of them, called to name, tame, and tend the other creatures. Thus humanity is to exercise "dominion,"[16] what Kuyper names the "cultural mandate," to create institutions and societies to guide and bring to its full potential all the primal powers of creation. That implies, by the way, that the good of all that is created is not created in a form that has actuated its fullest potential.

The creation is not a perfected steady state system but a dynamic set of potentialities ready for dramatic development, filled with powers whose possibilities are not fully realized, a point to which we shall shortly return. Humans have a special mandate, not given to any other creature, to make the potential more actual. No perfection or salvation can be reached by these, but things can be marginally improved and at least preserved from wanton destruction.

The implications are great. For one thing, if this claim is valid, then everything that is, including humanity, is real and to be taken seriously, yet it is limited and undeveloped. None are eternal, and all creatures, including us ourselves, are dependent and not autonomous. Moreover, nothing is to stay the same. Many things and many people have come and gone, and neither the world itself nor we will last forever. God invented and sustains nature, but it is unstable and unreliable on its own. Further, while no thing is totally constant or eternal, each thing has enough coherent order in it to be studied in some dimensions in a nomothetic way by the use of the gift of reason; but it also has enough freedom to be unpredictable or malleable in other respects. Science thus can seek to discover the patterns that, theologians say, reflect the intelligibility of the Creator behind the natural realm, but only stable ratios of probability can be found. Indeed, the sciences themselves have to be understood in terms of the shifting paradigms by which science proposes to grasp patterns in a partially contingent order and in the dynamic possibilities that it makes possible. Further, each part of creation, those now studied by a plethora of sciences, is a system that interacts with other systems in ways revealing enough contingency to show that nature appears to be not only ordered, but also malleable in some respects—evidencing not only a deep pattern that rationality can uncover, but also a kind of "natural freedom." Due to this "indeterminacy," humans can and do intentionally intervene in the operations of the biophysical world to control, within limits, this contingent interaction.

Not only is science possible, but so is technology, a matter of perhaps greater importance in generating our globalizing world. Indeed, if we take the "cultural mandate" seriously as a divine command, it is a theological duty to become as proficient as possible in technology in order to exercise our dominion. The practical implications of this belief allow a Christian theology to interact with nonbelievers and with other believers in a Creator God in discovering what we may call the "ontic laws of nature" while providing a stronger justification for stewardship in precisely that technological mastery of nature.[17]

The claim that God, in creating humanity, made humanity in God's own image reinforces the notion of malleability, for as mentioned earlier, humanity is differently capacitated than any of the creatures.[18] We can, in some modest measure, think in more abstract ways than the other creatures, discovering the patterns of nature and of morality, and engage in communication about them. We can also exercise some degree of freedom and, contemplating options, choose among possibilities in the ways we relate to our biophysical environment and our own bodies. Even further, we can find affinities and affectional passions that link us with beautiful things in our environment and to other humans. These themes are among the points signaled by the responses to the snake and the discovery of nakedness. Like the inner character of the triune God's own being, humans can be covenantal, both in response to God's relationship to us and in relationship to that beyond the self. Of course, the Genesis account points out these matters by showing how these capacities can be and prototypically have been distorted; humans can use the gifts given in creation, particularly by misuse of the capabilities given with the *imago Dei*, to violate the boundaries of the divine and created order and pretend, at least, to become the lord of all and judge of all good and evil, only to discover how ignorant (unreasonable), conditioned (unfree), and alienated (separated from others and from life) humanity can become, while blaming some subtle force of nature or some other human agent for the wrongs done.[19]

"OUT OF THE GARDEN"

Humanity does not live in, never historically did live in, and cannot return to the idyllic dreamworld of what believers think God must have had in mind for creation and the favored creatures. The departure from innocence is made possible and is almost "inevitable but not necessary"[20] by naturalistic distortions of the patterns of life given in the divine intent as those distortions interact, by means of the necessary contingencies of interacting systems, to allow both the possibility of freedom and the prospect of the kind of bonding that overcomes alienation. But the divinely intended gift of existence and human life is willfully disrupted further by the human complicity in transgressing boundaries, the exercise of freedom that distorts truth and justice, the consequent discovery that we are nakedly defenseless against life forces around and within us that alienate us from ourselves, our fellow humankind, and finally from God. Humans everywhere try to hide such facts from themselves, each other, and divine scrutiny; thus humanity is constantly under the threat of meaninglessness because we cannot fully perceive the splendor, order, responsible freedom, and bonding passions that stand behind the complexity of existence. We are also enslaved by all sorts of natural distortions and subject to suffering, pain, and nonexistence. For these reasons humanity must have a theology of history in which the end is different from the beginning, recognizing that nature itself is not only incomplete, needing tending and human dominion, but also distorted and thus needing restoration where possible and transformation where necessary.[21] At this point, things become quite interesting from the practical and ethical points of view, for two reasons.

One is the question of how to deal with established viewpoints whose holders do not accept this kind of account. In this connection, we need to recognize that all of the great world religions have a conception of creation, and they seldom see nature as the ultimate point of reference. That is, indeed, a distinguishing mark of "religions." We can debate with the representatives of a world religion the exact nature of this transcendence over nature and the ways in which we best come to know this, and we presume that our debates about these theological issues make sense. This is one of the primordial forms of public theology. Many could, in principle, debate these issues quite openly, implying a common possession of a rational capacity, although the will to do so is weak, and the alienating passions of loyalty to cultural traditions are quite strong, so that the institutional bonds between them that could facilitate such discussions are undeveloped. Still it goes on in fragmentary and episodic ways.

"MULTIPLY, AND FILL THE EARTH"

More difficult in a global era is the fact that some people sincerely doubt that a divine intelligence, a free will, and a loving affection are really behind the world. This is not the place to engage in a full-fledged discussion about theistic and antitheistic worldviews, but some parts of the scientific community and some who hold to non-Western world religions believe more in nature than in a creator God. Some reckon evolution to be a primal accident that, plus natural selection, made the earth, and that microbes, plants, animals, apes, and humanoids all evolved by mutation and adaptation until humans, with their industrial-sized brains, eventually appeared. Then these brains invented God to explain things we do not understand. These people do not believe that God made nature and us but that nature made us and we made God—in or out of our own imagination.[22] However, if humanity invented all the great worldview hypotheses involving an open universe, where transcendence is a force in the biophysical world, it can be argued that a closed universe, where there is no transcendence, is likewise invented and that those who claim a closed universe have a more difficult time accounting for the moral and spiritual character of their own intelligible, voluntary, and affectionate intuitions and interactions with each other and the biophysical universe than what the theological tradition conveys. And we can argue with equal plausibility that life can best be understood in terms of an open system, one where "spiritual realities" influence natural ones and where a morality that is prior to humanity's inventions can be structured into social and cultural existence. Kuyper railed against materialism, atheism, and pantheism: we simply find them unscientific and unconvincing.

Certain "religious" views also are nontheist yet superior to antireligious views, even if they are not all equally adequate when compared with Christian views. Buddhist metaphysics, for example, is in certain ways compatible with contemporary scientific views, as held by some Christians. The environmental scientist and philosopher William Cronon, for instance, has challenged the idea of a nonhuman nature that can be taken as a measure of the right order of things.

After all, humans have intentionally intervened in all sorts of natural processes for as long as these particular bipeds have been on earth. But not only have humans reframed their surroundings by material intervention in them; "nature" also is an idea. Cronon writes:

> Ideas of nature never exist outside a cultural context, and the meanings we assign to nature cannot help reflecting that context. The main reason this gets us into trouble is that (the view of) nature as essence, nature as naive reality, wants us to see nature as if it had no cultural context, as if it were everywhere and always the same. And so the word we use to label this phenomenon encourages us to ignore the context that defines it.[23]

Like the Buddhist, he sees the world of "nature" as an unsubstantial construct of human consciousness. But unlike the Buddhist, he does not want us to detach from the illusion: he wants us to engage the environment in a way that takes responsibility for the shape of that highly contingent reality toward which our construct points us. Indeed, he is closer to the ethic for laypersons who do not become monks or nuns and continue to live in this world, where responsible engagement in society and culture as well as with "nature" must continue. After all, it is from the laity that the begging bowls of the monks and nuns are filled. In brief, the difference is between the Buddhist idea of salvation and the idea of living in this life—a distinction that Christians often see in the tension between the ethics of eschatology and the ethics of protology.

Traditional Confucian teachings bear some similarity to this view as well. Such doctrines do not speak of where or what the source and norm of all existence is, as if there were a Creator God. The stratified existence of nature at the bottom, society in the middle, and heaven above is presumed to be a preexistent whole; it is a primal ontocratic order by which all can be integrated into a relative harmony. Of course, disorder erupts, in nature or in society, and sometimes from heaven, and the primal order must be restored by a "rectification of names." The devastation of floods, for example, must be repaired and the waters of the rivers returned to their proper channels and uses; fathers must be more fatherly, and sons must exercise greater filial piety; and the emperor and his literati officers must rule justly, exemplify virtue, and perform the appropriate rites to reestablish the harmony between nature, society, and heaven. The idea of transcendence over this ontic whole by a divine reality is a foreign and difficult concept even to articulate in that worldview.

That worldview did not provide for a view comparable to that of the vision of Eden, but it recognized something of a pregiven natural, moral, and spiritual order and thought that could be enacted in history. It thus made one of the world's greatest historic civilizations, constantly renewed by repeatedly realigning the order of things by natural intelligence, a disciplined will, and properly channeled affections that prompted efforts to cultivate a virtuous self in a virtuous society. Yet there were anomalies. Ancient technologies that built the massive irrigation system involved a fundamental intervention into the natural order (not entirely unlike China's Three Gorges Dam, built in 1994–2012), but it was justified by the desire to all the more adequately adapt society into its traditional ontocratic structures. Further, we notice that when the Confucian worldview first encountered the Western colonialists and missionaries, and then the Marxist revolutionaries, both with views that transcended the idea of a pregiven whole, the society collapsed. Here we see, as also in several traditions, that life cannot exist if it totally disrupts that which is biophysically pregiven; but it also fails if it does not recognize that some parts of the "natural order of things" are distorted ("fallen") and need to be transformed by human action that is obedient to a center of meaning and morality other than that order. The values that are to govern our lives do not come from nature: they come from culture, and at a deeper level the core of culture comes from the sovereign Creator—or they are merely imperial impositions.[24]

Currently, in China as earlier in Korea, both at the scholarly level and massively at the popular level, as in southern Africa, people are turning to Christianity as providing a better account of how to order society than Confucianism did and tribal cultures did, when they tried to preserve ontocracy, and better than Marxism does, when it tries to change everything by revolutionary action.[25] Neither can hold together a view of constant pattern in life and historically dynamic change. They each know some things about how the world works and about morality, but their accounts are sufficiently flawed that they both need each other and something more.

Cultures based on them cannot stand when faced with a better view. These excursions into modern scientific and ancient religious orientations challenging our theological perspectives actually reveal something that I believe the Kuyperian creational theology and ethics also allow us to see, something that some of his closest disciples and harshest critics did not recognize. In Kuyper (and the wider tradition), I think it is possible to see a helpful approach regarding the nature of things in the world and history, and regarding the human capacity to understand them: at one very deep level the world has an ontological and ethical order that scientists, logos theorists, natural law advocates, primal religions, Confucians, and Christians can in part discern. They can do this because the human capacities and the will and passion to do so are also present in humans in a way that is discontinuous with all other creatures. The most profound discoveries of modern science, such as Einstein's formula, and modern ethical insights, such as the need to defend universal human rights or the capacity to recognize virtues in people from all cultural and religious backgrounds—these are in fact universal and not a mere scholastic speculation. The idea of a common grace, given in creation by a Creator, offers the best account of this reality available. With Jonathan Edwards we can and must understand this grace as a fundamental "consent to being." We can confidently argue for such concepts in public discourse with nonbelievers and other believers.

At the same time and at the phenomenological level, "nature"—meaning that which is created but not conscious of a Creator—is divided against itself.

Disease corrupts, the wolf eats the lamb, entropy threatens being, and all life ends in death. Moreover, human nature is divided against itself if not integrated in God: reason asserts its arrogance over will and affection or is trumped by an assertive will, or the passions bind the will to degrading desires and irrational calculations. We are divided against ourselves. Meanwhile societies—tribes, cultures, political and economic orders—array themselves against their neighbors, dominate and exploit them, and bring untold suffering. In observing this, we can see why the Darwinians propose a natural, purposeless struggle for existence marked by "the bloody law of tooth and claw." We can understand why Marxists see life as an unmitigated story of the agonistic conflict of class interests. And the Christian can see why the Buddhists hold that the attachment to the illusory and passing "things" of the world brings suffering and is less authentic than a detached and pure consciousness. This level of existence, taken alone, is enough to make one believe in the total depravity in all things.

But what makes us not despair is not only the more ultimate promise of redemption in Christ, but also the more proximate fact that common grace can, in its various modes and in various degrees, constrain the degenerative tendencies in existence and provide the ontological and epistemic capabilities to create civilizations and, beyond that, to receive and accept providential covenants and vocations in this world. All such prospects are fragile; but they are possible, and given the disarray of existence, we can rejoice that common grace is given. It is this accent that makes scientific and political cooperation with nonbelievers possible. It is the willingness to engage the formation and constant reformation of civilizations, to form and reform covenantal bonds, to throw ourselves into our worldly vocations—that willingness has made the Reformed traditions influential in scientific and sociopolitical activities in a degree disproportionately above our numbers.

This tradition, thus, is confident in God's sovereignty and Christ's centrality but never utopian; realistic about sin and evil but never antinomian or nihilistic; practical and expectant in the confident quests for truth and justice but never certain that we have them in hand. Our globe needs a renewed, creationally informed Neo-Calvinism.

Chapter 10

Christian Ethical Distinctiveness, the Common Good, and Moral Formation

GEOFF THOMPSON

INTRODUCTION

The eloquent, albeit often pugnacious, prose of Stanley Hauerwas has provided the contemporary theological community with no shortage of quotable quotes, of which perhaps the most quotable, and arguably the most quoted, is his comment about the church's social ethics: "I am . . . challenging the very idea that Christian social ethics is primarily an attempt to make the world more peaceable or just. Put starkly, the first social ethical task of the church is to be the church—the servant community. . . . As such, the church does not have a social ethic; the church is a social ethic."[1] To the long, ecumenically broad tradition of Christian social involvement, such remarks are often heard with something approaching incredulity and quickly dismissed as sociologically sectarian. Where such social involvement has been intellectually grounded in some form of moral realism, Hauerwas's comments are likely to be even more quickly dismissed as epistemologically fideist. Above all, if such involvement has been nurtured in the Reformed tradition, with its ideas of common grace and civil responsibility, Hauerwas's approach is likely to be knowingly explained away as something potentially even worse than sectarian and fideistic: Anabaptist![2]

The essence of Hauerwas's response to these charges is captured in the sentence that I omitted from the above quotation: "Such a claim may well sound self-serving until we remember what makes the church the church is its faithful manifestation of the peaceable kingdom in the world."[3] Whether, in the end, Hauerwas's own developed position offers a theologically and philosophically coherent foundation for Christian involvement *in* the world will be a matter for ongoing debate, one that will not be taken up in this essay. Indeed, here I am not writing about Hauerwas. He is nevertheless a useful point of departure precisely because his work, among that of others, has generated one of the crucial tensions in contemporary Christian ethics: Does the Christian appropriation of communitarian ethics subvert the Christian commitment to the common good?

Of course, the problem is not simply one internal to the Christian community. In fact, it is even argued that the very idea of a common good that is genuinely common is both intellectually and socially implausible. The latter is so because the liberalism that has sustained discussions about the common good has been shown to be ideologically suspect. The neutrality and openness that was the foundation of liberal ideas of the common good have increasingly been exposed as obscuring hidden prejudices and unacknowledged strategies of exclusiveness. The critique is well documented in both theological and philosophical literature. Nevertheless, I know of few better or more pithy summary narratives of the decline of liberalism as a self-evident good than that provided by Andrew Sullivan.

> Liberalism began . . . as a way for politics to avoid settling profound and divisive issues of religion; in the modern Western world, where religious convictions have become generally less intense, the notion of cultural identity seems to have replaced them as the construct that gives the deepest meaning to many people's lives. And in its newest incarnation, liberalism is deeply implicated in the social warfare that this area inevitably leads to; indeed, it has begun to redefine politics and law as the means by which the problems of identity are finally resolved. *It has come, in other words, to resemble the problem it was originally designed to fix.*[4]

This is a telling critique. While it may not and should not render all liberal talk of the common good redundant, it is at least a reminder that discussions about Christian social involvement must assume a far less simple world than was possible when the idea of the liberal pluralist society was a more stable idea than it is today.

Within the debates that characterize the Christian community's attempts to negotiate its way into and through this more complex situation, the tendency is for distinctiveness to be played off against commonality. The more the distinctiveness of the Christian community is emphasized, the less likely, it is feared, will be the orientation to the common good, and vice versa. Indeed, the distinction can be even sharper than this: sacrificing the distinctive may mean promoting the banal, while sacrificing the common good may entail social alienation.

> In appealing to what is held in common, Christians may be sacrificing what is distinctive to their own identity in favour of notions whose general acceptance is based more on their vacuity and banality than their universal transparency. Yet, by speaking directly from their own tradition, Christians may succeed only in alienating other members of society, who hear no more than a religious group recounting special claims to authority and privileged sources of ethical guidance, rather than a community which genuinely seeks to contribute to the common human task.[5]

Against this background, the thesis of this essay is quite simple: Rather than play distinctiveness off against the idea of the common good, I argue that Christianity's strongest warrants for contributing to the common good derive from its most distinctive beliefs. Of course, this in itself does not say very much. More specifically, therefore, I want to take some of the language usually claimed by communitarians and import it into the discussion about social involvement. I argue that social involvement is as much a matter of, and dependent upon, processes of moral formation unique to the Christian community as are the identity-giving practices of forgiveness, reconciliation, worship, breaking bread, self-denial, and so forth. I want to propose that the Christian commitment to the common good is not an additional practice that the church might take up once it has been morally formed. Rather, it is intrinsic to the moral formation of the community. More specifically, appropriating Richard Hays's argument about the focal images of the New Testament's moral vision, I argue that the church's social involvement is fundamentally formed by its attention to cross, new creation, and community.[6]

The resulting proposal may or may not be immediately recognized as fitting the conventional contours of Reformed theology. Certainly, in broad terms, my approach to the issues is shaped by an ecclesial context—the Uniting in Australia—in which the Reformed tradition has already taken its place beside Methodist and Congregational traditions and is committed as a matter of course to engagement with the wider ecumenical traditions. At the same time it is shaped by the awareness of a social and cultural context that, as Clive Pearson's essay elsewhere in this volume has amply demonstrated, has little knowledge of, and often shows explicit hostility toward, the concerns and categories of classical Christian belief and practice, be they Catholic, Reformed, or anything else. In such a context the Christian community is forced to return to the narratives of Jesus' life, death, and resurrection in order imaginatively to rethink the manner of and rationale for its commitment to the common good.

Nevertheless, in order to locate my argument among the various concerns of the Reformed tradition, I first undertake two preliminary tasks. First I counter the view that the Reformed tradition is by definition suspicious of the common-good pole of the debate (and perhaps even responsible for the polarization of the debate). The other task is to explore two recent contributions, one Catholic and one Reformed, to demonstrate how the conventional ecumenical divide is playing out in this debate. With these tasks complete, I will offer my own proposal.

REFORMED CULPABILITY?

The Reformed tradition tends to be wary of either a real or imagined Anabaptist sectarianism,[7] and the Catholic tradition looks with suspicion toward the Reformed on account of the latter's criticism of the natural law tradition. Yet the history of the Reformed tradition bears strong and reliable witness to the fact that the absence of a developed natural law tradition has not prevented the development of an honorable history of social involvement.[8] Typically the doctrinal roots of this history are located in Calvin's "third use of the law" and his endorsement of the genuine wisdom to be found outside the church both in the political order and in the liberal and manual sciences.

Calvin's use of the law in the Christian life means that Christians encounter the law not only as a guide that brings them to Christ and is then redundant, but also as a continuing guide to the Christian life: "For no [hu]man has heretofore attained to such wisdom as to be unable, from the daily instruction of the law, to make fresh progress toward a purer knowledge of the divine will."[9] Through their knowledge of the law, they have, among other things, a mandate to honor and obey such structures and institutions that can be seen to be divinely intended for the whole human race (even if the divine origin of those structures and institutions is obscured from others who participate in and derive benefit from them). Calvin's exhortation to honor "civil government" is driven by both a strategy of protecting the church as well as a more unprejudiced desire for the peace of society as an end in itself. This twofold strategy reflects a prior twofold understanding of the "appointed end" of "civil government." On the one hand, that "end" includes "to cherish and protect the outward worship of God" and to defend sound piety and the position of the church. On the other hand, it is also the purpose of civil government "to adjust our life to the society . . . , to form our social behavior to civil righteousness, to reconcile us with one another, and to promote general peace and tranquillity."[10] Thus, through their participation in Christ, the fulfiller of the law, Christians have their eyes opened to the Mosaic law, which "asserts the very same things" as the "inward law, which [is] . . . written, even engraved, upon the hearts of all."[11] This includes a new awareness of the divine appointment of civil government.

Calvin's endorsement of wisdom from outside the church establishes the possibility that Christians can learn from non-Christians, both in the political order[12] and in the liberal and manual sciences:[13] "If the Lord has willed that we be helped in physics, dialectic, mathematics, and other like disciplines, by the work and ministry of the ungodly, let us use this assistance."[14] Although Calvin places the emphasis upon the fact that Christians can be "helped" by "this assistance," he has also implicitly laid the theological foundation for Christians to act in common cause with non-Christians on such matters.

Although these two strands of Calvin's thought are concerned with two different sets of issues, I argue that they are not unrelated nor merely random or ad hoc insights on his part. They belong to a coherent account of the interrelationship between creation, law, sin, salvation, and providence.[15] Because in Calvin's thought, the *imago Dei* has been corrupted rather than destroyed, the mind is therefore only "partly weakened and partly corrupted."[16] Nevertheless the level of corruption is sufficient to deprive it of access to "heavenly things." Thus "the human being is so shrouded in the darkness of errors that he hardly begins to grasp through this natural law what worship is acceptable to God."[17] On the other hand, it is not so great that "earthly things" have become inaccessible. So we read in the oft-quoted passage: "Whenever we come upon these matters in secular writers, let that admirable light of truth shining in them teach us that the mind of [the hu]man, though fallen and perverted from its wholeness, is nevertheless clothed and ornamented with God's excellent gifts."[18] The unity of these various strands of thought has been the basis for suggestions that it is possible, after all, to affirm that "for Calvin, as for the Catholic tradition, there is one moral law, and that it is 'written on the consciences' of all persons" and that, therefore, "a biblically based ethics can be an ethics for all, since its ultimate moral referent is 'written upon the hearts of all.'"[19] Thus, it is suggested, "constructive ecumenical ethics done from the perspective of Protestantism might best begin with Calvin."[20] So perhaps the Reformed tradition can breathe a sigh of relief that it can counter the objections of its Catholic counterpart.

One of the means for developing these insights has been the idea of "common grace." Richard Mouw has tracked the background of this idea and given an account of recent debates about it. Although more explicitly engaged with a specific strand of North American Calvinism, Mouw does, I think, summarize something of a more general Reformed sensibility around these issues, sentiments that can be argued to have stemmed from Calvin: "I think the main concern for Calvinists about general revelation, natural law, natural theology, and similar notions is that they can lead to a categorical endorsement of the moral and rational capacities of human beings in general."[21] He describes his own position as one of "a hermeneutic of caution, though not a hermeneutic of outright suspicion"; neither is it a "hermeneutic of solidarity in which we *presume* truth and goodness."[22] This is a reminder, I suggest, that Christian social engagement does not, in fact, require or depend upon a particular moral or ethical theory. Even if Calvin's various reflections on this matter can be shown to be internally coherent and inviting of some level of theoretical consistency (which I've suggested they can be), in the end the Christian trust for such encounters lies not in the wisdom of those who are wise but in God who, in faithfulness to all creation, has "clothed and ornamented] [the human mind] with such excellent gifts."[23] For this reason the tradition of thought formed by these seminal texts tends to exercise not systematic withdrawal from wider society but an ad hoc engagement with it. Thus, as I propose in the final section of my essay, Calvin reminds us that to be committed to social engagement, Christians must be morally formed by the narrative of God's faithfulness before they understand a theory of natural law or some variation thereof, be it even an idea of common grace.

Nevertheless, Protestant and Catholic contributions to the discussion remain shaped by the contours laid down through divergent attitudes toward natural law that emerged in the Reformation. For examples of this, I now turn to the recent proposals of Robert Gascoigne and David Fergusson.

CONTEMPORARY RESPONSES

These two relatively recent works are both highly erudite and sustained by sophisticated, subtle, and wide-ranging arguments. I will not even begin trying to summarize the full extent of their respective arguments within the space of this essay. Rather, I will seek to bring a few of their key concerns to focus, in order to draw some comparisons between them.

Gascoigne's *The Public Forum and Christian Ethics* (2001)

Gascoigne, an Australian Catholic theologian, does not set out to offer some generic Christian account of the church's commitment to the common good. He is explicitly oriented to the pursuit of that issue in liberal societies. He is, he writes, "concerned with the way the church understands and expresses its identity through ethical communication in liberal societies."[24] Moreover, as that very statement shows, his orientation is also toward the *communication* of Christian identity to and within liberal societies. This involves him in developing a particular account of revelation. Such an emphasis on communication is, of course, grounded in the mission of the church: "The church's mode of communication to the world is, at heart, a question of the nature of evangelization."[25] Clearly Gascoigne is of the view that the Christian faith has something very particular to say to liberal societies. Where such societies have, by definition, defined a "person's worth or dignity in terms purely of freedom from unwarranted interference,"[26] the Christian revelation, as the revelation of the triune God "who invites human beings to live in *communio* with the divine life and with each other,"[27] holds that the "freedom of persons is based in their relationship to the infinite God, a relationship which of its nature bonds them to other persons in community."[28]

Yet Gascoigne's emphasis on communication is also driven by another factor: the post-Kantian emphasis within liberal societies on discourse ethics where, in the absence of any appeal to the authority of any particular tradition, moral argument and decision depends upon the persuasiveness of the arguments themselves.[29] What Gascoigne does, however, is quite explicitly to redescribe this commitment to discourse ethics in terms of "natural law": "The communication of Christian ethics should be based on an understanding of consensus as the resultant of the influence of historical traditions, which converge on a number of principles which can receive strong community assent. Such mediating principles provide a new means of understanding the ancient concept of natural law."[30]

This leads to a further claim that such discourse ethics is ontologically grounded in the life of God. "The project of universal ethical dialogue and ethical community, as expressed in the Kantian notion of the kingdom of ends, receives its ontological grounding in the theology of revelation, in which the mutual respect of human persons is grounded in their community with the three-personed God and with each other."[31] Having already made the move of investing the mediating principles of liberal ethical discourse with the status of "natural law," and adding to that a conventional Catholic move of linking revelation to natural law, Gascoigne contends that such discourse also informs and is partly constituent of Christian identity. Thus the event of revelation includes not only the church's contribution to that discourse, but also what it receives from that discourse: "Christian identity is formed and re-formed in the process of understanding the relationship between the Gospel and all those moments of thought and action which call for reaction and response."[32] It is this element of his proposal that leads him to resist the communitarian approach of Hauerwas, which implies an understanding of revelation whose sources are solely internal to the community of faith, argues Gascoigne.[33]

As a concrete example of this approach, let me quote an extensive passage from toward the end of the book, where Gascoigne refers to the issues surrounding the ethical discussion of abortion.

> Ethical controversy in the public forum, since it is often not conducted on shared premises in such broader visions, must focus on the specifically ethical goods involved. References to the purposes of the creator are references to premises which are not shared, and whose relationship to the ethical question at stake is unclear for many participants in the debate. Communication of normative principles demands particularly stringent relevance and intelligibility. At the same time, Christians can communicate the meaning of those ethical goods in ways which are formed by their own religious vision—a vision which enables them to see the goods of human life in a particular light and in particular mutual relationships. Christian critique of abortion can develop and affirm understandings of human existence, which imaginatively links the desire for autonomy and self-expression with respect for the beginnings of human life. Motivated by their own narrative, but oriented towards the public forum, Christians can unfold the inherent ethical logic of a stance oriented towards the protection of innocent human life. This must be accompanied by words and action which seek to overcome the bitter history of conflict . . . through an affirmation of the rights of women, especially through a commitment to forms of service which welcome and support the bearing of children.[34]

For the purposes of the dialogue being developed here, a critical question to be put to this approach concerns the driving force behind Gascoigne's insistence on "particularly stringent relevance and intelligibility." Is it the motivation to evangelize through participation in ethical discourse? Or is it a desire to acknowledge the canons of post-Kantian discourse ethics, an acknowledgment that is reinforced by investing the "mediating principles" of that discourse with the authority, status, and function of "natural law"? If it is the former, should there be any hesitation about mentioning the Creator on the grounds of this being a reference "whose premises are not shared"? (Indeed, if reference to the Creator is deemed illegitimate, can the contribution actually be considered an instance of evangelization?) If the latter, are Christians "unfolding the logic of their stance" because they are "oriented towards the public forum" or because they are "motivated by their own narrative"? Indeed, the reference here to "public forum" could obscure the fact that Gascoigne has already made a decision to privilege a particular understanding of the public forum: a modern liberal society whose discourse is normed by post-Kantian ideas of discourse ethics. For all the obvious strengths of Gascoigne's argument, my query is whether investing the discourse of liberal societies with the authority of "natural law" has dented the normativity of the Christian community's own narrative.

Fergusson's *Community, Liberalism and Christian Ethics* (1998)

In large measure Fergusson's book is directed against the risk of ecclesial isolationism implicit in the communitarian approach of Hauerwas and others; to critique that approach, he uses the resources of the Reformed tradition, especially Karl Barth's account of Christ's presence *extra muros ecclesiae*.[35] Fergusson seeks to correct any tendency toward Christian isolation from the common good with an echo of Calvin's argument that I mentioned above: "For the church to function as a community which bears witness to the kingdom of God within a wider civil polity, some doctrine of the state is necessary. In this respect it seeks civil community space within which to practice."[36] Yet, in another echo of Calvin's arguments, Fergusson also recognizes that Christians are active contributors to "communities other than the Christian one" (presumably because of the intrinsic value of those communities) and "may need greater encouragement" for such involvement "than that found in wholesale denunciations of liberalism," which communitarians are often quick to provide.[37] They therefore are likely to seek some explanation of the fact that they often find themselves in moral agreement with non-Christians.

Fergusson explicitly rejects the appeal to natural law and orders of creation as a means of offering such explanation. In this rejection, he shows a sensitivity to communitarian concerns: "The arguments that have been rehearsed against liberal projects to establish the validity of moral principles independently of any particular tradition will also tend to destroy the more substantive and free-standing formulations of natural law theory or the doctrine of the orders of creation."[38] Therefore, in a move that eliminates any binding theological appropriation of the principles of discourse ethics, he acknowledges that there is "no free-standing natural theology governed by the presuppositions to which all rational inquirers can in principle give their assent."[39] At the same time, Fergusson has already set this discussion against the background of an extensive and sympathetic discussion of moral realism. He insists that his qualified defense of the ecclesial community in theological ethics does not involve any jettisoning of realism.[40]

Also in the background is a broadly defined Christian doctrine of providence, which is expressed in the "typical claim of the Christian tradition that God does not abandon the creation to the consequences of its worst excesses but is present, active and faithful to creatures beyond the domain of the church."[41] Indeed, Fergusson makes the obvious point that "without some such claim it becomes difficult to understand why or how common cause might be made with other forces, agencies and communities."[42]

With such concerns in place, he argues that even without a "free-standing" natural theology to resource such an approach, "it remains possible to offer a theology of nature which explains why moral perception and agreement can be found across traditions, cultures, and communities."[43] Such a theology is, for Fergusson, grounded in the "universal significance of God's action in Christ"[44] and can be viewed as a "theological expression of the commitment to ontological realism and epistemological contextualism." This position enables Fergusson to offer a theological rationale for Christians not only contributing to the common good, but also doing so in common cause with non-Christians. On this basis, it can be theologically possible for there to be "common moral ground in the absence of common theory."[45]

Clearly, Fergusson describes the Christian understanding of the common good with some very recognizable Reformed contours: the rejection of natural theology and/or natural law, the honoring of the state, and the appeal to a doctrine of providence (which is more fully and christologically developed through an explicit appeal to the "universal significance of God's action in Christ"). Yet I have a question to put to Fergusson's approach similar to the one I put to Gascoigne's. What is driving the explanation of common moral perception and agreement? Is it the "universal significance of God's action in Christ," or is it a prior commitment to moral realism? Even Fergusson's language invites comment: the appeal to God's action in Christ is a "theological expression" of a seemingly prior commitment to ontological realism. My concern is that by presenting the appeal to Christ's universal significance as an "expression" of ontological realism, Fergusson has also dented the primacy of the Christian community's own narrative as the foundation for engaging the common good.

Some Points of Comparison between Gascoigne and Fergusson

Obviously, some of the points of comparison have already been made obvious. Both writers are particularly concerned with avoiding ecclesial isolation. The arguments of both are sufficiently subtle to avoid any *simplistic* trading of commonality off against distinctiveness. There is no doubt that both writers seek to hold the two together. It is possible to see paradigmatic Catholic and Reformed attitudes to natural law working their way into the discussion about modern liberal ethics. In many ways, the lines drawn between these two approaches are rather fine, basically yielding to conventional Reformed-Catholic disagreements.[46] Nevertheless, this very distinction in relation to their respective assessments of the natural law tradition does make Fergusson more suspicious of modern liberal ethics than Gascoigne is. For similar reasons, Fergusson is more (albeit very cautiously) sensitive to the communitarian approach than Gascoigne. Indeed, I argue that Fergusson's proposal does offer some grounds for suggesting that a Reformed suspicion (as articulated by Mouw) of the natural law tradition might in its own way offer possibilities as a starting point for fruitful ethical reflection in contexts of radical pluralism. A strong adherence to natural law may actually force (as I fear it does in Gascoigne's account) levels of agreement and "stringent" demands for clear communication that risk skewing Christian ethical reflection. Fergusson demonstrates that, in the absence of common theory, common ground can be occupied and common causes undertaken.

What, then, of the question that I put to Fergusson's account? It certainly does not undermine his proposal. But it does raise the question of whether the appeal to the fact of Christ's work is sufficient to explain moral perception outside the church. My point is not at all that arguments for ontological realism should not supplement and help to interpret Christ's universal rule. Rather, in contrast to Fergusson's own formulation, I see ontological realism as an "expression" of Christ's universal rule. This brings me to the point of identifying how the church begins its ethical reflection, not least its reflection about the common good. In the end the church's commitment to the common good will not be sustained by separate theories of the common good; it will be stimulated and sustained by Christian people being formed by and in the conviction that God remains faithful to the whole creation. This brings me to the final section of my essay.

THE MORAL FORMATION OF SOCIALLY INVOLVED CHRISTIAN COMMUNITIES

The issue that emerges from the foregoing is that of how the contribution to the common good is related to the moral formation of the Christian community. It is my contention that commitment to the common good is not a special case or discrete area of ethical responsibility. It ought to be woven into the fabric of the Christian community's moral formation from which all its ethical activity and reflection flow. In proposing this view, I am suggesting that our continuity with the New Testament in moral matters lies not in the replication of all of its specific beliefs and practices but rather in sharing with them in the process of formation initiated by hearing and responding to the proclamation of Jesus' life, death, and resurrection.

Here I am appropriating some of the specific insights of Richard Hays's *The Moral Vision of the New Testament*. Employing a narrative approach to moral formation, Hays argues that the vision of the New Testament in moral matters is not limited to the explicit ethical teachings of its various documents. Rather, "the church's moral world is manifest not only in *didachē* but also in the stories, symbols, social structures, and practices that shape the community's ethos."[47] Obviously, however, the diversity of the New Testament means that alongside and emerging from its theological variety is a significantly differentiated moral vision. On the other hand, some measure of unity seems to be demanded if these texts are to be regarded as constitutive and not merely illustrative of Christian ethics.[48]

Nevertheless, says Hays, even within such constitutive unity certain tensions must be allowed to stand. For instance, in relation to the tension between Romans 13 and Revelation 13, Hays suggests that these two texts "are *not* two complementary expressions of a single principle or a single New Testament understanding of the state; rather, they represent radically different assessments of the relation of the Christian community to the Roman Empire."[49] These texts cannot, he continues, be "averaged out" in order for us to occupy some "middle position" that would "allow us to live comfortably as citizens of a modern democratic state."[50] Rather, "if these texts are allowed to have their say, they will force us either to choose between them or to reject the normative claims of both."[51] It is the latter option that Hays proposes: "Whatever synthetic account we give of the unity of the New Testament witnesses, it must be sufficiently capacious to recognize and encompass tensions of this kind."[52] In fact, however, by merely observing and honoring the "tensions" within the New Testament, Hays actually risks obscuring the fact that the New Testament communities are involved in a *process* of moral formation. Hays's suggestion leaves open the possibility that Romans 13 and Revelation 13 represent the poles of a static spectrum about "the state" in which contemporary reflection must work.

I suggest that the issue is somewhat more complicated than this, as is suggested by reflection on the "differences" between Galatians 3:26–29 and the hierarchical passages of, for instance, Colossians 3:18–4:1. If the latter is seen to be an exact mirror reflection of Roman domestic and social arrangements, then clearly the text hardly manifests a community fully exhibiting a penetrating gospel-driven moral formation. On the other hand, if, as is argued by some scholars, closer inspection of such passages reveals a subtle reordering of the Roman and domestic and social arrangements under the influence of the gospel, "then what we are witnessing in these texts is the criticism and gradual transformation from within of Jewish and pagan household ties in the light of Christ."[53] They do not, in other words, merely represent the poles of a tension that must be replicated in the contemporary church. Analogously, I suggest that the "differences" between Romans 13 and Revelation 13 do not reflect a perennial and defining tension about Christian attitudes to the state. Indeed, they could only be that if the "state" presented itself to Christian communities as a fixed and homogeneous object of inquiry. Rather, they suggest to us that the church's relationships to the structures and institutions of civil society were an object of diverse moral reflection in the light of Christ.[54] The contemporary church finds its continuity with the New Testament, therefore, through participating in an analogous process of moral reflection and formation as believers take their bearings in relationship to the various structures and institutions of civil society. Moreover, if Hays's proposal about the "constitutive" rather than "illustrative" status of the New Testament texts is to be given full weight (the weight it warrants being given, in my opinion), then the continuity with the New Testament communities will also lie in being formed by the moral vision of those communities.

Hays argues that that moral vision emerges from and is grounded in a sequence of three focal images: community, cross, and new creation. *Community* "points to the concrete social manifestation of the people of God," a people "called to embody an alternative order that stands as a sign of God's redemptive purposes for the world."[55] *Cross* refers to Jesus' death on the cross as being the "paradigm for faithfulness to God in the world."[56] Hays is not unaware that the cross has been used ideologically to "ensure the acquiescent suffering of the powerless," but he argues that the New Testament writers themselves "consistently employ the pattern of the cross precisely to call those who possess power and privilege to surrender it for the sake of the weak."[57] *New creation* refers to the eschatological framework in which the Christian community lives. It recognizes that since its own existence is to be understood as the appearance of the new creation, "all attempts to assert the qualified presence of the kingdom of God stand under the judgment of the eschatological reservation."[58]

This is not all. Hays goes a stage further: these three focal images belong, and make sense, in *this* sequence.

> By placing *community* first, we are constantly reminded that God's design of forming a covenant people long precedes the New Testament writings themselves, that the church stands in fundamental continuity with Israel. By placing *cross* in the middle, we are reminded that the death of Jesus is the climax and pivot-point of the eschatological drama. By placing *new creation* last, we are reminded that the church lives in expectation of God's future redemption of creation. In other words, the images are to be understood within a plot: they figure for the story of God's saving action in the world.[59]

With *these* foci set in *this* sequence, the Christian community will find itself oriented to the world beyond its walls in quite particular ways. If abstracted from this sequence, "community," "cross," and "new creation" could all form the Christian community in particular and strongly demarcated ways. Set in this sequence, however, the moral imagination formed by "community," "cross," and "new creation" is in one stroke oriented to the wider world. The church is indeed concrete and particular, but it is no longer discontinuous with that history of election in which the called community is to be a blessing to the whole world. The church is indeed cruciform in its life, but only as a witness to the pivotal event of God's self-giving for the whole world. The church indeed lives in hope, but given what it hopes for it cannot limit the realization of redemption to itself.

A church formed by *these* foci held together in *this* sequence will not treat the issue of the common good as an add-on to other (internal) dimensions of moral formation. Nor will it set such a commitment in antithetical tension with other tasks of the church (as, for instance, "evangelism" and "social justice" often are). With a moral imagination formed by *these* foci in *this* sequence, such a church would encounter the structures and institutions of society with responses ranging from critique, suspicion, and solidarity. Such responses would be held together not by a range, even a tension-filled range, of New Testament teachings on "the state," or on theological appropriations or rejections of "natural law," but on the plot of the New Testament teachings about the status and form of the church in the wider purposes of God. None of this would deny the importance of the kind of theoretical work carried out by Gascoigne and Fergusson. Indeed, such theoretical work could itself be seen as a particular instance of moral formation as Christian theoreticians encounter and then "transform and criticize from within" the world of ideas "in the light of Christ."

No doubt, a critical response to this proposal could well be that I have simply repeated the Reformed tradition's rejection of, or suspicion toward, natural law as a framework for thinking about Christian social involvement. Nevertheless, I argue that the approach taken here challenges *both* the respective proposals of Gascoigne and Fergusson. The *sequence* of the New Testament focal images suggests that the work done by "natural law" and "ontological realism" in Fergusson might be better framed in terms of God's faithfulness. The world may not understand this language (as per Gascoigne's fear), but it is this language that will be heard by Christians as integrally related to the narratives of Jesus' life, death, and resurrection, and therefore more directly formative of their moral imagination.[60] At the same time, the *particular focal images* define God's faithfulness not in terms of some generic appeal to providence (as it risks being done in both Calvin and Fergusson) but in terms of the specific narratives of Jesus' life, death, and resurrection. It is true that Fergusson certainly seeks to render something more than a generic appeal to providence as the basis for making common cause with non-Christians. He appeals to Trinitarian doctrine to propose an understanding of the rule and presence of Christ beyond the church. Yet on closer inspection this apparently more doctrinally complex approach still yields an affirmation of the *fact* of Christ's presence outside the church, not its form nor its status in relation to the church. The focal images of the New Testament narration of Jesus' life, death, and resurrection offer a thicker description of both the form and function of the church. In summary, therefore, Christian ethical distinctiveness need not be traded off against a Christian commitment to the common good. The possibility of both features is grounded in the narratives of the New Testament and in their formation of the moral imagination of contemporary Christian communities. This approach may well be more "Reformed" in its insistence on starting with Scripture and "the world" of the church's own text, but it also suggests a way into the debate not constrained by conventional debates about "natural law." Discussions about moral theory are not resisted but are relativized to, and seen to belong within, a wider ecclesial process of moral formation.[61]

Chapter 11

The Reformed Church and the Environmental Crises

JONG-HYUK KIM

INTRODUCTION

In this essay the Reformed church's faith and lifestyles are elaborated as a way of remediation for the current environmental crises. The status of present environmental crises threatens not only the lives of human and nonhuman beings, but also the very life-carrying ecosystem itself. In short, the current staggering environmental crises have resulted from a series of incoherent lifestyles and activities committed by all human beings. The resulting incoherent activities have, in turn, interacted, compounded, and accumulated as the phenomena of pollution in the ecosystem. It is like aged sick persons whose ailments have been the result of their lifelong lifestyle, eating habit, intrinsic physical condition, locality of hometown, kind of vocation, and so on. Likewise, the present worldwide environmental crises are the result of every human being's lifelong activities in the world of nature as a resident of Earth.

It is absolutely impossible for us to locate one single cause for complex and cumulative phenomena like the environmental crises. However, from the discussion above, we can briefly surmise that the phenomena of pollution and thus the environmental crises can be understood as a kind of revelation or disclosure.

The scope and level of the phenomena of environmental crises indirectly disclose some of the fundamental mistakes and errors that we human beings have committed against the ecosystem and the earth environment. The phenomenon of pollution reveals that human beings individually and collectively have persistently engaged for a long duration in the one-sided exploitation of the world of nature. Human beings, even in their innocent but basically incoherent lifestyles and activities, have disrupted the delicately balanced organic system of the world of nature. Also, those incoherent elements locally and innocently produced by human beings have gradually accumulated and interacted, and in turn they have generated a chimera, a third generation of pollutants, which we do not know how to manage.

Thus we cannot single out a particular country, lifestyle of a nation, or scientific culture and blame only its wrongdoings for contributing to the phenomena of the environmental crises. The phenomena of pollution have resulted from the life-related activities of all human beings who have inhabited this fragile and delicately balanced ecosystem ever since the formation of Earth. The ultimate scope and universal level of the ecosystem's crises reveal them to be basically a multilateral question involving not only human beings but also the creation itself. Therefore it is a question for religion. It is a question of beliefs and values of human beings' hearts and minds. It is a question of the creation itself.

In this study I elaborate on the nature of the delicately balanced organism of the world of nature, the ecosystem, and the generation of incoherent elements known as pollutants in the world of nature. In conclusion, I advocate the importance of the Reformed church's faith and lifestyles of the Christian community for remediating the environmental crises. Here the terms of the Reformed church's faith have largely the connotation of biblical faith.

To respond properly to the environmental crises, we need to go back to the biblical descriptions of creation and redemption. Also, to comprehend the genesis of the phenomena of pollution, we have to reflect closely upon the biblically elaborated story of the fall of human beings. By studying the passages about human beings' fall, we might understand that in every process of creation or ordering, there is also an accompanying element of disorder or chaos in it. And somehow we human beings thus far have never succeeded in avoiding the elements of disorder creatively in the daily activities of our lives. We can see that the accumulation of disordered edges have reached the point of presenting nearly insurmountable crises in the environment of our lives.

THE DELICATELY EQUILIBRATED AND AUTONOMOUS ECOSYSTEM

Here are a few typical and exemplary phenomena of nature to demonstrate the autonomous structure of the ecosystem.

It has long been known that the constitution of the air is approximately 78% nitrogen and 21% oxygen. However, out of this amount of oxygen, approximately 7.6 mg (milligrams) of oxygen is dissoluble in every liter of water. The minimum oxygen requirements for living species in the water to breathe are 5 mg of oxygen per liter of water. Thus, if we assume that our air were to consist only of 10% oxygen, the resulting dissolved amount of oxygen in the water would be less than 3.8 mg per liter, and the lives of the living species in water would be greatly endangered. However, if we raise the amount of oxygen in the air to 40% for the benefit of aqueous species, then the ecosystem would be prone to very hazardous fires. In this sense we are fortunate that we have such a delicate and balanced environment for the lives of all living species, including human beings.

The amount of oxygen in our environment is provided by the process of photosynthesis in plants, including the green leaves of trees. Thus we are told that the primeval forests in the Amazon River basin provide 15% of the oxygen in the ecosystem. However, the most dramatic provision of oxygen is the nearly 40% of oxygen for the earthly environment produced through photosynthesis by the numerous microplankton, which stay near the surface of seawater for the sake of incoming sunrays. Plankton are essential for small fish to eat. Who would dare think that these hardly visible, fine, and delicate microplankton play such a major role in providing oxygen for the entire ecosystem?

However, such plankton are adversely affected when we cover the sea's surface with crude oil and constantly contaminate our body's waters by dumping chemically polluted wastewater into them. The oceans are vast (71% of Earth's surface), but when we pollute an ocean's active zones or surfaces, we actually pollute the entire ocean.

If we compare the subtleness of all components of the ecosystem, water will probably rank first. Water is not only the most abundant but also the most plain and nontoxic substance among all parts of the entire ecological system. Due to its versatile structure and according to ambient condition changes, it can freely transform into solid ice, liquid water, and gaseous vapor. Within a single state such as solid or liquid, water has various substructures. For instance, water can consist of fragmented and dispersed single water molecules, clusters, or hexagonal structures. It is known that appropriate concentrated clusters of water molecules contribute to the longevity of the residents who drink such water. And it is also known that water having a hexagonal molecular structure plays a role as a soothing agent for internal injuries that can develop into further disease. The versatile molecular structures of water can be mobilized into an activated state so that we can use such water for washing clothes without requiring detergents. Also, water can be encoded with information because of these complex molecular structures.

Because of water's unusual characteristic of maintaining its highest density near (at 4 degrees C) its freezing point, the water in rivers and lakes does not freeze all the way to the bottom and thus the fish and other living species in the water are able to survive safely during the cold winters. In addition, water can protect against drastic temperature change between daytime and nighttime by absorbing and retaining heat during the day. Water can also be carried deeper inland by way of rain and thus can protect lands from becoming deserts. Among other subtle characteristics of water is its sensitivity and response to gravity. Because of that, we rely on water streams for generating energy by hydroelectric power plants. However, by the same gravitational sensitivity of water, we pollute the life-carrying water of our oceans by the unintended diverse daily acts of contamination of local rivers and streams through production activities of factory work, chemical cultivation of farmland, automobile washing, sewerage, canalling, spreading of rock salts on snowy days, and so on.

THE VIOLENT MODE OF MODERN PRODUCTION TECHNOLOGY

In the early stages of our exploration of atomic energy, we were greatly heartened at the possibility of having an unlimited amount of clean energy. This was particularly seen when considering that one gram of uranium can generate energy equivalent to the energy produced by burning thirty tons of coal, an activity creating dust and producing the sulfuric gases responsible for acid rain. However, up to this very moment we do not have any complete answers for the problems of persistent radiation and thermal pollution from generated radioactive substances. We can barely harness reactor systems and radioactive substances. Nuclear reactors can erupt at any time like Mount St. Helens, generating radioactive rays and heat, due to the activity of earthquakes, or overheating within the reactor itself through a defect of the cooling system, which would cause a return to chaotic and desolate states.

In order to improve quantities and qualities of such products as fruits, corn, wheat, potatoes, flowers, domestic fowl, livestock, and fish, a series of modern life-science technologies have been actively sought and developed. Among these modern technologies, two areas are briefly summarized here. The first is cell fusion technology, which involves two different kinds of cells. For instance, a cell is taken from a tomato and another is taken from a potato, each inherently containing the characteristics of the tomato and potato, respectively. The two cells are directly docked together through the employment of chemical bonding agents such PEG (polyethylene glycol), which allows a hybrid cell to be formed. Because of such technologies we are able to produce a hybrid plant that yields tomatoes in the branches and potatoes in the roots.

The second technology is that of nuclear transplantation. This is known as cloning technology and involves a receiver and a donor. An egg cell as a receiver has its nucleus removed through irradiating ultraviolet rays and instead receives a nucleus from the donor; then a series of processes for preparing the nuclear transplanted embryo for further development are completed. By cloning technology we are able to multiply a given species.

Human beings have devised and employed technology to respond to their societal demands. Therefore, the technological endeavors are meant to achieve freedom from social restrictions and limitations such as food shortages, rampaging epidemics and diseases, energy requirements for extreme climatic changes, impediments to long-distance transportation and communication, and so on. However, despite such well-intentioned efforts for societal reasons, these modern technologies have caused problems for the entire family of ecosystems. The two modern scientific technologies mentioned above weaken the interrelations among structures and in the end destroy entire structures of the ecosystem. Cell fusion technology tries qualitatively to improve a biological species to enhance human societal conditions by eugenically combining the desired elements to form a kind of chimera. Such chimeras are not known to exist naturally except in a few instances and with limited capabilities, such as the donkey, which is not capable of natural reproduction. Nuclear transplantation technology tries quantitatively to improve human beings' societal condition by duplicating desired elements of certain biological species in potentially unlimited quantities. While cell fusion technology combines and thus reduces the uniqueness of species, the latter technology exaggerates the presence of particular species, thereby potentially disrupting the balance of the ecosystem.

Likewise, when we constantly apply chemical fertilizers on farmland to increase the harvests, the end result will be self-defeating due to the deterioration of the soil structure because of the induced chemical fertilizers. The farmland to which chemical fertilizer is applied constantly becomes acidified, weakening the spontaneous and naturally self-supporting capacity of the land, thereby more than ever increasing the dependence upon the chemical fertilizers. In such a barren situation, we cannot ultimately expect healthy crops, fruits, or vegetables. If we human beings take nutritiously barren foods, our health will in turn become barren. In our living situation we find wrong use of all kinds of addictive phenomena, originating from drinking, smoking, coffee, drugs, gambling, work, sex, or even religion: the end result is similar. The addicts will lose their natural, self-supporting capacities and will be unable to perform reasoned thinking, sound judgment, effective speech, or self-determined actions, which will lead addicts to rely on increased use of the addictive substance. In so doing, ordered systems and structures become disordered via the induced energy from without, whether the form of energy be an elaborate tool like modern technology, chemical fertilizer, drugs, alcohol, coffee, gambling, work, or a conviction or an ideology.

THE GENESIS OF CUMULATIVE AND COMPLEX PHENOMENA OF DISORDER

The elementary causes of the environmental crises are, as shown above, partly due to the nature of industrial production techniques and tools. The crises are also due to the one-sided and objective ways of using the tools by human beings.

However, in the twentieth and twenty-first centuries the environmental crises have been radicalized, and the rate of the ecosystem's degradation has been exponentially accelerated by population growth, the decline of natural resources, and the introduction of violent, high-energy-oriented production technology. The pollution of Earth's environment and the acceleration of the rate of ecological crises cannot have resulted from mere misuse of the techniques and a certain particular mind-set of the users of the technologies. The ultimate scope and the universal level of the ecological crises suggest that the environmental crises are the outcome of an all-out battle between humankind and the world of nature, like the battle of Armageddon. Because of the extent and the destructive nature of the battle, there will be no winner in this confrontation, contrary to Darwin's anticipation.

In the areas of physics and chemistry we find the common subject of thermodynamics or the science of energy. Entropy is a concept for measuring the disorder of a system. In short, the greater the degree of disorder in a system, the higher the value of entropy. If a physical system, for example, is subjected to an elevated temperature, the molecular structure of the system becomes disordered. In general the more we put energy or unfamiliar or foreign chemicals into the system, the more the internal structure of the system becomes disordered or disrupted. This can be conjectured as the reason for the deterioration of the environment and ecosystem as well. Thus in our time the ecosystem has more quickly and severely deteriorated through the introduction of more energy and chemicals by the more energy-intensive and chemical-dependent modern industrial technologies. The weakened ecosystem, like a senior patient whose symptoms frequently become aggravated into complications induced by the very act of treatment, has become more destabilized by the very act of remedy offered by modern technological activities. The aggravation of the disorder or deterioration of the ecosystem develops precisely because the ecosystem has a limited or closed structural system. In a practical sense the total energy of Earth in terms of natural resources is limited. Rifkin and Howard have emphasized:

> As entropy increases, then, that means a decrease in "available" energy. Every time something occurs in the natural world, some amount of energy ends up being unavailable for future work. That unavailable energy is what pollution is all about. Many people think that pollution is a by-product of production. In fact, pollution is the sum total of all of the available energy in the world that has been transformed into unavailable energy. Waste, then, is dissipated energy. Since according to the first law [of thermodynamics,] energy can neither be created nor destroyed but only transformed, and since according to the second law it can only be transformed one way—toward a dissipated state—pollution is just another name for entropy; that is, it represents a measure of the unavailable energy present in a system.[1]

In the temptation story in Genesis 3:1–7, we encounter the story of the fall of the first human beings. They became fallen because they were not able to resist the temptation contrived by the crafty serpent. The serpent presented Eve and Adam with the one of most fundamental issues that threatens the desire for the human being's survival. So the tempter began by saying to her (and him), "Did God say, 'You shall not eat from any tree in the garden?'" The tempter then continuously insinuated to her every human being's desire, which is the state of "not dying" and having abundant life. However, the most fatal and thus most original sin among all the sins was that the serpent had contrived to convince the human species that they can competently solve their desires by themselves in the realm of the created without consulting the Lord God. The suggestion made to the first human beings by the tempter was absolutely a bad scheme.

In the created world of nature considered without any awareness of God's sovereign care, there is an interrelated system or network that is prone to degradation by any of a number of local or minor disturbances. Hendry indicates that in the event of the fall, humanity "is offered the chance to exchange . . . freedom for God for freedom from God."[2] One of the world's renowned ecologists, Barry Commoner, has eloquently described the structural system of the world of nature in terms of "laws of ecology." Commoner indicates that four laws are operating in the world of nature, three of which are very much related to our discussion: the first law of ecology is that everything is connected to everything else; the second law is that everything must go somewhere; and thus Commoner stresses in his fourth law that "there is no such thing as a free lunch" in the structured system of the world of nature. Commoner's third law asserts that nature knows best: it is his conviction that even if a technology were to be developed with the intention of improving nature, then such change in due course will most 'likely to be detrimental to that [natural] system."[3]

The absence of human beings' freedom in the world of nature can be observed in the following instances. We employ industrial production technology for societal reasons. For instance, there will be a situation of an increased demand for the food with the increased population. Thus the increased demand for food should expand the farming industry. Then the expanded farming industry in turn demands expanded farmlands, more mechanized machines, fuels, fertilizers and herbicides, and so on. Like the ecosystem or an ailing person, human society has a structural system in which each part is related to the rest of the parts, and thus it is more prone to the aggravation of symptoms by induced complications from without. So in a given system, any remedial effort by a certain part for a given problem tends to always generate another new problem in the rest of the system.[4]

Before the first Industrial Revolution in the eighteenth century, the phenomenon of environmental pollution was regional. However, in the twentieth century these regional environmental crises reached a critical point and became pervasive and universal in scope. Under the globalized phenomena of pollution, every member of the ecosystem is now subjected directly to the corrupting power of technology. From this critical juncture, all participants in the interrelated ecosystem—such as the ocean waters, air, soil of the land, climate, and the human and nonhuman species—are completely affected by the deteriorating power, and thus no partial or temporary remedial program known to us is suitable to resolve these universal crises.

THE REFORMED CHURCH'S FAITH AND THE ENVIRONMENTAL CRISES

To respond properly to the pervasive status of the environmental crises in our time, we indeed need to return to the saving faith of the Reformed church. The concepts of faith and conviction frequently are understood as subjective power and dominant authority. We are in need of strength to endure the rampant corrupting power that deteriorates the ecosystem, as shown in the foregoing discussion. However, if our response to the environmental crisis is with strong dominating power and intentional measures, using modern high energy-intensive technology, in the end we will be confronted with nothing less than a greatly aggravated state of deterioration. The reason for such a negative prognosis is that the world has become a battlefield between the unquenchable societal desire of human beings and the limited and structured ecosystem of the world of nature. This war has continued ever since the fall of the first human beings in the garden of Eden. From the 1980s onward, however, with the globalization of the economic and industrial activities of human societies, the war has become global. The present human condition is indeed very close to the vision of the world of nature that was depicted by Paul a long time ago.

> For creation waits with eager longing for the revealing of the children of God; for the creation was subjected to futility, not of its own will but by the will of the one who subjected it, in hope that creation itself will be set free from its bondage to decay and will obtain the freedom of the glory of the children of God. We know that the whole creation has been groaning in labor pains until now; and not only the creation, but we ourselves . . . groan inwardly . . . for . . . the redemption of our bodies. (Rom. 8:19–23 NRSV)

One of the perennial issues that we have repeatedly confronted in our study is the nothingness of freedom or the "does not exist" situation of liberty for human beings in human society and the ecosystem in the world of nature. In the event of the fall, our first human beings stumbled by ignoring the "does not exist" sign that was put in the middle of Eden, and we are still repeating the same mistakes by evading the signs that were put in the middle of modern human societies and of the ecosystem.

According to the indications of Paul, we human beings have been granted the opportunity of obtaining freedom by becoming the children of God. In the Greek usage of the New Testament, this concept is expressed with *teknon*, which means "child" (or *tekna*, "children") in relation to the parents or family. Thus the term "the children of God" has this relational context. Redeemed, we become the children of God (Rom. 8:16). Thus one cannot understand an individual apart from understanding the family in which one holds membership. And also in Matthew 18:2–4, the children's unhesitating and immediate response to Jesus' call is quite contrary to the attitudes of the first human beings, who were afraid of the Lord God and hid from God in the event of the fall.[5]

Therefore, the only way that human beings can become truly free persons is by being the children of God. With the granted freedom and liberty, for the first time in human history, we can be liberated from bondage to decay and are able to respond coherently and comprehensively to the environment and ecosystem of Earth without disturbance and without the generation of incoherent elements.

However, in order to have further understanding of the notion of becoming the children of God, we may have to go on the scriptural descriptions about the event of Jesus' temptation by Satan in Matthew 4:1–11 and Luke 4:1–12. In these passages Jesus strongly emphasizes that "one does not live by bread alone, but by every word that comes from the mouth of God" (Matt. 4:4). In the context of Jesus' temptation the issue of human beings' desire for eternal living comes up once again. And Jesus responds decisively with a complete answer to the tempter. However, in the instance of the temptation of the first human beings, they ignored the importance of and evaded the word of God for their survival and freedom.

God's word is the power by which the universe was brought into existence. It is by the word of God that God expresses his presence with his people. Thus the word of God cannot be separated from God's personal presence and his power. As the word of God, Jesus was incarnated to "save his people from their sins" (Matt. 1:21). Also, Jesus as the word of God incarnated (John 1:14) was to be "God with us" (Matt. 1:23 RSV). Therefore the word of God is the only source of power or energy that makes it possible to regenerate the degraded environment and recuperate the weakened structure of the ecosystem.

The word of God is the only source of freedom that enables human beings to participate in the most comprehensive and redemptive manner in the process of re-creating the first creation, which has been in bondage to the forces of decay and futility ever since the fall of the first human beings.

In this way we now can see that the only way of restoring the creator God's degraded creation is through God's own initiated reconciliation, to himself, of the estranged creation as indicated by Paul:

> So if anyone is in Christ, there is a new creation: everything old has passed away; see, everything has become new! All this is from God, who reconciled us to himself through Christ, and has given us the ministry of reconciliation; that is, in Christ God was reconciling the world to himself, not counting their trespasses against them, and entrusting the message of reconciliation to us. So we are ambassadors for Christ, since God is making his appeal through us; we entreat you on behalf of Christ, be reconciled to God. (2 Cor. 5:17–20 NRSV)

The estrangement of human beings and the rest of creation from the creator God has been the case ever since the fall of the first human beings in the garden of Eden. Under this condition of estrangement from God, human beings and the rest of creation can only perform one thing: the aggravation of the crises within creation. This is because, as we have observed through Commoner's laws of ecology, one of the most characteristic phenomena of the ecosystem is that everything is connected to everything else. Therefore, maintenance of the ecosystem's function is possible precisely through the elaborate and multiple interconnectedness of participants of the system. So even a single momentary incoherent act that causes estrangement will in the end be a crucial problem for the whole ecosystem. Furthermore, because of the structurally closed or confined and systemic nature of human society and the ecosystem, no human action is free from distorting the ecosystem and aggravating the environmental crises. With the structurally confined human society and world of nature, no human being and no institution is infallible or irreformable or has absolute authority.[6] Thus, as fallen human beings, it is absolutely impossible for us to engage in the work of reconciliation. As Paul stressed, the reconciliation can only be done by God in Christ. The reconciliation is the work of God in Christ Jesus and done for God. Therefore, here the term reconciliation does not merely have the meaning of reconciliation between ourselves and an estranged neighbor or friend, through a persuasive dialogue or an apology. The estrangement that Paul is mentioning is the estrangement from God, and it reflects the sinful status of the fallen human beings and the rest of creation. Human beings are not the only species that are estranged from God. According to Paul the world and the rest of the creation are also estranged from God (perhaps exemplified via tragic natural catastrophic events in the form of earthquakes and tsunamis, such as in the Indian Ocean on December 26, 2004). Thus reconciliation as God's work of redemption in Christ recovers God's relationship not only with men and women, delivering them from their sinful status, but also with the rest of creation, freeing it from its futility and decay.

Therefore, through God's reconciliation work in Christ, human beings and the rest of creation "have become new," with restored relationship with God; hence, it "is a new creation" (2 Cor. 5:17). Redeemed human beings will be given a place in the family of God, becoming the children of God. Only as this happens will the degraded creation—human beings and the rest of creation—be fundamentally and completely restored from the fallen condition and be put into personal relationship with God. Thus the crises cannot be resolved completely by any known social, cultural, political, or ethical crash program, and thus any such approach may well only delay the resolution. So many contingent factors—political, economic, self-interest—can be at work and are always liable to compromise the best of ecological intentions.

Our environmental problem has originated from structural distortion. Yet in the nascent state the problem seemed to begin by a momentarily committed transgression by a particular person in a particular place (Gen. 3). The environmental crisis ironically is not only a crisis of the environment. It is deeply rooted in fallen humankind and creation. Therefore human beings and the rest of the creation have transgressed the word of the creator God, and crises of the environment and the ecosystem are the outcome. The following theological argument can be made: All of our suffering from the environmental crises and its ramifications are the consequences of our transgressions of the word of God. As the fallen race, we human beings are so completely oriented by our self-centered desire and will that we can hardly find any alternative route in this hardened human condition and will continue repeating the act of transgression of the word of God, just as the first human beings did.

Paul declares that all works of reconciliation have come from God. He also admonishes that we have been given "the ministry of reconciliation" and entrusted with "the message of reconciliation" by God (2 Cor. 5:18–19). One of the most important tasks for the Christian church: witnessing to the message, which is the work of explaining reconciliation as the basic process for restoring fallen or alienated human beings and the rest of the creation back into relationship with God. To bear witness to a message or a fact, one should have firsthand experience and familiar knowledge of the message or fact. Therefore, for us to fulfill the task of witnessing to the message of reconciliation, we ourselves should possess some experience or intimation of comprehension of God's work of reconciliation. This can be done with hermeneutical work on the notion of reconciliation. In order to do so, we have to go back to the instance of the first human beings' fall in the garden of Eden.

Two of the most deeply cherished doctrines of the Reformed church tradition are the notions of the sovereignty of God and the grace of God. Through these theological themes of the Reformed church, we can understand the meaning of Paul's statements about all works of reconciliation having come from God and also that creation itself is made by God and has come from God as the gift of God. Thus far, since the fall of the first human beings, we human beings on our own have not been able to see creation as God's gift. Pressed by deterioration of the ecosystem, we have begun to think of an alternative way of approaching creation. And thus we begin to see creation as the gift of the creator God. At this moment it would be very helpful for us to consider the statements made by Don Postema about the characteristics of gratitude for a gift that is circular or spiral in nature:

> Gratitude recognizes that a gift has been given, a favor has been done by someone. There is a gift and a giver. But there is more. Gratitude also calls for a response to that gift. We thank the giver with an expression of appreciation—a handshake, a hug, a note. A gesture of gratitude completes the exchange, closes the circle, lets the love flow back to the giver. I (still) remember bringing a gift to a birthday party when I was a child. The birthday child met me at the door, grabbed the gift without a thank-you, ran into the room, and threw it among all the other gifts. . . . The gesture of thanks moves both the giver and receiver to another level. It expresses a unity; it solidifies a relationship. We start out with a giver, a gift, and a

receiver, and we arrive at the embrace of thanks. Thanks is expressed and then accepted by the giver. And in the final kiss of gratitude it's impossible to distinguish the giver from the receiver.[7]

Likewise the creation made by God in Christ has to be received by human beings with gratitude and appreciation because it is the gift of the Creator. As Postema indicates, with gratitude we can go closely to the Creator instead of hiding. With appreciation we respond gracefully and with caring minds to God's creation, allowing us to move to another level in which the entire creation can express the reconciled status between the Creator and creation. Therefore, through the human perceiver's appreciative response or answer to creation as to an art object, creation can be actualized as God's work of art.[8]

However, with the first human beings, exactly the opposite occurred. They did not come near with attitudes of gratitude and appreciation to the Creator, and thus they have fallen from the status of children of God. The fallen and estranged human beings cannot imagine and see creation from the aspect of God's grace and gift. And with creation estranged from God's care, creation itself has been in bondage to decay ever since the instance of the fall.

For the ministry of reconciliation and to be the witnessing community, the Christian church should be well versed in the notion of the personhood of Christ. Paul repeatedly stressed that "God . . . reconciled us to himself through Christ, and . . . in Christ God was reconciling the world to himself" (2 Cor. 5:18–19). The notion of "person" in the Greek term *hypostasis* has been interpreted as "a particular embodiment of certain qualities"; thus a "person" is an "individual being."[9] As with God the Father and God the Son, the Holy Spirit has never been mentioned in the Scriptures as an impersonal substance or principle. When we try to consider the Holy Spirit as an impersonal principle, we may implicitly exercise our power and domination over the Holy Spirit. In God's graceful creation and redemptive works, each of the three persons of the Trinity has participated in a distinctive way; also for Jesus' life of incarnation, the notion of person is significantly involved. In and through the person of Jesus, God has disclosed his love, grace, and care in creating the universe and redeeming fallen creation. With the idea of the person, God internalizes all of his works and actions within his own being.

God created his universe through his Word, and he has redeemed fallen creation in and through the same Word, God the Son. Thus God created the universe and redeemed fallen humanity in and through Jesus Christ. Therefore the work of God's creation cannot be separated from Christ's work of salvation. Thus we can understand that God created the universe in order to redeem it. And God in Christ redeemed the universe to complete his good creation. In this way we not only cannot separate the work of creation from the work of redemption, but also we cannot separate the two works from the person of Christ Jesus. The creator God has become the redeemer of creation in the person of Christ. In this way the Creator's work became one with the works of Christ Jesus. Thus

Paul was able to say that "in Christ God was reconciling the world to himself, not counting their trespasses against them" (1 Cor. 5:19).

Since the Holy Spirit is the community-creating Spirit, the gifts of the Holy Spirit to individuals are also meant to be used for the benefit and the service of the community as a whole (1 Cor. 12:7). Therefore the Holy Spirit is the Lord of the community, and his presence and activity are for the life of the community. Because of this nature of community creation, we need to trust the Holy Spirit to deter the power of community destruction (Rom. 8:20). The structure of nature's ecosystem is an organic one in which numerous members are assembled in a delicately balanced way. Certain members of the ecosystem have life, such as the various biological species, and others without life are inorganic substances, such as rocks and stones. Thus the communal nature of the ecosystem inevitably demands a variety of responses from human beings. From the ambient conditions, each member of the ecosystem is different by species or region.

Paul compared the church to the body of Christ, which has many different members. Each member has been given a specific ability for communal service. In the community each member has been equipped with a specific function. In cooperating, the community as a whole is to perform with a synchronized response to a given situation. In Jesus' life, the incarnation, divine nature, and human nature are inseparably joined together in one person. By being such a unique person, Jesus has been able most effectively to perform his mediatory ministry in the complex human world. For him, the uniting factor of the two natures was not in natural union but in the person of Christ.[10]

In the person of Jesus Christ, the two completely different natures of the divine and the human are uniquely joined. And thus Jesus, by being a living community in his person, was able to perform his mediatory ministry effectively in the world. When we perform our ministry as members of a Christian community, if the community is united in a natural or mechanical mode and not in the person of Jesus Christ, our ministry of mediation cannot be expected to be effective.

One of the most distinguished examples of self-reformation can be found in the Nazarene Jesus' life of incarnation. To be an effective reconciler, Jesus has had to belong to two parties needing to be reconciled, a friend to both God and human beings. Jesus displayed the distinct role in and through his person as the uniting factor in his life of incarnation, in which "Christ, being in the form of God, took the form of a servant, not in order to cease to be God, but in order to be God in human form."[11] In his person as the Son of God, Christ "chose to become man, and so to be God as man, living his life under the conditions of human life." In this way Jesus as both "God and man must be able to deal with man on behalf of God and with God on behalf of man."[12]

With the Trinitarian mode of redemptive work, God demonstrates his love and grace most effectively toward fallen humanity in and through three persons in the Trinity. In his creation and redemption, God has to remake his decision without rest and with suffering and self-denying love for each different circumstance. By bringing this difficult decision making and love into his person, God is able to demonstrate his love and grace most effectively toward human beings and creation. Because of the lack of such love and care in their response to the creation, human beings have brought about unprecedented crises in the world of nature. Hannah Arendt has lamented these circumstances: "Instead of objective qualities, . . . we find instruments, and instead of nature or the universe, . . . [modern] man encounters only himself" in the world of nature.[13]

To participate in the ministry of reconciliation with Christ, the Christian church should also share the burdens of the deteriorated ecosystem. Members of the Christian community should also live their lives with patience and endurance in the deteriorated condition of the ecosystem. However, the lives of Christians need to be lives embodied into the person of Christ and not simply lived out as individual persons. A life in the person of Christ Jesus means that we live and perform our lives in the saving faith in Christ. Without the saving faith in Christ, the community's life will be exactly like the lives of the estranged ones. The Christian church as the body of Christ subsists by the energy that is derived from the person of Christ (Eph. 5:25). Without the ceaseless supply of transcendental power from the person of Christ, this creation cannot be restored from its degraded and weakened state.

CONCLUSIONS

1. The most fundamental cause for the crises of the environment and the ecosystem is the estrangement of creation from God the creator, which was initiated by the fall of the first human beings in the garden of Eden.

2. To be a mediatory ministry for the estranged creation, the Christian community should first have a completely new style of life by being united with Christ through the work of the Holy Spirit (Rom. 6:5). The new style of life that the community cherishes does not, for its subsistence, completely depend upon energies that are mostly mechanically extracted from the world of nature.

3. The new style of life does not perform according to the exclusive authority and conviction derived from structured, systemic, and societal reasons alone.

4. The new style of life does not at will produce incoherent elements in the ecosphere and in the ambient environment with the spirit of "survival of the fittest."

5. The new style of life regards creation as a gift, responds with gratitude and praise to God, and participates in the created objects to actualize creation as his "very good" work of art.

6. The new style of life considers that "the world of nature requires care as a part of the care of the human" and "the purpose of the human is not competitive success but the achievement of that relation in which the Trinity can be manifest. By this means alone the Kingdom of God will come into being."[14]

7. With the inherent endurance of suffering involved, the ministry of reconciliation of the Christian community is redemptive but creative through the life of forgiveness.

8. In this way the church in Christ overcomes rejection by accepting it and achieves victory by submitting to defeat.[15]

9. The mission of each Christian community should always remain as the mission of God in Christ. Therefore the church's ministry should always be communal, yet specific and timely, one that is predescribed as "once for all" from the eternity in the Trinity of God.

10. Without having been reconciled or united with Christ, human beings' remedial action for the crises of the environment will always be partial and precarious and in turn will mostly enhance the disorder in the ecosphere.

11. Therefore the Christian community should always hold on to the Lord Jesus Christ because all work of reconciliation "is from God" in Christ and the Holy Spirit. In this sense the Christian church "is called to do no less, and no more, than to bear witness to what God has done and is doing to renew creation."[16]

12. To be an effective witnessing community, the Christian church should continuously be in prayer, "consent to become anonymous" or transformed, and depend upon the grace of the Lord Jesus and the work of the Holy Spirit.

13. This study concludes by quoting Cochrane's statement of reasons for the decline of the Roman Empire. Likewise, the reason that restorative efforts for the environmental crises "thus far have been retarded is due . . . solely to the blind and obstinate resistance of [hu]mankind."[17]

Chapter 12

Reformed Resources for Practical Theology
The Christian Life and Consumer Capitalism

CAMERON MURCHISON

The question of how Reformed theology might specifically engage practical theology comes to important expression at the intersection of the life of faith with life in any economic order. The conversation largely stimulated by Max Weber's *The Protestant Ethic and the Spirit of Capitalism*[1] provides ample evidence that the Reformed theological tradition has the possibility of bringing profound practical consequences, psychological, social, and thus economic. Notwithstanding vigorous contention about exactly what these consequences may be and how unique they in fact are,[2] some significant consequences stemming from Reformed theology in a capitalist economic order seem inescapable.

This essay is not the same as a developed, practical theology. Economic consequences flowing from dispositions, behaviors, and practices, nurtured by certain theological convictions, do not constitute an explicit practical theology. (At most they might be said to comprise an *implicit* practical theology.) Rather, practical theology can properly be said to be at work when theological convictions are consciously affirmed as disclosing the truth of God's way in the world, thus providing practical directives or guidelines for the conduct of faithful Christian life in particular human endeavors.

One of the obstacles to the development of a practical theology concerning faithful Christian life in the economic domain has been the tendency since the Enlightenment to differentiate between the private and public realms, limiting the accepted reach of theology to the private sector.[3] The effect of this has been effectively to forestall the development of an explicit practical theology for faithful Christian life in the economic sphere (since economics is par excellence about the public realm). One ironic result has been that while such explicit practical theology was ruled out in spheres of Enlightenment influence, its implicit form was being analyzed for all manner of practical consequences in the economic order.

In the effort toward identifying Reformed resources for practical theology, it is instructive to pause over this irony. A first step is to trace some of the implicit developments arising from Reformed theological understandings in the progress of capitalism. A second step is to examine more explicit attempts to frame Reformed theological claims as disclosive of how God would have Christians live faithfully in the economic order of capitalism, both historically and contemporarily.

At least for a casual reader of Weber, the general thesis that certain attitudes and habits engendered by Calvinism contributed to the development of capital has a certain cogency. That is, Calvin's emphasis on industry and frugality,[4] when translated to broad reaches of society, inevitably would have consequences for capital accumulation, providing the launching pad for capitalist production. "The rigid limitations on consumption on the one hand and the methodical intensification of production on the other could have but one result—the accumulation of capital."[5] As long as the basic economic issue is production, the Calvinist legacy for the economy is supportive and nurturing. But there is already visible in Calvin's addressing of economic issues a feature that contends with some manifestations of capitalism, such as its consumption orientation.

This feature is the conviction, shared with the greater part of Christian tradition,[6] that there are limits on the use of wealth. For Calvin, "wealth was given by God to meet the needs of community, notably those of its neediest members."[7] Hence "luxuriating wantonly in abundance"[8] was explicitly forbidden. According to Albert Hyma, this demonstrates Calvin's "decidedly anticapitalistic attitude in frowning upon all attempts to secure a superabundance of temporal riches, and by condemning the consumption of luxuries."[9]

Thus, if Calvinism nurtured some dispositions and habits conducive to some aspects of capitalism (i.e., those that stimulate the accumulation of capital, a result necessary for production-oriented capitalism), it appears likewise to nurture others antithetical to other features of capitalism (those that avoid indulging in abundance, an indulgence that appears necessary for certain forms of consumption-oriented capitalism).[10] Thus, while Weber's thesis can be sustained with reference to production-oriented capitalism, it is less certain that it is coherent in relation to the consumption-oriented dynamic of capitalism.[11]

But since a primary characteristic of capitalism since the Industrial Revolution has been consumption, it is worth asking whether any alternative theological convictions were nurturing dispositions that support this "consuming passion." Rodney Clapp sees an answer in British sociologist Colin Campbell's argument[12] that later Calvinists, the Puritans, took matters in a quite different direction by stressing the need not only for a confession of faith but also for an experience of the work of grace in the believer's heart. By thus associating true faith with deep, emotional sensibility, "a link was forged between displays of feeling and assumptions about the fundamental spiritual state of an individual which was to long outlive the decline of Calvinism and to influence profoundly the eighteenth-century movements of sensibility."[13]

As Calvinism thus came to be reinterpreted sentimentally, it produced what Campbell calls "another protestant ethic" that "stresses fervent feeling, sentimentality, luxurious introspection and an abiding emphasis on self-fulfillment."[14] This begins to furnish some of the missing ingredients needed to sponsor not production-oriented but consumption-oriented capitalism. Clapp invokes the historian Jackson Lears[15] to make the link to consumption patterns. Since this "other protestant ethic" shaped the quest for salvation into "a state of constant, feverish, spiritual yearning,"[16] "people were exquisitely attuned to intense emotion and so primed to stimulate it and repeatedly play infinite variations on it."[17] Expanding consumption requires such feelings of longing and yearning for satisfaction that buying something may momentarily deliver, "followed by dissatisfaction and renewed longing."[18] Just such stimulation of a cycle of satisfaction-dissatisfaction is a major dynamic that makes consumption-oriented capitalism possible. Thus a supplementary "protestant ethic" supplied some of what was lacking in the ethic identified by Weber. Weber's "Protestant ethic" identified Reformed convictions that made possible capital formation and thereby would undergird production. This "other protestant ethic" created the longings that would undergird consumption.

Clapp further argues that this supplementary ethic was also reinforced by the emphases of revivalism (sanctifying choice and encouraging rapturous feelings in a self, open continuously to the choice for conversion and reconversion) and by the advent of leading Christian businessmen whose marketing vision was likely connected to involvement in national and international Christian missions (Asa Candler) and whose translation of luxuries into necessary commodities extended to the commodification of Christmas and Easter (John Wannamaker).[19] Thus "Protestantism in clear if sometimes strange ways 'was excellent preparation for the pleasures of . . . modern consumer hedonism.' It sanctified choice. It brought Christianity lock, stock, barrel and Bible into the marketplace and redefined faith in terms of the marketplace."[20] Wedded to the "original" Protestant ethic, these factors guaranteed the continuing, if implicit, contribution of some lines of Reformed thought to the practice of a life of faith in the capitalistic economic order.

If the foregoing can stand as an account of the de facto (and implicit) way in which Reformed thought has had practical consequences for faithful Christian living in the economic order, it is worth asking how matters might be if such a Reformed practical theology were more explicitly pursued. One intriguing point of departure for such an effort is the dividing line already drawn between the way Calvin's own thought supports some requirements of production-oriented capitalism and the way his thought contends with some versions of consumption-oriented capitalism.

Perhaps the heart of Calvin's contribution to such production-oriented capitalism is his theological view of creation and calling.[21] The latter meant that people are to direct their God-given energies primarily to their work. This doctrine of calling also promoted a division of labor such that no one was required to presume to do everything, relying instead on the providence of God, which places people in a variety of occupations that together accomplish important ends. The corollary doctrine of creation affirmed that work and industry were principal reasons for being that made "languishing in idleness" shameful.[22] These explicit theological claims about creation and calling thus frame (and commend) a pattern of life that regards work as fundamental, thereby serving the needs of any economic order but especially that of production-oriented capitalism.

Calvin's accompanying theological concerns of frugality and temperance[23] represent the middle space between Reformed theology's support of production-oriented capitalism and its contention with some versions of consumer-oriented capitalism. One effect of frugality is capital accumulation, an acknowledged necessity for production-oriented capitalism to get underway. Another effect of such temperance in economic matters is limitation on material indulgence, an indulgence strongly commended if the prosperity fueled by consumer demand is to be sustained. Weber's thesis, as we have already observed, tends to affirm the first result and overlook the second. But it is questionable whether Calvin's insistence on such frugal and temperate economic behavior can be easily dismissed as stemming from an unfortunate "ascetic" emphasis.[24]

Whatever may have become the fate of frugality at the hands of later Calvinists, including the Puritans, it is arguable that in Calvin the concern is not so much personal asceticism as it is communal justice. That is, the reason for Calvin's exhortation against "luxuriating wantonly in abundance" is that the right use of wealth is determined by the obligations of human community. Calvin echoed the voices of many early church theologians in his claim that "what is left over is meant not for intemperance or luxury but for relieving the needs of" others in the church community.[25] This is in clear accord with the summary, virtually unanimous, judgment of Christian teaching in the first four centuries of the church: "To accumulate wealth is to pervert it, not only because real wealth must always be moving and active, but also because the purpose of wealth is to meet human need. Therefore, those who accumulate wealth as if it were an end in itself or who accumulate it in order to live in comfort and ostentation are misusing wealth."[26]

It is not too much to suggest that the focus on community is critical for Calvin's framing of theological convictions that guide economic practice.

Certainly, in the larger discussion of Calvinism and capitalism, it is an underacknowledged focus. But with almost every mention of economic matters, Calvin invokes or alludes to this communal framework for faithful Christian living.[27] Thus, though he accepts a certain material inequality as inevitable, those living in a position of relative abundance are expected to "do so 'temperately, not failing others,' and taking care of the poor."[28] As Bouwsma observes, Calvin takes money so much for granted that he even described the lives of the saints in economic metaphors.[29] Yet this very description expresses the manner in which the economic order serves the purposes of human community:

> Those who expend usefully what God has deposited with them are said to trade. For the life of the godly is aptly compared to business, since they ought to deal with one another in order to maintain their fellowship; and the industry by which each person carries out the injunction laid on him, and his very calling, the capacity of doing right, and his other gifts, are regarded as merchandise, since their purpose and use [are] to facilitate intercommunication among men.[30]

While a reader may be excused for noticing the eerie sense that theological descriptions were being colonized by an economic vocabulary at such an early stage, it is significant that it is not a consumer economy that Calvin has in view. It may be more aptly called a neighborly economy in which the purpose is not *acquisition but fellowship* and *intercommunication* among people.

Even Calvin's oft-noted acquiescence on the matter of usury is normed by his theology of community. As Bouwsma tells Calvin's story, the allowance for usury (charging interest on loans) was judged acceptable among the rich but was explicitly constrained when it came to burdening and oppressing debtors. "Hence it follows that usury is not now unlawful, except insofar as it contravenes equity and brotherly union."[31] Albert Hyma adds that for Calvin (and Luther as well), it was always prohibited to charge interest to a poor person, always enjoined by Christ to do unto others as one wanted done to oneself, and always urged that "the desire for personal gain must . . . remain subordinate to that Christian spirit of brotherly love which seeks to aid the poor and the outcasts, for they are to receive all the property and profit which exceed one's moderate needs."[32]

Calvin did not need to await the maxims of Benjamin Franklin to link wealth and time ("Time is money"), yet he did so not with reference to individual achievement but with reference to both wealth and time as scarce resources for communal needs. "God has joined and united us together so that we might have a community, for men should not be separate. . . . It is too great a cruelty on our part if we see a poor and afflicted man and do not try to help him but rather turn away from him."[33] In this context he did not hesitate to use the metaphor of the yoke to describe the "mutual obligation of parties" in society,[34] thereby stressing a theological purpose for such social and economic interdependence.

Thus the theological convictions that framed economic matters for Calvin do not all run in unanimous support of all features of capitalism. It is true that certain important theological claims sponsor habits and practices that can lead to capital accumulation, thus supporting production-oriented capitalism; yet other equally important theological claims sponsor habits and practices that tend to curb material acquisition due to the communal obligation to use excess wealth not for self-satisfaction but for the needs of others—thus contending with a version of consumer-oriented capitalism that relentlessly attends only to consumer demand and may generate new consumer desires.

Transposing all of this into an intentional practical theology of faithful living in economic matters brings us to some important affirmations. God's creation and calling of people to productive, industrious lives, reflecting the image of the Creator in the creature, does undergird important economic values such as productivity and the co-generation of wealth. However, precisely because this doctrine of creation and calling has reference to the Creator—who has communal purposes for us as people, who are necessarily yoked to our neighbors—productivity and wealth are not abstract, unfocused, and individualized but concrete and aimed exactly at the construction of human community.

The result is a nuanced embrace of capitalism that calls us to undertake productive economic lives while simultaneously insisting that we resist the excesses of acquisitive desire that encourage "luxuriating wantonly in abundance" in the face of massive deprivation in much of the world. Therefore a Reformed practical theology of faithful Christian living in the economic domain will answer the challenge posed at the end of Justo González's *Faith and Wealth* in a way that shows a fundamental consistency of Reformed practical theology with Christian practical theology in the early church.

González concludes with a striking comparison of the world faced by Christians of the first four centuries with the world Christians face today. "They lived in a world in which contrasts between the rich and poor were staggering; we live in a world populated by a few who have millions and by millions who have nothing. For them, these issues were indissolubly connected with the meaning of salvation."[35] He then translates all of this into an affirmation and a challenge. Asking whether the world has changed so much that what these Christians of the first four centuries had to say is no longer relevant, he answers, "I believe not." Asking whether the commitment of contemporary Christians has waned to such an extent that we do not take seriously what they say in our use of the world's resources, he pleads, "I hope not."[36]

This investigation of the ways in which Reformed theology might more explicitly be developed to frame the concern for faithful Christian living in the economic domain leads to the affirmation of some elements of the "Protestant ethic" identified by Weber, appropriately nuanced and formulated not just as resulting economic behaviors but also as commended frameworks for economic practice consistent with production-oriented capitalism and a disciplined consumer-oriented capitalism. It also leads to a serious questioning of some aspects of the "other protestant ethic" that, by sanctifying choice and stressing concerns for self-fulfillment, nurtured relentless consumer-demand capitalism. As Calvin has been seen to argue, in concert with the early Christian church, acquisition (hence consumption) needs always to be constrained by the needs of the broader human community. Thus if there is a practical theology of consumption, it is an abiding theology of suspicion regarding "luxuriating wantonly in abundance."

The further development of such a practical Reformed theology of faithful Christian living in the economic domain faces a severe challenge from at least one contemporary Reformed theologian who has written extensively on the matter. John Schneider, as earlier indicated, agrees both with González's summary of early Christian teaching and the argument of this essay about Calvin's caution against the accumulation and selfish use of wealth. But Schneider persists in the argument that these theological claims may be safely disregarded.

Schneider argues that this consensus, as wise and good as it may have been, is largely a "product of its time." That time, he believes, was one in which "a very small minority of people were rich in relative terms (and had more than they needed), and the vast majority were either poor or facing poverty (did not have, or barely had, enough to live on) as a constant danger."[37] He further believes that modern market economies present an altogether different situation in which "the vast majority of ordinary people have become rich by any literal or historic measure, while the small (by comparison) minority are materially poor."[38] Thus a new Christian ethic and a new spirituality need to be formed in contrast to most of what has gone before, with the present recognition that "a new species of acquisition has been born that not only does not naturally oppress other human beings but actually liberates them."[39]

The new ethic and spirituality that Schneider sees as necessary for Christians in the changed environment of modern market economies can reclaim acquisition and enjoyment as desirable goals. Although Schneider acknowledges that "the entire weight of historic Christian tradition seems to be against the integration of faith with the habits of acquisition and enjoyment," he argues, "We must have a distinctly Christian way to affirm the economic habits of acquisition and enjoyment of affluence as they necessarily exist within the culture of modern capitalism."[40]

While Schneider's alternative poses a host of important questions that are beyond the scope of this essay, several must be addressed that concern key ingredients in a Reformed practical theology of faithful Christian living in the economic order. Vis-à-vis economic questions, Schneider makes a major claim in his aim to construct a quite different Reformed practical theology than the one I have argued as grounded in Calvin's thought. He proposes that the weight of Reformed (and Catholic) theological tradition, not to mention the plain sense of Scripture, can be set aside on the strength of new historical realities revolving around the alleged magic of capitalism. Embracing Dinesh D'Souza's "new way of thinking about inequality," Schneider argues (again with D'Souza) that capitalism creates wealth that did not exist before.[41]

Schneider thus sets out to frame a new ethic and a spirituality that will support what the historical legacy cautions against: celebration of acquisitiveness. He proceeds to ground this spirituality of acquisition in a reading of Old and New Testament texts and early church narratives.[42] His project is to turn Calvin's counsel on its head, urging a form of "luxuriating wantonly in abundance." Ironically, he appears to do so by invoking forms of the doctrines of creation and calling, as well as God's purposes for human community that, we have argued, Calvin also invoked. However, his doctrine of creation takes a decidedly anthropological turn as he concentrates on the creation of wealth. "The truth is that in modern market economies the main way people acquire wealth is not by taking it away from someone else, but by taking part in its creation."[43] Since such creation of wealth is "what the habit of acquisition is essentially all about under working capitalism,"[44] it becomes the calling of the Christian person. However, not only does Schneider's way of talking about creation focus on the human agency involved; it also implies that human creation is like God's creative work, that is, "from nothing." To this end he cites with approbation D'Souza's rhetorical question: "What if the rich are getting richer *because they have created new wealth that didn't exist before?*"[45] By contrast, Calvin's stress on creation has been seen to take the tack not of humans' imitating God's creation ex nihilo, but rather that of humans imitating God's industry in fashioning a world deemed "good."

In addition to the allusions to creation and calling, Schneider even expresses some sense of obligation toward community, upon which Calvin insists, as we have seen. "Acquisition and enjoyment in an economy such as this are not just ends for oneself alone; they are also the means to similar ends for others."[46] Robert Wuthnow has commented on how, at the end of the nineteenth century in America, as the moral conversation about the economy went into eclipse: "Preachers, journalists, and other moralists worried more about getting the lower classes to work harder than they did about greed and ambition among the middle classes."[47] In contrast, Schneider seems to worry more about placing the greed and ambition among the middle classes on a sounder theological and moral footing. His words resoundingly echo the political economists of the nineteenth century who regarded the economy "as a domain that happily regulated itself for the good of all."[48]

Yet the telling element in his appeal to the benefits accruing to the community in democratic capitalism is that the benefits are solely expressed in economic terms and exclusively related to the individual. The "wealth" that is produced is measured only in economic categories. The noneconomic "costs," especially the costs that are charged against human community, never come into view.[49] Indeed, the community he imagines is not one that has the features of fellowship but only features of economic benefits delivered to an aggregate of individuals. Thus, though he appears to embrace the theology of community that we have seen in Calvin, in the end it turns out to be a very different affirmation.

When Calvin speaks of the norm of human community that should constrain the way one behaves in the economic domain, he consistently speaks of the *relationships* that obtain among neighbors. Even money itself was important as "a medium for reciprocal *communication* among men, principally used for buying and selling merchandise."[50] The language and images of union, joining, and yoking are elemental to what he means when he says, "God has joined and united us together so that we might have a community, for men should not be separate."[51] In contrast, Schneider's attempt to give moral support to the acquisitive habits required for consumption-oriented capitalism to function at peak efficiency appeals not really to community but to an aggregate of individuals. His argument is that this form of capitalism makes certain economic goods available to more and more individuals. "Acquisition and enjoyment in an economy such as this are not just for oneself alone; they are also the means to similar ends for others."[52] But nowhere does he engage the fact that global economic development at the beginning of the twenty-first century has increased rather than ameliorated the economic disparities among the peoples of the world.[53] Thus the "community" Schneider invokes to warrant acquisitive economic behavior is not a matter of relationships among people but merely a matter of the common interests they may have in various economic goods—goods that are globally distributed in a way that reinforces hierarchy more than community.

What we confront in Schneider's proposal is indeed a Reformed practical theology respecting faithful Christian living in the economic domain. But the overwhelming oddity of his proposal is that it has to contend explicitly against the weight of Reformed and Catholic tradition when it comes to constraints on acquisition. Instead of joining those elements of the tradition that have called into question the demands of consumption-oriented capitalism for a repetitive cycle of consumption-satisfaction-dissatisfaction-consumption, Schneider claims that the genius of capitalism compels us to retrieve the elements of Christian tradition that can support a spirituality and ethic of acquisition. However, his way of invoking theology to frame practical habits in economic life appeals to creation, calling, and community in ways distant from the appeals that Calvin made respecting the same themes.

The fatal flaw in Schneider's reading of capitalism is that he holds a view of capitalism that does not square with its actual history as it has evolved, notably in the U.S. context. As already mentioned, he claims that what is needed is "a distinctly Christian way to affirm the economic habits of acquisition and enjoyment of affluence as *they necessarily exist* within the culture of modern capitalism."[54] In the United States, however, habits of acquisition and enjoyment have existed in different ways over the twentieth century and into the twenty-first. For example, Lizabeth Cohen traces an important difference between such habits manifest in the "citizen consumer"[55] just before and during World War II and the habits evident in the "purchaser as citizen"[56] in the immediate postwar period. In the first phase of this capitalist development, when consuming was defined by citizenship, the habits of acquisition and enjoyment were not unalloyed but combined with commitments to a larger public good, especially in the case of disciplining consumption first to overcome the Great Depression and then in support of the war effort. Clearly this represents a pattern of consumer behavior that is consistent with the emphases on creation, calling, and community as articulated by Calvin.

In the second case, when citizenship was defined by purchasing, the habits of acquisition that Schneider promotes surely came more fully into play. However, even in the postwar era, it was possible for consumption to be turned to more public ends than merely personal acquisition and enjoyment, as in the civil rights movement that showed "the Consumers' Republic had its liberating side, as it offered the protection of a mass market whose success depended on attracting consumers previously excluded from it."[57] Cohen's careful analysis of how the consumption side of capitalism has functioned differently even in a prominent "culture of modern capitalism" suggests that there is not the inevitability that Schneider assumes about a new ethic and spirituality of acquisition and enjoyment of affluence. Indeed, it is rather the case that there is a need for a fresh (even alternative) imagination of how theological claims of creation, calling, and community might guide the patterns of consumption that Christians practice in the "culture of modern capitalism."

Chapter 13

Human Dignity and Human Cloning
Perspectives from the Reformed Tradition

KANG PHEE SENG

New scientific knowledge and technological breakthroughs are among the most remarkable human achievements in the twentieth century and onward. More significantly, their impact is not confined merely to our physical realm of existence. Every aspect of our existence, be it social or political, economic or cultural, moral or religious, has come under the influence of science and technology. Not only have they conditioned the way we live and relate to the material world; they have also challenged the way we think and act. Not only has our understanding of the world been completely changed; our perception of humanity and who we are has also been radically questioned. Indeed, the future of humanity will very much depend on decisions we make with respect to the possibilities that science and technology offer.

GENETIC REVOLUTION

Robert F. Curl Jr. of Rice University, Nobel laureate in chemistry in 1996, was reported to have said that the twentieth century was "the century of physics and chemistry. But it is clear that the twenty-first will be the century of biology."[1] To be sure, scientists will continue their quest for the Grand United Theory (GUT), which when found will hopefully explain all laws of physics and chemistry, perhaps even help us "know the mind of God," as the Cambridge physicist Stephen Hawking believes it will.[2] Computer chips will continue to challenge the limits of speed, capacity, and size, and within a couple of decades they will send all of today's hardware and software to the museum of science and technology. Our grandchildren can only wonder, What concourse can there be between a mouse and a computer? And few can imagine what a cyber-society will be like half a century from now. If, however, Robert Curl Jr. is right, and few will think that he is not right, a yet greater challenge and transformation will come in the field of biotechnology. Indeed, the curtain of the new century of biology has been drawn by the advent of genetic engineering. Many financial analysts believe that the financial miracles of IBM in the 1960s and Microsoft in the 1990s will be repeated in the genetic engineering industry and that genetically modified products will be frantically sought after within the first half of the twenty-first century.[3]

Genetic engineering in the 1980s and 1990s was still very much a technical term used and understood by only the professionals. With the announcement of the successful cloning of a Scottish ewe in 1997, the public has suddenly been made aware of a new scientific revolution that is at hand.[4] Aside from the excitement of a scientific breakthrough, what really concerns the public is the immense impact this has on society, and in particular the moral controversies it raises.

Genetic engineering encompasses wide-ranging applications, including genetically modified food, transgenic organisms, xenotransplantation, cloning, and research in human stem cells and preembryos. The issues involved in each are often different and complex. The corresponding ecological, social, and moral implications, together with the agricultural potentials or medical benefits, have to be studied and evaluated on their own merits. Genetic engineering therefore is not a technology to which we can give a simple "yes" or "no" answer. Each application needs to be considered carefully, thoroughly, and seriously.

REFORMED, EVANGELICAL, AND CATHOLIC

Anyone who is engaged in a discussion of Reformed theology in, say, an ecumenical dialogue will be faced with the difficult if not impossible task of defining what Reformed theology is.[5] There is no one single confession or creed that defines the essential elements of Reformed faith for all Reformed churches. The Scottish theologian David Fergusson once pointed out that "attempts to define the essence of the Reformed tradition have generally failed to stand the test of time," and he concluded that "it is not possible . . . to give a simple definition of the predicate Reformed."[6] The Westminster Confession (1647), once the definitive statement of the Reformed faith for the English-speaking world, is now no longer so. Even in the Church of Scotland, which has it "as the *de jure* subordinate standard of faith," it is "*de facto* . . . neither respected nor studied. It is no longer read by Divinity students except in those optional courses which deal with Scottish theology."[7] With the exception of its notion of assurance, Westminster Confession is rejected by R. T. Kendall as un-Calvinistic: "Calvin's thought, save for the decrees of predestination, is hardly to be found in Westminster theology; only the notion of assurance itself seems traceable to Calvin. . . . Westminster theology hardly deserves to be called Calvinistic—especially if that term is to imply the thought of Calvin himself."[8]

However, to reflect theologically on the issue of human cloning, it is not necessary for Reformed churches to draw from resources that are distinctively and exclusively Reformed. After all, Reformed churches do not stand alone: they belong to the holy catholic church.[9] For our purpose, we will therefore use resources that are acceptable to most if not all Reformed churches. For example, we will draw insights from the doctrine of Trinity and the doctrine of incarnation, the twin doctrine that is the evangelical foundation for the whole catholic church.

WHY THEOLOGICAL REFLECTIONS?

Cloning, if applied to humans, will be the culmination of a risky trend of transforming human procreation into a mere biotechnological operation. Since economic consideration now is the dominant concern of almost all societies, our culture has become increasingly overwhelmed by technology and production, by "making." Cloning is the extension of this "making" culture to the realm of human procreation. It is telling that we have come to replace the use of the word "procreation" with "reproduction," substituting "the generative act of a Creator and Giver of life" by "a metaphor of the factory."[10] New developments in reproductive techniques have indeed provided many alternate ways to "having" or "producing" a child. "Making babies" is becoming increasingly acceptable and fashionable.[11] While the end "product" may look the same, this does not imply that what we have, or what we have done, is the same.[12] As O'Donovan warned as early as 1984, these biotechnological breakthroughs have the potential to change "not merely the conditions of our human existence, but its essential characteristic.[13] They challenge our self-understanding as human beings and our understanding of human relationships, understandings that have most of their roots in the Christian tradition. As such, they raise profound moral controversies and have significant philosophical and theological implications. Theologians together with philosophers and ethicists are therefore called to reflect upon these developments, as are colleagues from other academic disciplines and professions, so that society as a whole may know how to respond.

We shall now turn to some of the challenges posed by human cloning and related technologies to the Christian tradition.

"BEGOTTEN NOT MADE": EQUALITY OF HUMAN BEINGS

In the fourth century the early Christian church used the phrase "begotten not made" to describe the unique relation between Jesus Christ and God. In declaring that Christ was "begotten not made," the Christian church proclaims the "equality of being" between the Son and the Father. Thus, what is ascribed to the Father can be, and must also be, ascribed to the Son.[14] That is to say, the Son, who is born of the Father, is truly and fully God and is what the Father is. That which is "made" belongs only to the creaturely realm, between whose being and the being of "the begotten" a sharp distinction must be drawn.

Only the begotten can be said to be truly the same and coequal with the begetter. In contrast, that which is made is ontologically different from its maker. The maker stands above that which is made. Similarly, what we *beget* is like ourselves, sharing our own nature, and with them we enjoy a fellowship based on radical and unconditional equality. In natural procreation there is a delicate balance of our child truly coming from us and yet being different from us. While there certainly is a biological relationship with both parents in terms of genetic continuity, the child is a new creation in the true sense of the word because of being a chanced combination of the parents' genes. The child replicates neither the father nor the mother. The genes of every child constitute a new and unique combination. To the parents, a newborn is an unknown. The infant begins life from birth with a kind of "genetic independence" from the parents. Because of this, the child demands to be treated as our equal, as an independent and unique person, of equal dignity with us and not at our disposal.

Our child does not live a life for us or for anyone else. Each child lives a life that is their very own.[15] On the other hand, what we *make* is alienated from us. In the case of human cloning, the clone is the result of a programmed project realized with the aid of technology. The genes have already existed before cloning. It is difficult for a clone really to have a life that truly belongs to the clone. The clone will not only live in the shadow of the donor but also in fact be the shadow of the donor.[16] Hence the clone cannot declare, "I am unique" or "I shall be who I shall be," because the donor is the original and the prototype. The cloned child is made in the image of the donor.[17] Experience tells us that many children suffer under parents who try to live vicariously through them. "If most parents have hopes for their children, cloning parents will have expectations."[18] The clone is "the product of our free decision, and [the clone's] destiny is ours to determine."[19] In natural birth, we give existence to a being by what we are, but in human cloning, we do so by what we intend and design. Unfortunately, "as with any product of our making, no matter how excellent, the artificer stands above it, not as an equal but as a superior, transcending it by . . . will and creative prowess."[20] Thus human cloning is fundamentally "an assertion of power over another human being, exercised without consent," hence "power not just over the clone's liberty or privileges, but over [that] very being."[21] As such, it is the usurping of dominion over another person, usurping dominion held rightfully only over the rest of the creation.[22]

PRIESTHOOD OF ALL BELIEVERS: HUMANITY NOT COMMODITY

The Christian doctrines of creation and redemption put all humankind on the same ontological ground: all are created in the image of God, all are fallen, and all are justified on the same divine ground by grace alone. As fellow recipients of God's unconditional grace, we are each seen as inherently valuable and absolutely equal in the sight of God. This radical and unconditional equality between all members in a community is further expressed by the Reformers as the doctrine of the priesthood of all believers. It is in the form of a suffering servant that the high priesthood of Jesus Christ was manifested, and his high-priestly prayer was offered just before he laid down his life for all. In Christ all believers are called to be priests, sharing in the one priesthood of Christ.[23] No one therefore is above the other. We are to see each as a priest to every other and to respect the dignity of every person within the community. Even the least among us is to be honored as a royal priest because of being "chosen and precious in God's sight" (1 Pet. 2:4 NRSV). In fact, Jesus has always identified himself with the weakest in society, not least when he said: "Truly I tell you, just as you did it to one of the least of these who are members of my family, you did it to me. . . . As you did not do it to one of the least of these, you did not do it to me" (Matt. 25:40, 45). Moreover, as priests we are also to serve one another. It is thus only within such a community of serving priesthood that persons, in Kantian dictum, are treated as "ends in themselves and not simply as means," and our dignity and worth as persons can be truly treasured and upheld.[24]

Cloning, however, reduces procreation to a project of producing children. Genes are selected for cloning because they have certain values or meet certain needs. Gradually and perhaps inevitably, such children are seen as products over which we feel the need to exercise "quality control,"[25] and as commodity priced for what they can do or be used for.[26] In the final analysis, we may learn to think of these persons in terms of a "genetic bar code" and reduce them to simply a biochemical entity. As such, cloning runs the risk of dehumanizing the cloned child. In fact, advocates of procreative liberty like John A. Robertson have defended the employment of biotechnology to determine the *quality* of offspring desired.[27] Philip Kitcher believes that "some form of eugenics is inescapable" and calls for the development of "utopian eugenics." He even argues for the genetic enhancement of the human species as a social responsibility.[28] According to Gregory Pence, eugenics is indeed the best argument for cloning so that the child can have better genetic advantages.[29] Singer and Well express support for only "single cloning" of an individual yet reveal their eugenic bias in advocating the "multiple cloning" of exceptionally gifted people.[30]

No doubt, with the memory of Nazi scientists and their genocide programs still fresh in people's mind, not all who advocate cloning subscribe to positive eugenics, to genetic enhancement. However, once the possibility is there, the temptation is almost irresistible. The new eugenics is driven by "something more like consumer choice. Parents, putting themselves in a consumer posture, are demanding increased genetic knowledge in order to give birth to designer babies."[31] Though seldom publicly acknowledged, genetic testing is being used by some parents to decide if a developing fetus is worthy of life. As recently reported, "a small but increasing number of women [are] choosing preimplantation genetic diagnosis (PGD) to avoid giving birth to children who carry mutations in the BRCA genes, which increase the risk for breast and other cancers."[32] Thus it would not be surprising if eugenics is in fact the main driving force behind the development of cloning technology.

It is hideous to think of a future scenario of couples in a genetic clinic making choices about the genetic constitution of their children.[33] The rapid growth of assisted-reproduction clinics, sperm banks, and the like points to the commercialization of "making" babies. If cloning is made possible, human nucleus banks or DNA banks would surely join the ranks. Such commodification and commercialization will seriously violate the dignity of human beings, who are created in the image of God.

FREE GRACE: FAMILY AS A PLACE OF UNCONDITIONAL BELONGING

Reformed theology depicts the divine-human relation in terms of a covenant between God and humanity. This theology of the covenant has the effect of transforming humanity's salvation away from a dark center in the divine decree of predestination, turning it to an evangelical center in God's loving heart in grace. Nothing can purchase the free grace of God. What matters most here is the "unconditional binding of God's self to the human partner." As such, it is the most significant development in Reformed theology after Calvin's death.[34] However, in the sixteenth and seventeenth centuries, this biblical concept of the divine covenant of grace in Reformed tradition was much influenced by the idea of contract law in contemporary political and juridical theories. In turning covenant into contract, federal theology in effect made divine grace conditional upon human works of obedience, hence substituting a legalism for the evangelical proclamation of God's unconditional love.[35] Instead of being gracious gifts from God, human responses like repentance and faith became the conditions for the covenant. In other words, humanity is thrown back upon itself to secure its worthiness before God for entering into a life-relation with God.

The God of the evangelical covenant is a God of filial Trinitarian relation, a heavenly Father who reveals himself in his eternal Son and Spirit, who in his Son and Spirit unconditionally loves his human children, and who truly is "the Father, from whom every family in heaven and on earth takes its name" (Eph. 3:14–15). This fatherhood of God is the foundation of all human parenthood, and the unconditional covenantal relationship that God establishes between humanity and himself is the ground for human family relationship.[36] Children are unconditionally assumed into communion with parents and are enabled to respond as persons grounded in unconditional love and grace. "No conditions were originally stipulated, nor did any require to be stipulated—not a contract but an assumption into a life-relationship."[37] Here lies the evangelical message: The gift of new life is to be accepted gratefully in its totality. Nothing stands between the child and her parents.

Viewed in this light, a family in the natural order of things is a place of unconditional belonging. It is not a collection of arbitrary, unrelated spousal, parental, filial, and fraternal relationships. From the one-flesh unity of a wife and her husband there unfolds an openness to the begetting of their children.[38] Parents do not choose their children any more than children their parents. Children are "gifts from God" and are unconditionally accepted by their parents for what they are, regardless of their sex, health, intelligence, physique, or looks. The parents' unconditional acceptance of the child is reciprocated by the child's unconditional acceptance of the parents. The child cannot preselect her parents any more than the parents can prescreen their child. The unconditionality that characterizes the parent-child relation is the foundation of love and grace, a reflection of the absolute unconditional love and grace of God.

In nature's providence, this unconditionality is secured by the randomness of the so-called genetic lottery at conception. Cloning and other efforts of genetic enhancement will break this chance determination and for it substitute a genotype that is completely or partially known and meets the expectation of the would-be-parent, often in the name of securing a head start for the child. But by so doing, the integrity of the family as a place for unconditional belonging and acceptance is compromised. For now the child is made rather than begotten, sought and attained rather than given and received. If the quality and desirability of a child's genotype is the *condition* of her inclusion into a family, there is no guarantee that the quality and desirability of her parents or family will meet her expectations. In other words, if a couple can choose to have a child with a potential IQ of 200, why can't that child prefer to be born to a couple with an equal or even higher IQ? If children need to qualify themselves in prescreening, they might now show their dissatisfaction if they think that the family is not good enough for them. This reproductive right of choosing a desirable child is purchased at a high cost of *unconditional belonging and acceptance of the family.*

DIVINE ACCOMMODATION: MAKE ROOM FOR THE WEAK

Paul Tillich holds that for Calvin, the majesty of God is the central doctrine of Christian faith.[39] Granted that it may be so, one must add that for Calvin, God is never locked up in the infinity of his divine majesty, only to be deistically related to this created universe at the singularity point of the big bang. Though transcendent and infinite in himself, God is free to reveal himself to us and indeed free to make himself available for us in our creaturely existence. This "divine accommodation" of God in revelation and redemption is one of Calvin's immense contributions to Reformed theology.[40] In making room for us in our dark and frail existence, God reveals himself in Jesus Christ to be truly worthy of all honor and praise. For not only is he the God of the rich and the strong; he is also the God of the poor and the weak. In other words, the God of the Christian faith is not impassible nor immutable. Rather, he is "invariant in love but not impassible, constant in faithfulness but not immutable."[41] In his great passion and incarnational movement for humanity, he was made poor and weak for human's sake in order that we through his poverty may be made rich and through his weakness might be made strong. In a *mirifica commutatio* (as Calvin calls it) that only he himself can perform, the incarnate Word is clothed with our wretched (in)humanity and (in)personhood so that we may be clothed by his authentic humanity and personhood:

> This is the wondrous exchange (*mirifica commutatio*) made by His boundless goodness. Having become one with us as the Son of Man, He has made us with Himself sons of God. By His own descent to the earth He has prepared our ascent to heaven. Having received our mortality, He has bestowed on us His immortality. Having taken our weakness upon Himself, He has made us strong in His strength. Having submitted to our poverty, He has transferred to us His riches. Having taken upon Himself the burden of our unrighteousness with which we were oppressed, He has clothed us with His righteousness.[42]

The question of the status of embryos has been the focus of attention again in recent debates over human cloning. The assertion that embryos are not persons will no doubt offer much-needed relief in easing the conscience of many who fear a rise in the number of abortions. With new technologies now available at hand, it is a matter of pressing concern that embryos and preembryos are artificially created daily in industrial numbers in laboratories and later discarded for research in cloning and in human stem cell experiments.[43]

In a testimony to the National Bioethics Advisory Commission, Reformed theologian Ronald Cole-Turner presents the view of the United Church of Christ in the United States that it is "open to the possibility that somatic cell nuclear transfer be used to create embryos for research," while noting that the church has perhaps deliberately avoided any official declaration on the status of embryos.[44] On the other hand, Scottish Reformed theologian Thomas Torrance argues in a different context for the personhood of embryonic existence. For Torrance, if the incarnation is the coming and presence of the creator Word in the fullness of his Spirit, he cannot be less human or personal even in his mother's womb. As he himself is the personalizing Person and humanizing Human who constitutes in himself the ground of our personhood and humanity, the incarnation has the effect of sanctifying the whole course of our human existence, including the embryonic (and preembryonic) phases.[45] In other words, the status of an embryo must be sought beyond its dark and frail existence in the mother's womb, sought in him who for the embryo's sake has graciously identified himself with it in assuming its form and existence, yet without ceasing to be the Giver of Life.[46] As such he has made room for it and made it worthy to receive life and acquire moral status.

Seen in this light, the embryo is the very weakest member of the human race, crying out for accommodation to be properly placed and nurtured to full term in the mother's womb. "No community, whether family, village or state, is really strong if it will not carry its weak and even its very weakest members."[47] Gilbert Meilaender, quoting these words of Barth, calls for an inclusive understanding of the human species and argues that "the embryo is . . . the weakest and least advantaged of our fellow human beings."[48] As such, no community is really strong if its weakest members are reduced only to biological tissues and treated simply as means, not as ends in themselves.

We have earlier mentioned the importance of serving priesthood in honoring the dignity and worth of others. We could do well to further deepen this serving priesthood in terms of an "anthropological accommodation," making room for the weakest and the poorest from among us in order that they may become persons and humans, and be one of us. "Once you were not a [person], but now you are; . . . once you had not received mercy, but now you have" (cf. 1 Pet. 2: 10). It is ironical that in an age of tremendous medical advancements, even more embryos have been intentionally abandoned. Should not the least among us be protected so that their personhood and humanity will not be exploited just for our own benefits in the name of medical research?

CONCLUSION

Nearly five decades ago, in a paper titled "Moving Toward the Clonal Man: Is This What We Want?," James Watson, Nobel laureate and first director of the Human Genome Project, warned that "if we do not think about it now, the possibility of our having a free choice will one day suddenly be gone."[49]

When the possibility of human cloning was first suggested in the media, the most common words used in people's reaction were "offensive," "grotesque," "revolting," "repugnant," "repulsive." Even Wilmut, the creator of Dolly, the first cloned sheep, said that he "would find it offensive" to clone a human being. Leon Kass aptly coins this "the wisdom of repugnance," but he also warns at the same time that "yesterday's repugnances are today calmly accepted."[50] Our theological reflection aims to provide some rationale behind this sense of repugnance.

We have argued that human cloning is not just merely another alternative for human reproduction provided by modern technology. If unchecked, it threatens the dignity of humanity and runs the risk of depersonalizing and dehumanizing the cloned child. It is, however, not our intention in this essay to conclude that under no circumstances should human cloning be allowed, or that all research in human stem cells and preembryos with possible applications in human cloning are to be categorically opposed.[51] It is not to establish an eleventh commandment: Thou shalt not clone. It should not be construed as an attempt to elevate the human genome into a sacred cow since it would violate a central concern of the Reformed faith to distinguish clearly between the Creator and the creation.

The fundamental issue here is not that of science versus Christian theology. Theologians, like scientists, do not have only one voice about this. Some theologians and churches, Reformed included, are more receptive to the new cloning technology, while others have more reservations.[52] To be sure, the complexity of the problem defies a quick and simple "yes" or "no" as answer. What is urgently needed is a prolonged period of intense and open public discussion, for "all such research should be subject to broad public comment and . . . should only proceed within a context of public understanding and general public support."[53] Our theological reflections should be part of that wider context of public response and discussion.

REFORMING MINISTRIES

Chapter 14

Renewal of the *Imago Dei*
Hope for the Depleted Self

CORNELIUS PLANTINGA JR.

INTRODUCTION

Despite the infrequent and often cryptic appearance of the phrase "image of God" in Scripture, the corresponding biblical and Christian *doctrine* possesses great power to secure not only human rights and dignity, but also to epitomize the human relation to God. So John Calvin, for example, sees the image of God as a summary of humanity's status before God not only in creation, but also in redemption,[1] where it is renewed, in part, by means of "mortification" of the old self and "vivification" of the new.[2] These movements may be said to "keep the rhythm going" for people who have already died and risen with Jesus Christ in their baptism. In fact, given Christ's godliness, perhaps dying and rising with him not only renew the image of God but also exhibit it. In a remarkable and improbable turn of events, disciples of Jesus who "put to death" their old nature and "clothe themselves" with their new nature are acting like *God*.

But here a notorious problem arises: if mortification and vivification are both God's gift and also the Christian's calling, how do defeated or depleted believers answer their calling? From a moral and pastoral point of view, doesn't it seem futile or even cruel to call such brothers and sisters to self-denial, say, or to some other form of dying with Christ? Perhaps they feel as if they are already half-dead. So wouldn't they properly reproach the preacher of self-denial? "Look," they might say, "I've barely got any self left, and you're telling me to kill it?"[3]

But what if within the theology of dying and rising as means and exhibit of a renewed image of God there might be resources not only for avoiding insult to depleted believers, but also for comforting and strengthening them? What if pastoral care providers knew how to help in these ways not just because they were adept at clinical pastoral education (CPE), but also because they had read their Paul and Calvin and had been "renewed in knowledge according to the image of [their] Creator" (Col. 3:10)?

In what follows, I want to consider these themes and questions. I do so in hope that "faith seeking understanding" may, along the way, sometimes find healing as well.

JESUS CHRIST AND THE RENEWAL OF THE IMAGE OF GOD

Suppose that even though the Bible uses the phrase "image of God" sparingly, it nonetheless presents godlikeness as a motif and does so in a range of contexts. One possible conclusion is that, for theology, the image of God consists not merely in responsible dominion, or fellowship, or speech, or "respondability to love," or rationality, or self-consciousness, or self-transcendence—each of which has been isolated and championed by one or another theologian as the image of God—but rather in the whole set of these (and many more) likenesses. Suppose, in other words, that neither God nor the ways of resembling God are simple.

In this way of thinking, the image of God will then emerge as a rich, multifaceted reality, comprising acts, relations, capacities, virtues, dispositions, and even emotions. Within this array of godlikenesses, a few are scripturally highlighted and existentially crucial to the Christian life, and among these perhaps the top rank includes those that tie believers not just to God *überhaupt* (generally), but particularly to Jesus Christ and to his death and resurrection.

In the New Testament, Jesus Christ appears as the preeminent image of God the Father (Col. 1:15; 2 Cor. 4:4). He is the "exegesis of God" (John 1:18, Greek), bears the very stamp of the divine nature (Heb. 1:3), and prekenotically exists "in the form of God" (Phil. 2:6). Believers are in turn to be conformed to the image of this Son and Lord (Rom. 8:29; 2 Cor. 3:18).

Some of these conformities appear in the context of those "renewal of the image" passages that connect vast tracts of Pauline redemption teaching to the image theme. In these passages (Col. 3:10; Eph. 4:24) "knowledge" and "righteousness and holiness" stand for the whole new life in Christ that Paul wants believers to "put on." In these passages Paul[4] is talking especially about self-giving love, the ligament of the new community (Eph. 4:15–16; Col. 3:14). He is talking, most generally, about the Christlikeness that allows believers to present *his* image to the world and to each other. For, as Paul can say alternately (Rom. 13:14), it is somehow Christ himself that believers have put on like a garment.

From these passages, I believe, one properly concludes that the New Testament image of God in believers includes not only loving, forgiving, and being perfect—all specifically linked to God or Christ by "just as" clauses (*kathōs* in Eph. 4:32 and Col. 3:13; *hōs* in Matt. 5:48). It also encompasses the whole range of ways in which believers obey God by imitating Christ, involving all the virtues, all the fruit of the Spirit, every generous lifting of a cup to someone's thirst, every resourceful attempt to shore up a sagging spirit, all compassionate attempts to struggle and suffer with people in distress. The idea here is that Paul's virtue lists are only exemplary. When he speaks of renewal in knowledge, or in righteousness and holiness, the emergent image of God is every conceivable form of godliness: it is "concretely visible sanctification."[5]

And that sounds wonderful. How wonderful it is to tell young Christian persons that when they are compassionate, kind, gentle, or patient with somebody who is driving them crazy, then *they are like God*. The trouble is that conformity to Jesus Christ includes suffering as well as glory, frustration as well as liberation, death as well as life.[6] In fact, in each of these cases, the former seems to be a condition, or at least an antecedent, of the latter. What Abraham Heschel says about the pathos of the God of the prophets[7] comes home to us in Jesus Christ. God suffers: so will those who are godlike and Christlike. God the Son dies: so must those who hope, like him, to be raised to new life.[8] Disciples are not greater than their master. For both, strength is displayed in weakness; believers who lose their life will find it; those who are humbled will be exalted; the one who dies shall live.

DYING AND RISING WITH JESUS CHRIST

Let's say that Jesus' resurrection, the "second exodus" (see Luke 9:31, Greek), proclaims to the world one more time that God has set people free. But to profit from this event, people need to get *into* it. So in the sacrament of baptism the followers of Christ deliberately reenact his dying and rising, and most include infants in this reenactment, believing that they too belong to the covenant of grace. To be baptized, a person is immersed in water or sprinkled with water (my own opinion is that sprinkling is only an appetizer) in a near-death experience that publicly marks the new believer as belonging to Jesus Christ. Each believer is "lowered into death" and is then "raised to life" in an identity-forming event that says to the world, "This is a person who belongs to Calvary, to Easter, to Christ." Their confession is not only "I am a person formed by Exodus and Sinai," but also "I am a person formed by the cross and the resurrection." These are my events because I belong to the Lord of these events and to the *people* formed by these events. Because I have died and risen with Jesus Christ, I live with the people of Christ, under the shadow of Christ, in a world that has been changed by Christ, and that will one day be wholly transformed by Christ.[9]

Let's say further that baptism is the sign of belonging to a new world, a "promised land" where people may enjoy "the glorious liberty of the children of God" (Rom. 8:21 RSV). Everybody wants liberty. The problem is that everybody wants it on their own terms. But salvation does not work that way. God does not save people (from slavery, from addiction, from sin and shame) and then cut them loose to do what they want because without the guidance of God, "doing what we want" is a recipe for falling right back into slavery.

So to prevent a relapse, God preserves those who die and rise with Christ in baptism, those who respond to their baptism with faith (or to their faith with baptism). How? The Spirit of God empowers believers to "keep the rhythm going" where dying and rising are concerned.[10] Yielding to the Spirit of God, believers seek the death of their old self and the resurrection of their new self. That is, they put arrogance to death and raise humility to life. They put envy to death and raise gratitude to life. They put rage to death and raise gentleness to life. When they break this good rhythm for a time, they confess their sins, which is another form of dying with Christ because it kills us to admit that we are in the wrong. What is wonderful is that the person who goes through the "little death" of confession to imitate Jesus' big death at Golgotha—this person also rises toward new life, like Jesus walking out of his tomb. Confession of sin is an enormously *freeing* thing to do.

The Christian life always needs reforming. Perhaps even our reforms need reforming, especially when we grow proud of them or despairing of them. In any case, the main instrument of reform is dying and rising with Christ, practiced over and over till it becomes a way of being.

Take compassion as an example of dying and rising. A compassionate Christian feels distress at another's suffering and wants to relieve it. Such willingness to take on the suffering of others represents the death of aloofness, of scorn, and of much else. Her bestowal of sorrowing love on a sufferer may cause new life in them both, a new life they may be able to connect to the sorrowing and suffering love of God, who does not remain aloof but gains our trust by becoming vulnerable.

In the view of Calvin and of such standard Reformed confessions as the Heidelberg Catechism,[11] the dying of our old self and the coming to life of our new self are God's gift and also our calling. The Christian's vocation is (among other things) lifelong repentance in a big sense of that term, including constant attempts to starve ungodly impulses and dispositions and to feed the new self that has been "created to be like God in true righteousness and holiness" (Eph. 4:24 NIV).

HOW CAN DEPLETED CHRISTIANS ANSWER THEIR CALLING?

In *Facing the Truth, with Bill Moyers*, a documentary film of the Truth and Reconciliation Commission and of its principal participants,[12] Tandy Shezzi tells of her degradation by white government agents. She tells of sexual torment too awful to imagine and of how it was deliberately designed to assail her dignity. At one point, she says that in order to cope with her ordeal, she removed her soul and spirit from her body because she could not bear its violation. After years, she said she would like to go back "and collect my soul." Imagine what it means to say, in effect, "I am a woman without a soul. I don't have the strength, the substance, the core of my humanity anymore. Maybe God calls me to drop the anger I have a right to have, and maybe I'd like to do it, but I'm too numb now. I'd have to collect my soul first."

The call to crucify one's pride, envy, anger, sloth, avarice, gluttony, and lust is seemingly a call that can be answered only by a believer with considerable resources.[13] It takes a kind of spiritual muscle to slay the impulses and dispositions of the old self. People who have been abused may lack these resources. In fact, their "too-little self" may have gone into hiding.[14]

Perhaps something like the same goes for people who have been depleted not by attack on them, but by neglect of them. North American pastoral theologians speak of believers who share in a more general social phenomenon, the "emptying of the self." Perhaps some of these believers were raised by parents or others who didn't supply enough "oxygen" for them to draw upon: not enough attention, not enough empathy, not enough sheer enthusiasm for them as persons.[15] Perhaps their parents were gone too much (some of them out of necessity). Perhaps their caretakers were more interested in taking care of themselves than of their children because they, too, felt deprived. In any case, whatever has emptied it out, a depleted self emerges into adulthood without the conventionally Christian set of spiritual coordinates: such persons experience less faith than anxiety, less hope than fear, less love of others and more of a need to be loved by others. They feel little guilt. For them, feeling guilty would be an achievement. Instead, they feel shame: a sense of distress at their deficiencies, deformities, or absurdities, and especially at the uncovering of these things before the eyes of others.

This may be a narcissistic person, whose self-absorption arises from insecurity. Such persons may think about themselves a lot not because they think they are wonderful, but because they think that they are not, that they do not measure up in some way.

Remarkably, in both clinical and more everyday forms of narcissism, the empty self may overinflate in order to compensate, and perhaps most especially if they think they need a high profile to attract the kind of attention they want. What may then emerge is the kind of mating call that sometimes shows up in the personals section of papers and magazines:

> **A Delicate Beauty**
>
> Captivating, head-turning, petite, slim, successful artist and writer. Compelling combination [of] intelligence/sensuality. Fun, funny, and talented. Known for clever, silly rhymes, gracious entertaining, caring heart, beautiful hands. Passionate and radiant widow. Lots of style and flair. Entrepreneurial, philanthropic, high-profile . . .[16]

Of course, only the Lord knows whether the caring heart and beautiful hands belong to a poor self who is starved for attention or to a grandiose self who is overstuffed with it. All I know is that I have quoted only half the ad.

In sum, if believers include many who, whether from assault or neglect or some other cause, lack a sturdy self, if they already have "a sense of mortification for having failed to live lives of significance,"[17] then what earthly good will it do to call such folk to "the dying-away of the old self and the coming-to-life of the new"? To paraphrase Donald Capps, what can possibly be gained by preaching repentance to the shamed, the drained, and the bereft?

RESOURCES FOR HEALTHY REPENTANCE

I am not brave enough to attempt a real answer to this question, but I do wish to address it in a series of what seem to be pertinent observations. I will make five of them:

1. Repentance, including dying and rising with Christ, is not a self-help program. Nobody is asking a depleted self to huff and puff to be good. A Christian's virtues derive from the goodness of Jesus Christ, who is the original vine, and from the sanctifying Spirit, whose secret work bears fruit within (and without) the church. Humility, kindness, and the ability to cope with people who tell us jokes that we first told them are gifts deserving quiet gratitude. For the whole run of life—beginning, growth, flowering, dying in peace—a Christian depends on the gracious impetus of God. All human virtue is born and grows up in the cradle of God's grace.

2. Let us say that the object of faith of a Christian person is Jesus Christ, or Christ "clothed with the gospel," or "Christ and his benefits," or, more generally put, the grace of God. Faith attaches not to God's threats or to God's displeasures or to God's ways with donkeys that talk and axheads that float, but to God's grace. It was a conviction of John Calvin that grace must be the proper object of faith because that is the thing on which faith can repose: God's mercy for the miserable, God's forgiveness of the guilty, God's benevolence toward his children. And repose is welcomed by the restlessly proud and the restlessly despairing alike.

What follows, I think, is that the depleted heart could be called to faith in God's grace first and for a long time. Repentance arises from the conviction that it reposes in the cradle of grace, that it is OK to risk a little, to try a little, to fail a lot, provided that one rests within the grace of God. Virtues arise in the context of this same faith that binds Christians to Jesus Christ. For example, their gratitude—their blended sense of blessedness and nonentitlement—arise from their faithful recognition of God's benevolence to them. Gratitude motivates a Christian life just because faith does. A grateful Christian cannot repay God for redemption. But like good children of good parents who want to pass on healthy home life to their children, grateful Christians can direct the energy from their gratitude out toward others. Those who trust "Jesus Christ, God's only Son, our Lord" therefore trust that (contrary to appearances and to Nietzsche) kindness is a form of strength and humility a species of wisdom. They trust that obedience to God exalts a life instead of stifling it and that a glad habit of spending oneself for others (washing the feet of disciples who would not dream of doing the same thing for each other) can in a godly community excite a near carnival of goodwill and self-irony.

Here, as always, cautions are in order: Jesus Christ assumed the form of a servant, not a doormat, and Christians in union with Christ need to recognize that distinction, particularly in abusive settings. True humility extends respect yet also wants respect. We do not serve people if we merely reinforce their arrogance or if we give them submission when what they really need from us is resistance. Endless deferring to others can stop life's traffic (not the least at intersections with four-way stop signs). Still, given the necessary precautions, Christians may trust that self-spending love—with all its kin among the middleweight virtues—is a mark not of the fool but of the redeemer.

3. In such paraenetic contexts as Colossians 3, Ephesians 4, and Romans 12, Paul exhorts those who are "one body in Christ" to adopt virtues appropriate to building their communal unity. Union with Christ is ipso facto union with others, and a more perfect union with them will take a lot of virtue on the part of the members. Thus Paul counsels humility, not particularly because the humble person will then find others more interesting and human life more engaging than can those curved in on self, but because Christians need to respect each other's dignity and each other's complementary gifts in order to function as a healthy body. Paul exhorts forgivingness not particularly because the person who drops (justifiable) anger against an offender will then be able to get a night's sleep (though true enough and worth noting; Eph. 4:26), but because we cannot have a reconciling community unless those who have been forgiven by God believe, and act on their belief, that it would be superbly fitting for them to forgive each other. And Paul exhorts believers to "weep with those who weep" (Rom. 12:15), not particularly because compassion is a sign that a person possesses a full and healthy range of emotion (and that whoever can cry is an up-to-date character), but because compassion is the kind of "wound," as Julian of Norwich called it, that helps to heal other wounds in a body.

A corollary: as we have mentioned above, practicing virtues in union with Christ represents the image of God. Compassion, patience, humility, and the rest of the virtues compose not the ambition of spiritual entrepreneurs but the vocation of godliness by people elected to follow it. There are a number of ways to image God. One of them is to live in communal love. Because God is triune, the image of God is social as well as personal—a truth we can find not only in John 17, which appears to make the church the official biblical analogue of the Holy Trinity, but also in the "renewal of the image" passages in Ephesians 4 and Colossians 3.

There Paul writes to churches that are divided or in danger of division and calls them to renew the image of God by such means as telling the truth, practicing the difference between indignation and mere irritability, working hard so as to have something to give to the poor, and adopting a tenderhearted attitude toward sinners. The idea is that doing these things is being like God. To act like this is to act like God. More specifically, to act like this is to represent Jesus Christ, the preeminent image of God the Father. We image God by imaging Christ, and we do it by showing godly knowledge, righteousness, and holiness (Col. 3:10; Eph. 4:24). Paraenesis is just a way of spelling out righteousness.

Considerations of this kind help us to see the paraenetic sections of Scripture in the same way as we see the church, as a part of the gospel and not a mere addendum to it. The reason is that these sections present us with the counsels of grace by the God of grace, who knows how life flourishes in union with Christ and wishes to share the recipe. God's commands orient us to covenant living and tell us how to make it sing. It is part of Karl Barth's enduring spiritual genius to see this truth and to insist upon it. God's command is "the form of the gospel" that invites "joyful participation" in good life with God and each other. God's call to compassion is itself compassionate. When we refuse God's commands, it is grace we are refusing; it is freedom we are refusing. We think we are refusing a bad death and that as depleted persons we cannot handle any more death, but we are actually refusing the good death that leads to resurrection and life.[18] "The good command of God," writes Otto Weber in a luminous treatment of paraenesis, comes to us not out of pique, and not out of the blue, but "in Christ," "in the Lord Jesus," "by the name of our Lord Jesus Christ," "by the mercies of God." Forget about "principles," "duties," and even "virtues," if you must, and let your Christian ethics amount to "thought-out paraenetics" in which indicative mercy gets transformed into imperative mercy.[19]

4. When Paul (or the Pauline) counsels believers to put to death pride, anger, greed, and lust, those sins are only samples of disunion with Christ. Perhaps these are not the besetting temptations of depleted believers, and perhaps preachers and pastoral care providers will be diligent to know their audience. To whom do they preach humility? To major players or minor ones? To those who strut or to those who cower? To men or to women? Knowing the audience, perhaps discerning preachers or pastoral care providers will counsel depleted believers in tones adapted from Jesus, who spoke quite differently from those who piled burdens on others than he did to those who had to carry those burdens. Perhaps the Christian helper will assist the burdened to off-load not pride, malice, and greed so much as despair, fear, and the terrible sense that they are less a person than a shadow of a person.

5. Following Colossians 3:10, Calvin left a place for knowledge in the renewed image of God. We are "renewed in knowledge according to the image of [the] Creator" (RSV). Given that God's knowledge is always discerning, dynamic, adaptive through changing contexts including appalling ones, it might not be too much to say that one of the most enduring and resourceful signs of God's image shining through the church is that the pastoral ministry adapts to changing personal and cultural circumstances. The name of such knowledge is wisdom, which includes a kind of knack for knowing when to rebuke and when to encourage, when to urge and when to caution, when to stiffen and demand the whole of justice, and when to salvage as much justice as one can, leaving something to the justice of God.

I believe we could say that one of the functions of the doctrine of God's image is that it helps to orient us human beings in the cosmos: the doctrine positions humanity between extravagant and demeaning estimates, between soaring humanisms and reductionist naturalisms, between the view that we are gods who create the worlds and the "nothing but" philosophies that reduce our humanity to chemical and electric systems and events. In this view we are "naked apes" or "digestive tubes." Against all Promethean presumptions of ultimacy, we are not God but only secondary images of God. Yet against all materialist reductions we are images of God. Depending on the audience, we hope the pastoral care providers will use their wisdom to know where to put the accent.

Chapter 15

Preaching in the Age of the Holy Spirit

JANA CHILDERS

Poet-theologian Amos Wilder said that going to church should be like "approaching an open volcano where the world is molten and hearts are sifted. The altar is like a third rail that spatters sparks. The sanctuary is like the chamber next to an atomic oven. There are invisible rays and you leave your watch outside."[1] Though the lines are more than forty years old, they capture something of the yearnings of the moment.

These days all kinds of people are spiritually restless. Harvey Cox is writing on Pentecostalism,[2] Youth Ministry's Mark Yaconelli is leading teenagers to rediscover Christianity's ancient spiritual disciplines,[3] the Faith and Politics Institute is hosting a weekly spiritual reflection group for U.S. senators and members of the House of Representatives in Washington, D.C.,[4] and throughout the U.S. "performance consultants" are beginning meetings at Dell and IBM and Motorola with prayer. Popular San Francisco author Carol Lee Flinders claims that feminism is at a "fourth turning."[5] Voting rights, economic opportunity, and sexual freedom, she says, are being followed by a fourth phase of the movement, a turning toward spirituality.

All kinds of people are searching, even church people. Something, it seems, is sending them up the steps at 11:00 o'clock on Sunday morning with renewed hope. It is as if they expect to catch a glimpse of the glorious church without spot or wrinkle, if not Wilder's phantasmagoric version. As the great preacher Fred Craddock predicted, they come and say, "Maybe there will be a word from the Lord today."[6] Even some in the churches usually counted among the least restive of tribes, are wondering.

The "age of the Holy Spirit," some have called it, noticing a rising tide of interest in the larger culture that seems to float a number of boats, the church's among them. Some say that Christianity is due for the shift. After two thousand years of focus on the first person of the Trinity, followed by two thousand years of focus on Christ, some see the new millennia we have entered as the age of the Holy Spirit.[7] Perhaps it is.

Pentecostalism celebrated its centenary (1906, Azusa Street Revival, Los Angeles) with exponential growth. From T. D. Jakes's Potter's House in Dallas (boasting a membership of 28,000 in its first six years) to Yoido Full Gospel Church in Seoul and its one million members, Pentecostalism is a lively tribe with an impressive record.[8] The largest religious movement in history, it numbers 580 million souls. In just a hundred years, it has become the most globally diverse and fastest growing expression of Christianity. Given the rate of growth, some researchers see their numbers reaching one billion by 2025.

At the same time, something is indicated by the unrest within Reformed tradition churches and the reforming of worship going on right and left throughout the Protestant churches of the United States. Something is stirring. Even the Presbyterian Church (U.S.A.) website has featured something called "Emerging Worship," which defines itself as any practice of worship that is expressive, faithful to tradition, and attentive to local context. It is meant, it says, to provide an alternative to classical, traditional, and contemporary understandings of worship. Perhaps it would not be too much to say that the alternative church worship styles, upbeat music, and let-your-hair-down preaching that are currently taking the church, or some segments of it, by storm point to the Holy Spirit's stirrings. Of course, while some turn to churches with their spiritual longings, it must be admitted that more do not. Bette Midler was among the first to say it publicly, some years ago, in front of Johnny and Doc and half the country: "I'm not religious, but I'm very spiritual." It's been repeated countless times since, achieving near mantra status in California, where only 4.6 percent of the population attends mainline denominational churches. These days many people in California and elsewhere are expressing their spirituality outside the church. They may not know what they are spiritually, but they know they are not Jimmy Swaggart or Robert Schuller, not "Presbyterian" or "Methodist."

The problem is not that preaching is not interested in addressing the needs of the age. There is no shortage of preachers trying to deliver the message of hope and spiritual power that many are longing to hear. There are any number of folks fairly standing on their heads in the pulpit to get a hearing. The Message is being Sent, week by week, zip code by zip code. The problem is that it is failing to reach the Receivers, often wafting over empty pews instead. Though the decline of mainline churches in North America may be rather well explained in terms of the sea change in attitudes toward institutions, tradition, and authority, not all of the current malaise can be laid at the feet of the 1960s. Some of it we have yet to parse.

PREACHNG TO THE HOPEFUL AND THE JADED

This essay explores the question of what preachers within the Reformed tradition might have to contribute to an age that is both more hopeful of and more jaded about spiritual experience. Does being Reformed make a difference in how we will preach our way through the twenty-first century? What does the Reformed tradition have to say to or learn from the age of the Holy Spirit? Is there anything that can be said to be "distinctive" about our preaching, especially anything that would be helpful to this peculiar age?

Before tackling those questions directly, I will explain how I came to be interested in them. Postmodernism has taught me something of the value of speaking from my own location, and it seems particularly appropriate to disclose that although I have been Presbyterian for just more than half of my life, I was not born into the Reformed tradition. I was born into the Pentecostal church at, as far as I can tell, the exact nadir of its popularity. I am the daughter and the granddaughter of Pentecostal families. Not only was it not chic to be Pentecostal in the New Jersey public school system of the 1960s, but it also was impossible to imagine then that there would ever be a Religious Right or a 700 Club, much less a Tammy Faye. It was the age of Madeleine Murray O'Hare, Dean Martin, and, of course, modernism. If there ever was an institution more modernist than the New Jersey public school, I do not know what that would be. Richard Nixon was President when I graduated from that system, and nobody had ever heard of Jimmy Carter. It may seem that spending half your life—all of the Sunday mornings and the Sunday, Wednesday, and Friday evenings of the first half of your life (with occasional Saturdays thrown in)—kneeling around Pentecostal altars might qualify a person to talk a bit about dramatic spiritual phenomena or at least to comment on Wilder's phantasmagoric vision of worship. I bring up my social location because I want to make two small observations or claims:

1. People of this generation of the Reformed tradition know something about social change; in that facility and familiarity with the phenomena of spiritual resources, perhaps even an *Anknüpfungspunkt* (point of connection) for the Holy Spirit, may be found.
2. The Reformed tradition does indeed have something essential to offer the age of the Holy Spirit, something that no other movement seems in a position to provide.

We will look briefly at the phenomenon of social change and say a bit more about why it might be useful to think of this as the age of the Holy Spirit and then move to the substance of this thesis: what the Reformed tradition in preaching has to offer this peculiar age.

SOCIAL CHANGE AND THE AGE OF THE HOLY SPIRIT

The pendulum swings. If there is one thing that our generation has learned over the course of our lives, it is that cultural shifts you could not have imagined occur. Kennedys are replaced by Bushes. Peaceniks fade and Yuppies appear. O'Hare yields the stage to Falwell. For the most part, of course, these are physical, political, social, and economic matters that can be seen to be pushed along by physical, political, social, and economic forces. The Klan falls and the NAACP (National Association for the Advancement of Colored People) rises. The DAR (Daughters of the American Revolution) fades and the ranks of women CEOs grows. The terror of AIDS begins to give way to the power of several new medicines. Society changes. However, to those of us who identify with the Reformed tradition, they call up two ways of parsing the phenomena of change: social and theological. They get us thinking about the phenomena in two of the deepest grooves of our minds and hearts. And as such, they serve as *reminders* to us of the unseen, the surprising, and the unpredictable. They serve as reminders of the province of the Holy Spirit.

I am not saying that this generation or people of the Reformed tradition know more than any other group about social change, only that we know a good deal, more than we might think, and that, in learning to be sensitive to change, we may have developed skills that will help us in the age of the Spirit. The facilities we develop in sniffing out the beginnings of change, in riding change through and absorbing its movement into our lives, may have interesting spiritual analogues. This generation of the Reformed tradition is a people who live with numerous built-in pneumatic devices that, at the very least, should help us to remember to ask, "Is it possible that the Holy Spirit might be moving?" The Holy Spirit is indeed all about change, and though you hardly ever know till much later whether a particular set of changes can be rightly ascribed to the Holy Spirit (hence 1 John 4:1 says, "Test the spirits"), change should make us wet our spiritual finger and put it up in the air.

Let me put it less colloquially and more precisely. Michael Welker reminds us that in pneumatology the concept of "emergence" is important.[9] It is a concept that describes something of the unique ability of the Holy Spirit to "make all things new." According to this concept, God the Spirit is experienced as a power that effects certain kinds of change "by appearances and processes that are difficult to grasp—experiences and processes that can be termed 'emergent.'"[10] Welker's work with the concept of "emergence" calls up Alfred North Whitehead and a number of others who have kept the notion in play and endeavored to refine its definition over the last several decades. In his seminal work *God the Spirit*, Welker offers first the words of mid-twentieth-century philosopher

G. H. Mead and then his own definition. Both are helpful in describing this distinct and constitutive element of the Holy Spirit's character and providing background for a word that has taken on new valences in early twenty-first-century worship.

Mead defined emergence as "the presence of things in two or more different systems in such a fashion that its presence in a later system changes its character in the earlier system."[11] Now for Welker: "I characterize as 'emergent' those constellations, conditions, and structures whose appearance on the scene cannot be derived from preceding constellations, conditions and structures, although diverse elements that define both conditions persist in them."[12] The point of the philosophical discussion of "emergence" and the "emergent" is that one of the essential characteristics of the Holy Spirit is the Spirit's unique ability to orchestrate change, especially by bringing about new understanding, reinterpretation, and redefinition.

Whitehead, Mead, and Welker are commenting on a slice of a much larger and classic understanding of the Holy Spirit as change agent, an understanding held virtually throughout the Reformed Tradition. Emil Brunner defined the Holy Spirit as "creative power, that produces new life, new will, new feelings, new spiritual, psychological and even physical power."[13] Karl Barth described the church's need to be a community of the Spirit: "The Christian community can and must be the scene of many human activities which are new and supremely astonishing to many of its own members as well as to the world around it."[14] And Calvin himself said, "As long as Christ remains outside of us, and we are separated from him, all that he has suffered and done . . . remains useless and of no value to us. . . . It is true that we obtain (this benefit) by faith, yet since we see that not all indiscriminately embrace that communion with Christ which is offered through the gospel, reason itself teaches us to climb higher and to examine into the secret energy of the Spirit, by which we come to enjoy Christ and all his benefits" (*Institutes* 3.1.1).

It thus may be useful for those of us in and around the Reformed tradition to consider the possibility that the twenty-first century may be seen in some sense as the age of the Holy Spirit. Certainly we live in an era characterized by dramatic, frequent, wide-reaching, and often unpredictable change, the very kind of change that causes one to rethink one's original categories. It ought to make us think of what we say we believe about the Holy Spirit. And it may, in fact, be helping us develop sensibilities and *habitus* that will serve to deepen our life in the Spirit as the Spirit moves across the face of the new millennium.

THE REFORMED TRADITION

I take the position that there are at least three "soft" distinctives of Reformed tradition preaching. Its preaching is distinguishable from other contemporary preaching in terms of its priorities, purpose, and nature. Taken together, these distinctives may suggest a model of preaching with potential to speak to the peculiar problems and yearnings of the age.

The Reformed Tradition. I can hardly make myself capitalize the "t." Is there such a thing as a theological animal so distinct from other species that it deserves all those capital letters? The question has already received a good deal of attention. George Stroup has described five approaches to defining Reformed identity. The tradition may be understood in terms of its polity, "essential tenets," themes, *habitus*, or theological grammar, he claims, arguing for a combination of the last three—using the metaphor of a family's photo album. What we are looking for, he says, are "the distinctive features of the family."[15] Stroup tries his hand at reframing traditional concepts into "distinctives," softening, for example, the "essential tenet" concerning the sovereignty of God to an affirmation of the "priority of God in God's relation to human beings."[16]

Stroup's essay is written with an eye toward enabling ecumenical dialogue. This may go a ways toward explaining why his "distinctives" strike some readers as a bit fuzzy. However, the soft approach suggested by his photo-album metaphor is useful for the purposes of this essay. In considering the strengths most often associated with the Reformed tradition—in flipping through the album—it is striking to see that a few family members do indeed have pronounced features. Long noses and strong chins stand out. Among these more "strongly featured" branches of the Reformed family are certainly Uncle Homileticus and Auntie Praedicatio. There is no doubt to whose family they belong. In terms of its priority, purpose, and nature, preaching is a distinguished and distinguishable branch of the Reformed tradition family.

A PRIORITY ON THE WORD

Praedicatio verbi Dei est verbum Dei.
—The Second Helvetic Confession (1562)

On any list of hallmarks of the Reformed tradition, an emphasis on preaching is near the top. The symbolic importance of preaching in the Reformed tradition is affirmed, even where the reality is different. There can be little doubt that from a historical point of view, one of the Reformed tradition's most significant contributions to Christian worship has been the priority it places on preaching.

"Preaching the Word of God is the Word of God," the Second Helvetic Confession declares. Calvin, who defined the church as a place where the Word is purely preached and the sacraments rightly administered (*Institutes* 4.1.9), is said to have preached more than seven thousand sermons himself. Karl Barth, too, preached frequently and thought of his theology as a preacher's theology. John Leith lists preaching among nine motifs that have "shaped the Reformed style of being a Christian."[17] Implicit in John de Gruchy's view—Reformed theology is "essentially an attempt to restate the biblical message within ever-changing historical contexts"[18]—is a suggestion of preaching's significance. Hughes Oliphant Old puts preaching at the "head of the list" of Reformed worship traditions.[19] There is wide agreement that the proclamation of the Word is of primary importance in the worship of the Reformed tradition.[20]

The Reformed tradition's reputation for preaching is closely tied, of course, to its *ad fontes* interest in Scripture. The Reformed tradition's preaching is not just any kind of preaching. It is preaching that is avidly interested in the biblical text. Expository preaching, it is often claimed, is the form most appropriately used by Calvin's homiletical children. (Calvin was, indeed, a great practitioner of the method, although he knew and practiced others.) However, while the expository sermon provides a fine example of text-centered or text-serious preaching, it is clear that in the contemporary period of the Reformed tradition, a priority on Scripture and the preaching of Scripture-based sermons is more important than any one homiletical style.

A MAJESTIC PURPOSE

The greatest single contribution which the Reformed liturgical heritage can make to contemporary American Protestantism is its sense of the majesty and sovereignty of God.[21]

—Hughes Oliphant Old

Preachers in the Reformed tradition preach with a peculiar purpose in mind: the glorification of God. When this is seen in combination with the Reformed tradition's emphasis on God's sovereignty, the peculiar "flavor" of Reformed tradition preaching begins to make sense. If our sermons are somber, responsible, dignified, it is partly because we preach under the aegis of a Very Big God.

If there is one thing that Reformed tradition preachers know, it is dignity. Not everyone practices it or practices it all the time, but it would be difficult to be a Reformed tradition preacher in the United States and not know what is expected of you in this regard. Sobriety, rigor, dryness, rationality, and learnedness are part of the same stereotype.

People expect a certain kind of deportment from preachers in the Reformed tradition, it seems. Some say we are the people Garrison Keillor had in mind when he described some folks of his acquaintance as having "the emotional range of Lucite." Or the ones Jim Wall meant when he referred to preachers who "would rather sound like bank presidents than prophets." It is not without reason that the oldest imaginable chestnut linking Presbyterians with "the frozen" and "the chosen" still gets a good laugh. We are indeed the bank presidents of preachers. The scholars. The Jesuits of the Protestant world. There is truth in the jest.

One of the reasons why we are the way we are is that we value dignity, and one of the reasons we value dignity is that we are shaped by a tradition emphasizing God's sovereignty. God's prevenience, power, and "size" are themes upheld in good Reformed preaching. Not in content only, but in process and form, preaching in the Reformed tradition focuses on God. And it does so in a way that focuses the listener's attention on God. At its best, Reformed preaching is characterized by magnitude, or what some preachers call "size." This way of focusing attention on God and on God's majesty elicits, from both the preacher and the listener, a profound response. Not trivial, not casual, not folksy, and not small, but profound—the kind of response that is associated with the word "dignity."

Preaching that focuses on God in this way provides a needed corrective in contemporary preaching. So Paul Scott Wilson says, "Most current preaching is deficient in its presentation of God and God's action in our world. God has revealed Godself in Scripture, has intervened in history in Jesus Christ, and remains active in the world in the Holy Spirit, yet many of us who are pastors, ministers or priests aim our homiletical cameras in the other direction, at human activity."[22] Contemporary preaching is known for its anthropocentrism and Pelagianism. Listeners are exhorted, soothed, or analyzed but often left ultimately to their own devices. God's activity in the world on our behalf gets short shrift.

Paul Scott Wilson describes a volume of sermons published recently as part of a noteworthy series. The theological diversity of the church was well represented; the sermons were models of excellence. However, of the twenty sermons in the collection, Wilson found that six did not mention God in any meaningful way and seven made only brief mention of God. The remaining seven sermons devoted several paragraphs each to the subject. However, in no case was any more than 10 percent of the sermon's content found to contain significant language about God and God's activity on our behalf.[23]

A theological tradition that is able to keep preaching focused on God has a timely and significant contribution to make.

A SACRAMENTAL NATURE

Homileticians in the Reformed tradition in the United States do not make free use of the term "sacramental." Yet the concept is close to home for us. After several trips around large theological barns, we end up using other words to describe the same phenomena. We talk about "mystical union," the "divine exchange," and *Christus praesens*. "Mutual indwelling" is a safe phrase; it is fine to talk about how Christ is present in the believer, how the believer is present in Christ, and about the role preaching might play in that. But when it comes to saying the obvious—that a sacramental model of preaching captures much of what is important to and even distinctive about the Reformed view of preaching—we are sometimes a bit shy, a bit bound by old quarrels and ancient lexica.

We are aware that other traditions have made much of "sacramentality"; while in some ecumenical dialogues, the commonality provides a useful starting point for dialogue, in others it hold us back. We hold ourselves back; we hesitate to use language that has been more famously associated with Luther and Rahner.

There is no one sentence in the *Institutes*, after all, where Calvin says, "Preaching is a sacramental act" or "The preached word effects what it signifies." It is easy to say that Calvin holds a "very high view" of preaching and to quote his *Institutes* (4.1.5, trans. F. L. Battles here and below), "For, among the many gifts with which God has adorned the human race, it is a singular privilege that he deigns to consecrate to himself the mouths and tongues of men in order that his voice may resound in them." But we stop short, as Calvin did, of speaking explicitly of preaching as sacrament.

To the Reformed tradition mind, however, preaching *is* a sacramental act. Though it would have been lovelier for us if Calvin had said so in the most direct terms, it is nonetheless a legitimate interpretation of Calvin's view. Calvin regards the sacraments and the preaching of the Word of God as having the same modus operandi. "Therefore, let it be regarded as a settled principle that the sacraments have the same office as the Word of God: to offer and set forth Christ to us, and in him the treasures of heavenly grace" (4.14.17). Dawn DeVries, who along with Brian Gerrish has done much to elucidate this aspect of Calvin's thinking, explains: "What do we mean when we say Calvin had a doctrine of the sacramental word? We mean, in short, that the Word can be understood to operate in the same way a sacrament does and can be said to convey the same gift a sacrament does, namely, Jesus Christ and all his benefits."[24]

Following Augustine's treatment of the Gospel of John (chiefly John 6, with connections to 1 John 1 as well as to the prologue of the Gospel), Calvin sees "sacrament" as the Word of God made visible. The Word is made visible in preaching, Calvin claims, in a way that effects what it signifies. He is saying that in preaching, the Word is made present, brought into the room, made hearable. "If for Calvin the sacraments are the visible word of God, it must be underlined that they are effectual," as Hughes Oliphant Old says.[25] Yet Calvin's view of the sacramental nature of preaching goes farther still. Not only is the Word made hearable and effectual, but for Calvin "visible" may even imply "embodied." Calvin's famous statement—arguably the line of Calvin most beloved of preachers—makes the point: "The preacher's lips are the very lips of Christ."[26] It is hard to imagine a line more suggestive of a full-blown "sacramental" view of preaching. Indeed, when taken all together, the picture hints at the possibility that Calvin's view of preaching was not only sacramental but, at least nascently, incarnational.[27]

On the basis of the argument made so far, Calvin's homiletical nose and chin may or may not be distinguishable from those of other families. However, there is one feature of Calvin's (and of his homiletical children) that adds significantly to the colorfulness of the family album. For Calvin, preaching is not simply a sacramental act: it is a sacramental act that dramatically depends on the Holy Spirit.

It is doubtful whether any other major theologian has written more extensively of the role of the Holy Spirit in preaching than John Calvin. The word, in Calvin's view, needs the Holy Spirit in order to be efficacious. It is not the sacraments that confer the Holy Spirit upon us, Calvin makes clear: "The only function divinely imparted to [the sacraments] is to attest and ratify for us God's good will toward us. *And they are of no further benefit unless the Holy Spirit accompanies them*" (4.14.17, emphasis added). For Calvin, preaching is "the administration of the Spirit" (4.3.3). There can be no question that Calvin has both sacramental activity and the Holy Spirit in mind when he says, in the same paragraph, "This office could not be more splendidly adorned than when [God] said, 'He who hears you hears me, and he who rejects you rejects me' [Luke 10:16]."

Preaching requires the agency of the Holy Spirit to be effectual, Calvin believes, and he sees that role played out in two ways: creating entrée and sealing. First of all, the Holy Spirit creates entry to the human heart. "Indeed, the word of God is like the sun, shining upon all those to whom it is proclaimed, but with no effect among the blind. Now, all of us are blind by nature in this respect. Accordingly, it cannot penetrate into our minds unless the Spirit, as the inner teacher, through his illumination makes entry for it" (3.2.34). Second, the Holy Spirit seals the human heart against doubt.

> For the word of God is not received by faith if it flits about in the top of the brain, but when it takes root in the depth of the heart.... But if it is true that the mind's real understanding is illumination by the Spirit of God, then in such confirmation of the heart his power is much more clearly manifested, to the extent that the heart's distrust is greater than the mind's blindness. It is harder for the heart to be furnished with assurance than for the mind to be endowed with thought. The Spirit accordingly serves as a seal, to seal up in our hearts those very promises the certainty of which it has previously impressed on our minds. (3.2.36)

When Calvin's emphasis on the "creating-entrée" and "sealing" roles of the Holy Spirit are painted into his sacramental view of preaching, a distinctive picture emerges. Preaching is rightly understood in the Reformed tradition as a peculiarly powerful and mysterious Holy Spirit event, which effects what it signifies. Not only that, but we are talking about an event in which the Holy Spirit does not merely inspire, delight, persuade, or move, but also creates access into human consciousness. The image is of an aperture being widened. The Holy Spirit's role as a modifier of consciousness is part and parcel of the Word being heard. In other words, the way the Holy Spirit ensures that the Word will be heard has something to do with the modifying of consciousness.

Here, then, is the answer to the question we have posed. What does the Reformed tradition have to contribute to an age where people are more desirous of and more jaded about spiritual experience? A belief that the Holy Spirit is in charge of their apertures. And that the same Spirit may be trusted to make use of this unique ability in the service of the Word. For, as Chrysostom most pointedly says, "Many boast of the Holy Spirit, but those who speak their own thoughts claim him falsely. As Christ testified that he spoke not from himself, because he spoke from the Law and the Prophets, so let us not believe anything that is thrust in under the title of the Spirit apart from the gospel. For just as Christ is the fulfillment of the Law and the Prophets, so is the Spirit the fulfillment of the gospel" (via *Institutes* 4.8.13). While other Christian brothers and sisters agree with the pieces of Calvin's picture, no one sketches just the same portrait.

IMPLICATIONS FOR PRACTICE

There is no guarantee that the distinctive features of preaching in the Reformed tradition we have discussed—a priority on textual preaching, a God-centered purpose, and a sacramental nature—will add up to an attractive picture for the scrapbook or contribute to the age of the Holy Spirit. On any given day, the Homileticus branch of the family may or may not be very photogenic. A great deal depends on how the features discussed here are combined in practice. In practice, preaching in the Reformed tradition does several things, as suggested here:

1. Sets a priority on the study and careful interpretation of the text. This is the obvious implication of the claim I have made that RT preaching sets a priority on textual preaching. While others claim to base their preaching on a careful interpretation of biblical texts, in practice it is the churches of the Reformed family who focus preachers' training in this area. To the evangelical church's zeal, the Reformed tradition adds a few resources in hermeneutics and theological methods. And we maintain a pneumatology that emphasizes the role of the Holy Spirit in interpreting Christ's work.

2. Corrects contemporary tendencies toward trivial and narcissistic preaching by keeping the focus of the sermon on the gracious activity of God among us. This is the implication of the claim I have made that RT's distinctive sense of the purpose of preaching highlights God's majesty. Sermons that combine a God-centered focus with a textual emphasis (#1 above) will concentrate on finding a record of God's activity in the biblical text and generating story, metaphor, and narrative that lives up to the "size" of God's ways of being with us. Again, it is hard to imagine a purpose of preaching more connected to and supported by the Holy Spirit than one that focuses on God's mighty and tender acts.

3. Explores *embodied* preaching. This is the natural consequence of my claim that RT preaching really is sacramental preaching. Preachers in the RT preach with confidence that the Holy Spirit is using their hearts, minds, *and bodies* (famously, as per Calvin, their very lips!) to make the Word present. The promise of such an approach is that it yields authentic preachers, those whose expression faithfully communicates their experience. Such preachers "outer what they

inner," and it is obvious to everyone in the room. It is imputed to them as "sincerity," "naturalness," and "credibility." Howard Rice describes this phenomenon, potentially so important for this age and time, in clear and simple terms: "The preacher's task is to be so personally present that the people can see the connection between the words that are spoken and the person doing the speaking."[28]

The more preachers find ways to combine and recombine the distinctive features of the Reformed tradition in practice, the more opportunity the ecumenical church will have to test our contribution against the peculiar needs of the age. However, in an era where hunger for an experience of the Holy Spirit is afoot, where preachers are critiqued as being narcissistic or inauthentic, and where the two-dimensional screen threatens the intimacy of worship, Calvin's model seems uncannily timely—and worth everything preachers can give it.

Chapter 16

The Aesthetic Profile of Reformed Liturgy

RALPH KUNZ

Over the past few years, I have studied the Zwinglian worship service intensively.[1] This investigation of the roots of our tradition opened for me the sparse beauty of the Zwinglian liturgy, as well as its problems. For Zwingli, a worship service was to be a "pauper's theater." Sensual aspects were reduced to the essential. This was more than an asceticism of the senses: it was a matter of devotion. A worship service is an event calling for awareness and concentration. My question: How is this worship tradition presented in contemporary culture? Stimulated by interaction with dramaturgical theory and theatrical aesthetics,[2] I propose considering the question, To what degree did the late medieval ideal of worship seek to realize a timeless aesthetic principle that also has contemporary relevance?

LITURGICAL EROSION: SIDELIGHTS OF A DEBATE

In the Swiss Federation of Protestant Churches' bulletin, a column was published in 2002 with the title "Liturgical Erosion." There the author Ruedi Heinzer reported an alarming decline in the awareness of form in Swiss Protestant worship services. The little that gives the Reformed worship service its identity is flushed away by the effusion of personal feelings of the worship leaders. The Lord's Prayer is missing; where once the final blessing was spoken, creative wishes and Irish weather aphorisms sprout up. Heinzer called on church and university to erect a dam of education against the disintegration of the awareness of form.[3] The appeal found approval yet also met with criticism and triggered a proper little debate. Three ministers protested against Heinzer's analysis. They could not see any purpose in this lamentation on the decline. That ceremonies change is a typical Protestant approach. Whoever demands more unity, more awareness of form, or more respect for tradition should visit a museum. In a similar direction, but a little less pointed, is David Plüss's contribution to this discussion. He countered Heinzer by saying that in the postconventional society there could no longer be a "right" and a "wrong." Liturgical pluralism is a fact, and it therefore is pointless to fight against it. In the German Swiss Protestant churches, the Sunday sermon-liturgy is one form among others. The worship meetings are also conducted in totally different styles. The criteria by which a worship service could be evaluated must be determined based on the internal style. Therefore, to speak of erosion does not make any sense.[4] The debate continues up to this day.[5]

What does this debate show? The publicly carried-out quarrel on the form of church service reveals the dissension that prevails among Protestant Christians concerning liturgical questions. Of course, Catholics, Lutherans, and Methodists also have their liturgical debates. But I believe the controversy within the German Swiss Reformed community is especially controversial. The rift is deep between those who support more the *awareness of the ceremony's form* and those who accept only the *liberty of arrangement* as the guiding criteria. Thus Theophil Müller arrives at a totally different conclusion from Heinzer in his analysis of the liturgical situation. For his part, he warned of a re-Catholicization of the Protestant worship service tradition![6]

I believe a critical distance from liturgism is part of the Reformed identity. But a liberty of form does not mean an absence of form. I see the liturgical situation in German-Switzerland symptomatic of a genuine Protestant problem. In the present cultural situation it is difficult to advocate a worship service that has a Reformed profile—simply because it is not easy to define the "liturgical" that is apparently threatening to erode in the Protestant church's worship service, or has long been eroded and forms itself anew in different styles. Protestant Christians must decide to determine their own profile, or else others will do it for them.

CHRISTIAN WORSHIP IN REFORMED CHURCHES, PAST AND PRESENT

The right to name the characteristic features of a recognizable and unmistakable Reformed form of celebration is raised in one of the publications by Lukas Vischer. The goal is defined like this: "This book can help many of us Reformed

Christians to sense the global scope of the Reformed branch of the Christian church. . . . This book helps us understand how the Reformed tradition need not be dependent on a particular ethnic or cultural context."[7]

What gives the Reformed worship service its profile? To find an answer to this question, around twenty Reformed theologians and worship leaders from all over the world met at the John Knox Center back in January 2001. It was agreed that the connection between ethnic and confessional identity has become brittle. It was also methodically agreed that drawing up a picture of the present situation of the Reformed worship service tradition can be done only by exploring the historical backgrounds in the different regions. This multicolored picture—Vischer speaks of a bouquet of flowers—is foundational in the search for ingredients that distinguish the Reformed church service tradition and make up its special color in the larger bouquet of ecumenism. Behind the book project one recognizes a concern of many of today's Reformed theologians. It has to do with marking the Reformed identity. Since the church service is a public representation of faith, this concern receives a special relevance and urgency in respect to the liturgy. Is there something that makes the Reformed worship service recognizable around the world? And what is that "certain something"?

In the manifesto "A Common Reflection on Christian Worship in Reformed Churches Today," the consultants try to track down a common heritage in the bewildering choices of Reformed worship service practices. They are seeking to discern impulses for the renewal of liturgy, impulses that can be guidelines for the Korean, South African, Scottish, Hungarian, and all other Reformed churches. Some things formulated in the study group remained correspondingly vague. Yet they still arrived at some clearly defined statements, such as a clear confession for an evangelical catholicism: "What makes our worship 'Reformed' in every time and place is . . . the continued attempt to respond in worship, in the light of the Holy Scripture, to the presence of Jesus Christ in the power of the Holy Spirit. Our primary concern is not that worship should be Reformed but that it should be truly Christian worship."[8]

What is further mentioned under the title "Searching for Authentic Christian Worship Today" is correspondingly universal: the emphasis on the Trinity,[9] the adherence to baptism as a basic sacrament,[10] and the use of liturgical dramaturgy. Despite the differences between the liberal church book tradition and the liturgically formed way of praying (traditional table of readings and prayers in the church year), the following maxim applies: "Each element has its own value, and all are indispensable parts of the whole movement leading from gathering to being sent again."[11]

The position paper contains some points that call for deeper discussion. The refusal to focus on a specific target audience is very strict: "We should resist the tendency to ignore certain age groups in our worship or to offer different styles of worship for different generations."[12] This resistance to splitting the worshiping congregation sheds light on the idea behind the book. There should be *one* worship-service theology for *all* Protestant churches. That is a very high demand, but for the Protestant community it is an important stimulus for discussion. Therefore it is commendable that the publishers have dared to tackle this huge task.

A PROTESTANT PROFILE

The suggestions from the manifesto are, however, only of limited help with regard to the difficulties in the liturgical situation outlined at the beginning. If the common awareness of the *form of worship service* has become weak, *aesthetic criteria* would need to be found that offer orientation for fashioning the form. Even if I now appeal for a Protestant profile of the liturgy, I also accept the prerequisite condition of liturgical liberty. We have no official office for propagating doctrines in our church. No church body has the authority to trim down the liturgical right of the individual congregation. I interpret this freedom positively and not only negatively. It is a right anew to rediscover aesthetic impulses that exist in the Reformed worship tradition, to take pleasure in them, and to cultivate them together with other Christians.

Going back to the ideas of Calvin, the Geneva-based reformer, might be promising.[13] He submitted a worship service concept that was much better thought out and less improvised than Zwingli. Concerning the differences between both strands of tradition within the Reformed churches, I refer to Elsie McKee.[14] That I claim to come across such forward-looking impulses in the church of Zwingli, of all places, needs to be explained. I therefore deal briefly with the latest chapter of German Swiss liturgy history in order to present an aesthetic access to liturgy, through which the special character or distinctiveness and also the charm of Zwingli's tradition can be more clearly appreciated.

The fact is that the liturgical *awareness of the form* in the evangelical Reformed church of German-Switzerland represents a relatively new phenomenon.[15] There was a string of protests when the joint speaking of the Lord's Prayer was introduced on a trial basis in the course of the Zurich worship service reform in the last 1960s. This was too catholic! And there was not yet any mention of responsories, creed, confession of sin, or *Kyrie*. The worship service was the way into the sermon, and that was that. If one looks at the situation before the worship service reform, something becomes clear: in Zwingli's church whoever talks about erosion, decline, and ruthless exploitation of liturgical awareness of form is only thinking of the relatively short phase of the last thirty years. In other words, Heinzer, whom I quoted at the beginning, is not defending the Reformed tradition but the reform of this tradition.

An important basis of this reform is the so-called Zurich liturgy of the late 1960s. The main concern of this worship service order was the introduction of a five-part structure. Every worship service is performed in steps of the call to worship, worship, proclamation, intercessory prayer, and dismissal. With this order, liturgy becomes comprehensible and understandable as events along the way. Inspired by the liturgical movement and the Second Vatican Council, the Reformers were interested in the *dramaturgy of the worship service*. One can view the introduction of a firm structure also as a maneuver or compromise. The concept that liturgy has an ordered structure had not played an important role in the Protestant theology of worship service up to then. This was new. On the other hand, the liturgy stayed open, open also for something new. So over the past thirty years certain items found their way back into the Reformed liturgy, without affecting the liberty of form. A glance into the new song book, the church books, and the worship service order, which have been produced since then, underline this in an impressive way. No fewer than thirteen proposals for the Lord's Supper, including Mass and Zwingli's original Lord's Supper, are collected in the German-Swiss liturgy's volume of material for the Lord's Supper.

The characterization of the liturgy as events along the way corresponds with the Protestant worship-service theology, even if it would be an anachronism to claim that the Zurich reformers, and above all Zwingli, had this model in mind when working on the reform. However, it is just as wrong to impute that the Protestant reformer had no sense for beauty in the worship service. That this picture of the Zurich worship service reform is wrong becomes clearer at the Lord's Supper worship service than at the service of the Word. Something is meant to be made visible in the liturgy. Faith is to be publicly displayed in the meeting of the congregation. Zwingli was fully aware of this. Whoever searches through the sparse sources for links between these considerations and liturgy, however, has to do some translation work.

An impressive example of such translation work was supplied by Lee Palmer Wandel. The subjects of his investigation are two wood engravings published in Zurich in 1525 and 1526, during the time when Zwingli was working on a new draft of the Lord's Supper worship service. The portrayal of the Last Supper of Jesus with his disciples and the Lord's Supper in Zurich make clear on the basis of which examples the Eucharist is celebrated in Zurich.

> In replacing the Eucharistic wafer of late medieval liturgy and processions with common bread, these wood engravings eliminate a central symbol of the late medieval construction of the sacred. The simple loaves of bread resting on plain tables contrast with the visual display of late medieval Eucharistic rituals. Gone is the carefully moulded Eucharistic wafer, whose size, shape, and composition were carefully regulated. Gone are the ornate monstrances and patens of late medieval liturgy. Gone is the elevating of the host and the invocation of the crucifixion. And gone are the elaborate, formalised rituals and the distance they represented between the laity and the Eucharist.[16]

But Wandel does not see only the scenic example of the new liturgy in the wood engravings. They are not representations of Zwingli's Lord's Supper but rather interpretations. In contrast to the portrayed scenes this is "still structured, temporally, spatially and socially; it retained certain divisions, between genders and spatial distance, between the congregation and the table." Wandel believes that he can also recognize the communicants' idea of Christ's presence during the Eucharist.

> The two images suggest, albeit tacitly, that Christ was to be located among those who join him at the table, who break bread with him, who share the cup with him each time. They suggest, in other words, that Christ was present within the ritual that sought to re-enact the specific context of the Last Supper, its implements, its rude table, its simplicity—the context of the Zwinglian communion.[17]

WORSHIP SERVICE AS A PRODUCTION

Zwingli's Lord's Supper is a production. Wandel's discoveries in the Reformed worship service tradition cast a light on this fundamental understanding of liturgy science. More formally expressed, liturgy is an action that is carried out in a specific room, at a specific time, by protagonists, and witnessed by others. With that, the worship service fulfills the minimal conditions of a theatrical production. A comparison based on such minimal definition and making liturgy a subject of discussion *as* a religious production does not add anything to the worship service that would be foreign to it. That this form has a theatrical frame is obvious. The worship service has the purpose and task of giving the inner experience an outer form.[18]

That some irritation arises from the comparison between a play and a worship service has to do with the piece that is to be interpreted. The lead role in the church service play cannot be embodied either by the stage play itself or by an actor. Zwingli points that out over and over again: God is the protagonist, and it is to him that one is pointed. His presence will be celebrated in song and witnessed and interpreted in the light of the gospel. However, it is only portrayable, and not producible, because God is *spirit*. The worship service is a performance, but God cannot be performed. He himself is present through his name. Because God is certainly present but is neither to be heard nor to be seen, he needs representatives who remind us of his saving intervention and thereby convey the Holy, but he never lets himself be portrayed or performed.

The typical irritation of the religious production emerges because of this paradox. The worship service offers a peculiar dramatic play between art and religion.[19] Poor rhetoric or poorly played organ music can interfere with the presence of the Spirit. The presentation of the Holy has to be learned, however, and not "only" be presented; otherwise it would not be a worship service. Authenticity and trustworthiness of the worship service production are at risk if someone gets the impression that they are witnessing only playacting! The liturgical play is unusual because the representation of that which is represented is of great importance, but at the same time it is unclear which role the representatives have to play on the stage of the Holy. Also the role of the *witnesses* of the play is not settled right from the start. Is the congregation cast in a spectator's role? Are the worship service "visitors" allowed to draw attention to themselves or not? Don't they belong as "common priesthood" to the cast as well?

It is obvious that religion must be produced. However, in the Judeo-Christian tradition there is always something conflicting that clings to religious productions. A worship service must not be perceived as a kind of show but as a performance of truth. When something religious is produced, the play has to be truthful. When comparing a worship service and a theater play, irritating similarities and dissimilarities show up. Tensions are brought to the fore. All of that also applies to the Protestant liturgy. However, it is exactly their austerity that makes the production's conflict visible. In the Reformed worship service culture, which is substantially influenced by the prophetic cult critique, I think we find an interesting performance of this tension. To recognize the aesthetic value, it is necessary to take a walk through present-day culture, where the Christian worship service has its home.

ALL ONLY PLAYACTING? AN EXCURSION IN PRESENT-DAY CULTURE

Such a visit uncovers the cultural framework of the media society, in which the production's authenticity has to become a topic. The suspicion that everything is "only show," the question whether what is shown is true or not, by no means concerns only the worship service. Productions are controversial because the conflict between what is shown and what is reality can be veiled faster and better, thanks to polished *media* technique. Everything that is produced must be checked for genuineness because the *professional image cultivation* has developed into a successful industry.

The concept of overstaging marks a border crossing, which repeatedly becomes a subject in the media society. It describes the condition of increased medialization (increased use of media in every aspect of daily life). How long will the spectators watch when they are informed (please note: by the media) at the same time that a story was overstaged? The question of spectator interest is relevant because productions are for the market. It is also valid since many put on a show, but not all of them get to be seen. Only what is of interest in the world of spectacles and media events will be performed. Therefore a differentiation must be made between a general theatrical approach, which permeates the entire social life,[20] and the spectacle for the media public, in which this life is put on stage in order to win more spectators by means of increased action. The latter raises the question of whether one should go back to the authentic. The question is justified because medialization has become an anthropological reference point, making the question of genuineness highly charged.

The American sociologist Erving Goffmann described the field of daily interaction as a stage where people portray themselves.[21] Goffmann's theater metaphor has been criticized in the meantime and replaced by the more open term of production.[22] The basic idea is the same: Whoever performs in public and takes on a role must have a good command of the play of self-projection. But it does not always work. Whoever is too good at it, whoever is overstaging, cannot be trusted at all. There are good and bad performances; there are lies and truth, distortions and simulation. The naive demand for authenticity in all productions or for the real face behind the mask, however, would cover up the conflict, which shows up in any attempt at self-projection.

Since we all must put on an act, an across-the-board condemnation of the category of production is out of the question. The theatrical does not only take place in the public of the media. The question is not *that* it will be played, but *what* we actually put on an act *about*. These are focal points of today's culture and are also of significance for discussing religious productions. The success of media productions depends mostly on the form of presentation. The measure of success is the interest of the audience. In the struggle for this interest, the aspect of entertainment seems to be becoming increasingly important, but no final verdict on this has been passed yet (against Postman)[23] because the question of whether what is shown is truthful or false cannot be answered by reference to the entertainment value of a production.[24] The question, What, in which context, and with which means should be publicly produced? cannot be answered either with a sweeping critique nor with a general justification of the medialization. The medialization is the framework and not the measurement of successful productions.

The Protestant reform of worship service in the Reformation was based on the prophetic cult critique, which was opposed to the clear show of piety. According to their credo, what is shown or produced in worship service will last only if it complies with the true worship in spirit and truth (John 4:22–24), a favorite formula of Zwingli. Therefore the cultural memory of the Protestant rite takes place mainly by word.

Everything that is shown must serve the Word of God and be understandable. The Reformers were convinced that the conflict with the religious production could be met by means of explanation and annotation of Scripture. Under different circumstances, this view of liturgy has gained in importance, and since the Second Vatican Council also in the Catholic rite. In today's culture the crisis in the Word-based and interpreted-service has, of course, raised doubts about the predominance of the verbal. The resistance against theater and the secular cultural scene[25] long ago gave way to a critical interest.[26] Discussions with media scientists and theater specialists have become a matter of interest for worship leaders. This is also reflected in the liturgical science discussion of the past few years.

EMBODIMENT OF TRUTH IN LITURGY AND THEATER

Marcus A. Friedrich (2001) presented an impressive study, showing how nourishing the reception of drama theories is for liturgical theory and practice. Three paradigmatic dramaturgical-aesthetic models are introduced and presented as a basis for pastoral aesthetic considerations. Especially informative is the condensed description of the creative drama aesthetic of Konstantin Stanislawski, Bertold Brecht's theory of the epic theater, and the spiritual drama aesthetic by Jerzy Grotowski. The drama theorist's thorough treatment unmasks precisely those wrong alternatives of genuine and artificial that are always present under the surface of the discourse about staging worship. Genuineness in expression is not to be equated with ignorance and missing craftsmanship in dramatic art. And vice versa, professional appearance on stage does not necessarily lead to less authenticity.

This becomes especially impressive in Stanislavsky's drama aesthetic, where the art of experiencing is the focal point of both theatrical perception and embodiment.[27] With the emphasis on experience, Stanislavsky turns against the art of performance, against the mere craft that conducts an illusion through practiced gestures, frozen tricks, and sleight of hand. A good actress does not just perform: she is an artist of perception. The ideal is to intuitively take over a role in the most natural and relaxed way. The art of experiencing implies an inner creative contact with partners, objects, and oneself. It guides the actor toward embodying the spiritual life of the role. At the end he should not feel himself in the role, but the role itself in him.[28] Consequently, Stanislavsky distinguishes between actors who have fallen in love with art and want to know that this love is confirmed by the audience, and those true actors of experiencing, who love the art in themselves.[29] In Stanislavsky's aesthetic the irritation of religious production emerges as a theatrical problem. It concerns the truthfulness of the scenic embodiment:[30] "Without this truthfulness, without faith in that which is happening on stage, all logical and consistent physical actions become conventional, that is, they create a lie, which cannot be believed."[31]

Brecht takes a different path with his epic theater. He too is occupied with the truthfulness of drama. In contrast to Stanislavsky, Brecht proposes a method he calls alienation. The purpose of this technique is to give the audience an investigative, critical attitude toward the portrayed event.[32] Not the experiencing and empathizing, enthusiasm and faith, but rather the distance of the actor toward his role is the guarantee for an honest play. The actor behaves as a demonstrator.

The third aesthetic approach to acting by Grotowski opposes both Stanislavsky's idealization of the creative condition and Brecht's pedagogical concept of theater. Neither any plausible transformation nor the actor's reflection of his social responsibility bring real life on stage. Grotowski demands of the actor a *via negativa*. The actress has to become a holy spectator, able to have a sensuous spiritual cognition of what happens in her embodying act with and to her.[33] The goal is the total self-immersion, but to achieve this result, one is (paradoxically) not allowed to look for it.[34] Theater has to become a "pauper's theater," without frills and without props. The dramatic art adds nothing. Staging functions like sculpturing and carving. By way of elimination the artist works through to the form that has been prefigured. Under the superficial pseudo-identity of the masked person, the human entity becomes visible through the theatrical action.

Friedrich's work shows how exciting and complex the discussion about religious staging is. The question about the importance of the representation is not detachable from the role of the representatives, neither in the secular nor the religious area. The advantage of dramaturgical-aesthetic analysis of religious productions is that it makes categories available for the classification of this role. The three types of the experience-like, epic, and spiritual aesthetic prescribe a heuristic pattern, with which, in my opinion, one can also ask for a specific and unmistakable form of the Reformed worship service. That has to be done, at least in initial stages.

LITURGY WITH PROTESTANT PROFILE: AESTHETIC VIEWPOINTS

Protestant Liturgy Is Not Stilted

Opposition to handicraft and the artificial, as is demanded by the Stanislavsky school of drama, corresponds to the demand for authenticity on the part of the minister and worship leader. There should be no double play in the Reformed liturgy. Whoever speaks in worship service should speak loudly and distinctly, so as surely to be understood. Above all, whatever will be said should be truthful and understandable. Of course, this demand for authenticity could be expressed in the following way: that one can understand the role of minister as a contrast to that of an actor. Zwingli resisted the "show piety" of his time. Staged and performed faith becomes hypocritical. The Protestant form of the ceremony, however, is not the renunciation but the reduction of an expression. Faith can have a sense of urgency and may find its way to the outside. But it is not expressionless. It has to do with the truthfulness of the scenic embodiment of *all the faithful*. Therefore, bearing in mind the inescapability of the performance character of liturgy, the forms become more important.

That the participation of everyone in the liturgy should be possible was a central concern of the reform in worship service. This *participatio plena et actuosa* should not be a show by a liturgical ensemble. That is the point of the *ascetic aesthetic*. Zwingli, for example, resisted psalm singing, although he loved and appreciated music. But in the worship service the faithful are distracted from their prayers by the incomprehensible, slow, Latin psalm-chanting of monks. If Zwingli had known Luther's chorale (and if he had not fallen out with the man), he probably would have agreed to joint singing in worship service. The church music that Zwingli knew was far too contrived. It created a wrong frame of mind and was not real and natural.

Liturgy Keeps the Memory of Prophetic Cult Critique Alive

Bertold Brecht's epic theater can illuminate a further feature of the worship service. It should not be that church service visitors will be so charmed by the beauty of liturgy that they forget to pay attention and follow someone's train of thought. A critical distance from the liturgical action is also required from worship leaders. They should maintain a distance from their role. They are not priests. And, as the actor in Brecht's play who acts like a demonstrator, the liturgy in Zwingli's worship service should also make clear that someone has a message to convey in public.

The analogy with epic theater can help one appreciate the critical gestures and expressions in the religious production, not as a contrast but as a principle of performing. The prophet who criticizes the cult should perform in the worship service. The liturgy is the place where the memory of Amos, Isaiah, Jeremiah, and certainly Jesus is to be kept alive. Therefore, in the Reformed tradition the sermon is central, and so is celebrating the Lord's Supper.

Reformed Liturgy Reflects the Image of God

Besides the ascetic and critical profile, the Reformed liturgy has an unmistakable spiritual dimension that can be traced with the help of Jerzy Grotowski's drama aesthetic. What Grotowski demands of actors is also required in the Reformed worship service with the participation of the Eucharist. The congregation should become holy spectators, able to have a sensuous-spiritual perception of what is happening with and to them in the embodying act. The self-immersion, which is the worship service's goal, is not only the private business of the individual; it is also a gift of Christ, who is present in the gathering of the faithful! If one transfers Grotowski's notion of "pauper's theater" into the religious production, it is therefore an attitude of being "poor in spirit" (Matt. 5:3) that is required. The worship service is a performance without frills. Only the most necessary props will be used. Liturgy adds nothing but is a symbolic reduction; it eliminates the unnecessary and penetrates through to the essential: the present Christ, who is in the midst of those who gather in his name (Matt. 18:20).

What is shown in the liturgy should not cover up this mysterious presence. The consequence to be drawn for the Protestant liturgy is the following: when people meet one another in the worship service, they should not produce themselves; they should not continue playing out their daily routine, should not represent, should not portray, and should show or perform nothing. The worship service is a community where a face is shown in which Christ is reflected. The worship service, therefore, has a form in which one may stay poor or can once again become a pauper.

CONCLUSION

Nowadays there are more intensive, more emotional, or more ecstatic forms of celebration, and it is taken for granted that one will experiment with these forms within the Protestant churches. However, Protestant Christians do well not to forget their own specific forms, to justify them in inner-evangelical and ecumenical conversations, and above all to make use of them.[35] They can only do this when they have an idea of which aesthetic impulses from their ascetic, critical, and spiritual liturgy can contribute to a strengthening of faith.

Chapter 17

On Not Offering Psychological Banalities as God's Word

A Reformed Perspective on Pastoral Care

CYNTHIA JARVIS

A PASTORAL CONTEXT

For six weeks, I had driven daily to the bedside of a young member of my congregation who was doing battle with his inevitable death at a university hospital.[1] He had celebrated his thirty-second birthday on New Year's Day and, two weeks later, his death day arrived. In the scant three months since his diagnosis, I had become a minister to his geographically scattered family as they gathered in shifts to keep vigil night and day. Their alleged minister had also been a husband and a stepfather until he had left them to take up with the Christian educator a few years earlier. Each member of the family had a story to tell of the struggle back to faith and the church, stories recounted amid the morphine-induced sleep of a son and brother who was determined not to go gentle into that good night.

My congregant and his family were all medical professionals of one stripe or another themselves. Not surprisingly, they were surrounded by the best medical team rank could pull together, and they were supported, as well, by colleagues and former classmates wanting to be of help. Furthermore, this incredibly erudite young man not only monitored every pill dispensed and IV bag hung, but also took to instructing the new residents as they made their rounds, praising them or correcting them on their bedside manner as though he were the attending doctor. There were also the promised visits of a pastoral counselor to whom I had referred him when his wife announced her departure from the marriage a few months before his diagnosis. "We made sure to tell the counselor that we would pay her for her visits," one sister assured me, "because we know her time is valuable." As far as I know, she made one visit before the unpredictable balance of his wakefulness and deep sleep made the trips not worth anyone's while.

The point is that my congregant's condition was addressed clinically from every angle. Had I embraced the pastoral self-definition imposed and rejected long ago in clinical pastoral education [CPE] or had I perfected the pastoral responses taught in my post-1960s seminary classroom, then awash with sensitive Rogerian prompts, I would have been one in a long line of technically trained (with the emphasis on technique) professionals on the team around his bed. My part would have been to translate what he called the "issues"—edema, bowel obstructions, fluctuating white blood cell counts, nausea—into "feeling statements" offered back with scant comment. The conversations could have been a CPE supervisor's verbatim heaven.

I was, instead, his minister. As I said to him one day after he had listed the particular medical issues for the day, I was not much good at dealing with anything on that list, but might be of some help with the "God issues." He nodded and said, in what was now labored speech, "That's a plan. That's a good plan." Having been raised in strictly Presbyterian territory, he chose to die as he had lived: thoughtfully and with no excess of emotion. "Avoidance" would have been the analysis of my training: make him deal with his feelings about death! My Reformed theological instincts told me otherwise.

In the end, the God issues were issues that only briefly made it onto a list, for his pain began to demand more and more morphine. So now I made my daily pilgrimage simply to listen for the "sighs too deep for words"—not only his, but [also] those of his family—and to offer in response the images and language of Scripture (Psalm 91, for instance, on the day when he said he was being pushed off the edge of a cliff), the substance of the church's confessions (when the only comfort to be had, body and soul, in life and in death, was belonging to God), and the familiar lines of the church's hymns suggested by the angst of the moment ("I want to sing 'The strife is o'er, the battle done,'" I said on one particularly pain-filled night. "Not yet!" he retorted as he refused to give in to death). And I was there to pray, no matter his state of wakefulness or deep sleep. Though one time, when I thought he was politely saying I had stayed a little too long by suggesting that we pray, I took his hand and, before I could invoke God's name, he began to pray, simply and eloquently, a prayer of thanksgiving for friends by his side and far away.

To borrow the subtitle of John Leith's *The Reformed Imperative*, I was there to say what the church says that no one else can say. I was there as one who had learned in thirty years of pastoral ministry that "It is evident that they do not need us to help them live, but seem rather to need us to help them die, . . . the whole reason that they come to us, strange as it may seem, for wisdom, is because they know the whole network of their life is hung upon a thread like gossamer. They suddenly awake to a realization that they are walking upon a ridge between *time* and *eternity* that is narrower than a knife-edge."[2]

Robert Coles made the same point long ago in *Harvard Diary: Reflections on the Sacred and the Secular*. In an essay entitled "Psychiatric Stations of the Cross," Coles tells of a medical school classmate in a teaching hospital in Boston who had been diagnosed with a cancer that would eventually take him. The man had "always been a rather quiet and thoughtful person—a stoic temperamentally. But he is also a deeply religious man."[3] This was my congregant precisely, whose reading material while undergoing an extreme form of chemotherapy was Dietrich Bonhoeffer's *Ethics*. "When I came to see him," Coles writes of this encounter with his friend, "he was angry, and quite ready to tell me why. A priest had just come by, and indicated a strong interest in how the doctor/patient was managing to 'cope.' My friend said he was doing 'fine' the way (he assumed) any of us had the right to say 'fine.' . . . For the visiting clergyman, however, such asserted poise and reticence were not to be accepted at face value. The priest persisted in asking questions which, in sum, amounted to a relentless kind of psychological inquiry. How was the patient "feeling"? How was his "spirit"? How was he "managing," in view of the stress he had to "confront"? Did he want to "talk about" what was "happening"?[4] Though the direct questioning of a patient likely would have been critiqued in CPE from the standpoint of methodology, I offer Coles's account simply as evidence that this characterization of clinical pastoral training, pastoral counseling, pastoral care and its resultant technique, poorly or properly practiced, has some wider warrant than my own individual recollections. According to Coles, his friend "had wanted to talk with the priest about God and His ways, about Christ's life and death, about the Gospel of Luke (a particular favorite), about Heaven and Hell—only to be approached repeatedly with psychological words and phrases."[5] The underlying and unexamined anthropology of one trained in the practical art of active listening, or in the more tangible categories of so-called pastoral psychology, denies the central theological claim we are ordained to represent. Namely, the one to whose side we are summoned as Christian clergy is one who, first and foremost, has been addressed by God in Jesus Christ. Either we come to bear witness to a word not our own or we might as well not come at all. "He comes here with a Roman collar," roared Cole's dying friend, "and offers me psychological banalities as God's word!"[6]

Within the confines of this brief essay, and with only a recovering academic grasp on the subject, I want to explore the distinctive understanding of pastoral care and the cure of souls rooted in the rich theological heritage of the Reformed tradition, a perspective which has been, for the most part, eschewed over the last thirty years in favor of the professionalization of the ministry and its captivity to a culture of technique.

AN HISTORICAL CONTEXT

In the recently translated 1923 lectures of Karl Barth on *The Theology of the Reformed Confessions*, the Confessio Tetrapolitana (1530) is explicated by Barth in such a way that it seems a fit, if obscure, beginning for naming the unique perspective of Reformed theology on the practice of pastoral care. Noting the subtle but significant distinction between the Augustana Confession and the Tetrapolitana as regards the doctrine of justification, Barth notes that the Augustana asks, "How shall I be saved?," whereas the Tetrapolitana asks, "Who saves me?"[7] Clearly the first question could imply a technical answer, albeit theological as God and the church are confessed to be the significant actors in pulling off the "how." But, if later the crack in the door swings our way, then the move simply shifts the means of our self-help from the institution to the individual. The Tetrapolitana's question presumes the initiative of God alone toward us and therefore leads with the theological and scriptural claims of faith. Both battling the Roman church's peddling of the means of grace, the Lutheran and Reformed confessions differ, according to Barth, in that, "If the Augustana warns against false trust, the Tetrapolitana warns against false gods. The direction in which the polemical interest of the Reformed confession is to be sought is plain: It battles Catholicism as an attempt at self-help, and it sees in this desire to help oneself an arrogance and presumption that do not lead to the goal but rather are an insult to God and thus make genuine help impossible. For God desires to help. But he helps as the one who alone helps. To believe means to affirm that God alone is our helper."[8] From the beginning, then, Reformed theology reframed the question to which a distinctly different understanding of pastoral care was the response. Pastoral care was not interested in personal psychology or the internal state of an individual soul but in turning the individual or the community toward the God who alone is our helper.

In the second place, Reformed pastoral care led with the word written, proclaimed, and explicated in the context of the public and personal lives of those in need of help. Prior to the Reformed movement, late medieval culture, according to David Cornick, was "intensely visual and tactile rather than cerebral."[9] Pilgrimages to shrines, pieces of relics (which according to Peter Brown replaced the pilgrimage to Rome with God's tangible dwelling in a village church), the sacraments that ordered a believer's life from birth to death, and supremely the repeated sacrifice of the Eucharist characterized popular piety. In addition, the ritual of confession wherein "the penitent was guided through a check-list of the seven deadly sins, the Ten Commandments, the five senses, the seven works of mercy, the seven gifts of the Spirit, the seven sacraments and the eight beatitudes"[10] offered an answer to the question of *how* a person could be forgiven and ultimately saved. This was the self-help that only the church could dispense.

"This landscape," says Cornick, "was to be irrevocably changed by the reformations. As 'justification by faith alone' laid waste the penitential system, the whole panoply of confession and works of satisfaction fell into disrepair, for they were no longer needed. . . . The guts of popular religion had been surgically removed."[11] In their place was the church's preaching and teaching of the Word, the sacraments of the Lord's Supper and baptism, and an understanding of pastoral care that began to raise up a flock seeking to understand and inhabit the narrative of salvation as put forth in Scripture.

Not surprisingly, preaching for the first Reformers and for Ulrich Zwingli, in particular, was pastoral care. In all of his writing, he says little directly about pastoral care, but rather subsumes all into the work of the preacher: "Preaching was not a rarified academic activity, although in Zwingli's eyes it demanded the very best of scholarship. Applying the Word of God to the life of God's people, indeed of God's world, was at its heart a pastoral activity, just as it was for the Old Testament prophets in whose works he delights. It was all of a piece—public, prophetic, private, consoling, broken into the multiplicity of the minister's work, baptizing, administering the sacraments, visiting the sick, caring for the poor from the Church's resources, but above all teaching."[12] That Zwingli began his ministry at the Grossmünster in Zurich with a *lectio continua*, and so a sermon series lasting twelve years, suggests that, by way of his preaching and teaching, he longed for his congregation to hear in the narrative of God's saving history the address of the God who alone is their help. That was the supreme care a pastor could give a people.

In addition, such an understanding of pastoral care also imposed a pastoral responsibility for the holiness or ethical dimension of a congregation's response to the gospel. This involved not only the personal but also the public lives of Christian witnesses. Zwingli believed the minister's work was not to be exhausted by preaching, for he must

> prevent the washed sheep falling to the excrement, that is, after the believers have come into a knowledge of their savior and have experienced the friendly grace of God, they should hereafter lead a blameless life so that they no longer walk in death. . . . Sheep need a shepherd when they are in danger. So they are to defend their sheep from idolatry and unrighteousness, and "attack and destroy all buildings which have raised themselves against the heavenly Word," and do "eternal battle with the powerful and the vices of this world."[13]

Pastoral care was more than a private affair between minister and congregant and even more public than between minister and congregation. The care for the well-being of the flock required a preacher to do battle with the powerful of the world, even unto death! Zwingli also implied that the minister would do well to be on guard for such abuses of power, and also for idolatry (giving people a god who is not God as though they were being of help: psychological banalities instead of God's Word) within the church and among fellow clergy. Following the Johannine image of the good shepherd, Zwingli's Sixty-Seven Theses of 1523 warns against the Christlessness of the so-called clergy who would lead the flock to enter a door (such as church doctrines and tradition) other than Christ.[14]

Though the brevity of this essay will allow for only a cursory treatment of John Calvin, we can discern, through his pastoral practice, the distinctively Reformed character of the care he gave to the souls entrusted to him. As Jean Daniel Benoit observed, the Genevan Reformer "was a theologian in order to be a better pastor,"[15] or as Cornick put it, "he was a theologian only in so far as theology supported and grew out of his pastoral work."[16] From his life, we can glean that he was well-acquainted with the brief and broken nature of human existence: the death of a wife and child, the unsuccessful marriages of stepchildren, the ruthless critique of a community, these human difficulties were known to him personally.[17] Yet his own life's circumstances drew no mention from his pen except as they could be presumed to be the personal crucible out of which the urgency of his preaching, teaching, and pastoral care were wrought.

Two aspects of his pastoral practice warrant mention as we catalog the development of a Reformed understanding of pastoral care. The written record of his care and advice to his congregants was in the form of letters. In these we see that his counsel is deeply rooted in Scripture. "First, he writes in an atmosphere totally impregnated by the Bible," says Benoit, "and assumes an intimate knowledge of it on the part of the receivers of his letters. Second, he continually urges the reading of, and meditation on, the Scriptures. Third, he dwells upon the doctrinal points of his biblical faith, writing with a certitude that leaves no place for doubt."[18] Behind the assumption that his correspondents are as intimate with the biblical text as he, there is an understanding of pastoral care that, once again, rests upon the spadework of scriptural preaching and teaching. Only with that foundation can the church provide the rich and deep soil in which the Christian life may take root. Thus counsel from out of Scripture is at the heart of the Reformed practice of pastoral care, not as literal moral injunction, but as the metaphor and narrative over which human beings trace the troubles and trials of their common life, so as to trust God's leading and discern life's meaning and purpose.

In the second place, Calvin's understanding of the pastoral relationship between minister and member, a relationship still reckoning with the Roman system of confession and penance, also underlines the ethical dimension of a distinctively Reformed understanding of pastoral care. Calvin understood himself as a "spiritual director" in the sense that he was a physician of the soul, called in at times of crisis rather than as a permanent guide: "He expect[ed] his patient to recover and normally to control his own health."[19] The advice he gave was not the advice that was meant to lead toward perfectionism but was "advice that tends to Christian living."[20] McNeill cites Hermann Strothmann in suggesting that Calvin's pastoral work with souls involved him in the process of moral transformation and renewal.[21] Not the inner psychological workings of an individual's personal life but the outward response of a forgiven Christian in the world was what engaged Calvin's pastoral practice and theological reflection.

Hence he was less interested in "the retrospective of sin" and more taken by the "transformation of repentance."[22] This is why, when asked for spiritual direction, a Reformed minister will often suggest a night spent with the homeless or a day given to feeding the hungry rather than signing up for a prayer retreat or taking a labyrinthine walk.

No examination of the distinctive practice of pastoral care in the Reformed tradition would be complete without attention to the author of *The Reformed Pastor*. Richard Baxter's little treatise, written to his pastoral colleagues some 350 years ago, is still read today. According to Andrew Purvis (commenting from the perspective of today's Reformed pastor who believes a minister's job encompasses five days a week—or less, if one is to be compensated in time off for attendance at evening meetings), Baxter's method of pastoral care "appears to be an exercise in compulsive overwork and a recipe for exhaustion."[23] Yet the most salient observation of Purvis in relation to this study is that we are given, in Baxter's writing, not "pastoral technique skillfully applied" but rather the application of "a spiritual and theological understanding of human beings to the work of pastoral ministry, which begins with the continuing conversion of the pastor and leads to the conversion of the parishioner."[24]

Theologically, Baxter was an admixture of Roman, Reformed, and especially Arminian influences,[25] believing that though salvation had been accomplished in Jesus Christ, the faith of the convert remains a condition and so a necessary aspect of imputed righteousness. Out of this, he developed a doctrine of continuous justification and a somewhat Pelagian spirit as regards moral effort[26]—both on the part of the pastor as well as the parishioner. From these theological premises, his pastoral work followed: continuous visitation! He is best known for his rigorous schedule of calling on families in his parish. He and his "faithful unwearied Assistant" personally called upon eight hundred families numbering about four thousand people once a year while envying his colleagues in smaller parishes who could visit once a quarter! Yet it is the content of those visits that should both interest and instruct us in our present ecclesial malaise.

While Baxter no doubt befriended and gave comfort to his people, his primary concern was that their faith would grow in understanding to the end that they know themselves as persons who must stand before God. "Baxter reminds us that trying to bring comfort in the midst of life's tragedies but failing to address a person's life in and before God is no care at all."[27] He, therefore, became a teaching elder in the most demanding sense of that office, an office renamed in Reformed circles today to the detriment of our distinctive Reformed pastoral self-understanding. While many Reformed ministers may not share the theological perspective that propelled Baxter into his parishioners' homes, nevertheless we would do well to imitate the catechetical thrust of his calling.

In addition, Baxter's admonition concerning regular pastoral visitation was aimed not only at his colleagues' slothful practice of the same, but also at the church's understanding of the pastoral office.

> Little do they know that the minister is in the church, as the schoolmaster in his school, to teach and to take an account of every one in particular, and that all Christians, ordinarily, must be disciples or scholars in some such school. They consider not, that all souls in the congregation are bound, for their own safety, to have personal recourse to him, for the resolving of their doubts, and for help against their sins, and for direction in duty, and for increase of knowledge and all saving grace; and that ministers are purposely settled in congregations to this end, to be still ready to advise and help the flock.[28]

As though he were writing of pastoral practice today, he notes that most church members commonly think a minister exists to preach, to administer the sacraments, and to visit them in sickness. In these times, the misconception is not always the fault of the minister, but often the result of a person's casual commitment to the community of faith. Yet even this Baxter traces to poor pastoral visitation. His own visitation resulted in a church so crowded on Sunday mornings that an addition had to be built to accommodate the well-over one thousand souls for whom worship became a habit. This should offer itself not as a technique to be added to church growth seminars but a starting point for the substantive renewal of a theological tradition and a pastoral office marked, historically, by a faith that seeks understanding.

Baxter enjoins the regular visitation of families for instruction and care within a church whose ministers had apparently quit this discipline in favor of time misspent "in unnecessary discourse, business, journeys or recreations. It will let them see that they have no time to spare for such things; and thus, when they are engaged in so much pressing employment of so high a nature, it will be the best cure for all that idleness, and loss of time."[29] Even more to the point of the church's current woes, "It will be some benefit, that by this means we shall take off ourselves and our people from vain controversies, and from expending our care and zeal on the lesser matters of religion, which least tend to their spiritual edification!"[30]

Finally, underlying all that he would have ministers do, Baxter's most pressing concern is the faith of the minister. As Purvis notes, "Baxter's unambiguous conviction concerning the conversion and spiritual renewal of the pastor can hardly be overemphasized, for that emphasis is rarely found today in much pastoral theology literature. Today the focus is more likely to fall on the pastor's mental health,"[31] a focus recast presently in the church's uncritical embrace of cultural spirituality and the "how" of spiritual technique. Baxter speaks rather of the minister's own growth in understanding, emphasizing theology in the service of pastoral practice. Clearly the point of a pastor's biblical and theological study is the strengthening of faith which, in turn, will strengthen the faith of the flock.

> O what sadder case can there be in the world, than for a man, who made it his very trade and calling to proclaim salvation, and to help others to heaven, yet after all to be himself shut out! Alas! that we should have so

many books in our libraries which tell us the way to heaven; that we should spend so many years in reading these books, and studying the doctrine of eternal life, and after all this to miss it! . . . And all because we preached so many sermons of Christ, while we neglected him; of the Spirit, while we resisted him; of faith, while we did not ourselves believe.[32]

From Baxter, we jump almost three centuries to Dietrich Bonhoeffer. The subject of the faith of the minister appears also in a series of lectures given at Finkenwalde, one of the seminaries of the Confessing Church, between 1935 and 1940. Published under the title *Spiritual Care*, we find Bonhoeffer's own reflections on the understanding and practice of pastoral care within the Reformed theological tradition. In an introduction to *Spiritual Care*, Jay Rochelle pointedly observes that "Unlike the traditional preachers' seminaries, in which only the practical aspects of ministry were taught in a technical school setting, Bonhoeffer wrestled theologically with his students in order that they might confront the impact of the theology of the Word on pastoral work."[33]

Given this starting point and, I daresay, the sociopolitical context of doing theology at that time in history, Bonhoeffer directly dismisses the role of psychology in the training and practice of pastoral care. For the pastor, the parishioner is "a sinner whom God's mercy wants to encounter. That is the difference between spiritual care and psychotherapy, for which the method of investigation is all-important. Spiritual care puts no stock in such methods. . . . There are no 'psychologically interesting cases' for spiritual care. . . . The pastor remains fundamentally premethodological and prepsychological, in the best sense, naive."[34]

Rather the very delicate representation of law and gospel in the minister's encounter with the person estranged from God, or indifferent to God, takes us on a different tack. Spiritual care begins with "bringing to speech" the point at which a person has become indifferent to God's Word. This is the grace of personal confession which frees us from ourselves and for discipleship, taking up Calvin's interest in the transformation of forgiveness rather than the retrospective of sin. The counsel given includes counsel toward discipline and practice, Scripture and prayer, forgiveness and then "the risk of a decision."[35] Though the pastor bears the other person's sin and struggle, the other is set free for the possibility of obedience and of a renewed relationship with the God whose service is in the world.

To put this another way, for Bonhoeffer, the office of Word and sacrament becomes personal address in spiritual care, "announcing that the search for God has been ended—in the Word which was effective in creation, now become incarnate in Jesus the Christ."[36] Yet this announcement, notes Jay Rochelle as he draws out the implications of Bonhoeffer's spiritual care for our day, takes place within the context of the community of faith, thereby differing both from psychological counseling and from pastoral counseling centers that function as a community service.[37] More significantly, spiritual care is not an end in itself, but "is aimed at freeing persons for service to God and world through their apprehension of the many dimensions of faith. It is aimed toward faith active in love."[38]

Perhaps the most powerful explication of the goal of spiritual care in the life of the individual, the church and the world is to be found in the *Letters and Papers from Prison* where Bonhoeffer writes of *metanoia* on the day after the unsuccessful attempt on Hitler's life:

> I discovered later, and I'm still discovering right up to this moment, that it is only by living completely in this world that one learns to have faith. One must completely abandon any attempt to make something of oneself, whether it be a saint, or a converted sinner, or a churchman (a so-called priestly type!), a righteous man or an unrighteous one. By this-worldliness I mean living unreservedly in life's duties, problems, successes and failures, experiences and perplexities. In so doing we throw ourselves completely into the arms of God, taking seriously, not our own sufferings, but those of God in the world-watching with Christ in Gethsemane. That, I think, is faith; that is *metanoia*.[39]

When this is read through his earlier reflections on spiritual care, we can conclude that for Bonhoeffer, the goal of such care in the lives of the people served by Reformed pastors is a community thrown into the arms of God that lives for others and takes God's suffering in the world as their cue for action. At the end, Bonhoeffer clearly is speaking not only of nurturing such faith in those given into a pastor's care, but also of the faith of the pastor. Hence at the end of these lectures to his seminarians in Finkenwalde, Bonhoeffer acknowledges that those who have been called to exercise spiritual care also live in the greatest need of spiritual care themselves:

> Whoever takes the office seriously must cry out under the burden. One has to make visits, listen to and bear the needs and sorrows of many people, one has to carry on numerous conversations with those one accompanies on life's way and always with those who encroach on one's time. . . . One has to find the right word with the dying, at the graveside, for a wedding. One should—and here is the heaviest responsibility of all—preach out of genuine certitude in order that others are led to certitude. . . . The mission is huge and our skills are small.[40]

Here he counsels prayer, but he counsels more. For at the end of the day, the "greatest difficulty for the pastor stems from his theology. He knows all there is to be known about sin and forgiveness. He knows what the faith is and he talks about it so much that he winds up no longer living in faith but in thinking *about* faith."[41] One cannot help but read what follows from the perspective of the end of Bonhoeffer's own life. Since Reformed ministers live so much in their heads, the danger is that faith becomes an abstract reflection upon a leap we have never taken personally.

Reaffirming that our mission is not to preach our experience but from Scripture, he still insists that the gospel cannot be proclaimed with integrity when our own experience "lags so far behind the Word." The concern was not an idle one for a German pastor in the 1930s. No doubt Bonhoeffer had reason to believe that, when theology becomes an academic exercise, it can be easily used toward evil ends. If the minister is living at a remove from the risk of faith in the world, Satan is not and, according to Bonhoeffer, is a great theologian: "He keeps your understanding three steps removed from your body."[42]

The spiritual care he recommends for pastors in this situation is congruent with the care he has instructed them to give their flocks. Bonhoeffer's final thoughts on the spiritual care of ministers will leave us only to offer some final reflections on the practice of pastoral care in our times:

> The only help is to call a person to the simplest things of Scripture, prayer, confession, and to concrete obedience in one definite matter.... The life of the pastor completes itself in reading, meditation, prayer and struggle. The means is the word of Scripture with which everything begins and to which everything returns. We read Scripture so that our hearts may be moved. It will lead us into prayer... which leads us into the world in which we must keep the faith. Where Scripture, prayer, and keeping the faith exist, temptation will always find its way in. Temptation is the sign that our hearing, prayer, and faith have touched down in reality.[43]

A PASTOR'S CONTEXT

What distinct hope do ministers in the Reformed tradition have to offer those who seek our help because "they are walking upon a ridge between *time* and *eternity* that is narrower than a knife-edge"? What is it that we have to say in our postmodern, pluralistic, multicultural world that no one else can say? What may we reclaim from out of our theological tradition that will be of help to people that need our help in order to die that they may truly live?

In the first place, I think that we, who also are dying and are in need of help, will be given the help we need only as we do business, throughout our lives, with the substance of the faith for ourselves. As we have ceased wrestling with that substance, we have grown ashamed of the gospel in the sense that we are no longer able thoughtfully to articulate the complexity of the Christian claim in the midst of this pluralistic age. As we have allowed all the other demands of running an institution to crowd in, we have quit the discipline required to plumb the depths and dare the heights of Scripture and so cannot compellingly present the meaning of the biblical narrative for our day in the pulpit or the classroom or the hospital room. Once the door has been shut leading out of any formal theological education, too many of us try to make due on the little theology grudgingly read in the classroom. We have little to offer of help because we are running on empty!

As all of our Reformed forebears knew, pastoral care begins in the study leading to the pulpit, the font, the table and only then to the home, the hospital, the office. In an oft-quoted sentence which has to do not only with preaching, but also with the renewal of the Reformed practice of pastoral care, John Leith reminds us that "the renewal of the church will come with the recovery of the sermon that is not moral advice or political rhetoric or personal therapy or entertainment but the means of God's grace to forgive and to sanctify, to heal and to fortify human hearts for the great crises and challenges of life."[44] We will only be able to preach such sermons as we renew our minds and our hearts through the disciplined study of Scripture, a lively engagement with the substance of our theological tradition and a seeking of the means of grace for the nurture and enlivening of our own faith. We need to reclaim the space and the time which has been given to "unnecessary discourse, business, journeys or recreation" for the sake of acquainting ourselves anew with the substance of God's grace to forgive and to sanctify, to heal and to fortify the human hearts given into our care.

In the second place, I believe pastoral care that offers the help people really need, which is to say, introduces them to the God who is their only comfort body and soul, in life and in death, rests on the nurture of a biblically literate congregation. Zwingli preached through the biblical narrative from his pulpit in Zurich. Calvin wrote letters to those under his care that were rich in biblical instruction. Richard Baxter organized his week around catechetical visits to parishioners who seemingly were as ignorant of Scripture as most postmodern congregations. Bonhoeffer viewed all of life's duties, problems, successes and failures, experiences and perplexities as the occasion for minister and parishioner to throw themselves into the arms of the God made known through Scripture.

We need to rethink how and where we tell the story of God's renovation of the world to the generation of our peers and, in turn, to their children and their children's children. What are the realistic means at hand that would allow us to sustain an adult's attention such that, at the end of a year or two or three, we could talk the same language, invoke the parables as stories that lend meaning to our own, offer the images of a psalm to name the rage or the sorrow or the deep joy which connects us with the depths of our human existence before God?

Finally, we need to wake to the urgency of our calling. What has been entrusted to us is the news that those who come to us "on the knife-edge" have been addressed by God in Jesus Christ. If we do not know the knife-edge ourselves, if we do not listen to our own crying out of the burden of the care we cannot give, then we will have missed the strange coincidence between those called out to speak of God's faithfulness and salvation and those left to wonder in the dark alone on Sunday night. We have been given to one another in Christ's church that we might together ask after our only comfort. "Those who do not ask," writes Karl Barth to theological students in Göttingen, "very radically what is their one and only comfort in life and death, must be told to their faces that they also do not believe. Believers are not secure people. They are those who first know what questioning means. To be rid of the questioning is to be rid of revelation and not to be addressed by God, or to be addressed by him no longer."[45]

Therefore, at the prospect of the care I am to give, the word I am to speak, I am haunted by Graham Greene's whiskey priest who, on the way to his execution, is asked by his jailer if he were hoping for a miracle. "No," he answers.

"You believe in them, don't you?" "Yes," says the whiskey priest, "but not for me."[46] I am accompanied to the hospital bed by Georges Bernanos's country priest who cried out, "Oh miracle—thus to be able to give what we ourselves do not possess—sweet miracle of our empty hands! Hope which was shriveling in my heart flowered again in her; the spirit of prayer which I lost in me forever was given back to her by God. . . . Lord, I was stripped bare of all things as you alone can strip us bare, whose fearful care nothing escapes nor your terrible love!"[47] Finally, I am bowed down by the psalmist whose words were written on my heart by my colleague of many years: "I have told the glad news of deliverance in the congregation, lo I have not restrained my lips, as Thou alone knowest. . . . I have not concealed Thy steadfast love and Thy faithfulness from the great congregation. Do not thou, O Lord, withhold Thy mercy from me; let Thy steadfast love and Thy faithfulness ever preserve me."

Chapter 18

Temples of the Spirit
Reforming the Reformed Congregation in Europe

WILLIAM STORRAR

What does the Reformed tradition bring to my work in practical theology in Europe today? In part, it brings the empirical problem that most concerns me as a practical theologian: the rapid decline of the Reformed churches in Europe since the 1960s, including my own Church of Scotland.[1] And in part it frames the way I interpret that problem and offers some practical theological criteria for addressing it constructively in the twenty-first century. In this chapter I explore the resources of this tradition to *reform* the Reformed congregation in Europe today in the face of this problem of institutional decline. I do so through a case study of one particular local parish church within my own Church of Scotland that is re-forming its life and witness in significant ways. I suggest that the changes in this local congregation in Scotland can best be understood in terms of three key Reformed concepts. First, the local church in the case study displays a particular type of innovative *leadership*. Second, it displays a *freedom* to develop appropriate local forms of church life. And third, the new social form of the local congregation that emerges out of this innovative leadership and freedom to reform gives *priority* to the worship of God. All three concepts can be traced back to the Reformation.

From a practical theological perspective, what is notable about the Reformed movement within the wider Reformation is the way in which the first Reformers combined theological with organizational leadership in their own local settings in Zurich and Geneva. At the same time they refused to prescribe their own local reforms in worship or church order for the other Reformed churches of Europe that were being set up under their influence. Rather, they actively fostered local autonomy and diversity in such matters. As John Calvin himself wrote to the refugee members of the French church in London, "[Do not] make an idol of me, and a Jerusalem of Geneva."[2] The historian Philip Benedict has put it this way:

> Clearly, the small corners of the European continent that had embraced Reformed worship by 1555 would not have assumed the importance they did had they not become home to several talented and deeply committed theologians, men who were capable of writing a body of treatises that won them admirers and disciples across national and linguistic boundaries. The organizational and theological accomplishments of Bullinger, à Lasco, and especially Calvin directly inspired the great explosion of Reformed churches that would follow.[3]

My own conviction is that the characteristic features of Reformed church leadership identified here by Benedict are still vitally important for the reform of congregations today: *we need a combination of theological and organizational leadership that is free and able to develop appropriate and varied local forms of church life*. However, the diverse congregations nurtured by such leadership will still be identifiable as creatures of the Word of God, affirming the primacy of divine agency in the midst of their own innovative human agency. As the theologian Alan Lewis put it, in an essay on a Reformed view of the church as the community of the Word of God, *ecclesia ex auditu* (church of the hearing): "The church-creating relationship between the Word and those who listen to it, is essentially asymmetrical. The Word which calls, elects and creates the community has, in its utter freedom and graciousness, an immutable theocentric priority over the human, hearing response which it evokes."[4] In other words, in any such *reforming* Reformed congregation, we should still be able to discern an *asymmetrical* pattern in its new life and social forms, with priority given to the worship and word of God. Before we turn to the case study of one such congregation in contemporary Scotland, to consider if it can bear the weight of such a threefold Reformed practical theological analysis, we must set it in the wider historical context of the Church of Scotland and its inherited and dominant model of the local church.

THE CHURCH OF SCOTLAND AS A MEMBERSHIP BODY

The apostle Paul famously describes the church as the body of Christ, with every vital part contributing to the body's flourishing under its head, Christ himself (1 Cor. 12:12–27). It is one of the most influential ecclesial metaphors in the history of the church, not least in the Reformed tradition. As Christian

Link observes, in an essay on the Reformed understanding of the *notae ecclesiae* (the marks of the church), "Calvin employs this image pointedly to characterize the congregation of the Lord's Supper and to ground church discipline."[5] In recent decades this image has been particularly influential in recovering the New Testament and Reformation vision of the priesthood and ministry of all believers. The body metaphor has contributed greatly to congregational vitality in many Reformed communities around the world, not least in my own Scottish context. However, it may increasingly be a problematic image of the church for many Scottish Presbyterian congregations in the early twenty-first century, when wedded to institutional and cultural forms of local church and congregational life inherited from the preceding two centuries, the era of modernity. This combined biblical and cultural image of the local congregation as a membership body, with its associated panoply of membership requirements and activities, can be a disabling and demoralizing image and inheritance for Reformed congregations experiencing the full impact of secularization. The struggle to maintain and operate such a model of the congregation is now overwhelming for many if not yet most local churches and ministers in the Church of Scotland.

The Church of Scotland is a national Church with a Presbyterian form of government and Reformed confession of faith, recognized but not established by the British state. As such, it is committed to a territorial ministry ensuring the ordinances of religion to the whole of Scotland and to a national role, "representative of the Christian faith of the Scottish people."[6] It went through a short period of postwar growth from 1946 to 1956, with one in three adults in Scotland in its membership, and then into a prolonged and accelerating period of decline after 1956. From 1957 it has declined from 1.32 million members to around 400,000 and still falling in 2015. In a church attendance census taken in 2002, only a third of those Church of Scotland members were at worship on a Sunday, with women between 20 and 40 being the largest group dropping out of membership and attendance.[7] This rapid decline has happened in a total Scottish population that has shown modest growth to 5.3 million in 2015. In this religious and demographic context, the thousand and more parishes and congregations of the Church of Scotland are now undergoing a crisis of historic and fundamental proportions in their institutional form and religious purpose as the local units of a national parish system, predating the Reformation in its twelfth-century origins in medieval Scotland. In the second decade of the twenty-first century, the Church of Scotland is moving from retrenchment to collapse. It has as many bureaucrats in its national offices as congregations funding the wider church.[8]

What would the continuing vitality of the Reformed congregation look like in such a situation?[9] Elsewhere I have argued that in postmodern Scottish society, the Reformed congregation of the twenty-first century must become both "sustainable" and "habitable" as a social expression of the Christian life within such a changing, globalizing world.[10] First, the institutional form of the *sustainable* congregation must be one that the church can sustain and its participants find sustaining, in both economic and spiritual terms. And, second, the *habitable* congregation must be a form of social and religious life that contemporary postmodern Scots do not find culturally alien and alienating. It must be one that the neighbor and stranger can enter as a welcoming social space that embodies God's concern for all of humanity and communicates the good news of Jesus Christ. For increasing numbers of Kirk ministers and members and for the majority of people in the wider society, the present national parish system is neither sustainable nor habitable as a contemporary social form of Christian faith and practice in Scotland.

Until the early nineteenth century, affiliation with and participation in the life of a local congregation of the national Church of Scotland was typically through birth into the local parish community. Financial responsibility for the payment of the parish minister and the maintenance of the church properties lay with the local land and property owners legally responsible for the provision of a parish church and ministry. The parish minister was there to provide "the ordinances of religion" to the local community, and the local governing Kirk Session of ministers and elders was there to ensure moral discipline, poor relief, and the provision of a day school and teacher in the parish. This territorial parish model, with its communal and civil notion of membership, was increasingly undermined in modern Scotland by the rise and growth of dissenting Presbyterian and evangelical churches from the second third of the eighteenth century onward; these groups separated themselves from the established national and parish church system and provided for their own ministers and church buildings through the voluntary giving of members in "gathered congregations." Congregational affiliation became a matter of choice and rivalry among several competing denominations for many Presbyterian Scots. The rise of an unchurched urban poor population and the immigration of large numbers of Irish Catholics in search of work, especially into the industrial West and central belt of Scotland, also broke the religious monopoly of the national parish system under the empirical weight of religious pluralism. More than that, the scale of poverty, disease, and social need in a rapidly industrializing and urbanizing Scottish society overwhelmed the welfare resources and capacities of the ancient parish model of the congregation in Scotland, inherited from a preindustrial and rural society of the Reformation and the medieval Catholic Church.

By the mid-nineteenth century, these ecclesiastical and economic factors, along with a characteristically Victorian concern for statistical measurement of institutional strength and religious observance and an evangelical concern to mobilize the laity for local mission and welfare work, led to a new model of the Reformed congregation as an *activist membership institution*. As such, it was concerned to encourage the membership requirements of regular church attendance and financial giving. For the dissenting Presbyterian denominations like the United Presbyterians and the Free Church of Scotland, and even for the established Church of Scotland, the local church was increasingly seen as a membership body, where everyone had to play a part as active and committed Christians. The Reformed congregation, its ordained ministry, elders, and other officeholders were there to mobilize church members in a range of Christian work: Sunday school teaching and "Band of Hope" temperance meetings for children; local evangelistic visitation, home mission, and social welfare programs among the unchurched poor and working class; activities on behalf of foreign mission work; and revival meetings like those of Moody and Sankey to win back the lapsed and indifferent, especially the young adult male members of church families from the 1870s onward.[11]

Responding to the social, cultural, and economic forces of modernization in an urbanizing and industrial society, two further trends in congregational life are discernible. First, a range of *lay religious organizations* were started to meet the spiritual and social needs of particular groups within late Victorian and Edwardian Scotland. New para-church and church organizations like the uniformed Boys' Brigade and the Woman's Guild, for example, must be seen in the changing social context of a militaristic British Empire and campaigns for women's suffrage and access to university education. Second, the Scottish Presbyterian congregation of the later nineteenth century and the first half of the twentieth century also became a *leisure center* for church members, their families, and local communities, especially in the new affluent suburban communities. As the Scottish Presbyterian middle class moved to the suburbs, they abandoned their evangelical activism among working class and poor neighbors, characteristic of early and mid-Victorian Presbyterian congregational life, and increasingly pursued their own bourgeois interests. The social historian of Scottish religion Callum Brown has explained it thus:

> The suburban exodus of the 1880s, 1890s and 1900s changed the nature of bourgeois religion. The middle classes became commuters on the new trams, retreating from the inner-city areas their parents had evangelised. The suburban churches symbolised their prosperity and their cultural concerns, with newfangled church halls constructed to act as the busy recreation centres of suburban leisure. Pursuits and organisations catered for all ages and tastes.[12]

Brown cites one example of such changes:

> Suburban churches of the 1880s and 1890s were built with multiple church halls—as many as five—to cater for the new plethora of pastimes. At St Matthew's Church of Scotland in Morningside in Edinburgh, the following activities were on offer: Sunday Schools with 441 children, five Bible classes with 120 teenagers, Young Men's Guild (with Fellowship and other sections) with 202 members, Woman's Guild with 463 members and ten different activities, a Self-Help Society, junior and senior Literary Societies (with drama sections), Golf Clubs for men and ladies with over a hundred members, together with curling, holiday "retreats" and a clutch of summer picnics. The minister of this congregation regarded these activities "as links in the chain of full Church membership."[13]

But such changes in the cultural form of congregational life were not restricted to the middle-class suburbs. Local church life and evangelistic activities among the working class and poorer communities also experienced the leisure revolution described by Brown:

> The period between 1870 and 1914 witnessed the growth of organised commercial leisure on an undreamt-of level: the music hall, variety theatre, organised rules sport, the cinema and many other forms of recreation. Attendances at Sunday School and mission stations were starting to fall whilst "secular" leisure was booming. Participant football also became enormously popular and religious organisations (notably the Bands of Hope and the Boys' Brigade) had by the early twentieth century organised their own teams, leagues and knock-out cups. The churches were being drawn inexorably into competition with commercial and social leisure.[14]

I have quoted Brown's evidence at some length to emphasize the fundamental changes that congregational life underwent in the Scottish Presbyterian denominations around the turn of the twentieth century. As he astutely observes: "Religious organisations were starting to compromise with secular pursuits, moving from 'improving' educational classes in religious instruction, or revivalism, to sport, outings and militaristic youth movements. Goal displacement was occurring: voluntary organisations' religious goals were being displaced by secular pursuits originally introduced as mere enticements."[15] This was a move to a model of the congregation as *"recreation centre."*

But this was not the whole story in the first half of the twentieth century. Anxious about the perceived alienation or indifference of Scots of all classes to institutional religion, the Presbyterian churches continued to engage in theologically diverse forms of home mission, including aggressive evangelism campaigns as well as gentler "missions of friendship," to win "the unchurched million" back to the fold.[16] In targeted missions to working-class communities in the interwar years of economic depression in the 1920s and 1930s, and especially after the Second World War, in the "Tell Scotland" movement of the early 1950s, local congregations were once again mobilized to take part in lay witness to their neighbors or to invite them to mass evangelistic meetings like those Billy Graham famously held in Scotland in 1956.[17] By the mid-twentieth century the national Church of Scotland had been reunited with the vast majority of dissenting Presbyterians from the earlier secessions of the eighteenth and nineteenth centuries. In 1956 its membership peaked at 1.32 million communicant members, embracing around one in three adults out of a total Scottish population of five million.

What kind of congregational vitality lay behind this seeming success? The typical Church of Scotland congregation of the 1950s could be described as a "hybrid membership body," synthesizing the legacy of these three different Reformed models of the local church since the eighteenth century that I have identified. In its nineteenth-century heyday, each of these models had contributed to the vitality of Reformed congregations in Scotland and had influenced the shape of this hybrid late modern form of local Presbyterian church life, which appeared to be so successful as late as the mid-1950s. At the core of this hybrid membership body was the notion that *the parish church* was there to provide the ordinances of religion to the local community in Scotland through its territorial ministry, serving parishioners as well as church members in parish weddings, funerals, and pastoral care. But around that core, and often in tension with it and with one another, were notions of the congregation as both a *social leisure center* for members and their families and an *activist outreach team* to win the lapsed or unchurched back to religious commitment. Such commitment meant institutional involvement as church members, with a growing emphasis on financial stewardship and giving.

What impact did socioeconomic and cultural changes have on the typical Reformed congregation in Scotland, as it tried to be a *purveyor of the ordinances of religion* to the parish through its ordained ministry, a *leisure center for its members* and local community, and a *spiritual assault team* to recruit the lost and recover the lapsed into active church membership? This hybrid membership body, as I have called it, went into crisis and decline from the 1960s onward.[18] The general picture in the opening decades of the twenty-first century is one of an aging membership and ministry, struggling and increasingly failing to maintain this inherited hybrid model of congregational life in the Church of Scotland, albeit with some notable exceptions to this trend. This is now true of its suburban heartland, as well as in its once dominant and vigorous working-class parishes. It is acutely the case in areas of multiple economic and social deprivation, where the population of postwar public housing schemes have suffered the triple blow of postindustrial male unemployment, poorly paid female part-time employment, and the onslaught of drug trafficking. This hybrid model is in terminal decline on all fronts, although it is in vigorous remission in some suburban and small-town areas.

With fewer ministers and larger, amalgamated parishes, the Church of Scotland's ordained ministry is experiencing high levels of stress and loss of vocation under the increasing workload of providing ordinances of religion like parish funerals and weddings to a society otherwise indifferent to their role or contribution as ministers of the gospel.[19] Church halls can no longer compete as recreation centers for their own members, never mind the wider community, in a postmodern world of sophisticated local and online leisure options. The range of congregational activities in youth work and adult social life, often based on organizations developed to meet the needs of eighteenth- and nineteenth-century children and women, are of dwindling attraction to twenty-first-century people of any age. And the small, committed group of church members typically at the heart of the activist congregation find it a growing burden to staff and run traditional church organizations or engage in innovative outreach activities to recruit new members. This may be due to the infirmities of age, the burden of financial reporting and legal compliance for congregations that must now register as charitable bodies, or the lack of time and energy that postindustrial working and social patterns impose on those of all ages at work. We are witnessing the religious enervation, bureaucratic overloading, cultural redundancy, and institutional decline of this *hybrid congregational model of public ordinances, private recreation, and active membership* in the Church of Scotland. But is there any Reformed alternative to this entrenched pattern? And are there any other biblical images of the church that may be more fruitful and appropriate to describe a process of reform in such a church and social context? We now turn to a local Scottish congregational case study to address these questions.

RICHMOND CHURCH: A TEMPLE OF THE SPIRIT?

I first visited the Church of Scotland parish church of Richmond in the city of Edinburgh in early 2001. I was leading a fieldwork visit with a group of divinity students from the University of Edinburgh, observing the changing pattern of ministry in this local church as part of their course work. I made two other such visits with students in 2002 and 2003, returning alone as a researcher in April of 2003 to conduct a recorded interview with its parish minister and church-employed project worker. At that meeting they decided that I should not impose anonymity on my account of their story but identify them and the congregation with minimal ascription. As a piece of practical theology, my account is both an exercise in congregational studies and a wrestling with the institutional implications of my own Reformed tradition's theological commitment to continuing reform. But why choose this case study in considering a successor to the hybrid model of the Reformed congregation as a membership body? The reason was not immediately obvious to me on my first or second visits.

On that first visit in 2001, Richmond seemed like so many parish churches and ministries in urban areas of multiple deprivation in Scotland. The minister, Liz, and Jessie, her close colleague and full-time church project worker, had recently opened a café in the church building for local people, as well as running a clothes store and a food cooperative in the church hall. Jessie was from the local community, and her local knowledge and rapport made her a supportive and wise guide to Liz as she in turn sought to develop appropriate ways of being an ordained minister in the poorest church and community in Edinburgh. With the university students, I worshiped with Liz and Jessie and the small local congregation on the Sunday morning of our first and subsequent visits over the three years of this study. We gathered in a large, cruciform sanctuary built in the arts and crafts style of the 1930s, and by 2001 somewhat shabby and cluttered with the bric-a-brac of church life, but brightened by the modern seating, warm welcome, and lively worship and preaching in an engaging contemporary and local idiom.[20]

The story could be repeated throughout Scotland, which is not to devalue the unique work and contribution of Liz and Jessie in that particular locality and situation. It is the remarkable story of what were then termed "UPA Churches and Ministries" in the Church of Scotland, which always struggle and so often succeed against all the odds to maintain lively and innovative worshiping, witnessing communities of faith, and service in government-designated "urban priority areas" (UPA) of multiple deprivation. However, as I returned each year and listened to the latest developments in the life of the Richmond congregation, as told by Jessie and Liz, something more than another UPA story of costly and creative ministry in a poor community was being described to me. From the poorest of the poor in Scotland, a new model of the Reformed congregation in the twentieth century was slowly emerging in front of me, literally before my eyes. Liz and Jessie were not sure how to describe what they are engaged in or what is emerging in Richmond Church, and so what follows is my interpretation as a practical theologian of their still unfinished and unfolding story. It draws on limited participant observation of the life and worship of the church over three years, an essay titled "From Monochrome to Colour" that Liz wrote about her ministry for a Scottish ethnography project, and an extended semistructured interview with Liz and Jessie that I conducted and recorded at the church in April of 2003.[21] It is an interpretation of the Richmond story and a proposal for a Reformed congregational model for the twenty-first century that at this stage can only be suggestive and exploratory.

Since her arrival at Richmond Parish Church in 1997, Liz has been responding pastorally to untimely and often tragic deaths in this community, from drugs and sometimes from violence. In response, at Jessie's initiative, they have created a memorial chapel and bronze "tree of remembrance" for the bereaved families and members of their community. In June of 2003 they opened "Richmond's Hope," a professionally staffed bereavement counseling center for children who have lost family members to untimely death or continuing drug addiction.[22] This center is the first of its kind in Scotland, and Jessie raised its initial three-year costs of £307,000 herself, with Liz. Both the chapel and the center are located *within the sanctuary* of the church building: the chapel is in a side aisle and the counseling center at the rear, with upper-floor windows intentionally built to look down into the worship area. The minister is quite clear on why the new Richmond's Hope counseling project for bereaved children should be situated at the rear of the sanctuary and look directly into it. Worship is the heart of all that they do:

> There is a theory about doing things off the premises and starting up say a shop or something in the community, particularly in communities like this. People have gone into the idea of house churches and moving away from buildings. I think if you scrape the surface of most of the people in the church, they still feel that it should be around the church, ... and I feel it should be in the church, not because I want to draw everything in here but because I think it is important to make that connection, to be honest about it and say, "This is who we are," and that the project will be run by people who ... it doesn't matter if they have faith or not, we need them to do this job for the children, but there is something about linking it in to the Memorial Chapel and the Tree.... Can we offer these rituals, can we offer new rituals to people that meet needs that they're expressing?[23]

If I were to suggest to Liz and Jessie that they are like Solomon, building a temple to the Lord, they would laugh at such pretension, with characteristic modesty and pastoral focus on Christ's compassion for their suffering neighbors. However, if the apostle Paul argues that our bodies as whole persons should not be violated by evil because they are the temple of the Spirit—the holy place where God dwells, the precious place that Christ bought with the cost of his own body and blood (1 Cor. 6:9–20)—then the Richmond story is about building up *such a spiritual temple*, the physical bodies and lives of whole persons, in the sanctuary light of the Gospel, *within the church walls.*

In interpreting the life of the Richmond congregation as that of a spiritual temple, I look in the Gospels to the physical temple in Jerusalem, rather than to the synagogue in Capernaum, to reconceive the Reformed congregation today. In part, I refer literally to the life and ministry of a physical temple, where people encounter God through their embodied religious and social practices, in the range of its courtyards and sanctuary spaces: like Joseph and Mary making their offering in the temple after the birth of Jesus (Luke 2:22–38); or the boy Jesus listening and talking with the teachers in the temple, on the threshold of adult life (2:41–51); or later teaching there himself in his public ministry (20:1–8; 21:37–38). By calling it a spiritual temple, I interpret this congregation's life in spatial terms: it is a set of physical and social spaces within which people encounter and glorify God in their bodies. Understanding the congregation in this way, as a carefully delineated literal and sacred space, affirms the occasional but deliberate participation in religious and social practices by all those who move within its physical walls, in a particular place.[24] Such practices focus on the embodiment of the whole person in life and in death and the renewing presence of the Spirit within the embodied community of persons, in the light of Christ's sacrifice: "for you were bought with a price" (1 Cor. 6:20 NRSV).

Such congregations are therefore not constituted primarily by maintaining the formal requirements or institutional infrastructure of church membership, as developed by mainline denominations since the nineteenth century. They are constituted by bodily participation in the social and religious life within their literal walls and sacred spaces. In theological terms, they are therefore closer to Paul's understanding of the physical body and embodied person as a "temple of the Holy Spirit within you" (1 Cor. 6) rather than to his metaphor of the spiritual body of "many members" (1 Cor. 12). Both metaphors are central to understanding the nature of the Christian church and Christian life. The question here is, Which might be more fruitful in analyzing and understanding congregational vitality in this particular local and postmodern context? In sociological terms, drawing on the work of Robert Wuthnow, this congregation in its social relationships and approach to religion can be characterized as a temple of "loose connection and spiritual practice." As such, it may be better attuned to being gospel communities in a postmodern culture. Such a culture finds the heavy commitments of institutional membership and the inherited conventions of institutional religion alien and alienating. It may be more open to discovering the riches of Christian traditions of faith through exploration and dialogue and through the voluntary discipline of personal practice.

In pursuing this goal, Liz has consciously abandoned the attempt to maintain the congregation according to the inherited model of a Church of Scotland parish church, what I have termed a hybrid membership body.[25] Reflecting on her experience in her previous parish, a typical hybrid membership body, she wrote:

> On a day-to-day basis ministry in my first charge was not a matter of choice. The report that I presented to the Annual General Meeting of the congregation each year was often structured around the statistical information that evidenced the work I was engaged in. Ninety funerals a year, fifty housebound, ten weddings, fifteen baptisms and fifteen new members a year were the average amounts. Beyond these tasks was the responsibility of ensuring the smooth workings of the inherited machinery of a local parish church. . . . The harder task was trying to find people willing to make up their numbers and thus ensure that there were people to lead the organisations, to fill the elders districts, to tend the property, to deal with administration, to distribute the flowers and so on. As resources of people and money shrink these tasks become more onerous. The concept of simply not having a choir or flowers or a property committee would have left the church feeling that it was falling down [in] some invisible league table of churches.[26]

Nearly all of these organizational activities had collapsed in Richmond Church when Liz came there as minister in 1997. Such a membership-body model of the congregation was no longer applicable or relevant. Trying to revive or operate such a model would have locked the congregation and minister into a permanent sense of failure and decline. More fundamentally and theologically, it would have offered them the bad news of institutional and cultural demands that alienated them from hearing and receiving the liberating good news of Jesus Christ in Word and Sacrament. In place of the classic modern Church of Scotland hybrid membership body model of the congregation, Liz is seeking to find another way of being a Reformed congregation.

With Jessie and the small number of formal church members, and through vital partnerships with the local community and nonchurch funding bodies, the minister turned a shabby and rundown building with holes in the roof, perceived as having a declining membership body, into a place of healing encounter with God for those with bruised bodies and broken spirits in the local community. This is not another church social work center, because everything revolves around worship in the sanctuary, at least for Liz, Jessie, and the few members of the congregation. For many other people who pass through the church each week, most will only enter the café at the side door, or the clothing store and food co-op in the church hall, the meeting room used by the community health and social workers, and now the child bereavement center. Occasionally individuals and families will venture into the sanctuary itself, to grieve and mourn in the memorial chapel around the bronze tree, or to sit quietly and pray around the Lord's Table and baptismal font and preaching pulpit. And sometimes the local community will crowd into the sanctuary for another funeral, to mourn another tragic and premature death.

As I have observed and listened and tried to understand what is happening here, I think I see the emergence of a new way of being a Reformed congregation. This is a temple, with its outer and inner courtyards and its sanctuary and sacred spaces. The clue to this new identity is an incident Liz records when a local person working as a waiter approached her while she was dining in a restaurant. The local person asked Liz to confirm to some skeptical work colleagues that she, the waiter, belonged to Liz's congregation. Although she was not a formal member of the Church of Scotland, she identified herself as belonging to Richmond Church because she came to the church café. Liz observed that the merging of church and community in the café, as in other parts of the church building, is intriguing. In Richmond they are witnessing a new understanding of what it means to belong to the Reformed congregation, through participation in the practices of its sacred spaces rather than in the demands of formal church membership.

In the temple in Jerusalem there was a series of courtyards, allowing people different stages of proximity to the inner sanctuary. As we know from the Gospel story of the cleansing of the temple, a range of activities went on within its precincts, for good and ill. In Richmond Church, the café functions as the "outermost courtyard" of the spiritual temple. Occasionally Jessie has had to throw people out for attempted drug dealing. But those who work and spend time in the café often consider themselves as fully part of the church as the active formal members. The invitation and the hope is that such people will draw closer to the worship at the heart of its life. The same story could be repeated about the other occasional or regular participants in the life of this church who come into its other "courtyards," sometimes the "outer sanctuary," in the Memorial Chapel but rarely the inner sanctuary, where the congregation worships each Sunday. In Richmond Church, we are witnessing a historic paradigm shift, from understanding the congregation as an activist membership body in time, *a temporal body*, to understanding the Reformed congregation as a spiritual temple in space, a *spatial body* with a focus on the central, defining place of worship, the sanctuary, around which everything revolves.[27]

CONCLUSION: A NEW MODEL OF THE REFORMED CONGREGATION FOR POSTMODERN EUROPE?

The American sociologist of religion Robert Wuthnow offers us two key concepts for understanding the social and religious changes that are taking place in Western society and represent a particular challenge to Reformed congregations like Richmond Church, described in our case study. First, he speaks of the new social culture of "loose connections" that has developed since the 1950s.[28] Up to the 1950s in America, as in Scotland, people were "joiners" who supported the tight social connections and activities of local and national membership organizations, like the mainline denominations or the Rotary Club for businesspeople. From the 1960s onward, we live in more fragmented communities of what Wuthnow terms "loose connections." However, he wants to stress that these looser social connections, where people are unwilling or unable to make lifetime organizational commitments, retain their moral and spiritual potential for expressing and enabling social action for the common good. Postmodern people will only participate in a voluntary or philanthropic activity if it is for a limited period that fits their schedule and allows them to express their own particular configuration of beliefs and values, with a sense of ownership and participatory voice or contribution. The postmodern social world of loose connection does not necessarily mean shallow convictions or lack of concern but rather a rejection of the typically modern hierarchical, time-greedy, and directive institutional culture that literally and metaphorically does not give postmodern people "space" to be themselves or express themselves.

The people who participate in the life of Richmond Church in our case study are such postmodern people, albeit in the socioeconomic context of a poor community. They are intensely and deliberately involved in one of the courtyards or sanctuaries of the temple, but they have loose connections with the church as a membership body. They are also people interested in exploring religious practices, and they play their part in shaping them in dialogue with the Reformed and ecumenical traditions of Richmond Church. In one moving story, for example, Liz describes how a young local boy planned and conducted his mother's funeral, at his own insistence and with her guidance as the minister. This is the model of ministry in such a congregation, functioning as a spiritual temple of "loose connection." The minister here is the "guide at the side" rather than the "sage on the stage," to borrow a phrase from the educational field to describe the changing role of the teacher. The Richmond congregation literally and metaphorically gives postmodern Scots space, within the walls of its spiritual temple, to encounter God in its courtyards and sanctuary of the living Word and Sacramental practice.

Wuthnow again offers us a helpful concept to understand this shift in the nature of religious experience since the 1950s in Western societies. In his book *After Heaven*, he describes the spirituality of the 1950s churchgoing generation as that of "settlers" and that of the post-1960s generation as that of spiritual "seekers."[29] But in the 1990s he detected a longing to return to the disciplines of "spiritual practice" carried by the great religious traditions. Although Wuthnow is describing the changing social and religious patterns of relationship and piety of Americans since the 1950s, in this instance such shifts are also typical of the cultural and religious changes experienced by the population of postmodern Scotland, within a far more secular northern Europe. The temple of the Holy Spirit that is Richmond congregation is a safe and hospitable space for people to encounter and engage with the Reformed tradition's rich and living heritage of spiritual practices.[30] It is also a place where, in an authentically Reformed way, such practices are being reformed in the light of the gospel and God's presence and work in the world.

What have I learned from this Reformed congregation as a practical theologian in the Reformed tradition? I think this case study shows clear evidence of exhibiting the three key Reformed practical theological concepts identified at the start of this chapter. The minister, Liz, and her colleague, Jessie, the local project worker, exercised a striking combination of theological and organizational leadership in their work. They did so by responding to profound pastoral needs in the community and directing the life of this congregation away from an inherited but failing and oppressive model of the parish church as a membership body. Instinctively at first, they reconceived the congregation and its ministry and mission in spatial terms. They showed the characteristic freedom of Reformed ecclesiology, quite literally rebuilding the sanctuary as a welcoming place and grieving space for the community, yet still firmly focused on the Word and Sacraments—such as the child bereavement counseling center open to all but with windows into the sanctuary. And they showed the Reformed pattern of asymmetry in the primacy and priority they gave to worship: restructuring the church building as public space for the parish, not as an act of social work but as an act of public worship.

In the spatial practices of Richmond's minister, affirming the church as place as well as people, I have witnessed the continuing vitality of the Reformed tradition to reform the Reformed congregation in Europe today. Richmond gives me hope.

IMAGINARY ENERGIES

Chapter 19

Practicing a Reformed Faith in a Land Down Under

CLIVE PEARSON

THE CONTEMPORARY CONTEXT

In our slice of theological geography "down under," the Reformed tradition is in trouble. Its tradition of a robust confessional theology and practice has not been able to protect its representative churches from the general demise of the Christian faith in a skeptical democratic society. In the past its Australian host culture has attracted the rather misleading claim that it might be the "most godless place under heaven." That assignation was largely a consequence of the convict origins of New South Wales and the need to establish the Christian faith as a "civilizing influence" in the new land, without the benefit of "many traditional supports" of a settled church.[1] It was arguably sustained by the manner in which religion in this country has subsequently been a "shy hope in the heart."[2] This particular cultural context is now self-consciously secular in the public domain, but with a strange difference. It is at the same time increasingly multifaith and full of options. There has been a "religious revitalization," but not along the lines of previous organized patterns.[3]

In his work on *The Australian Soul*, Gary Bouma has argued that various types of "spiritualties are rife and religious diversity is an accepted feature" of contemporary Australia.[4] Elsewhere Bouma has concluded that "everyday life [itself] has become religiously diverse."[5] That diversity is the "new normal."[6] The task facing adherents of any religion or spirituality in this Australian setting is seemingly then one of "living faithfully in the presence of the religious other."[7] And yet this claim is also not quite right. Bouma's sociological challenge to the secularization hypothesis—that is, the profession of faith in general will inevitably fade in the face of the relentless advance of the secular habits of the heart—is rightly made.[8] That "surprising trend" needs to be seen, nevertheless, in full view of the rising number of those who say they have "no religion" on their census return. Bouma describes them as the contemporary "nones."[9] They may also be variously designated as atheistic, agnostic, indifferent—or "apatherian." They can be post-Christian and now rather adept at living out what Philip Kitcher has described in his Terry Lectures as a "secular humanism in their life after faith."[10] The call Bouma identified to live faithfully must now be done in an everyday milieu that is both religiously diverse as well as secular, and it may well be more difficult to do so confessionally amid the steady advance of the secular.

This picture has been further complicated by other consequences arising out of changes in immigration policy. The strength of the Reformed tradition in terms of numbers and percentages was at its height when the Christian constituency was largely confined to an Anglo-Celtic society. That is no longer the case. In the wake of immigration from 1973 onward, the internal composition of existing denominations has been radically altered in race and culture. The largest single church is now Catholic rather than Anglican; there has been the emergence of other denominations that are closely bound to both the language and cultural history and memory of more recent migrant communities. The Christian faith itself is now expressed in Australia in a manner that is highly variegated. It lends itself to any and every denomination, being susceptible to what Hans Joas has identified as "competitive piety" and "transconfessionalism."[11] Joas was surveying the challenges facing the Western church more generally and not Australia, but his analysis resonates with Bouma's data. The capacity to transmit the ethos and tradition of a particular denomination from one generation to another has been compromised. There has been a "dissolution of milieu."

How to practice an applied theology of a Reformed nature in this demanding kind of cultural context is far from straightforward. The case is not helped by a point of definition. The label itself, "Reformed," may well be difficult to define in view of its sometimes competing claimants.[12] Those "distinctive emphases" in doctrine that Donald McKim has identified in his beginners' guide to a Reformed faith[13] are also lived out here in a society where the Christian faith and its practice is no longer "On Top."[14] That perspectival language belongs to the poet, Les Murray. Some years ago he informed his coreligionists in Australia that the plausibility of their patterns of belief and worship outside their institutional *habitus* relied at best on a "residual" cultural memory and frame of reference.[15] For many, the Christian option has thus become a default position in times of national disaster, civic worship, and the occasional personal tragedy and search for meaning.[16] It has lent its religious symbolism rather easily, for example, to the yearly liturgical service for Anzac Day, which commemorates the military action at Gallipoli in 1915.[17]

This shift in stance is reflected in the subsequent description of populist understandings of God that Charles Sherlock has identified in the period between the 1970s and the dawn of a new millennium. There has been a relative loss of transcendence at the expense of a more informal, chatty sense of diffused immanence.[18] The "bloke upstairs" and a "matey" Jesus who shares the sufferings of the "battlers" down below has given way to a more pluralistic, less clearly defined Deity who functions as a "spirituality sponsor." It is a way of relating far removed from responding to a conventional God of holy otherness.[19] The Reformed Christian life of call and obedience tied to the person and salvific work of Christ now competes not merely with other denominational and para-church claims but also with Murray's "paperback pilgrim" and Sherlock's enthusiasts for a spirituality that kicks in "after the doctor, psychiatrist, aerobics instructor, and social worker have had their go." In this kind of setting the pivotal a priori commitment to revelation that then releases a Reformed dogmatic and ethic has no immediate compelling authority. Those who imitate David Tacey and advocate an "Australian spirituality"—earthed in this red-centered landscape and open to Aboriginal experience and spirituality[20]—or count themselves among Rachael Kohn's somewhat syncretistic "new believers"[21] are full of hermeneutical suspicion; they have little or no apparent desire to step inside its revelatory circle of the Christian faith. For an understanding of faith littered with creedal positions and a confessional tendency that glorifies a majestic God, the dilemma is how to negotiate this personal desire to construct a patchwork spirituality that may have a more immediate apparent relevance to its advocates. The problem Bouma discerns lies in the way in which the Christian churches "are making demands that exceed the norms" of an Australian religious outlook that is inclined to be "subdued and laid back," "shy, withdrawn and not exuberant."[22]

The disenchanted are more likely to inhabit the social climate mapped by Steve Crittenden, writing in the wake of the Sydney Olympics. The opening ceremony was deemed to be a "kind of religious liturgy." Here the word "religion" was being used to describe "a whole lot more than going to church or to the mosque." It had to do with "our collective imaginings" and how we build ourselves as a "community, a people, a nation." The comparison was adversely made with the "politically correct" religious language of "brokenness." For a Reformed tradition of faith grounded in a soteriology that takes sin seriously, the prospect is not promising. According to Crittenden, Australians are "fed up" with this kind of talk; they want to be "happy and well" and, it would seem, that the compensating rhetoric and experience of grace has not entered into this equation.[23]

The problem here is partly one of language. The public discourse is no longer familiar with the ready and appropriate use of words like sin, grace, gospel, and holiness.[24] Their relative eclipse reflects the strength of alternative linguistic domains. In his most sobering description of the decay of public language

Don Watson has identified how the clichés, jargon, platitudes, and "weasel words" of managerial business and marketing have been imposed upon us and so readily embraced.[25] In his opinion there is less space for lyric, emotion, complexity, and nuance.

It is arguably the case that such language rather than theology now also shapes the polity and administration of a church ostensibly concerned for "funding" its "core business."[26] The practical effect is for the distinctive language of faith and its inherited polity to become more distant from experience and less intelligible. Faith's own language can, in fact, become a luxury or not well enough known to be used effectively. In this environment, not to be broken but happy and well could be made to fit some of these theological categories. And yet there must be some reserve lest faith is accused of a verbal sleight of hand. It is not all clear whether this ordinary, daily language signifies the same aspirations and experience as do key words like sin, grace, and holiness. Never that far away is the risk of special pleading on behalf of the Christian faith and in effect baptizing the experience of an unsuspecting public to a form of anonymous Christianity.

All the while hovering in the background is the mass attraction/distraction of sports. These societies, tucked away at the ends of the earth, are noted for their "religious" obsession and the capacity to let their character be shaped in the formative stages by what has been variously described as the "Games Revolution," the "Scramble for Sport," and the "Great Sports Craze." It is indeed no accident that the most thorough academic study of this "cornerstone" of the "business of being Australian" describes the host culture as a "paradise" and contemplates how those who were often excluded on the grounds of gender, ethnicity, intellect, or an artistic temperament were consigned to hell. Such is the sporting equivalent of double predestination. Not surprisingly the major stadia are likened to "cathedrals of sport."[27] For marketing purposes rugby union is even reputed to be the game played in heaven, and a variety of codes control miscreant on-field behavior through the use of a "sin bin." In a somewhat related manner social critics have also conceived of life in this culture in categories of the beach. Such is its place in the national imaginary of a country of coastal dwellers: Leone Huntsman reckons that we Australians have "sand in our souls."[28]

For sport and the beach to play such an iconic role in the construction of identity and attract this kind of metaphorical language poses quite a challenge to the Christian faith. They release messages seemingly directed toward competition, tribal loyalties, winning, and maybe hedonism that can sit uneasily with a Christian kerygma, Reformed or otherwise. The ambivalent value of sport was indeed explored in a series of lectures on ethics and sport on the eve of the Sydney Olympics. In the midst of rampant commercialism, national rivalries, fraught urban planning strategies, William James Baker addressed the topic of imaging if Christ came to the Olympics: Would the first now have been last and the last first?[29] Tony Kelly has observed that when the surf is up, the temperature is rising, and the beer is cool, moments of metaphysical reflection are rare.

In such a paradigm the transcendent nature of Christian claims is far from easy to advocate. We now inhabit a landscape that seizes upon indiscretions, inconsistencies, worrying statistics, and pronouncements of faith and then subjects them to a peculiar mix of critique and trivia. The former reserve regarding matters religious and maybe respect has gone. This lifestyle option of the elect and its basic convictions are fair game. It lends itself to the style of parody and witticism to be found in a column by Susan Maushart on "Bearing Gifts and Guilt." For a highly literate public keen to think for itself, well-loved and core Christian texts were interpreted with an eye to an essay that would engage the contemporary weekend supplement reader beyond the standard byte of attention. In contemplating what copy might fill a volume titled *Christianity for Mothers*, Maushart intoned:

> For verily, verily I say unto thee, blessed are the sleep-deprived. They know not what their PIN and username are. . . . For greater love hath no woman than she lay down, and get up again, and lay down and get up again for her baby. . . . Love bears all things, believes all things, endures all things. Love is a bit of a doormat really. . . . Faith, hope and love, these three abide. And the greatest of these is guilt.[30]

The comic element Maushart exploits masks a deeper, more serious reality. The Christian faith now occupies a rather ambiguous position in Australian society. It finds itself continuing to attract high-profile public attention due to controversial issues and personalities as well as the evident emergence of the religious right as a political force.[31] And yet, at the same time, one crisis after another, especially in the fraught area of clerical sexual abuse, has left the credibility of its institutional face somewhat in tatters. This state of play was captured well in a Cathy Wilcox cartoon that adorned the front page of the *Sydney Morning Herald* shortly before Easter 2002. It took the form of a caricature designed to expose the gap that exists between the highly intentional language of the Christian faith and harsh, less forgiving, down-to-earth realities. All that was required were a few lines. For those accustomed to matters of faith, the style was not too unlike those line drawings that litter the pages of the *Good News Bible*. There the similarity ended. This cartoon's message, its kerygma, was about as far removed from heroic and joyful scenes so often depicted in a relatively user-friendly version of the Bible as could be imagined. The outline of a figure, standing, looms behind a lectern ready to deliver. The audience is "us," the reading public, for there are no other characters on this enclosed space on the front page of one of Australia's leading newspapers. The caption beneath the "person" says it all in three brief monosyllabic words that hit home and strike a most vulnerable point: "Let us prey."

One of the difficulties accompanying this scandal is that all traditions bearing the label Christian are marked. The would-be practice and ethic of a Reformed faith bear these scars. It is not immune from the public gaze, even if and when the most high-profile offenses have usually occurred elsewhere.[32] These now well-documented traumas have effectively placed the Christian faith on the back foot and helped determine the cultural landscape in which the confession of the lordship of Christ and the scriptural Word are acted out. The ever-present risk is that the proclamation of faith and its practice have become seriously compromised. This hermeneutic of suspicion makes it even easier for the dominant discourse of the day to consign any talk of a creating and reconciling God to an in-house ecclesiastical audience and the realm of private choice. The popular opinion is that this is "the Australian way" and should remain so.

Writing indeed amid an unprecedented level of media coverage of matters Christian, the columnist Peter FitzSimons declared that God "is baaack!" Then he argued that these convictions should not be "ballyhooed around in public." The underlying assumption is that this is a democratic society whose civic character is defined by the idea of tolerance. The scandal of particularity that lies at heart of belief in the person and work of Christ is reckoned to undermine that ideal and is best thought of not as a public truth but rather as a personal choice. FitzSimons duly advised Christian leaders to "go tell [their story] on the mountaintop with the volume turned down." They were further informed that society in general is not on "the same trip as you," besides which "we are quite happy where we are."[33]

FitzSimons wrote with a degree of lightness and flair that often eludes expositors of faith. The apparent effortlessness of his position disguised a relatively recent reframing of the issues at stake. In the midst of his riposte he referred to "the Christian God." Once upon a time that would not have been necessary. The presence of the qualifying term "Christian" was a signifier of an altered religious landscape. The public and private discussion now takes place in a multifaith and multicultural democratic society. The much cherished civic virtue of tolerance leads to all religions being placed in the private bag; in so doing this binding value further relativizes Christian discipleship. Its effect is to call into question any hint of a public role for the Christian faith. FitzSimons's latest broadside is for the abolition of prayers before federal and state parliaments begin the day's business. "The God who is invoked is *your* God, not the God of the Australian Jews, the Australian Muslims, the Hindus, the Buddhists, Calathumpians, etc.—not to mention the pagans and witch worshippers—and certainly not the God of . . . many of us who believe that all these kind of things are only ancient superstitions anyway."[34] In theory a Reformed faith could now go into a dogmatic override and ignore the lie of this land, but in doing so it would lose its plausibility and become imprisoned in what is, in effect, a sectarian tactic.

RE-FORMING . . .

This description of the contemporary setting has been done for a purpose. Its origins lie in a reading of Peter Matheson's study of the role of rhetoric and imagination in the Reformation. The necessary hermeneutical leap between that past and our present is made through a concern for symbols, clusters of images, and figures of speech embedded in the life of a community. These are found in both the private and public spaces of a society and have the capacity to stir up and shape a renewed or new way of looking at the world and how to act. Rather than focusing on change in social, moral, and political structures and in doctrine, Matheson breaks with this norm and considers how this original Reformation effected a shift in the very perception of reality. The "iconoclastic splurge" of the Reformation is qualified by what he calls its "iconopoiac energies" that draw upon the creativity of "new allegories and metaphors for the divine and the human."[35] The manner in which these images are thrust together subverts one understanding of the cosmos "while paving the way for another." It lends itself to "elemental changes in spiritual direction" and a "reanimated, reactualised Bible." The "imaginative architecture" of a society has been turned upside down and inside out. This shift is popular: it is "signposted by the creative metaphors of the preachers and teachers, the images in literature and art, the rhythms and melodies of the popular ballads and chorales which sang the Reformation into people's souls."[36] These are metaphors that change a world, construct an alternative imagination, and grasp would-be adherents in a new way.

Exploring these themes, Matheson looks at us out of the corner of his furtive eye. In his view it is not just the Reformed tradition that is in trouble. It is also his conviction that

> outside the charmed world of Church and Academy the Reformation is viewed in almost exclusively negative terms. The most urgent concerns of the Reformers—justification by faith, the sole authority of Scripture—have become a closed book to most of us these days and are viewed with a bemused bafflement. The doctrinal archaeologists, busily unearthing layer after layer of controversy about the sacraments or shifts in the understanding of grace, have left most folk, even in the Church, far behind.[37]

From his observation tower Matheson is left to wonder whether this state of play is a symptom of a much wider unease. It gathers itself into a most discomforting question. Has Protestantism "reached its sell-by date and, to be judged by the pronouncement of media pundits, . . . [been] reduced to clear"?[38]

Matheson's contemporary diagnosis is concerned for "the Western world at least." The nature of this assessment is designed to be a more general overview and, in practice, the state of play on the ground will be more varied. The tendency Matheson has identified is not a uniform experience. This "most of us" he invokes is a mite deceptive. It is likely to provoke a reaction from those of the elect able to point to requisite numbers, the vitality of their local congregation or denomination, and a host society that possesses more than a Christian veneer and is not dogged by or so weighed down by an ambivalent historical legacy. Matheson's reading is also not necessarily going to commend itself to the "us" who form pressure groups and alliances deeply committed to the affirmation of evangelical, "orthodox," and reformed principles conceived in a particular way.

Their sense of loss and of being, at times, a "minority within a minority" is oriented toward a future realization of the very ways of life and belief that are now reckoned to be on the wane.

This reading of being Reformed in a land down under is conscious of how the politics of faith can construct a different vision even within the same tradition. The debate over sexual orientation and ministerial leadership on both sides of the Tasman Sea—in Aotearoa, New Zealand, as well as in Australia—has been highly divisive and demonstrated how fractured a confession can be both in practice and in basic outlook. In an acute form this particular "big little issue"[39] has raised the pressing ecclesiological and ethical question as to how any expression of faith preserves its own integrity and handles difference. It represents a variation on a theme proposed by Daniel Hardy, for whom the "moral future of theology" lies precisely in how we deal with one another in the height of controversy. According to the underlying assumption, how we conduct ourselves at such times is as theological as the positions we defend to the hilt.[40] Our actions betray our beliefs. It is indeed the kind of issue that presents us with the awkward vocation of being a moral community in our relationships with one another and being able to exemplify that to a skeptical public domain. This is now a media-driven society that knows the skeletons in the Christian closet. It knows our divisions and the weak points in our structures of plausibility. They make good headlines. Following one meeting of the presbytery of Sydney where there was a modest amount of jostling around the microphone, the front page of the city's *Morning Herald* proclaimed, "Fisticuffs for the Almighty."

The pressures of this particular debate and the struggle for institutional survival in an inhospitable climate of an aging membership and declining resources can be viewed in the light of Matheson's mapping of the present big picture. Arguably, his concern for the metaphorical and imaginative currents that inform a worldview require close scrutiny. Perhaps it is no longer sufficient merely to replay the hope for this tradition, in this location at least, in terms of theological and ethical arguments that do not engage with a much-changed imaginary. In this respect Matheson can be a source of worry for he does not allow us to hide from the awareness that images, symbols, and by extension maybe traditions can become burned out or lose their vitality.[41] Are we in that sort of *kairos* moment? Is it enough to restructure the institutional life of the church according to a range of unclear values and place so much confidence on alternative patterns of "leadership" and variations of how "to do church"?

The *habitus* for a Reformed faith is now far removed from the relationship of gospel and culture that lent itself to its classical confessional stances.[42] Its images and symbols no longer have the same popular currency; their status has been supplanted by those having to do with business, technology, sport, and science. Failure to strike up some engagement between the distinctives of a Reformed theology and ethic and this current concern for the imaginary will only further marginalize faith in this here and now.

The relative eclipse of this *habitus* is taking place while Australia is a society still caught in the process of reinventing itself. That description was used by Anthony Moran in writing on how Australia was leaving behind its Anglo-Celtic imaginary and becoming progressively more multicultural and multifaith.[43] Questions of identity and belonging are to the fore. The momentum possesses its own iconopoiac energies. It seldom, if ever, employs a Christian symbolism or iconic use of metaphor. In the circumstances, what are the options?

This turn to the popular imagination and cultural studies presupposes the practice of a self-conscious contextual theology. The pros and cons of such a way of doing theology are now well rehearsed. The fairly common recourse to the need for critical control has demonstrated the extent to which a Reformed understanding of faith has frequently sat uneasily with what has been described as the principle of contextuality. Karl Barth has often been cited as the authority for such a negative view.[44] It is reckoned that his understanding of revelation, the Spirit, Scripture, and the proclaimed Word depends upon "what is given." Seen from this perspective, theology "must not be allowed to become a religious variation on the everyday pursuits and values of a people, class, or gender raised to the level of universal experience."[45] It is a short step from this estimation to the conviction that Barth situates the gospel over and against culture. This general impression is now recognized to require revisiting. Daniel Migliore believes that claim to be a "colossal mistake."[46] Paul Louis Metzger likewise argues that Barth's response to the culture of his day was "by no means a dismissive reaction to modern concerns."[47] It was rather a "dynamic and carefully nuanced encounter" between the Word of Christ and the world of culture. The dialectical nature of his Christology did not allow for a divinization of culture at the expense of a gospel that always incorporates the "No" of God to the way the world is in its fallenness and need of redemption. Barth was ever wary of the possibility of those "ominous syntheses of Christ and culture." This form of theology preserves a strong sense of transcendence and a recognition of how this world must be addressed by the Word of God. It is also a theology where this "No" is set inside "a framework of the divine 'yes.'" Barth does not consign culture to the domain of the secular and nothing more, as can sometimes be implied. Through the condescension of God, humanity can "become a little more human." Metzger concludes that the Word of Christ in Barth's theology is both "against culture" and "for culture." It critiques, judges, and confirms and must do so because culture is ultimately "of Christ."

The Barthian idea of a critical engagement has often been represented through the analogy of the theologian with the Bible in one hand and the newspaper in the other. There is a sense in which this reading of living in a land down under has adopted aspects of that mode. The media and columnists have been repeatedly used. It has been assumed that the news media has something worth saying and that they do reflect and create a popular way of looking at the world. Media and columnists both mediate and form opinions. Their employment has not been for the sake of merely constructing a *prolegomena* that describes the soteriological necessity of a given society now awaiting a range of appropriate healing and reconciling doctrines to be applied. The reading of a contemporary society, nevertheless, requires a more sustained critical analysis than a romp through the daily newspapers and a much more careful description of the relationship between theology and the social sciences. The purpose has been to consider ideas, images, opinions, and metaphors to be found in one accessible pivotal medium of the public domain and contemplate how a Reformed imagination might then act itself out. It thus represents the beginning of a response to Matheson's study of the rhetoric and symbolism of the Reformation, albeit with one yawning difference. Matheson's world was one of competing visions of the Christian faith. The task before us is daunting in a new way, given the emergence of a media-driven world that is both secular and multifaith. The analogous task is to negotiate its way in and around this muddle of images and values.

The temptation facing theology and ethics is to let all the necessary critical work be done by a range of other disciplines and then append a theological idea or two. In his fine study on sin, Alistair MacFadyen described this tactic as a "Post-it label" theology. Some God-talk is added but in such a way that it is not really necessary. It makes little difference to the description whether the label is stuck on or removed.[48] The present task, then, is to avoid falling into the risk of either dumping a doctrine or moral code on a fairly unyielding society or "collapsing the transcendent into secular frames of reference—into ways of speaking about the world which pragmatically exclude God." MacFadyen senses the danger of us becoming "pragmatic atheists," almost without noticing it.[49] The point of entry in this territory is not easy. Being practical means taking the cultural location seriously and trying to find ways of allowing the habits of the Christian heart to be in critical tension with its images and rhetoric.

The issue at stake, then, is not so much the role of context in the task of theology but what kind. The work of Robert Schreiter and, more recently, Stephen Bevans and Angie Pears has identified a range of models of contextual theologies and diagnosed the jobs they do.[50] The tendency of an equivalent Roman Catholic theology is to focus upon a sacramental view of creation and how the doctrine of incarnation might inform a theory of inculturation or acculturation. For the sake of their signposts for a multicultural witness, Alberto Garcia and Victor Raj have been true to their Lutheran inheritance and opted for a theology of the cross.[51] Their emphasis on the redemptive and soteriological begs the question as to what organizing doctrines and threading (connecting) principles might a Reformed theology and ethic, then, privilege? What form might this theological response take, for Christ's sake, in an antipodean society tucked away in the southeast corner of the globe?

Writing on the Reformed inheritance of the Uniting Church in Australia, Gordon Dicker identified "some of the riches" of that tradition and "why we should be grateful for them."[52] Those he privileged were the emphases on the glory and majesty of God, the sovereignty of God with particular reference to providence and election, the fact of the incarnation, the divinity of Jesus and the saving work of Christ, the centrality of Scripture, preaching, godly scholarship, the life of holiness, and Calvin's polity and pastoral care. Maybe he could have added the priesthood of all believers; it was noticeable that he steered clear of certain Calvinisms like double predestination, which is not likely to travel well in this country.

The seemingly retrospective nature of Dicker's work was entirely understandable. This heritage had entered into union in 1977, and the passage of time has seen the emergence of a younger generation no longer deeply aware of, let alone formed by, its doctrinal emphases, practices, and what Dicker describes as its ethos, its way of doing things, and its spirituality. Now and then he reminded his readers of aspects of this heritage that should be recovered, though how that might be done was left unaddressed. There was no intention demonstrated of entering into the critical issues of our day in the light of these doctrinal markers, except for the acknowledgment of how pressing the issue of reconciliation with Muslim and Jew has become.

The main benefit of Dicker's work was the way it served as a reminder of some key Reformed concepts and how they might be interpreted and applied in a contemporary context. For a generation at a further remove from this inheritance and concerned for the well-being of God's gift of life, there was food for thought. Admittedly the Reformed ethos has far too often been inclined to "look within oneself to discern and reflect on the presence of God." Its imagination has often been introspective and lacked color and drama.[53] But that is not necessarily true for the broad spectrum of its theological trajectories. It possesses a "full agenda" of theological themes aspiring to "a more just world" that bears witness "to the glory of God."[54] William Dyrness has indeed recognized its "longing to see the world remade"; Albert Wolters has identified its biblical concern for creation and a creation restored;[55] it is a theology that at its best weaves together creation and covenant and expects participation;[56] its nature is, at least in theory, always to be reforming and resisting diverse forms of idolatry.[57] There is a Reformed spirit that is committed to engaging with the whole of creation—and this is certainly not a theme that has yet achieved its use-by date.

The practice of faith in a particular theological site involves attending to key public concerns as well as the life of personal discipleship and individual piety. The latter should, of course, not be underestimated or ignored. Dicker is adamant that the church for whom he is writing needs to place "greater emphasis on personal as well as social holiness," especially in a time of "an increasing blurring of the distinction . . . between the life of the world and the life of faith." This wise advice concerning the personal and indeed the subjective is timely given the immediate context. It is a time and place that is noted for an upsurge in a pick'n'mix approach to spirituality and matters of religious conviction. What has the Christian faith, let alone a Reformed ethical or practical theology, to offer in this competitive consumer market of ideas and lifestyles? How can those who profess to stand within this tradition speak with credibility if their grasp on the heritage Dicker has identified is weakening? The present debates in this country over homosexuality have exposed a worryingly low level of personal biblical and theological literacy.

If the Reformed expression of the Christian faith has anything distinctive to offer in this context, then the formation and nurture of the personal cannot be ignored. They are foundational and presently at risk and vulnerable. They need to stand alongside diverse commitments to issues of social justice and the common good and not be swamped or replaced by them. And yet, for all the merits of this argument, simply to be content with the personal could deepen the separation of the private and public. In so doing the church would become complicit in rendering an introverted faith that accepted the rhetoric of religion being something voluntary and what you choose to do for yourself, so long as it does not infringe the democratic code of tolerance.

It is an invidious task now to restrict the range of Reformed concerns and their intersection with the public context described. There is an element of the subjective. Nevertheless there are some recognizable issues that possess a *kairos* nature. These have to do with reconciliation between the indigenous Aboriginal inhabitants of what was once named a *terra nullius* and the dominant settler society,[58] care of the environment,[59] the protection of borders and the treatment of refugees, the rightness or otherwise of a revised theory of a just war, and how best to put into effect a policy of multiculturalism. Amid natural disasters such as fire, flood, and drought; plus human-caused crises such as railway strikes, footballers behaving badly, and political one-upmanship—these themes are relatively constant and repeatedly grab the headlines, inspire the columnists, and allow the cartoonists to indulge in their preferred brand of caricature. If faith were to be silent on any one of these matters, then the moment is lost in a further retreat away from the national imaginary. Even more telling would be the failure to live out the implications of a Reformed faith. The rhetoric and symbolism of this heritage have a role to play and may indeed be both redeemed and revitalized.

The emphasis upon the majesty and sovereignty of God open up the possibility of a deep-seated passion for a highly vulnerable land at ecological risk. The transcendent nature of this confession is bound to a belief in a creator and covenantal God. The salinity levels in the Murray-Darling Basin, the continuing erosion of land, and water catchment areas for the sake of urban development testify to a violated environment. It is a serious national matter, but it is more than that. The covenantal relationship between God and creaturely existence has been placed at risk. These are but a few episodes in a much larger global theological concern for the reversal of God's good creation and actually represent the risk of "uncreation." The distinctive Reformed understanding of majesty, sovereignty, and covenant do not constitute the primary discourse for this domestic ecotheology. It is much more common to hear about Aboriginal spirituality, the ecojustice principles upon which the Earth Bible has been established, perhaps the cosmic Christ, themes of Sabbath and Jubilee, and custodianship (rather than the problematic term "stewardship"). For the prospect of a future for a Reformed ethic in this particular theological geography, these high views of a majestic creator and covenant possess their own imaginative appeal and can be extended to embody the ecological reference. The gathering discourse surrounding climate change, and whether the time for effective action has already passed, only heightens the critical reference back to this transcendent God who creates and sustains.

The need for a local rereading similarly attends the Reformed confession of the lordship of Christ. It cannot be presumed that this titular claim is likely to secure a fair hearing in a society skeptical of honorifics at the best of times. The confession presumes a hierarchical order of authority and obedience. The public tendency is to espouse a deep-seated egalitarianism and a "fair go" for the "underdog." Furthermore the invocation of Christ is more usually associated with uttering expletives than declaring religious belief. The extent to which this has become so is disturbingly evident in a level of perceived generational difference. Work done by the National Church Life Survey has led Ruth Powell to conclude that the present cohort of school-age children is the first peer group with no residual memory of the faith they are rejecting. They know Jesus Christ better as "a swear word than as the Son of God."[60]

Faced with this kind of popular rhetoric, the time and place seem to require an antipodean, upside-down hermeneutic for theology and a consequent ethic. This is one that would allow for more sideways glances across the Tasman between Australia and Aotearoa, New Zealand, than usually occurs. The benefit of this bonding lies initially in the desire to take seriously the political and social contexts in which faith finds itself. These two societies are often referred to as being down under and the antipodes. That language belongs to the period of imperialism and colonialism, but it has survived into our here and now of global flows of peoples, ideas, and technologies. As an accessible metaphor that speaks into a popular culture of sporting, relationships, and travel, it is a part and parcel of cultural history and an icon of settler identity. Talk of being down under has an energy that suggests a perspective, a way of looking at things, and does not necessarily constitute a sense of inferiority, as an occasional critic reckons.

Conceived in the form of the antipodes, the term also has a theological history that goes back to Augustine. His conviction that there could not be such an inhabited place following on from his belief in "monstrous beings" was, in fact, shaped by his confession of the universal lordship of Christ and its salvific purposes.[61] In terms of a biblical exegesis, it lends itself to a view of lordship established in the inversion of Philippians 2:5–11. The saints are called to have the same attitude as that of Christ Jesus, who made himself nothing, taking on the very nature of a servant/slave, being made in human likeness, who through his humbling himself, his obedience, and his death is exalted by God so that "every tongue [should] confess that Jesus Christ is Lord." The lordship of Christ here is concerned with the "belowness" and underside of life as much as it is with their polar opposites.

It is arguably the case that this kind of lordship can play a critical role in the contemporary supermarket range of philosophies and lifestyle options that characterize this particular democratic society. It can do so partly because the hermeneutical principle of being down under establishes a bridge between faith and dimensions of cultural identity. In a society that has been described as being "rarely anti-Jesus" but often indifferent toward the church, theology, and religious moralism, these antipodean metaphors can stimulate the imagination. They can do so because they are not afraid to use the prepositions of being below and beneath jumbled up with the transcendent claims of a more overtly high Christology. They reflect the career of Christ, the humanity of God, who drew alongside those on the periphery. The Reformed fear that a practical, contextual theology and ethic can succumb too much to a cultural captivity is never entirely absent, but that necessary risk can be overplayed. The language of lordship with reference to the confession of Christ always presupposes a divine otherness. The symbolism of being down under can also become a form of cultural criticism in a land that has often seen itself as being a "lucky country." It provides a divine sanction and justification for a commitment to those most in need in such a society for Christ's sake.

There is no end of social, cultural, and political issues alive and well in the Australian setting that might now be subject to theological critique. Each and every doctrine can be engaged. Those selected here have been identified purely for the purpose of illustration. The dilemma to date has been to find a point of entry for a theological and ethical discourse that speaks to Australian realities in a society that is multicultural or multivoiced, multifaith, and in its public domain secular, which in the past has looked upon such discussion as an embarrassing subject. As a form of cultural criticism, the metaphor of being down under directs attention to that which is most vulnerable and disadvantaged. In this antipodean setting, in an Australia facing serious ecological threat, in need of reconciliation with its indigenous peoples, and relating its recent history of multiculturalism and treatment of refugees to the biblical and theological category of hospitality—faith's continuing interrogation is perhaps most urgently put in the form of the question, Who is Jesus Christ for us today?

The future prospects for a Reformed faith that can be converted into a practical ethic cannot in this location rest upon the laurels and spiritual capital of the past. The host society is too greatly changed. The task is to find ways in which a tradition can be released in a manner that continues to speak into contemporary issues and a present imaginative worldview. For that to happen involves a willingness to engage with the principle of contextuality and a desire to allow distinctive doctrines and practices to be viewed from a range of angles. It means cultivating the habit of a listening ear and paying close analytical attention to the images, rhetoric, and symbols that pervade a culture and not merely opting for a preachy theology and high-minded ethic that is no longer convincing.

Notes

Foreword

1. Stephen Happel and David Tracy, *A Catholic Vision* (Minneapolis: Fortress Press, 1988); Francis Schüssler Fiorenza and John P. Galvin, eds., *Systematic Theology: Roman Catholic Perspectives*, 2 vols. (Minneapolis: Augsburg Fortress, 1991).
2. David Willis and Michael Welker, eds., with Matthias Gockel, *Toward the Future of Reformed Theology: Tasks, Topics, Traditions* (Grand Rapids: Eerdmans, 1999) (Michael Welker and David Willis, eds., *Zur Zukunft der Reformierten Theologie: Aufgaben, Themen, Traditionen* [Neukirchen-Vluyn: Neukirchener Verlag, 1998]).
3. Wallace M. Alston Jr. and Michael Welker, eds., *Reformed Theology: Identity and Ecumenicity* (Grand Rapids: Eerdmans, 2003); Alston and Welker, eds., *Reformed Theology: Identity and Ecumenicity II: Biblical Interpretation in the Reformed Tradition* (Grand Rapids: Eerdmans, 2007).

Preface

1. See, e.g., Peter Matheson, *Argula von Grumbach (1492–1554/7): A Woman before Her Time* (Eugene, OR: Cascade Books, 2013).

Chapter 1

1. Hugh T. Kerr, "Where Are You From?," *Theology Today* 47 (January 1991): 361–64.
2. John H. Leith, *The Reformed Imperative: What the Church Has to Say That No One Else Can Say* (Louisville, KY: Westminster John Knox Press, 1988).
3. Michael Welker, "Globaliserung in wissenschaftlich-theologischer Sicht [Globalization from a Scientific-Theological Perspective]," *Evangelische Theologie* 68 (2008): 365–82.
4. Letty M. Russell, *Church in the Round: Feminist Interpretation of the Church* (Louisville, KY: Westminster John Knox Press, 1993), 12–13, 17–19, 35.
5. Daniel L. Migliore, *Faith Seeking Understanding: An Introduction to Christian Theology*, 3rd ed. (Grand Rapids: Eerdmans, 2014), 374–442.
6. Wallace M. Alston Jr. and Cynthia Jarvis, eds., "Preface," *The Power to Comprehend with All the Saints: The Formation and Practice of a Pastor-Theologian* (Grand Rapids: Wm. B. Eerdmans Pub. Co., 2009), xii–xiv.
7. Keith Riglin, Julian Templeton, and Angela Tilby, eds., *Reforming Worship: English Reformed Principles and Practice* (Eugene, OR: Wipf & Stock, 2012).
8. Lukas Vischer, ed., *Christian Worship in Reformed Churches: Past and Present* (Grand Rapids: Wm. B. Eerdmans Pub. Co., 2002).

9. Julian Templeton and Keith Riglin, "Ordered Freedom: English Reformed Worship," in *Reforming Worship: English Reformed Principles and Practice*, ed. Julian Templeton and Keith Riglin (Eugene: Wipf & Stock, 2012), 1–2.
10. Ernest Marvin, "Shaping Up: Reforming Reformed Worship," in Templeton and Riglin, *Reforming Worship*, 16.
11. Angela Tilby, "Foreword," in Templeton and Riglin, *Reforming Worship*, xi–xii.
12. Walter Brueggemann, *Finally Comes the Poet: Daring Speech for Proclamation* (Minneapolis: Fortress Press, 1989); Brueggemann, "Preaching as Re-imagination," *Theology Today* 52, no. 3 (October 1990): 313–30.
13. David Cornick, *Letting God Be God: The Reformed Tradition* (Maryknoll, NY: Orbis Books, 2008), 58–61. For Brueggemann there is a sense in which the Reformed and "evangelical imagination" seeks to provide the hearer "with an offer, as best we can, of an alternative to what is otherwise available in a livable world." See Walter Brueggemann, *The Collected Sermons of Walter Brueggemann* (Louisville, KY: Westminster John Knox Press, 2011), xxiv.
14. Fleur Houston, "Can a Sermon Be Boring? Metaphor and Meaning," in Templeton and Riglin, *Reforming Worship*, 84–94.
15. John W. de Gruchy, "Public Theology as Christian Witness: Exploring the Genre," *International Journal of Public Theology* 1, no. 1 (2007): 26–41.
16. John W. de Gruchy, *Liberating Reformed Theology: A South African Contribution to an Ecumenical Debate* (Grand Rapids: Wm. B. Eerdmans Pub. Co., 1991).
17. Dirk Smit, "Could Being Reformed Have Made A Difference? On Practical Theology and Ethics in South Africa," in *Essays on Being Reformed: Collected Essays 3*, ed. Robert Vosloo (Stellenbosch: SUN Press, 2009), 241.
18. John W. de Gruchy, "Toward a Reformed Theology of Liberation: A Retrieval of Reformed Symbols in the Struggle for Justice," in *Toward the Future of Reformed Theology: Tasks, Topics, Traditions*, ed. David Willis and Michael Welker (Grand Rapids: Wm. B. Eerdmans Pub. Co., 1999), 103.
19. Dirk Smit, "Can We Still Be Reformed? Questions from a South African Perspective," in Vosloo, *Essays on Being Reformed*, 423–40.
20. Smit, "Reformed Theology in South Africa: A Story of Many Stories," in Vosloo, *Essays on Being Reformed*, 201–16.
21. John H. Leith, *An Introduction to the Reformed Tradition: A Way of Being the Christian Community*, rev. ed. (Atlanta: John Knox Press, 1981), 7.
22. Douglas John Hall, *The Cross in Our Context: Jesus and the Suffering World* (Minneapolis: Augsburg Fortress Press, 2003), 2.
23. Ibid., 3.
24. Cornick, *Letting God Be God*, 10. For a historical account of "Who Are the Reformed," see 23–52.
25. Leith, *Introduction to the Reformed Tradition*; James K. A. Smith, *Letters to a Young Calvinist: An Invitation to the Reformed Tradition* (Grand Rapids: Brazos Press, 2010).
26. Dirk Smit, "The Trinity and the Reformed Tradition?," in Vosloo, *Essays on Being Reformed*, 35.
27. Bruce Gordon, *Calvin* (New Haven: Yale University Press, 2009); Randall C. Zachman, *John Calvin as Teacher, Pastor, and Theologian* (Grand Rapids: Baker Academic, 2006); Zachman, *Image and Word in the Theology of John Calvin* (Notre Dame: University of Notre Dame Press, 2009); Zachman, *Reconsidering John Calvin* (Cambridge: Cambridge University Press, 2012); Herman J. Selderhuis, ed., *The Calvin Handbook* (Grand Rapids: Wm. B. Eerdmans Pub. Co., 2009).
28. See Richard A. Muller, "Demoting Calvin: The Issue of Calvin and the Reformed Tradition," in *John Calvin, Myth and Reality: Images and Impact of Geneva's*

Reformer, ed. Amy Nelson Burnett (Eugene: Wipf & Stock, 2011), 3–18. In a similar vein Dirk Smit argues that Calvin should be honored not by "praising him, but rather by standing inside his living legacy." "Views on Calvin's Ethics from a South African Perspective," in Vosloo, *Essays on Being Reformed*, 2009), 33.

29. Gijsbert van den Brink and Harro Höpfl, "Calvin, the Reformed Tradition and Modern Culture," in *Calvinism and the Making of the European Mind*, ed. Gijsbert van den Brink and Harro Höpfl (Leiden: Brill, 2014), 3–24.
30. Richard A. Muller, *Calvin and the Reformed Tradition: On the Work of Christ and the Order of Salvation* (Grand Rapids: Baker Academic, 2012), 9.
31. Ibid., 10–20.
32. Leith, *Introduction to the Reformed Tradition*, 28–29.
33. John Reader, *Reconstructing Practical Theology: The Impact of Globalization* (Burlington, VT: Ashgate, 2008), 69.
34. Leith, *Introduction to the Reformed Faith*, 18–31.
35. William A. Dyrness, *Reformed Theology and Visual Culture: The Protestant Imagination from Calvin to Edwards* (Cambridge: Cambridge University Press, 2004).
36. Charles Taylor, *Modern Social Imaginaries* (Durham, NC: Duke University Press, 2004), 1.
37. Ibid., 23.
38. De Gruchy, "Toward a Reformed Theology of Liberation," 112.
39. Ibid., 109.
40. Daniel Migliore, "The Spirit of Reformed Faith and Theology," in *Loving God with Our Minds: The Pastor as Theologian; Essays in Honor of Wallace Alston*, ed. Michael Welker and Cynthia Jarvis (Grand Rapids: Wm. B. Eerdmans Pub. Co., 2004), 352–66.
41. Michael Welker, "Serving God in a Time When a World-View Collapses: The Pastor-Theologian at the Beginning of the Third Millennium," in Welker and Jarvis, *Loving God with Our Minds*, 74–75.
42. James Woodward and Stephen Pattison believe that it is probably "not very useful" to draw a distinction between pastoral theology and practical theology. James Woodward and Stephen Pattison, eds., "An Introduction to Pastoral and Practical Theology," in *The Blackwell Reader in Pastoral and Practical Theology* (Malden, MA: Blackwell, 2000), 4.
43. Bonnie J. Miller-McLemore, "The Clerical and the Academic Paradigm," in *Christian Theology in Practice: Discovering a Discipline* (Grand Rapids: Wm. B. Eerdmans Pub. Co., 2012), 160–84.
44. Elaine Graham, Heather Walton, and Francis Ward, *Theological Reflections: Methods* (London: SCM Press, 2005).
45. Dorothy C. Bass and Craig Dykstra, eds., *For Life Abundant: Practical Theology, Theological Education, and Christian Ministry* (Grand Rapids: Wm. B. Eerdmans Pub. Co., 2008).
46. Helen Cameron, Deborah Bhatti, and Catherine Duce, *Talking about God in Practice: Theological Action and Research Practical Theology* (London: SCM Press, 2010).
47. Claire Wolfteich, ed., *Invitation to Practical Theology: Catholic Voices and Visions* (Mahwah, NJ: Paulist Press, 2014).
48. Cameron, Bhatti, and Duce, *Talking about God*, 21; Woodward and Pattison, *Blackwell Reader*, xiii.
49. Wolfteich, *Invitation to Practical Theology*, 13.
50. Ibid., 2.
51. Ibid., 14.
52. Ibid., 3.

53. For another overtly Catholic approach to a practical theology, see J. Sweeny, G. Simmonds, and D. Lonsdale, *Keeping Faith in Practice: Aspects of Catholic Pastoral Theology* (London: SCM Press, 2010).
54. Reader, *Reconstucting a Practical Theology*, 4.
55. Ibid., 8–14.
56. Ibid., 1.
57. John Leith, *The Reformed Imperative: What the Church Has to Say That No One Else Can Say* (Louisville, KY: Westminster John Knox Press, 1988), 28.
58. Ibid., 22.
59. John F. Kilner, *Dignity and Destiny: Humanity Made in the Image of God* (Grand Rapids: Wm. B. Eerdmans Pub. Co., 2015), 3–36.
60. James H. Evans Jr., *We Have Been Believers: An African American Systematic Theology*, ed. Stephen G. Ray Jr., 2nd ed. (Minneapolis: Fortress Press, 2012), 115–38.
61. Joel Kovel, *White Racism: A Psychohistory* (New York: Pantheon, 1970). Kovel made a distinction between dominative and aversive racism. The dominative racist is "the type who acts out bigoted beliefs—he represents the open flame of racial hatred" (54).
62. John F. Dovidio and Samuel L. Gaertner, *Prejudice, Discrimination, and Racism* (San Diego: Academic Press, 1986).
63. Adam R. Pearson, John F. Dovidio, and Samuel L. Gaertner, "The Nature of Contemporary Prejudice: Insights from Aversive Racism," *Social and Personality Psychology Compass* 3 (2009): 1.
64. Ibid., 2.
65. Nancy J. Ramsay, "Faculty Colleagues as Allies Resisting Racism," in *Teaching for a Culturally Diverse and Racially Just World*, ed. Eleazar Fernando (Eugene: Wipf & Stock, 2013), 238–52.
66. Derald Wing Sue, *Microaggressions in Everyday Life: Race, Gender, and Sexual Orientation* (Hoboken, NJ: John Wiley & Sons, 2010).
67. John F. Dovidio, *Reducing Intergroup Bias: The Common Ingoup Identity Model*, Essays in Social Psychology (New York: Routledge, 2014), xii.
68. Pearson, Dovidio, and Gaertner, "Nature of Contemporary Prejudice," 4.
69. James M. Jones, John F. Dovidio, and Deborah L. Vietze, *Beyond Prejudice and Racism* (Malden, MA: Blackwell, 2014); John F. Dovidio, Miles Hewstone, Peter Glick, and Victoria M. Esses, *The SAGE Handbook of Prejudice, Stereotyping and Discrimination* (London: Sage Publishers, 2013).
70. Pearson, Dovidio, and Gaertner, "Nature of Contemporary Prejudice," 4–12.
71. Mahzarin R. Banaji and Anthony G. Greenwald, *Blindspots: The Hidden Biases of Good People* (New York: Delacorte Press, 2013).
72. Christena Cleveland, *Disunity in Christ: Uncovering the Hidden Forces That Keep Us Apart (*Downers Grove: IVP Books, 2013), esp. 178, 187.
73. Pearson, Dovidio, and Gaertner, "Nature of Contemporary Prejudice," 19.
74. Jennifer Harvey, *Dear White Christians: For Those Still Longing for Racial Reconciliation* (Grand Rapids: Wm. B. Eerdmans Pub. Co., 2014).
75. Fleur Houston, *You Shall Love the Stranger as Yourself: The Bible, Refugees, and Asylum* (New York: Routledge, 2015), 2.
76. Ibid., 1.
77. Susanna Snyder, *Asylum-Seeking, Migration and Church* (Burlington, VT: Ashgate, 2012), 93.
78. Linda Woodhead, "Religious Other or Religious Inferior," in *Living with Religious Diversity*, by Sonia Sikka, Bindu Puri and Lori G. Beaman (New York: Routledge, 2016), 3–16.

79. Sebastian C. H. Kim, ed., *Christian Theology in Asia* (Cambridge: Cambridge University Press, 2008); Jonathan Y. Tan, *Christian Mission among the Peoples of Asia* (Maryknoll, NY: Orbis Books, 2014); Felix Wilfrid, ed., *The Oxford Handbook of Christianity in Asia* (New York: Oxford University Press, 2014).
80. The reference to "center of gravity" is taken from Philip Jenkins, *The Next Christendom: The Coming of Global Christianity*, 3rd ed. (New York: Oxford University Press, 2011), 1. The way in which this shift is being reflected in increasing reference to a global Christianity can be seen in Sebastian Kim and Kirsteen Kim, *Christianity as a World Religion* (New York: Continuum, 2008); and Timothy C. Tennent, *Theology in the Context of World Christianity: How the Global Church Is Influencing the Way We Think about Doing Theology* (Grand Rapids: Zondervan, 2007).
81. L. H. Lalpekhlua, *Contextual Christology: A Tribal Perspective* (Delhi: ISPCK, 2007).
82. Hmar Vanlalauva, "Impact of the Christian Faith on the Socio-Political Context of Mizoram," *Mizoram Journal of Theology* 16 (April–December 2011): 28–42.
83. Ankur Barua is seeking to address this historic tension in the light of recent debates over the "significance and legal justification" of conversion: Are conversions to a "foreign religion" more than "individual resolutions of inner spiritual crises"? Can they be seen as "subversive acts that threaten to undermine national unity"? "Ideas of Tolerance: Religious Exclusivism and Violence in Hindu-Christian Encounters," *International Journal of Public Theology* 7, no. 1 (2013): 65–67.
84. Barua recognizes that Jesus Christ is "the normative criterion for deciding what is of salvific importance in the other religions." The obvious weakness of a recourse to the presence of Christ being somehow discerned in these religions is regarded as an act of paternalism. The invoking of a cosmic Christ in whom this presence can be situated is likewise perceived to be misleading. It presupposes an eschatological fulfillment: "these traditions are somehow oriented towards the eschatological consummation hoped for by Christianity." Ibid., 66.
85. Barua does not believe the comparative claim that Hinduism is more tolerant is ultimately true. The reason why Hinduism can appear to be tolerant is due to its "belief that the ultimate end of life can be attained over more than one life; hence, 'the cruciality of taking a stand here and now in this life is much less'" (ibid., 76). There is thus a hierarchy of tolerance: for Barua, the issues now become ones of what kind of tolerance and apprehension of reality we are talking about.
86. Diana Eck, *The New Religious America: How a "Christian Country" Became the World's Most Religiously Diverse Nation* (New York: HarperCollins, 2002).
87. Lenn E. Goodman, *Religious Pluralism and Values in the Public Square* (New York: Cambridge University Press, 2014).
88. David Miller, *Justice for Earthlings: Essays in Political Philosophy* (Cambridge: Cambridge University Press, 2013), 71.
89. Anne Elvey, "Interpreting the Time: Climate Change and the Climate in/of the Gospel of Luke," in *Climate Change, Cultural Change: Religious Responses and Responsibilities*, by Anne Elvey and David Gormley-O'Brien (Eugene, OR: Wipf & Stock, 2013), 78–91.
90. Clive Pearson, "The Purpose and Practice of a Public Theology in a Time of Climate Change," *International Journal of Public Theology* 4, no 3 (2010): 356–72.
91. Clive Hamilton, Christophe Bonneuil, and François Gemenne, eds., "Thinking the Anthropocene," in *The Anthropocene and the Global Environmental Crisis: Rethinking Modernity in a New Epoch* (New York: Routledge, 2015), 1–12.

92. Clive Hamilton, *Requiem for a Species: Why We Resist the Truth about Climate Change* (London: Earthscan, 2010).
93. Stefan Skrimshire, "Eschatology," in *Systematic Theology and Climate Change: Ecumenical Perspectives*, ed. Michael S. Northcott and Peter M. Scott (New York: Routledge, 2014), 157–74.
94. The term "wicked problem" was first coined by Horst Rittel and Melvin Webber, "Dilemmas in a General Theory of Planning," *Policy Sciences* 4 (1973): 155–69. It connoted a sense of being malignant, tricky, vicious, or aggressive. The contrast was made with "tame" problems. Rittel and Webber defined wicked problems as (1) difficult to define, (2) full of interdependencies and multicausal, (3) liable to unforeseen consequences, (4) constantly evolving and not stable, (5) without clear solutions, (6) socially complex, (7) not likely to sit within the responsibility of any one organization, (8) every wicked problem can be considered to be a symptom of another problem; (9) likely to involve changing behavior, and (10) characterized by chronic policy failure. Kelly Levin, Benjamin Cashore, Steven Bernstein, and Graeme Auld have defined climate change as a "superwicked problem." Such problems represent a new class characterized by four key features: (1) time is running out, (2) those who cause the problem also seek to provide the solution, (3) the central authority needed to address them is either weak or nonexistent, and (4) irrational discounting occurs and pushes responses into the future. Levin, Cashore, Bernstein, and Auld, "Overcoming the Tragedy of Super-wicked Problems: Constraining Our Future Selves to Ameliorate Global Climate Change," *Policy Sciences* 45.2 (2012):123–52.
95. Dale Jamieson, "The Nature of the Problem," in *The Oxford Handbook of Climate Change and Society*, ed. John Dryzek, Richard E. Norgaard, and David Schlosberg (Oxford: Oxford University Press, 2011), 40–42.
96. Ernst Conradie, "Climate Change and the Common Good: Some Reflections from the South African Context," *International Journal of Public Theology* 4, no. 3 (2010): 271–93.
97. Mike Hulme, *Why We Disagree about Climate Change: Understanding Controversy, Inaction and Opportunity* (Cambridge: Cambridge University Press, 2009).
98. Ernst Conradie, *Saving the Earth? The Legacy of Reformed Views on "Re-Creation* (Berlin: LIT Verlag, 2013); Conradie, "What Is the Place of the Earth in God's Economy? Doing Justice to Creation, Salvation and Consummation," in *Christian Faith and the Earth: Current Paths and Emerging Horizons in Ecotheology*, ed. Ernst Conradie, Sigurd Bergmann, Celia Deane-Drummond, and Denis Edwards (New York: Bloomsbury T&T Clark, 2014), 65–97; Neil Messer, "Sin and Salvation," in *Systematic Theology and Climate Change: Ecumenical Perspectives*, ed. Michael S. Northcott and Peter M. Scott (New York: Routledge, 2014), 124–40.
99. The consequences for an ecological rendering of theology can be far-reaching. It matters not just how each point of doctrine is to be understood but also how one point relates to another. It is perfectly feasible, for instance, to make a case for a Christian eschatology that seeks "redemption *from* the earth." In this instance there is no particular need to show any degree of concern for the salvation of the earth (whatever that might then mean): the existing creation is effectively disposable. That is one extreme—but it serves the purpose here to demonstrate the interrelationship of one doctrinal "chapter" with others. Writing from within a Reformed tradition, Conradie has argued that our human response must be seen from within "the whole work of God"—and for him it is likely that tensions between doctrines of creation and salvation are probably most sharply felt in matters pertaining to the problem of theodicy.

100. Sallie McFague, *Life Abundant: Rethinking Theology and Economy for a Planet in Peril* (Minneapolis: Fortress Press, 2001), 71–126; McFague, *A New Moral Climate for Theology* (Minneapolis: Fortress Press, 2008), 84–97. McFague is keen to relate the words economics, ecology, and ecumenicity to one another: "The three belong together" and have their origins in the Greek word for house, household: *oikos*.
101. McFague, *A New Moral Climate for Theology*, 86.
102. Ibid., 87.
103. Ibid., 83.
104. Ibid., 84.
105. Ibid., 85. Michael Northcott considers the implications of various types of economies in his chapter on "Climate Economics," in *A Moral Climate: The Ethics of Global Warming* (London: Darton, Longman & Todd, 2007), 120–56.
106. Sallie McFague, *Blessed Are the Consumers: Climate Change and the Practice of Restraint* (Minneapolis: Fortress Press, 2013).
107. Ibid., 2.
108. Ibid., 9.
109. McFague is of the opinion that "the world that greets us scarcely appreciates the meaning of the words *restraint, self-sacrifice, give-and-take, limitation*" (ibid., 141). The merit of a "kenotic way of life" lies in how it "respects and pays attention to the other"; it is "a spirituality of subtraction rather than a spirituality of addition." The kenotic way of life places over and against "the modern life of goal setting" the example and call of God's self-giving (151–62).
110. For a recent critical account of Weber's thesis, see Max Stackhouse, "Weber, Theology and Economics," in *The Oxford Handbook of Christianity and Economics*, ed. Paul Oslington (New York: Oxford University Press, 2014), 307–36.
111. Ibid., 313.
112. Joel Stillerman, *The Sociology of Consumption: A Global Approach* (Cambridge: Polity Press, 2013); Clive Hamilton and Richard Denniss, *Affluenza: When Too Much Is Never Enough* (London: Allen & Unwin, 2005); John de Graaf, David Wann, and Thomas H. Naylor, *Affluenza and How Overconsumption Is Killing Us—and How to Fight Back* (San Francisco: Berrett-Kohler Publishers, 2014); Oliver James, *Affluenza* (London: Random House, 2007).
113. Stackhouse cites the editorial introduction of Talcott Parsons to make the case for the "Romantic Ethic" being responsible for stimulating the "new desires and want that shaped the modern form of consumerism" ("Weber, Theology and Economics," 313).
114. The ambiguous legacy of the Reformation is captured by Brad S. Gregory's historical inquiry into "the world we have lost." Gregory identifies the following legacies: the exclusion of God, the relativization of doctrines, control over the churches, the subjective nature of morality, the manufacturing of "the goods life," and the secularization of knowledge. *The Unintended Reformation: How a Religious Revolution Secularized Society* (Cambridge, MA: Belknap Press of Harvard University Press, 2012).
115. Adam Withnall, "Pope Francis Says He Would Baptise an Alien," *The Independent*, July 21, 2015.
116. Brent Waters, *The Mortal Flesh: Incarnation and Bioethics* (Grand Rapids: Brazos Press, 2009), 15–48.
117. Ronald Cole-Turner, ed., *Transhumanism and Transcendence: Christian Hope in an Age of Technological Advancement* (Washington, DC: Georgetown University Press, 2011); Calvin Mercer and Derek F. Maher, eds., *Transhumanism and the Body: The World's Religions Speak* (New York: Palgrave Macmillan, 2014);

Michael S. Burdett, *Eschatology and the Technological Future* (New York: Routledge, 2015); Celia Deane-Drummond, "The Technologisation of Life: Theology and the Trans-Human and Trans-Animal Narratives of the Post-Animal," in *Technofutures, Nature and the Sacred: Transdisciplinary Perspectives*, ed. Celia Deane-Drummond, Sigurd Bergmann, and Bronislaw Szerszynski (Farnham, MA: Ashgate, 2015).

118. Neil G. Messer, *The SCM Guide to Christian Ethics* (London: SCM Press, 2006), 17.

119. Rachel Muers, *Living for the Future: Theological Ethics for Coming Generations* (New York: T&T Clark, 2008). Muers is writing out of a concern for intergenerational justice; in the light of her own pregnancy she was wrestling with the question "*What am I doing, bringing a child into a world like this?*"—a world that was becoming more used to terrorist attacks. What might it mean to be "mothering the future," and which vocation is likely to include sustainable thinking and passing on the genes?

120. Victor Lee Austin, *Christian Ethics: A Guide for the Perplexed* (New York: Bloomsbury T&T Clark, 2012), 23–43.

121. Therese Lysaught, "Becoming One Body: Health Care and Cloning," in *The Blackwell Companion to Christian Ethics*, ed. Stanley Hauerwas and Samuel Wells, 2nd ed. (Malden, MA: Wiley-Blackwell, 2011), 303–4.

122. Neil Messer, *The Ethics of Human Cloning* (Cambridge: Grove Books, 2001), 9.

123. Ibid., 12. Neil Messer has written more extensively on the relationship between theology and genetics: see *Theological Issues in Bioethics: An Introduction with Readings* (London: Darton, Longman & Todd, 2003), Messer, *Selfish Genes and Christian Ethics: The Theological-Ethical Implications of Evolutionary Biology* (London: SCM Press, 2007); Messer, *Respecting Life: Theology and Bioethics* (London: SCM Press, 2011).

124. Lysaught, "Becoming One Body," 304.

125. Howard Gardner and Katie Davis, *The App Generation: How Today's Youth Navigate Identity, Intimacy, and Imagination in a Digital World* (New Haven, MA: Yale University Press, 2013).

Chapter 2

1. Previously published in Dirk J. Smit, *Essays on Being Reformed: Collected Essays 3* (Stellenbosch: African Sun MeDIA Stellenbosch, 2009). Included here by permission.

2. W. D. Jonker, "Reaksie," *Nederduits Gereformeerde Teologiese Tydskrif* 32, no. 1 (1991): 119–23; in Piet Naudé's "The DRC's Role in the Context of Transition in South Africa," *Scriptura* 76, no. 1 (2000): 90.

3. Originally given as the 1990 Warfield Lectures at Princeton Theological Seminary but published as John W. de Gruchy, *Liberating Reformed Theology: A South African Contribution to an Ecumenical Dialogue* (Grand Rapids: Wm. B. Eerdmans Pub. Co., 1991).

4. W. D. Jonker, "Kragvelde binne die Kerk," *Aambeeld* 26, no. 1 (June 1988): 11–14.

5. See, e.g., J. F. Durand, "When Theology Becomes a Metaphor?," *Journal of Theology for Southern Africa* 111 (November 2001): 12–16; D. J. Bosch, *Transforming Mission: Paradigm Shifts in Theology of Mission* (Maryknoll, NY: Orbis Books, 1991); A. Boesak, *Farewell to Innocence* (Kampen: Kok, 1976); and esp. Boesak, *Black and Reformed: Apartheid, Liberation, and the Calvinist Tradition* (Maryknoll, NY: Orbis Books, 1984); C. J. A. Loff, *Bevryding tot eenwording*:

Die Nederduiste Gereformeerde Sendingkerk in Suid-Afrika, 1881–1994 (Kampen: Theologische Universiteit, 1997); J. C. Adonis, *Die afgebreekte skeidsmuur weer opgebou* (Amsterdam: Rodopi, 1982); T. A. Mofokeng, *The Crucified among the Crossbearers: Towards a Black Christology* (Kampen: Kok, 1983); L. R. Lekula Ntoane, *A Cry for Life* (Kampen: Kok, 1983); C. R. Burger, *Ons weet aan wie ons behoort: Nuut nagedink oor ons gereformeerde tradisie* (Wellington: Lux Verbi, 2001); H. R. Botman, "'Black' and Reformed and 'Dutch' and Reformed in South Africa," in R. Wells, ed., *Keeping the Faith* (Grand Rapids: Wm. B. Eerdmans Pub. Co., 1997), 85–105; P. J. Naudé, "Constructing a Coherent Theological Discourse: The Main Challenge Facing the Dutch Reformed Church Today," *Scriptura* 83, no. 2 (2003): 192–211.

6. A. MacIntyre, *After Virtue: A Study in Moral Theory* (Notre Dame, IN: University of Notre Dame Press, 1981), 222.
7. D. J. Smit, "Reformed Theology in South Africa: A Story of Many Stories," *Acta Theologica*, no. 1 (1992): 88–110.
8. D. J. Smit, "Rhetoric and Ethic? A Reformed Perspective on the Politics of Reading the Bible," in *Reformed Theology: Identity and Ecumenicity*, ed. W. Alston and M. Welker (Grand Rapids: Wm. B. Eerdmans Pub. Co., 2007), 385–418.
9. Karl Barth, e.g., would not approve. For his own appreciation of Calvin, see his early lectures, *The Theology of John Calvin* (Grand Rapids: Wm. B. Eerdmans Pub. Co., 1995); Barth, the short but instructive "Thoughts on the 400th Anniversary of Calvin's Death," in *Fragments Grave and Gay* (Glasgow: Collins, 1971; Eugene: Wipf & Stock, 2011), 105–10; and H. Scholl, ed., *Karl Barth und Johannes Calvin: Karl Barth's Göttinger Calvin-Vorlesung von 1922* (Neukirchen: Neukirchener Verlag, 1995). John Webster aptly comments: "Barth is evidently drawn to the Calvin whom he portrays as the theologian of Christian life and obedience." *Barth's Moral Theology* (Grand Rapids: Wm. B. Eerdmans Pub. Co., 1988), 3. Later he concludes: "It would be not too much to claim that in the Calvin lecture cycle Barth already and very quickly formed some of the lines of his later ethical thinking" (34). However, in several essays during the 1920s on being Reformed, Barth explicitly rejects all attempts to define being "Reformed" by focusing on historical figures, events, or motifs and argues for the "Scripture-principle" as the only way to being Reformed. See, e.g., several essays in *Vorträge und kleinere Arbeiten, 1922–1925*, Gesamtausgabe 3 (Zurich: Theologischer Verlag, 1990).
10. Even in South Africa, Calvin has been accommodated to the purposes of both apartheid and antiapartheid theology. F. J. M. Potgieter, a major representative of apartheid theology, was also an authority on Calvin. See H. S. A. Engdahl, "Theology in Conflict: Readings in Afrikaner Theology" (New York: Peter Lang, 2006).
11. R. A. Muller, *The Unaccommodated Calvin: Studies in the Foundation of a Theological Tradition* (Oxford: Oxford University Press, 2001).
12. See, e.g., the very important essay by H. R. Botman, "Belhar and the White DRC: Changes in the DRC 1974–1990," *Scriptura* (2001): 33–42. P. J. Naudé responded in "Constructing a Coherent Theological Discourse: The Main Challenge Facing the Dutch Reformed Church in South Africa Today," *Scriptura* 83, no. 2 (2003): 192–211.
13. F. L. Battles, *Analysis of the "Institutes of Religion" of John Calvin* (Phillipsburg, NJ: P&R, 1980), 14–16
14. P. C. Böttger, *Calvin's "Institutio" als Erbauungsbuch* (Neukirchen-Vluyn: Neukirchener Verlag, 1990).
15. E. T. Charry, *By the Renewing of Your Minds: The Pastoral Function of Christian Doctrine* (Oxford: Oxford University Press, 1997).

16. J. H. Leith, *John Calvin's Doctrine of the Christian Life* (Louisville, KY: Westminster John Knox Press, 1989; Eugene, OR: Wipf & Stock, 2010), 15–21.
17. S. Jones, *Calvin's Rhetoric of Piety* (Louisville, KY: Westminster John Knox Press, 1995). Several recent studies have emphasized the importance of rhetorical readings of Calvin, including R. S. Baard, "Constructive Feminist Critiques of Classical Sin-Talk: A Rhetorical Reading" (PhD diss., Princeton Theological Seminary, 2004).
18. Battles, *Analysis of the "Institutes,"* 14.
19. H.-J. Kraus, "The Contemporary Relevance of Calvin's Theology," in *Toward the Future of Reformed Theology*, ed. D. Wills and M. Welker (Grand Rapids: Wm. B. Eerdmans Pub. Co., 1992), 323–38. See also C. van der Kooi, *Als in een spiegel: God kennen volgens Calvijn en Barth* (Kampen: Kok, 2002); and D. L. van Niekerk, "Geloof as Cognitio en Fiducia by Calvin en die na-Reformatiese Ontwikkeling," ThD diss. (Stellenbosch University, 1991); and J. B. Krohn, "Knowing the Triune God" (Stellenbosch: Stellenbosch University, 2002).
20. See, e.g., P. W. Butin, *Revelation, Redemption, and Response: Calvin's Trinitarian Understanding of the Divine-Human Relationship* (New York: Oxford University Press, 1995).
21. See, e.g., Leith, *Calvin's Doctrine of the Christian Life*; R. S. Wallace, *Calvin's Doctrine of the Christian Life* (Eugene: Wipf & Stock, 1997).
22. See, e.g., W. D. Jonker, "Heilige Skrif en sociale etiek by Calvyn," *Bulletin Suid-Afrikaanse vereniging vir die bevordering van Christelike wetenskap* 39 (1997): 31–37; J. H. van Wyk, *Die etiek van Calvyn* (Potchefstroom: Pro Rege, 1980).
23. See V. E. d'Assonville, *Der Begriff "doctrina" bei Johannes Calvin: Eine theologische Analyse* (Münster: LIT Verlag, 2001); also P. Opitz, *Calvin's theologische Hermeneutik* (Neukirchen-Vluyn: Neukirchener Verlag, 1994).
24. A. C. Outler, foreword to *Calvin's Doctrine of the Christian Life*, by Leith, 9–11.
25. This motive is central in the first question and answer of the Heidelberg Catechism and forms the heart of the argument of the whole document. Barth acknowledged that this theme from the Catechism informed the Theological Declaration of Barmen's central claim (1934), that Jesus is the Lord, over church and life; and Barmen again informed the conclusion of the South African Reformed Confession of Belhar (1986). The Brief Statement of Faith of the Presbyterian Church (U.S.A.) from 1991 begins with the same words. For the text and commentary, see W. C. Placher and D. Willis-Watkins, *Belonging to God* (Louisville, KY: Westminster John Knox Press, 1992). At the Debrecen meeting of the World Alliance of Reformed Churches (1997), a liturgical litany was adopted to be used in the *processus confessionis* regarding economic injustice and ecological destruction, and this motive again informs the basic conviction of the litany. In South Africa, C. W. Burger has published a monograph on being Reformed: *Ons weet aan wie ons behoort* (Wellington: Lux Verbi, 2001).
26. G. J. Retief, *Die verhouding tussen mortificatio en vivificatio in die leer van die heiliging by Johannes Calvyn* (ThD diss., Stellenbosch University, 1984).
27. Battles, *Analysis of the "Institutes,"* 18.
28. This is the apt description by N. Wolterstorff, *Until Justice and Peace Embrace* (Grand Rapids: Wm. B. Eerdmans Pub. Co., 1993).
29. The literature on most of these aspects is overwhelming. See A. Biéler's *Calvin's Economic and Social Thought* (Geneva: WCC, 2005); and his *The Social Humanism of Calvin* (Richmond: John Knox Press, 1964).
30. R. S. Wallace, *Calvin, Geneva, and the Reformation: A Study of Calvin as Social Reformer, Churchman, Pastor, and Theologian* (Grand Rapids: Baker Book House, 1990).

31. Leith then lists nine characteristics of Calvin's theology, demonstrating this ability. Calvin deliberately and intentionally rejected all speculation in theology. (1) The purpose of theology is to edify and not satisfy idle curiosity. (2) His interpretation of Scripture reflects a hard-nosed sense for what is real, namely, the natural sense, to be expressed with simplicity and brevity. (3) Theology must deal with the concrete realities of human life in the language of ordinary human experience, not talking about a make-believe world, but addressing the actual situations of the people to whom it speaks, using the language of everyday, ordinary discourse. (4) It should be simple, moderate, sincere, concrete, and direct, "uncover(ing) reality for all to see." (5) Theologians should be willing to face realities, facts, particularly difficulties—from the inability of some mothers to nurse their babies to the unresponsiveness of listeners to sermons, 20 percent when taken optimistically, and 10 percent when taken pessimistically! (6) The purpose of theology is sanctification, including the edification of human beings and the church, the transformation of human life according to God's image, the concrete embodiment of theology in human life and community as well as in the structures of church and society, not simply believing but also doing: so that people who once took from society what they could now seek to live in such a way that God's glory is enhanced. (7) Theology should reflect the real life of the theologian, and the theologian's life should be congruent with the theology they do, since part of the power to persuade is the reality of theologians who actually believe and practice what they speak about. (8) Calvin's theological realism meant that theological doctrines correspond to reality, that the doctrine of the Trinity is the way God is, that the substance of theology takes precedence over theological method and rhetoric. (9) See J. Leith, "Calvin's Theological Realism and the Lasting Influence of His Theology," in *Towards the Future of a Reformed Theology*, ed. D. Willis and M. Welker (Grand Rapids: Eerdmans), 339–45.
32. For van Ruler, see C. Lombard, *Adama, Thora en Dogma: Die samenhang van aardse lewe, skrif en dogma in die teologie van A. A. van Ruler* (PhD diss., University of the Western Cape, 1996). For Torrance, see E. M. Colyer, *How to Read T. F. Torrance* (Downers Grove, IL: InterVarsity Press, 2001); A. E. McGrath, *T. F. Torrance: An Intellectual Biography* (New York: T&T Clark, 2006).
33. For Welker's thought, see B. Oberdorfer, "Biblisch-realistische Theologie: Methodologische Überlegungen zu einem dogmatisschen Programm," in *Resonanzen*, ed. S. Brandt and B. Oberdorfer (Wuppertal: Foedus-Verlag, 1997), 63–83; and A. Conpaan, "Kreatiewe pluralismes? 'n Kritiese analise van wet en evangelie in die denke van Michael Welker" (ThD diss., Stellenbosch University, 2002).
34. See D. Smit, "Seeing Things Differently: On Prayer and Politics," in *Theology in Dialogue: The Impact of the Arts, Humanities, and Science on Contemporary Religious Thought*, ed. L. Holness and R. K. Wüsenberg (Grand Rapids: Wm. B. Eerdmans Pub. Co., 2002), 271–84.
35. C. G. Burger, *Praktiese teologie in Suid-Afrika: 'n Ondersoek na die denke oor sekere voorvrae van die vak* (Pretoria: Raad vir Geesteswetenskaplike Navorsing, 1991).
36. This reminds me of the title of Thomas W. Gillespie's *Festschrift*, edited by Wallace M. Alston Jr., *Theology in the Service of the Church* (Grand Rapids: Wm. B. Eerdmans Pub. Co., 2000).
37. "(We achten) het onjuist om vanuit een theologische radicalisering van deze vakken de verantwoordelijkheid van de kerk voor de communicatie op menselijk vlak te bagatelliseren," in *Theologie en praktijk*, by W. D. Jonker (Kampen: Kok, 1968), 24.
38. Burger, *Praktiese*, 70, under the rubric of "the necessity of critical thinking."
39. Ibid., 66.

40. Ibid., 71–72.
41. D. E. de Villiers, "Challenges to Christian Ethics in the Present South African Society," *Scriptura* 69 (1999): 75–91; P. J. Naudé, "The DRC's Role in the Context of Transition in South Africa: Main Streams of Academic Research," *Scriptura* 76, no. 1 (2001): 87–106; N. N. Koopman, "Some Comments on Public Theology Today," *Journal of Theology for Southern Africa* 117 (2003): 1–19.
42. See, e.g., D. E. de Villiers and D. J. Smit, "Hoe Christene by mekaar verby praat: Oor vier morele spreekwyses in die Suid-Afrikaanse kerklike konteks," *Skrif en Kerk* 15, no. 2 (1994): 228–47; N. N. Koopman, "Freedom of Religion and the Prophetic Role of the Church," *Nederduits Gereformeerde Teologiese Tydskrif* 43 (March 2002): 132–47.
43. W. D. Jonker, "Reaksie," *Nederduits Gereformeerde Teologiese Tydskrif* 32, no. 1 (1991): 119–23; in Naudé's "DRC's Role in the Context," 90.
44. W. D. Jonker, "Suid-Afrika se verbondenheid met Europa: Die teologie," *Tydskrif vir Geesteswetenskappe* 28 (1988): 146–57. The observation certainly was not true of scholarly ethics in the black Dutch Reformed circles during the same years, where the awareness of context and contextuality was very strong indeed. For example, for an overview of the specific contributions of the Faculty of Theology at the University of the Western Cape, and in particular the Theological School of the (then) Dutch Reformed Mission Church, see D. J. Smit, "In diens van die akademie," *Koinonia* (February 12, 2000): 3.
45. The quotation is from D. Tracy, *Plurality and Ambiguity: Hermeneutics, Religion, Hope* (San Francisco: Harper & Row, 1987). Several South African scholars have used this, including Gerald West and Jan Botha. See D. J. Smit, "Rhetoric and Ethics: A Reformed Perspective on the Politics of Reading the Bible," in *Reformed Theology: Identity and Ecumenicity II*, ed. W. Alston and M. Welker (Grand Rapids: Wm. B. Eerdmans Pub. Co., 2007), 385–418.
46. D. M. Ackermann and R. Bons-Storm, eds., *Liberating Faith Practices: Feminist Practical Theologies in Context* (Leuven: Peeters, 1998). See also D. M. Ackermann, *After the Locusts: Letters from a Landscape of Faith* (Cape Town: David Philip, 2003).
47. The Reformed practical theologian from the Netherlands, Gerben Heitink, is a good example of this approach. See his lecture in honor of his predecessor Jaap Firet, *In helder inzicht en alle fijngevoeligheid* (Amsterdam: Vrije Universiteit, 1994); his inaugural lecture, *Om raad verlegen, doch niet radeloos . . .* (Kampen: Kok, 1988); his final lecture, *Tussen "oprit 57" en "afslag 03" de weg, het landschap en de praktische theologie* (Amsterdam: Vrije Universiteit, 2003); his monograph *Practical Theology: History, Theory, Action Domains* (Grand Rapids: Wm. B. Eerdmans Pub. Co., 1999); or his informative overview "Developments in Practical Theology in The Netherlands: A Historical Approach," *International Journal of Practical Theology* 3 (1999): 127–44. Within the helpful typology of five different streams (normative-deductive, hermeneutical-mediating, empirical-analytical, political-critical, and pastoral-theological), he describes his own approach as hermeneutical. For Jonker's theology and the crucial role of discernment, together with all other believers, see D. J. Smit, "Om saam met al die heiliges Christus te ken . . . ," in *Koninkryk, kerk en kosmos*, ed. P. F. Theron and J. Kinghorn (Bloemfontein: Pro-Christo, 1989), 11–32. C. W. Burger practiced his approach in several studies on the church, in different phases of the South African transformation processes, including *Dinamika van 'n Christelike geloofsgemeenskap* (Wellington: Lux Verbi, 1991); Burger, *Gemeentes in transitio* (Wellington: Lux Verbi, 1995); Burger, *Gemeentes in die kragveld van die Gees* (Wellington: Lux Verbi, 1999). Daniel J. Louw also explained and practiced his

hermeneutical and discerning method (of interpreting, communicating, doing, and embodying) in several publications, such as "Creative Hope and Imagination in a Practical Theology of Aesthetic (Artistic) Reason," in *Creativity, Imagination and Criticism*, ed. P. Ballard and P. Couture (Cardiff: Cardiff Academic Press, 2001), 91–104.

48. See J. W. de Gruchy, *Seeing Things Differently* (Cape Town: Mercer, 2000); D. E. de Villiers and D. J. Smit, "Hoekom verskil ons so oor die wil van God? Opmerkings oor Christelike morele oordeelsvorming," *Skrif en Kerk* 17, no. 1 (1996): 31–47; A. E. J. Mouton, "Remembering Forward and Hoping Backward? Some Thoughts on Women and the DRC," *Scriptura* 76, no. 1 (2001): 77–86; also D. J. Smit, "On Learning to See? A Reformed Perspective on the Church and the Poor," in *Poverty, Suffering and HIV AIDS*, ed. P. D. Couture et al. (Cardiff: Cardiff Academic Press, 2003), 55–70.

49. See D. J. Smit, "Can We Still Be Reformed? Questions from a South African Perspective," in *Reformed Theology: Identity and Ecumenicity*, ed. W. M. Alston and M. Welker (Grand Rapids: Wm. B. Eerdmans Pub. Co., 2003), 233–56.

50. M. Welker, "Travail in Mission: Theology Reformed according to God's Word at the Beginning of the Third Millennium," in *Toward the Future of a Reformed Theology*, ed. D. Willis and M. Welker (Grand Rapids: Wm. B. Eerdmans Pub. Co., 1999), 136–52.

Chapter 3

1. A version of this essay was published in "The Ethical Challenge of Identity Formation and Cultural Justice in a Globalizing World," *Scriptura*, 89, (2005): 536–49.
2. Michael Welker, "Globalisierung in wissenschaftlich-theologischer Sicht [Globalization from a scientific-theological perspective]," *Evangelische Theologie* 68, no. 53 (2008): 368.
3. Ibid., 372.
4. Ibid.
5. See Konrad Raiser, "Globalisierung in der ökumenisch-ethischen Diskussion," *Verkündigung und Forschung* 54, no. 1 (2009): 6–33. See also Raiser's excellent literature references. For a summary of statements up to about 1990, see Aart van den Berg, *Churches Speak Out on Economic Issues: A Survey of Several Statements* (Geneva: WCC, 1990). See also *Christian Faith and the World Economy Today* (Geneva: WCC Pub., 1992); essays on "technology" and "culture" in the *Dictionary of the Ecumenical Movement*; Júlio de Santa Ana, ed., *Sustainability and Globalization* (Geneva: WCC Pub., 1998); and *Ecumenical Review* 52, no. 2 (2000), devoted to "economic globalisation," 181; Welker, "Globaliserung," 375.
6. The Accra Confession (AC) was adopted by the World Alliance of Reformed Churches during its twenty-fourth General Council held in Ghana, Africa, in 2004. For a summary and discussion, see Raiser, "Globalisierung," 11–13.
7. This current essay is updated from the German version of Piet Naudé's "The Challenge of Cultural Justice under Conditions of Globalization: Is the New Testament of Any Use?," in *The New Testament Interpreted: Essays in Honour of Bernard Lategan*, ed. Cillliers Breytenbach, Johan C. Thom, and Jeremy Punt (Leiden: Brill, 2009), 267–87.
8. David Chidester, Philip Dexter, and James Wilmot, eds., *What Holds Us Together: Social Cohesion in South Africa* (Cape Town: HSRC Press, 2003; London: Global, 2004), vii.

9. See Welker's references in "Globaliserung" (368nn5–6) to the work of S. P. Huntington on the clashes of civilization and the cultural dimensions of globalization as discussed by Arjun Appudurai.
10. Heinrich Bedford-Strohm, "Zu diesem Heft," *Verkündigung und Forschung* 54, no. 1 (2009): 2.
11. Chirevo V. Kwenda, "Cultural Justice: The Pathway to Reconciliation and Social Cohesion," in Chidester et al., *What Holds*, 67–80.
12. I am not an expert in anthropology or cultural studies, yet I have found the following sources very helpful (without fully integrating them into this essay): Simon During, ed., *The Cultural Studies Reader* (London: Routledge, 1993), is an excellent collection of groundbreaking essays by authors like Theodor Adorno, Max Horkheimer, Roland Barthes, Michel Foucault, Jean-François Lyotard, Cornel West, and others. Specifically see part 4 as relevant for this essay. The somewhat older collection, edited by Frederick C. Gamst and Edward Norbeck, *Ideas of Culture: Sources and Uses* (New York: Rinehart & Winston, 1976), has a strong sociological focus with contributions by (inter alia) Émile Durkheim, Talcott Parsons, and Bronisław Malinowski. In *Understanding Global Cultures: Metaphorical Journeys through 17 Countries* (London: Sage, 1994), Maartin J. Gannon develops an interesting analytical instrument: significant social actions as metaphors for analyzing local and global cultures. For an example from the African continent, see chap. 16 on the Nigerian marketplace. I am deeply aware of my limitations in this exciting field of study.
13. Clifford Geertz, *The Interpretation of Culture* (London: Hutchinson & Co., 1975), 5, 14.
14. Kwenda, "Cultural Justice," 68–69.
15. Ibid., 68.
16. See Bedford-Strohm's reference in "Zu diesem Heft" (2) to "die Ambivalenz der Globalisierung [the ambivalence of globalization]"; and Welker's call in "Globalierserung" (372) that we should not be naive about the interconnectedness of the world, since globalization has both "Licht- und Schattenseiten [light and shadow sides]."
17. Elizabeth Gerle, "Contemporary Globalisation and Its Ethical Challenges," *Ecumenical Review* 52, no. 2 (2000): 159.
18. Konrad Raiser, *Ernstfall des Glaubens: Kirche sein im 21. Jahrhundert* (Göttingen: Vandenhoek & Ruprecht, 1998), 37.
19. Ibid.
20. De Santa Ana, *Sustainability and Globalization*, 14.
21. Daniel J. Louw, "A Practical Theological Ecclesiology of Relocalisation and Globalisation from Below: Toward a Viable African Renaissance," *Journal of Theology for Southern Africa* 112 (March 2002): 79.
22. Samuel Kobia, *The Courage to Hope: The Roots for a New Vision and the Calling of the Church in Africa* (Geneva: WCC, 2003), 138.
23. Miroslav Volf, *Exclusion and Embrace: A Theological Exploration of Identity, Otherness, and Reconciliation* (Nashville: Abingdon, 1996), 75.
24. De Santa Ana, *Sustainability and Globalization*, 16.
25. "Like any casino, this global game is rigged so that only the house wins." Fidel Castro in a speech to the South African parliament, September 4, 1998. See Chidester, *What Holds*, 10.
26. Peter Berger, *The Social Construction of Reality: A Treatise in the Sociology of Knowledge* (New York: Anchor Books, 1967), 152.
27. Ninian Smart, *The Phenomenon of Religion* (London: Mowbrays,1973).
28. David Tracy, *The Analogical Imagination: Christian Theology and the Culture of Pluralism* (London: SCM Press, 1981), 159.

29. Larry Rasmussen, "Cosmology and Ethics," in *Worldviews and Ecology*, ed. M. E. Tucker and J. A. Grimm (Maryknoll, NY: Orbis Books, 1994), 178.
30. Thomas Berry, *The Dream of the Earth* (San Francisco: Sierra Club Books, 1988), xi.
31. Welker, "Globalierserung," 376.
32. Chris Arthur, *The Globalization of Communications* (Geneva: WCC Pub., 1998), 3; see Dirk Smit, "Living Unity? On the Ecumenical Movement and Globalisation," a paper read at a joint consultation by European Food Safety Authority and the Evangelische Akademie in Tutzing, Germany, on "Consequences of Globalisation for Germany and South Africa," June 5–7, 2000, 15.
33. De Santa Ana, *Sustainability and Globalization*, 19.
34. Zygmunt Bauman, *Life in Fragments: Essays in Postmodern Morality* (Oxford: Blackwell, 1995), 99; See Volf, *Exclusion and Embrace*, 22.
35. Bauman, *Life in Fragments*, 156.
36. Smit, "Living Unity?," 15, emphasis original.
37. Two distinguishing features of societies in transition are a marked increase in socioeconomic inequality and a massive rise in violence and criminality. This is true of countries as diverse as Russia and South Africa. In the latter case, the new government resorted to a moratorium on the release of police statistics in a desperate bid to restrain the images of a "violent" new democracy. See Tony Addy and Jiri Sinly, "The Political Economy of Transition," *Ecumenical Review* 53, no. 4 (2001): 505, who state that in some cases Eastern European areas experienced a 400 percent rise in criminality over a ten-year period.
38. Ibid., 503.
39. The term "anomie" stems from Émile Durkheim in his groundbreaking study on social cohesion and suicide: "When society is disturbed by some painful crisis or by beneficent but abrupt transitions, the collective conscience is momentarily incapable of exercising restraint. Time is required for the public conscience to reclassify men [*sic*] and things. So long as social forces thus freed have not regained equilibrium, their respective values are unknown and so all regulation is lacking for a time. The state of de-regulation or anomie is heightened by passions being less disciplined precisely when they need more disciplining. See Émile Durkheim, *Suicide* (New York: Routledge Classic, 2002; French original, 1897; English trans., 1952), 252–53.
40. "It's all a question of story. We are in trouble just now because we do not have a good story. We are in between stories." Previously, with the old story (whether my own or the clear story of an oppressive regime) "we awoke in the morning and knew where we were. We could answer the questions of our children. We could identify crime, punish transgressors. Everything was taken care of because the story was there." Berry, *The Dream of the Earth*, 123.
41. In a different context, see Johannes Fischer's discussion of how the mode of knowledge emanating from the Enlightenment enabled humankind to make the world so habitable, so transparent, that it exactly loses its character as *Heimat* (home). "Der ärgste Feind der Verantwortung ist die Gleichgültigkeit. Gleichgültigkeit aber ist die Folge *existentieller Heimatlosigkeit* [the biggest enemy of responsibility is indifference. Indifference, however, is the result of an *existential homelessness*]" (emphasis added). He then pleads for a process of *Beheimatung* (providing a home) to restore responsibility. Johannes Fischer, "Christliche Ethik als Verantwortungsethik?," *Evangelische Theologie* 52, no. 2 (1992): 124.
42. See Welker's critical reference to a speech by the American William Timken, who states that the core of a consumer society is expressed by the dictum "We want more for less!," which is the engine for economic growth. Welker, "Globalierserung," 374.

43. John L. Comaroff and Jean Comaroff, "On Personhood: An Anthropological Perspective from Africa," in *Die autonome Person—Eine Europäische Erfindung*, ed. Klaus-Peter Köpping, Michael Welker, and Reiner Wiehl (Munich: Wilhelm Fink, 2002), 80.
44. Tony Balcomb, "From Liberation to Democracy: Theologies of Bread and Being in the New South Africa," *Missionalia* 26, no. 1 (April 1998), 71.
45. Kwenda, "Cultural Justice," 70.
46. Volf, *Exclusion and Embrace*, 78. Note the interesting debate about the wearing of Muslim head scarves in European schools, as well as the heated debate about "European identity" in the light of Turkey's possible entrance into the European Union. These are all interesting examples of disarranging cultural maps!
47. Tinyiko Sam Makulele in Balcomb, "From Liberation to Democracy," 70, emphases added.
48. Volf, *Exclusion and Embrace*, 23, emphasis added.
49. Bauman as quoted in ibid., 76.
50. Volf, *Exclusion and Embrace*, 76, emphasis original.
51. Richard Rodriquez, "Aria: A Memoir of a Bilingual Childhood," *American Scholar* 50, no. 1 (Winter 1981): 25–42.
52. Richard Rodriquez, *Hunger of Memory: The Education of Richard Rodriquez* (Boston: Godine, 1982), 23.
53. Ibid., 22–23.
54. Ibid., 29.
55. Ibid., 30.
56. Ibid., 31.
57. Ibid., 35.
58. Kwenda, "Cultural Justice," 71.
59. Addy and Silny, "Political Economy," 503.
60. Ibid., 505.
61. Ibid.
62. This process of being subject to the aesthetics of the Other is a vivid reality in the lucrative global tourism industry. See the illuminating analysis done by Sandra Klopper in which she highlights the marginalizing effect on local communities as the City Bowl area in Cape Town was turned into an international tourist destination. Sandra Klopper, "Global Tourism, Marginalised Communities and the Development of Cape Town's City Bowl Area," in Chidester, *What Holds*, 224–41.
63. See the very simple but informative discussion in Calvin J. Roetzel, *The World That Shaped the New Testament* (London: SCM Press, 1985).
64. As with most "topics" in the New Testament, there is a wide variety of witnesses to the relation between faith community and the state. See the clearly apologetic nature of Lukan views in the Gospel of Luke and Acts, the sayings attributed to Jesus, the varied responses in the Pauline corpus, and the obviously radical opposition to the state expressed in Revelation 17–18.
65. Wolfgang Schrage, *The Ethics of the New Testament* (Edinburgh: T&T Clark, 1988), 113.
66. In South Africa's recent history, Rom. 13:1–7 was a subject of severe hermeneutical struggle between those who cited it in support of subordination to the apartheid government that claimed to be Christian, and thus worthy of support, and those who (in 1985) called believers to pray for the fall of the government exactly because it did *not* fulfill the "criteria" for a godly government put forward in this passage.
67. See, e.g., Domitian, who claimed the divine honors of *dominus ac deus*.

68. Schrage, *Ethics*, 345.
69. See the attempt by Allen Verhey, in *Remembering Jesus: Christian Community, Scripture, and Moral Life* (Grand Rapids: Wm. B. Eerdmans Pub. Co., 2002), to reconstruct a New Testament ethics on the basis of the early church as a remembering and instructing community. He takes Rom. 15:14 as point of departure and aligns himself with eminent ethicists like James Gustafson, Larry Rasmussen, and (the more controversial) Stanley Hauerwas to develop the idea of early churches as communities of moral discourse.
70. See the clear "cosmic" bias of passages like the prologue to John, the exaltation in Eph. 1:3–14, the hymn in Col. 1:15–20, and the depiction of the cross as cosmic battle in Col. 2:6–15.
71. Welker, "Globalierserung," 382.
72. See Dirk Smit's overview of African contributions to the globalization debate where he emphasizes that "der wahre Prüfstein schliesslich die Praxis (ist) [the truest test-stone is the praxis]." Dirk Smit, "Schreie nach Leben: Eine (süd-) afrikanische Stimme," *Verkündigung und Forschung* 54, no. 1 (2009): 65.
73. See, e.g., the publications and later comments related to the well-known "three costlies" emanating from three conferences: costly unity (Ronde, Denmark 1993), costly commitment (Jerusalem 1994), and costly obedience (Johannesburg 1996). The three final statements were published in 1997 as *Ecclesiology and Ethics*, edited by Thomas Best and Martin Robra (Geneva: WCC, 1997). "The titles (of the three consultations) reflect *a progression of ecclesiological reflection and deepening of moral concern*: from realising that 'the unity we seek' will turn out to be *costly unity*; through recognizing that 'a *costly unity* requires *costly commitment* to one another' as Christians and as churches: to admitting that it is, finally, not a matter of programmes and institutions, even ecumenical ones, but of a *costly obedience* to our calling to be one and, as one body of Christ, to serve all humanity and creation" (ix, emphases original).
74. Bedford-Strohm, "Zu diesem Heft," 5.
75. As noted by Welker above, the notion of a "global village" is deeply ambiguous. On the one hand, it depicts the reality of a shrunk world through global communication and virtual closeness, such as we find in the traditional rural village; on the other hand, this village is highly exclusionary (think of the digital divide!), with false senses of belonging, and imbued with asymmetrical power relations.
76. Best and Robra, *Ecclesiology and Ethics*, 51–52.
77. Raiser, *Ernstfall des Glaubens*, 34.
78. As can be expected, and following the context of this passage, Luther in his commentary places heavy emphasis on the social implication of justification by faith alone: "Wie in Christus kein Ansehen der Person für die jüdische Richtung gilt, so gilt in ihm auch sonst kein Ansehen der Person. Es ist ein Zeichen menschlichen und gesetzlichen Gerechtigheitswesens, dass mann sich spaltet in Sekten und sich unterscheidet nach den Werken." Martin Luther, *Kommentar zum Galaterbrief*, Calwer Luther-Ausgabe 10 (Hamburg: Taschenbuch, 1968), 160.
79. F. F. Bruce, *The Epistle to the Galatians: A Commentary on the Greek Text* (Grand Rapids: Wm. B. Eerdmans Pub. Co., 2013), 187.
80. Such communities in Africa are exemplified by the so-called African Independent Churches, where tribal, cultural, and class distinctions are transcended in communities that represent far more than a mere "religious affiliation," including economic partnership and holistic healing as well.
81. Lewis S. Mudge, *The Church as Moral Community: Ecclesiology and Ethics in Ecumenical Debate* (London: Continuum, 1998), 140.

82. The confession was adopted in 1986 by the then Dutch Reformed Mission Church after acceptance of the ecumenically endorsed *status confessionis* on apartheid. For the English text (translation of the Afrikaans original) and initial explication, see G. D. Cloete and Dirk Smit, *A Moment of Truth: The Confession of the Dutch Reformed Mission Church 1982* (Grand Rapids: Wm. B. Eerdmans Pub. Co., 1982).

Chapter 4

1. T. A. Noble, "Our Knowledge of God according to John Calvin," *Evangelical Quarterly* 54 (1982): 2.
2. Edward E. Dowey, *The Knowledge of God in Calvin's Theology* (New York: Columbia University Press, 1952), 3.
3. Noble, "Our Knowledge of God," 4.
4. John Calvin, *Institutes of the Christian Religion* 1.1.3.
5. Richard Gamble, "Calvin's Theological Method: Word and Spirit," in *Calviniana: Ideas and Influence of Jean Calvin*, ed. Robert V. Schnucker (Kirkville, MO: Sixteenth Century Journal Publishers, 1988), 72.
6. Calvin, *Institutes* 1.2.1 and 1.5.11–15.
7. T. H. L. Parker, *The Doctrine of the Knowledge of God: A Study in the Theology of John Calvin* (Edinburgh: Oliver & Boyd, 1952), 25–26.
8. Cornelis van der Kooi, "Within Proper Limits: Basic Features of John Calvin's Theological Epistemology," *Calvin Theological Journal* 29 (1994): 381.
9. Calvin, *Institutes* 1.7.5.
10. Kooi, "Within Proper Limits," 382.
11. Calvin, *Institutes* 3.2.7.
12. Kooi, "Within Proper Limits," 365.
13. N. H. G. Robinson, "God," in *Dictionary of Christian Theology*, ed. Alan Richardson (London: SCM Press, 1969), 139.
14. J. Atkinson, "Hidden and Revealed God," in *A New Dictionary of Christian Theology*, ed. Alan Richardson and John Bowden (London: SCM Press, 1983), 300.
15. John T. McNeill, "Calvin after 499 Years," *Christian Century* 84 (1964): 703.
16. D. S. Watson, "Western Christian and Vedantic Thought on Mediated and Directed Knowledge of God," *Religion in Southern Africa* 5 (1984): 51–52; T. F. Torrance, "Knowledge of God and Speech about Him according to John Calvin," in *Theology in Reconstruction* (Grand Rapids: Wm. B. Eerdmans Pub. Co., 1966), 54; Gerald J. Postema, "Calvin's Alleged Rejection of Natural Theology," *Scottish Journal of Theology* 24 (1971): 425.
17. S. J. Samartha, "The Cross and the Rainbow," in *The Myth of Christian Uniqueness*, ed. John Hick and Paul Knitter (New York: Orbis Books, 1987), 79.
18. E. Davies Willis, *Calvin's Catholic Christology* (Leiden: E. J. Brill, 1966), 130.
19. Timothy George, *Theology of the Reformers* (Nashville: Broadman Press, 1988), 123.
20. Paul Heim, "Calvin (Zwingli) on Divine Providence," *Calvin Theological Journal* 29 (1995): 388.
21. John Hicks, *Evil and the God of Love* (London: Macmillan, 1985), 123.
22. A. N. S. Lane, "Calvin's Doctrine of Assurance," *Vox Evangelica* 9 (1979): 34.
23. John Calvin, "Prefatory Address to His Most Christian Majesty, the Most Mighty and Illustrious Monarch, Francis, King of the French," in his *Institutes of the Christian Religion*, trans. Henry Beveridge (Grand Rapids: Eerdmans, 1989), 6.
24. James Orr, *The Progress of Dogma* (London: Hodder & Stoughton, 1902), 292–93.

25. Garret A. Wilterdinck, "The Fatherhood of God in Calvin's Thought," *Reformed Review* 30 (1976): 111–12.
26. John H. Leith, *John Calvin's Doctrine of the Christian Life* (Louisville, KY: Westminster John Knox Press, 1989), 138.
27. Jane Dempsey Douglass, "Christian Freedom in Calvin's Theology: The Foundation and Significance of Christian Freedom," *Princeton Seminary Bulletin* 4 (1983): 83.
28. Heim, "Calvin (Zwingli) on Divine Providence," 388–90.
29. J. L. Neve, *A History of Christian Thought* (Philadelphia: United Lutheran Publication House, 1943), 36, 45.
30. Ibid., 148.
31. Bengt Hägglund, *History of Theology* (St. Louis: Concordia Pub. House, 1968), 65.
32. T. H. L. Parker, "Predestination," in Richardson and Bowden, *Dictionary of Christian Theology*, 266.
33. Thomas Oden, *The Living God* (San Francisco: Harper & Row, 1987), 271–79.
34. Thomas B. Mozley, *A Treatise on the Augustinian Doctrine of Predestination* (London: John Murray, 1983), 128–30.
35. John Hick, *Evil and the Problem of Love* (London: Macmillan, 1985), 120.
36. Karl Barth, *Church Dogmatics, The Doctrine of God, Volume 2 Part 2* (Edinburgh: T&T Clark, 1957), 111–12.
37. Charles Partee, "Calvin on Universal and Particular Providence," in *Readings in Calvin's Theology*, ed. Donald K. McKim (Grand Rapids: Baker Book House, 1984), 69–88.
38. Sallie McFague, *Models of God: Theology for an Ecological, Nuclear Age* (Philadelphia: Fortress Press, 1987), 65.
39. Ibid.
40. Calvin, "Prefatory Address," 51–52.
41. Ibid., 6.
42. Jorge Lara-Braud, "Reflection on Liberation Theology from the Reformed Tradition," in *Major Themes in the Reformed Tradition*, ed. Donald K. McKim (Grand Rapids: Wm. B. Eerdmans Pub. Co., 1992), 413.
43. Calvin, *Institutes* 1.13.17.
44. Eric Lott, *Vedantic Approaches to God* (London: Macmillan, 1980), 35; Nagaraj Rao, "The Concept of God in Shri Madhav's Vedanta," *Indian Philosophical Manual* 7 (1971): 167–68.
45. F. A. Klein, *The Religion of Islam* (New Delhi: Cosmo Publications, 1978), 58.
46. Rev. Dr. Zairema, "The Mizos and their Religion," in *Towards a Tribal Theology: The Mizo Perspectives*, ed. K. Thanzauva (Jorhat: Mizo Theological Conference, 1989), 39.

Chapter 5

1. Elaine Graham, "Pastoral Theology," *The Oxford Companion to Christian Thought*, ed. Adrian Hastings, Alistair Mason, and Hugh Pyper (Oxford: Oxford University Press, 2000), 520.
2. A. Dible, *Theological Dictionary of the New Testament*, ed. Gerhard Kittel and Gerhard Friedrich, trans. Geoffrey W. Bromiley (Grand Rapids: Wm. B. Eerdmans Pub. Co., 1971), 7:980.
3. For further commentary along these lines, see Tan Yah-hwee, "The Hemorrhaging Woman: A Case for Women's Alternative Leadership," *In God's Image* 12, no. 1 (March 2002): 38–39; Teresa Okura, "The Will to Arise: Reflections on Luke

8:40–56," in *The Will to Arise: Women, Tradition and the Church in Africa*, ed. Mercy Amba Oduyoye and Musimbi R. A. Kanyoro (New York: Orbis Books, 1992); Mary Ann Tolbert, "Mark," in *The Women's Bible Commentary*, ed. Carol A. Newsom and Sharon H. Ringe (Louisville, KY: Westminster/John Knox, 1992); Ched Myers, *Binding the Strong Man* (Maryknoll, NY: Orbis Books, 1988); and Elisabeth Schüssler Fiorenza, *In Memory of Her* (New York: Crossroad, 1983).

4. John H. Leith, *An Introduction to the Reformed Tradition: A Way of Being the Christian Community* (Atlanta: John Knox Press, 1977), 71.
5. John W. de Gruchy declares, "The Reformed Tradition, when it is faithful to its original vision of the gospel of the kingdom of God, most truly exists only in the process of being re-formed in relation to the struggles and issues facing it in its various historical contexts." *Liberating Reformed Theology: A South African Contribution to an Ecumenical Debate* (Grand Rapids: Wm. B. Eerdmans Pub. Co., 1991), 13.
6. Michael Weinrich, "The Openness and Worldliness of the Church," in *Reformed Theology: Identity and Ecumenicity*, ed. Wallace Alston and Michael Welker (Grand Rapids: Wm. B. Eerdmans Pub. Co., 2003), 413, 427–28.
7. In Gregory of Nyssa's words in *An Answer to Ablabius (On Not Three Gods)*, God's nature "cannot be named and is ineffable. We say that every name, whether invented by human custom or handed down by the Scriptures, is indicative of our conceptions of the divine nature, but does not signify what that nature is in itself." Cited in Ellen T. Charry, *By the Renewing of Your Minds: The Pastoral Function of Christian Doctrine* (New York: Oxford University Press, 1997), 10.
8. For another perspective on the issue of pluriformity, see Edmund Za Bik, "The Challenge to Reformed Theology: A Perspective from Myanmar," in *Toward the Future of Reformed Theology: Tasks, Topics, Traditions*, ed. David Willis and Michael Welker (Grand Rapids: Wm. B. Eerdmans Pub. Co., 1999), 75–86.
9. John de Gruchy argues that theology is ideological insofar as it is inescapably a human enterprise. It invariably serves the interests of a particular group, whether than group be one of race, gender, or class. It can do so in ways that are contrary to the gospel. *Liberating Reformed Theology*, 34-39.
10. See Calvin, *Institutes* 4.10.6, 32.
11. My older brother was active in Detroit politics in the 1960s and 1970s, including orchestrating a television campaign against gun ownership. He eventually dropped plans to run for mayor of the city.
12. Jane Dempsey Douglas, "Wholeness of Life: Becoming Human in a New Community," *Reformed World* 52, no. 4 (December 2000): 182–83.
13. E. M. Uka, "The Second Millennium: An African Theological Agenda," *Reformed World* 48, no. 4 (December 1998): 162.
14. Isabel Apawo Phiri, "Doing Theology in Community: The Case of African Women Theologians in the 1990s," *Journal of Theology for Southern Africa* 99 (November 1997): 68.
15. Audre Lorde, "The Master's Tools Will Never Dismantle the Master's House," in *Sister Outsider: Essays and Speeches* (Trumansburg, NY: Crossing Press, 1984), 110–13.
16. Letty M. Russell, *Church in the Round: Feminist Interpretation of the Church* (Louisville, KY: Westminster/John Knox Press, 1993), 12.
17. The 200,000+ people in Maine of Franco-American descent have been systematically stripped of their language and culture, to a great extent their Catholic faith, and their pride. A growing movement to regain their heritage has given many back what they lost at school and church. For further information, see the Franco-American Women's Institute at fawi.net.

18. Musa W. Dube, "Unsettling the Christian Church," *Journal of Theology for Southern Africa* 99 (November 1997): 165–76.
19. Delores S. Williams, *Sisters in the Wilderness* (Maryknoll, NY: Orbis Books, 1993).
20. Emilie M. Townes, ed., *A Troubling in My Soul* (Maryknoll, NY: Orbis Books, 1993).
21. Deborah F. Mullen, "Baptism as a Sacrament of Struggle and a Rite of Resistance," *Ending Racism in the Church*, ed. Susan E. Davies and Sr. Paul Teresa Hennessee (Cleveland: Pilgrim Press, 1996).
22. Phiri, "Doing Theology in Community."
23. Nyambura J. Njoroge, "The Missing Voice: African Women Doing Theology," *Journal of Theology for Southern Africa* 99 (November 1997): 77–83.
24. Leith, *Introduction to the Reformed Tradition*, 72.
25. Elsie Anne McKee, *John Calvin: Writings on Pastoral Piety* (New York: Paulist Press, 2002), 4.
26. Horace Bushnell, *Christian Nurture* (Cleveland: Pilgrim Press, 1994).
27. Calvin, *Institutes* 3.2.7, as cited in Donald K. McKim, *Introducing the Reformed Faith: Biblical Revelation, Christian Tradition, Contemporary Significance* (Louisville, KY: Westminster John Knox Press, 2001), 159.
28. McKim, *Introducing the Reformed Faith*, 159–60.
29. D. W. Waanders, "Reformed Pastoral Care," *The Dictionary of Pastoral Care and Counseling*, ed. Rodney J. Hunter (Nashville: Abingdon, 1990), 1051.
30. Cf. Albert Curry Winn's observation that "Reformed theology was originally a theology of the oppressed." "The Reformed Tradition and the Liberation Theology," in *Major Themes in the Reformed Tradition*, ed. Donald K. McKim (Grand Rapids: Wm. B. Eerdmans Pub. Co., 1992), 406.
31. See Marie Fortune, *Is Nothing Sacred?* (Cleveland: Pilgrim Press, 1999). The website for the Center for the Prevention of Sexual and Domestic Violence, now known as the FaithTrust Institute, is faithtrustinstitute.org. They have many very helpful resources, including videotapes, materials in Spanish, and some in Korean.
32. The WARC's (World Alliance of Reformed Churches') journal, *Reformed World*, is an excellent resource for pastoral theologians and ethicists as we consider these and many other issues facing both the church and the world.
33. Johanna W. H. van Wijk-Bos, *Reformed and Feminist: A Challenge to the Church* (Louisville, KY: Westminster/John Knox Press, 1991), 15.
34. Eleanor H. Haney, *The Great Commandment: A Theology of Resistance and Transformation* (Cleveland: Pilgrim Press, 1998), 131.

Chapter 6

1. Peter Randall, "Not without Honour: The Life and Work of Beyers Naudé," in *Not without Honour: Tribute to Beyers Naudé*, ed. Peter Randall (Johannesburg: Ravan Press, 1982), 1.
2. His lecturer in sociology was Dr. H. F. Verwoerd, later the prime minister of South Africa who was responsible for the development and consolidation of the policy of apartheid.
3. Randall, "Not without Honour," 10: *Afrikaner Broederbond* means "Afrikaner Brotherhood/Fraternity."
4. Beyers Naudé had an important influence on his colleague Ben Marais in the Pretoria East Congregation. Marais's book *Die Kleur-Krisis en die Weste* (The color crisis in the West) raised critical questions regarding segregation, race, and human dignity in the church. A further influence was Prof. Barend Bartholomeus

Keet's book *Suid-Afrika—Waarheen?* [Whither South Africa?] (Stellenbosch: Universiteits-uitgewers), published in 1955, caused a stir in the DRC as it held that apartheid was a betrayal of the Christian calling.
5. "Coloured" was the term used during apartheid times to describe people of mixed racial origins.
6. Peter Walshe, "Mission in a Repressive Society: Christian Institute of Southern Africa," in Randall, *Not without Honour,* 52.
7. Denis E. Hurley, "Beyers Naudé—Calvinist and Catholic," in Randall, *Not without Honour,* 71.
8. Randall, "Not without Honour," 17.
9. Johan Kinghorn, "Modernization and Apartheid: The Afrikaner Churches," in *Christianity in South Africa: A Political, Social and Cultural History,* ed. Richard Elphick and Rodney Davenport (Cape Town: David Philip, 1997), 148.
10. Randall, "Not without Honour," 19.
11. Kinghorn, "Modernization and Apartheid," 148.
12. Ibid., 148–49.
13. John W. de Gruchy, "Grappling with a Colonial Heritage: The English-Speaking Churches under Imperialism and Apartheid," in Elphick and Davenport, *Christianity in South Africa,* 167.
14. Randall, "Not without Honour," 22.
15. Alan Paton commented as follows: "One is forced to conclude—because one does not reach such a conclusion lightly—that this is the work of the Holy Spirit and that Beyers Naudé was struck down on some Damascene road." See "Church and State in South Africa," *Christianity and Crisis,* September 1974.
16. Randall, "Not without Honour," 29.
17. Ibid., 41.
18. Beyers Naudé, *My Land van Hoop* (Cape Town: Human and Rousseau, 1995), 124. All quotations from this work are translated by me.
19. *Oom Bey,* literally "Uncle Bey," was the name by which he was affectionately known by the many South Africans who knew and loved him.
20. Nico Koopman, "Some Comments on Public Theology Today," *Journal of Theology for Southern Africa* 117 (2003): 3–19.
21. David Hollenbach, "Editor's Conclusion," *Theological Studies* 40 (1979): 700–715.
22. Martin Marty, "Foreword," in *Religion and American Public Life,* ed. R. Levin (New York: Paulist Press, 1986), 1–4, esp. 1.
23. Robert G. Simons, *Competing Gospels: Public Theology and Economic Theory* (Alexandria, NSW Australia: E. J. Dwyer, 1995), xv.
24. Denise M. Ackermann, "'Doers of the Word'? Public Theology as Public Practical Theology," a paper read at the Centre of Theological Inquiry's (CTI) Conference on Public Theology in Central Europe, Prague, June 2003.
25. Ronald F. Thiemann, "The Public Theologian as Connected Critic," a paper delivered at the CTI Conference on Public Theology in Central Europe, Prague, June 2003.
26. C. F. Beyers Naudé and Dorothee Sölle, *Hope for Faith: A Conversation* (Geneva: WCC, 1986), 4.
27. Ibid., 11.
28. Ibid., 9.
29. Beyers Naudé, "Die Christelike Instituut en die Kerk," *Pro Veritate* 6, no. 8 (December 1967).
30. Ibid., 4.
31. International Commission of Jurists, ed., *The Trial of Beyers Naudé: Christian Witness and the Rule of Law* (London: Search Press, 1975), 10.

32. Naudé and Sölle, *Hope for Faith*, 21.
33. See International Commission, *Trial of Beyers Naudé*, 55. Recounting this event in his autobiography (100), he recalls how he refused to pay the fine imposed on him and instead went to jail for a night, where he read Amos and then slept like a log (*soos 'n klip geslaap*) before a friend bailed him out the next morning.
34. *Pro Veritate* 13, no. 1 (May 1976): 10.
35. International Commission, *Trial of Beyers Naudé*, 11.
36. *Pro Veritate* 13, no. 1 (May 1976): 10.
37. Beyers Naudé, "On Majorities and Minorities," *Pro Veritate* 14, no. 11 (April 1976).
38. Quoted in Roelf Meyer and Beyers Naudé, "The Christian Institute: A Short History of a Quest for Christian Liberation," in *The Long March: The Story of the Struggle for Liberation in South Africa*, ed. Ian Liebenberg, Fiona Lortan, Bobby Nel, and Gert van der Westhuizen (Pretoria: HAUM, 1994), 164.
39. Naudé, *My Land van Hoop*, 115–16.
40. Naudé and Sölle, *Hope for Faith*, 15.
41. Naudé, *My Land van Hoop*, 116.
42. *Pro Veritate* 9, no. 6 (October 1970).
43. Beyers Naudé, "Die skeiding van die weë," *Pro Veritate* 9, no. 6 (October 1970).
44. Thiemann, "The Public Theologian," 11.
45. Ackermann, "Doers of the Word?"
46. Dirk Smit, "The Paradigm of Public Theology: Origins and Development," a paper given at the International Conference on Contextuality and Intercontextuality in Public Theology, University of Bamberg, June 22–23, 2011.
47. In a sermon delivered to his congregation in Aasvoëlkop in 1962, Beyers Naudé set out his credo. He had to counter suggestions that he was propagating a false gospel. Taking 1 Cor. 2:2 as the text for this sermon, he set out his beliefs. The Bible is the only true Word of God given to humanity as the guiding principle for belief and life: as such it has authority over our lives. He confessed his faith in Christ, "the eternal and only Son of God." Naudé confessed his faith in an inclusive church, which shares communion with all its members equally and calls us to love our neighbors in all our differences. He affirmed his belief that a group, nation, or civilization can only be assured of God's care if it practices justice and seeks the truth. Last, Naudé affirmed the prophetic calling of the church to speak on matters of justice, charity, and compassion. Then he asked his congregation: "Do you believe this?" Thus his sermon was nothing more than simple statement of Reformed faith.
48. Naudé, *My land van Hoop*, 159.
49. Ibid.
50. Ibid., 160. When this sermon was quoted at his trial ten years later, the advocate for the defense asked him: "Now, Mr. Naudé, in the ten years since you preached that sermon, have you had any reason to change your opinion in any way?" He answered, "No. In the past ten years that opinion has only been deepened, broadened, and confirmed." See International Commission of Jurists, *The Trial of Beyers Naudé: Christian Witness and the Rule of Law* (London: Search Press, 1975).
51. Duncan B. Forrester, *Truthful Action: Explorations in Practical Theology* (Edinburgh: T&T Clark, 2000), 139.

Chapter 7

1. John Leith, *Introduction to the Reformed Tradition* (Atlanta: John Knox Press, 1977), rev. ed. (1981).

2. Wendy Farley, *Tragic Vision and Divine Compassion: A Contemporary Theodicy* (Louisville, KY: Westminster John Knox Press, 1990); Nancy J. Ramsay, "Compassionate Resistance: An Ethic for Pastoral Care and Counseling," *Journal of Pastoral Care* 52, no. 3 (1998): 217–26.
3. Douglas J. Hall, *Imagining God: Dominion as Stewardship* (Grand Rapids: Wm. B. Eerdmans Pub. Co.; New York: Friendship Press for Commission on Stewardship, National Council of Churches of Christ, 1986).
4. Fumitaka Matsuoka, *The Color of Faith: Building Community in a Multiracial Society* (Cleveland: United Church of Christ Press, 1998), 124.
5. Marianne Bertrand and Sendhil Mullainathan, "Are Emily and Brendan More Employable than Lakisha and Jamal? A Field Experiment on Labor Market Discrimination," *American Economic Review* 94, no. 4 (2004): 991–1013.
6. Affirmative Action / Equal Employment Opportunity (AAEEO): http://oirap.rutgers.edu/msa/Documents/oee-staff-recruitment-guidelines.pdf; https://www.eeoc.gov/laws/regulations/.
7. David Wellman, *Portraits of White Racism* (Cambridge: Cambridge University Press, 1993), 7–8.
8. Farley, *Tragic Vision and Divine Compassion*, 44.
9. Stephen Ray, *Do No Harm: Social Sin and Christian Responsibility* (Minneapolis: Fortress Press, 2003), 1–36.
10. Ronald Takaki, *A Different Mirror: A History of Multicultural America* (Boston: Back Bay Books, 1993).
11. Ibid., 58.
12. Ian Haney López, *White by Law: The Legal Construction of Race*, 10th anniversary ed. (New York: New York University Press, 2006), 1; cited in Richard Delgado and Jean Stefancic, *Critical Race Theory*, 2nd ed. (Philadelphia: Temple University Press, 2000), 626–34. The Naturalization Act of 1870 extended the naturalization law to "aliens of African nativity and to persons of African descent."
13. Matsuoka, *Color of Faith*, 35–36.
14. James R. Barrett and David Roediger, "How White People Became White," in *White Privilege: Essential Readings from the Other Side*, ed. Paula S. Rothenberg (New York: Worth Publishers, 2001), 4th ed. (2012), 29–34.
15. Matsuoka, *Color of Faith*, 38–41.
16. Ibid., 98.
17. Garth Baker-Fletcher, *Somebodyness: Martin Luther King, Jr., and the Theory of Dignity* (Minneapolis: Fortress Press, 1993).
18. Daniel Day Williams, *The Spirit and the Forms of Love* (New York: Harper & Row, 1968), 134.
19. Wendell Berry, *The Hidden Wound* (New York: North Point Press, 1989), 3–4.
20. Williams, *The Spirit and Forms of Love*.
21. Martin Luther King Jr., "On Being a Good Neighbor," in *Strength to Love* (Philadelphia: Fortress Press, 1963), 26–35.
22. Lois Mark Stalvey, *The Education of a Wasp* (New York: Morrow, 1970; Madison: University of Wisconsin Press, 1989).
23. Catherine Fosl, *Subversive Southerner: Anne Braden and the Struggle for Racial Justice in the Cold War South* (New York: Palgrave, 2002, 2006).
24. Charles Foster and Theodore Brelsford, *We Are the Church Together: Cultural Diversity in Congregational Life* (Valley Forge, PA: Trinity Press International, 1996).
25. Beverly Daniel Tatum, *"Why Are All the Black Kids Sitting in the Cafeteria?" And Other Conversations about Race* (New York: Basic Books, 1997).

Chapter 8

1. Coenie Burger, *Ons Weet Aan Wie Ons Behoort: Nuut Gedink Oor Ons Gereformeerde Tradisie* (Wellington: Lux Verbi, 2001), 89–104; J. H. Leith, "The Ethos of the Reformed Tradition," in *Major Themes in the Reformed Tradition*, ed. Donald K. McKim (Grand Rapids: Wm. B. Eerdmans Pub. Co., 1992), 8–11; H. Richard Niebuhr, *Christ and Culture* (New York: Harper & Row, 1951), 190–229; Dirk J. Smit, "Wat beteken 'Gereformeerd'?," in *Vraagtekens oor Gereformeerd*, ed. W. A. Boesak and P. J. A. Fourie (Belhar: LUS Uitgewers, 1998), 30–34; Ernst Troeltsch, *The Social Teaching of the Christian Churches* (Chicago: University of Chicago Press, 1981), 2:576–691.
2. Leith, "Ethos of the Reformed Tradition," 8.
3. This paper, read at the conference on Reformed Theology: Identity and Ecumenicity, organized by the Center of Theological Inquiry in Stellenbosch in April 2004, was subsequently published as "The Vocation of Reformed Ethicist in the Present South African Society," *Scriptura* 89, no. 2 (2005): 521–35. In the decade since the conference, I have further developed certain themes touched upon in this essay: (1) The public role of churches and public theology in South Africa: "The Interdependence of Public Witness and Institutional Unity in the Dutch Reformed Family of Churches," *Verbum et Ecclesia* 29, no. 3 (2008): 728–43; "Kan die NG Kerk nog 'n konstruktiewe rol in die Suid-Afrikaanse samelewing speel? [Can the Dutch Reformed Church Still Play a Constructive Role in the South African Society?]," *Verbum et Ecclesia* 29, no. 2 (2008): 368–86; "The Public Role of Churches in Present Democratic South Africa," in *Crossroad Discourses between Christianity and Culture*, ed. Jerald D. Gort, Henry Jansen, and Wessel Stoker (New York: Rodopi, 2010), 197–214; "Public Theology in the South African Context," *International Journal of Public Theology* 5, no. 1 (2011): 5–22; "Public Theology in the South African Context," in *Contextuality and Intercontextuality in Public Theology*, ed. Heinrich Bedford-Strohm (Münster: LIT Verlag, 2013), 87–105. (2) Prophetic witness as a legitimate mode of public discourse: "Prophetic Witness: An Appropriate Mode of Public Discourse in the Democratic South Africa?," *HTS [Hervormde Teologiese Studies] Theological Studies* 66, no. 1 (2010): art. #797, 8 pages; "Do the Prophetic and Reformist Approaches in Christian Ethics Exclude One Another? A Responsibility Ethics Attempt at Reconciliation," *In die Skriflig / In Luce Verbi* 46, no. 1 (2011): art. #38, 8 pages. (3) Contemporary Christian ethics developed as an ethic of responsibility: "Prospects of a Christian Ethics of Responsibility (Part 1): An Assessment of an American Version," *Verbum et Ecclesia* 27, no. 2 (2006): 468–87; "Prospects of a Christian Ethics of Responsibility (Part 2): An Assessment of Three German Versions," *Verbum et Ecclesia* 28, no. 1 (2007): 88–109; "Perspektiven einer christlichen Verantwortungsethik," *Zeitschrift für Evangelische Ethik [ZEE]* 51, no. 1 (2007): 8–23; "The Recognition of Human Dignity in Africa: A Christian Ethics of Responsibility Perspective," *Scriptura* 104 (2010): 263–78; "An Ethics of Responsibility Reading of Eduard Toedt's Theory of the Formation of Moral Judgement," *Nederduits Gereformeerde Teologiese Tydskrif* 54, Supplement 5 (2013): 138–46. (4) The relation of Christian ethics to secular modes of ethics: "Christian and Cosmopolitan Ethics: Friends or Foes?," in *Cosmopolitanism, Religion and the Public Sphere*, ed. Maria Rovisco and Sebastian Kim (New York: Routledge, 2014), 161–74.
4. The theocratic ideal as part of the faith tradition of the DRC and the negative impact the transition to the new constitutional dispensation had on this

ideal—both are discussed in a report on "Church and State in the Present Constitutional Dispensation," in the "Proceedings of the General Synod of the Dutch Reformed Church, October 1998," 83–87. See also D. Etienne de Villiers, "The Influence of the DRC on Public Policy during the Late 1980s and 1990s," *Scriptura* 76 (2001): 51–61.

5. In his book *Ontluisterde wêreld: Die Afrikaner en sy kerk in 'n veranderde wêreld* [Disenchanted world: The Afrikaner and his church in a changing world] (Wellington: Lux Verbi, 2002), 32–39, J. Durand traces the roots of this close relationship back to the influence of the Reformed pietism prevalent in the Netherlands at the time Jan van Riebeeck founded a Dutch settlement in Africa at the Cape.

6. One of the national objectives set out in the constitution was "to maintain Christian values and civilised norms and to recognise and protect freedom of worship." G. Lubbe, "Religio-Political Changes in South Africa," in *No Quick Fixes: Challenges to Mission in a Changing South Africa*, ed. D Kritzinger (Pretoria: IMER, 2002), 64.

7. D. Etienne de Villiers, "Kerklike standpunte sedert die instelling van die wette," in *Op die skaal: Gemengde huwelike en ontug*, ed. D. Etienne de Villiers and J. Kinghorn (Cape Town: Tafelberg, 1984), 58–59.

8. Allan Boesak, *Black and Reformed: Apartheid, Liberation and the Calvinist Tradition* (Johannesburg: Skotaville Publishers, 1984), ix–x.

9. Jürgen Moltmann, *Man: Christian Anthropology in the Conflicts of the Present* (London: SPCK, 1974), 37–41.

10. D. Etienne de Villiers, "Die NG Kerk en die oorgang na 'n nuwe Suid-Afrika," in *Skrif en Kerk* 200, no. l (1999): 23–24.

11. D. Etienne de Villiers, "The Influence of the DRC on Public Policy during the Late 1980s and 1990s," in *Scriptura* 76 (2001): 51–52.

12. John Tomlinson, *Globalization and Culture* (Chicago: Chicago University Press, 1999), 106–49.

13. Robert N. Bellah, Richard Madsen, William H. Sullivan, Ann Swidler, and Steven M. Tipton, *Habits of the Heart: Individualism and Commitment in American Life* (Berkeley: University of California Press, 1985; here updated ed., 1996; 2007), 32–35.

14. Peter Beyer, "The Global Environment as a Religious Issue: A Sociological Analysis," in *Religion and Social Transformations*, ed. David Herbert (Aldershot: Ashgate, 2001), 273.

15. In *Christengemeinde und Bürgergemeinde*, Barth has the following to say about the purpose of the state: "Die in seiner Existenz stattfindende Auswirkung göttlicher Anordnung besteht darin, dass es da Menschen (ganz abgesehen von Gottes Offenbarung und ihrem Glauben) faktisch übertragen ist 'nach dem Mass menschlichen Einsicht und menschlichen Vermögens' für zeitliches Recht und zeitlichen Frieden, für eine äusserliche, relative, vorläufige Humanisierung der menschliche Existenz zu sorgen." Karl Barth, *Christengemeinde und Bürgergemeinde* (Zollikon-Zurich: Evangelischer Verlag, 1946), 14. See Karl Barth, *Community, State, and Church: Three Essays; With an Introduction by Will Herberg* (New York: Anchor Books, 1960), 160–61. "The effect of the divine ordinance is that men are entrusted (whether or not they believe it to be a divine revelation) to provide 'according to the measure of human insight and human capacity' for temporal law and temporal peace, for an external, relative, and provisional humanisation of man's existence." See also Karl Barth, *Community, Church, and State: Three Essays by Karl Barth; With a New Introduction by David Haddorff* (Eugene: Wipf & Stock, 2004).

16. Max Weber, "The Profession and Vocation of Politics, in *Weber: Political Writings*, ed. Peter Lassmann and Ronald Speirs (Cambridge: Cambridge University Press, 1994), 309-69.
17. D. Etienne de Villiers, "A Christian Ethics of Responsibility: Does It Provide an Adequate Theoretical Framework for Dealing with Issues of Public Morality?, in *Scriptura* 82 (2003): 23-38.
18. The need to acknowledge "that human beings do not develop theological convictions free of the influence of environments, subsystems, and associations in which they live and in which they commit themselves to action," while at the same time preserving "theology within communities of faith from being diverted from its actual content and object and from losing sight of speech about God"— that need is also stressed by Michael Welker, "Is Theology in Public Discourse Possible outside Communities of Faith?," in *Religion, Pluralism, and Public Life: Abraham Kuyper's Legacy for the Twenty-First Century*, ed. Luis E. Lugo (Grand Rapids: Wm. B. Eerdmans Pub. Co., 2003), 120-21.
19. William Schweiker, "Responsibility in the World of Mammon: Theology, Justice, and Transnational Corporations," in *God and Globalization*, vol. 1, *Religion and the Powers of the Common Life*, ed. Max L. Stackhouse with Peter J. Paris (Harrisburg: Trinity Press International, 2000), 128-39.
20. Johannes Fischer, *Leben aus dem Geist: Zur Grundlegung christlicher Ethik* (Zurich: Theologischer Verlag, 1994), 110-23.
21. Wolfgang Huber, *Kirche in der Zeitenwende: Gesellschaftlicher Wandel und Erneuerung der Kirche* (Gütersloher: Gütersloher Verlagshaus, 1999), 156; Nico Koopman and Robert Vosloo, *Die ligtheid van die lig: Morele oriëntasie in 'n postmoderne tyd* (Wellington: Lux Verbi, 2002), 8-10.
22. Dirk J. Smit, "Comments and Questions (unpublished presentation on a research project under the auspices of the Center for Theological Inquiry, Princeton Theological Seminary, 2002), 8.
23. Gerrit G. de Kruijf, *Waakzaam en nuchter: Over Christelijke ethiek in een democratie* (Baarn: Ten Have, 1994), 40-52, 236-40.
24. Ibid., 182.
25. Ibid., 183, 195. For the distinction "thick" and "thin" used with regard to morality and ethics, see M. Walzer, *Thick and Thin: Moral Argument at Home and Abroad* (Notre Dame, IN: Notre Dame Press, 1994), xi, n. 1. Walzer utilizes the term "thick" to point to a kind of moral argument that is "richly referential, culturally resonant, locked into a locally established symbolic system or network of meanings." "Thin" is simply the contrasting term.
26. Beyer, "Global Environment as a Religious Issue," 266.
27. Bellah et al., *Habits of the Heart*, 142-63.
28. Dawid Venter, "What Is Sociology That Religionists Should Be Mindful of It? The Relevance of the Sociology of Religion for Studying Change in South Africa," *Journal for the Study of Religion* 15, no. 2 (2002): 174.
29. José Casanova, *Public Religions in the Modern World* (Chicago: University of Chicago Press, 1994), 39.
30. Abdulkader Tayob, "Religion, Culture and Identity in a Democratic Society," *Journal for the Study of Religion* 15, no. 2 (2002): 12.

Chapter 9

1. These questions are taken up in *The Spirit and the Modern Authorities*, ed. Max Stackhouse with Don S. Browning, vol. 2 of *God and Globalization* (Harrisburg: Trinity International Press, 2001); see, in particular, Ronald Cole-Turner,

"Science, Technology and the Mission of Theology in a New Century", 139-65; and Jürgen Moltmann, "The Destruction and Healing of the Earth: Ecology and Theology," 166-90.
2. David J. Bosch, "The Afrikaner and South Africa," *Theology Today*, 43, no. 2 (July 1986): 203-16. He is quoting from A. Kuyper, *Lectures on Calvinism* (Grand Rapids: Wm. B. Eerdmans Pub. Co., 1961), 35-36.
3. A convenient summary of much of the current social-scientific discussion of this phenomenon can be found in Malcolm Waters, *Globalization* (London: Routledge, 2000).
4. See Peter Berger and Samuel Huntington, *Many Globalizations: Cultural Diversity in the Contemporary World* (New York: Oxford University Press, 2002).
5. Stackhouse, *The Spirit and the Modern Authorities*.
6. I am much indebted to Mark Heim, *Salvations: Truth and Difference in the World Religions* (Maryknoll, NY: Orbis Books, 1999). He moves the whole discussion beyond "inclusivism, exclusivism, and toleration." See also *Christ and the Dominions of Civilization*, ed. Max Stackhouse with Diane Burdette Obenchain, vol. 3 of *God and Globalization* (Harrisburg: Trinity Press International, 2002).
7. Abraham Kuyper, *Maranatha*, in *Abraham Kuyper: A Centennial Reader*, ed. James D. Bratt (Grand Rapids: Wm. B. Eerdmans Pub. Co., 1998), 207-8. Also Vincent Bacote, *The Spirit of Public Theology: Appropriating the Legacy of Abraham Kuyper* (Grand Rapids: Baker Academic, 2005).
8. Max Stackhouse, "The Common Good, Our Commons' Good, and the Uncommon Good," in *Theology and the Common Good*, ed. Patrick Miller and Dennis McCann (New York: T&T Clark International, 2005), 279-300.
9. Kuyper, *Maranatha*, 213.
10. Ibid., 246.
11. See Michael Cromartie, *A Preserving Grace: Protestants, Catholics, and Natural Law* (Grand Rapids: Wm. B. Eerdmans Pub. Co., 1997).
12. See Gunther Hass, *The Concept of Equity in Calvin's Ethics* (Waterloo: Wilfrid Laurier University Press, 1997); and Harold Berman, *Law and Revolution* (Cambridge, MA: Harvard University Press, 1985).
13. In a fuller treatment, one would have to treat the Holy Spirit in relation to creational, providential, and eschatological themes, as did Abraham Kuyper in *The Work of the Holy Spirit* (Grand Rapids: Wm. B. Eerdmans Pub. Co., 1900, 1976). This is particularly important in view of current Pentecostal and charismatic movements in the churches and among the peoples who have undergone "liberation" from colonialist rule, their effects in personal and social change, and the way it influences the relationship of Christianity to certain elements of the world religions. See David Martin, *Pentecostalism: The World Their Parish* (London: Blackwell, 2001).
14. I am grateful to Reinhold Niebuhr's understanding of how a nonliteralist view of key biblical "mythic" symbols can reveal more than the literalist ones. See his "As Deceivers Yet True," in *Beyond Tragedy* (New York: C. Scribner's Sons, 1937), 1-24. Niebuhr, incidentally, shares with many Kuyperians a critique of the Barthian perspective on many of these matters.
15. This is the one central and valid insight of "Creationists." They, like the wise of all the world religions, know that a purely naturalistic account is not sufficient to render an adequate worldview. Yet they often seek to force the scientific data into a literalist account of what is otherwise seen as an adequate worldview. But the Genesis story is not about how and when the earth and the life on it emerged. In fact, the best of the Reformed tradition has always had a high respect for science and held that, under God, we must be honest with scientific findings and that

the Christian view has gotten itself into trouble when it denied the validity of scientific efforts. Indeed, it tends to claim that the evidence tells us that scientific hypotheses with high levels of evidence, such as evolution, are valid in some areas of understanding. It tells us how change took place and produces evidence as to when things must have developed; although new evidence continues to modify our best scientific theories, nothing has been discovered that refutes evolution as a process. But these theories do not claim to know the source or reason for all that is. The protological account of creation does; it offers to all humanity the hypothesis that God did it and why. Without God, everything would be nothing and mean nothing. But not even the most secular and antireligious scientist lives as if everything is illusion or has no meaning. The story of creation, Christians hold, gives humanity the best insight about an intelligent, free, and loving God behind the universe who, by grace, made it possible for us to know, choose, and love the Creator and our neighbors, and to care for and cultivate the potentialities in creation. God's wise and loving will is behind everything, and that is why it is good. This story offers a metaphysical-moral vision of possibility, a worldview, so to speak, universal in implication and scope.

16. I do not pause to debate the charge made famous by Lynn White Jr. that Christianity's view of dominion is the source of our contemporary ecological crisis. I have elsewhere shown that the "lordliness" of "dominion" is not a matter of wanton "domination," except in those humanistic frames of reference where adherents do not know that human stewardship of the biophysical order is to be conducted by humans not as sovereigns, but under a loving Lord.

17. At this point I am deeply indebted to several scholars, two of whom have made contributions to the discussions of these matters at an Abraham Kuyper Center Consultation (see *Princeton Seminary Bulletin* 24, no. 1 [2003]). See also theologian Thomas Derr, *Environmental Ethics and Christian Humanism*, Abingdon Series on Christian Ethics and Economic Life 2 (Nashville: Abingdon Press, 1996); cf. http://journals.ptsem.edu/id/PSB2003241/dmd010; and environmental engineer Brad Allenby, *Observations on the Philosophical Implications of Earth Systems Engineering and Management* (Charlottesville, VA: University of Virginia, Bratten Institute, 2002); cf. http://journals.ptsem.edu/id/PSB2003241/dmd011.

18. This is one of the key disputes about the work of the Princeton philosopher Peter Singer. See his *Animal Liberation* (New York: Avon, 1991). However, at points he admits that humans have a consciousness about their sensate capacities to suffer pain, a rational will to change social conditions when pain is suffered, and relational capacity for empathy for other humans and for other creatures—all capabilities that animals do not have, at least to the same degree.

19. In a 1990s series of conversations titled "The Hope That Is Within Us," the Working Group of the UCC-EKU delegates of the United Church of Christ (USA) and the Evangelische Kirche der Union (Germany) identified several of the themes in this section and the next; I was the author of several of the proposed theses and the scribe of the whole discussion. Changes in the ecclesiological order of the member churches East and West ended the project.

20. This is a repeated phrase in the work of Reinhold Niebuhr, specifically targeting the "fortunate fall" view of his friend and sometime colleague Paul Tillich.

21. For reasons of length, at this point I must desist from my original plan for this chapter, which was to draw attention to certain globally pertinent themes contained in the "third creation story." After the Priestly and Yahwistic accounts in Gen. 1–3, then Gen. 4 deals with the "providential" creation of the city, the division of labor in the economy, and the development of the crafts and professions.

For a theological view of social ethics, this is very important and much neglected. Notably, Gen. 4 ends with the creation of religion, the capstone of cultural creations. No society is complete without a religion to guide it, and which Lord we depend upon is decisive for these cultural realities.

22. See J. Wentzel van Huyssteen, *Alone in the World: Human Uniqueness in Science and Theology*, the 2004 Gifford Lectures at the University of Edinburgh (Grand Rapids: Wm. B. Eerdmans Pub. Co., 2006).
23. William Cronon, ed., *Uncommon Ground* (New York: W. W. Norton, 1996), 35.
24. These comments on Buddhism and Confucianism are informed by the essays written on the responses of these traditions to, and possible contributions to, globalization—one by Kosuke Koyama, "Observation and Revelation: A Global Dialogue with Buddhism," and the other by Sze-Kar Wan, "Christian Contributions to the Globalization of Confucianism (beyond Maoism)"—included in Stackhouse and Obenchain, *Christ and the Dominions of Civilization*.
25. See David Aikman, *Jesus in Beijing: How Christianity Is Transforming China and Changing the Balance of Power in the World* (Washington, DC: Regnery Press, 2003).

Chapter 10

1. Stanley Hauerwas, *The Peaceable Kingdom: A Primer in Christian Ethics* (Notre Dame, IN: University of Notre Dame Press, 1983), 99.
2. Here I am echoing Richard J. Mouw's remarks in *He Shines in All That's Fair: Culture and Common Grace* (Grand Rapids: Wm. B. Eerdmans Pub. Co., 2001): "When the going gets tough in an intra-Reformed controversy, there frequently comes a point when one of the parties reaches into the rhetorical arsenal and employs what seems for all the world to be one of the worst insults one Calvinist can toss at another: they call their opponent an Anabaptist" (21).
3. Hauerwas, *Peaceable Kingdom*, 99.
4. Andrew Sullivan, *Virtually Normal: An Argument about Homosexuality* (New York: Vintage Books, 1995), 154, emphasis added.
5. Robert Gascoigne, *The Public Forum and Christian Ethics* (Cambridge: Cambridge University Press, 2001), 1.
6. Richard B. Hays, *The Moral Vision of the New Testament: A Contemporary Introduction to New Testament Ethics* (San Francisco: HarperSanFrancisco, 1996), 193–205.
7. Hauerwas, in an article coauthored with J. Alexander Sider—"The Distinctiveness of Christian Ethics: A Review Article on John Colwell, *Living the Christian Story: The Distinctiveness of Christian Ethics*," *International Journal of Systematic Theology* 5 (2003): 225–33—has recently chided mainline Protestants for a tendency toward misrepresentation of the Anabaptist tradition: "Frankly, we have to admit, we are sick and tired of mainline Protestants, who advocate 'engaging the world,' accusing Anabaptists of 'sectarian withdrawal.' As Daniel L. Smith-Christopher points out, these mainline Protestants 'typically undervalue, or are not even aware of, the worldwide involvement of these supposedly withdrawn Christian activists in direct service projects that are not mediated by any state authorities'" (232).
8. In his work *Rediscovering the Natural Law in Reformed Theological Ethics* (Grand Rapids: Wm. B. Eerdmans Pub. Co., 2006), Stephen J. Grabill argues that there is a developed, if circumscribed, tradition of natural law in the Reformed tradition with its roots in Calvin; but it was obscured during the twentieth century by Barth's rejection of natural theology and by the polemics of Barth and others

against the rationalism of the Reformed scholastics as a deviation from authentic Reformed theology.
9. John Calvin, *Institutes of the Christian Religion*, trans. Ford Lewis Battles, ed. John T. McNeill (Philadelphia: Westminster, 1960), 2.7.12.
10. Calvin, *Institutes* 4.20.2. In his *Sovereign Grace: The Place and Significance of Christian Freedom in John Calvin's Political Thought* (Oxford: Oxford University Press, 1999), William R. Stevens Jr. has written: "Calvin finds the effort to distinguish sharply between the sacred law and secular law to be, in many ways, an artificial endeavour. Although Christian conscience does set Christian individuals apart from thoughtless obedience to institutional structures, it ends up freeing them for thoughtful awareness of their need for such structures. Through his law God provides for church, family, work, school and civil polity" (50).
11. Calvin, *Institutes* 2.8.1.
12. See ibid., 2.2.13.
13. See ibid., 2.2.14.
14. Ibid., 2.2.16.
15. For a detailed study of the interrelationships between the *duplex cognitio Dei*, the *sensus divinitatis*, the *semen religionis*, the *lex divina*, the *lex naturalis* in Calvin, see Grabill, *Rediscovering the Natural Law*, 70–97.
16. Calvin, *Institutes* 2.2.12.
17. Ibid., 2.8.1. That Calvin does indeed have an idea of "natural law" and "natural revelation" is often obscured in Protestant polemics. That such natural law and natural revelation does not attain its intended purpose does not alter the fact that it exists. Indeed, the coherence of Calvin's ideas quoted above collapses if such an idea of natural law or natural revelation were to be ultimately denied by Calvin. In a recent study Edward Adams also appeals to the coherence of these strands in Calvin's thought. Although focusing on the arguments in *Institutes* 1.2–5, he argues that Protestants often miss the nuances of Calvin's ideas around this theme by reading book 1 of the *Institutes* filtered through book 2. Adams concludes: "Calvin attempts to develop an approach to natural theological knowledge which is philosophically informed as well as biblically based." Edward Adams, "Calvin's View of Natural Knowledge of God," *International Journal of Systematic Theology* 3 (2001): 281–92, esp. 292.
18. Calvin, *Institutes* 2.2.15.
19. James M. Gustafson, *Protestant and Roman Catholic Ethics: Prospects for Rapprochement* (London: SCM Press, 1979), 19–20.
20. Ibid., 19. For an interpretation of Calvin that would justify this claim, again see Grabill, *Rediscovering the Natural Law*.
21. Mouw, *He Shines in All That's Fair*, 92.
22. Ibid., 93.
23. Calvin, *Insitutes*, 2.2.15.
24. Robert Gascoigne, *The Public Forum and Christian Ethics* (Cambridge: Cambridge University Press, 2001), 2.
25. Ibid., 1.
26. Ibid., 5.
27. Ibid., 3.
28. Ibid., 5.
29. Of such discourse ethics, as shaped by Habermas, David Horrell has written: "The emphasis on argumentation as the process by which norms are discerned is founded on the conviction that norms are only valid if they are arrived at without coercion. Ideological, power- or interest-based distortions would invalidate

any consensus or norms." David Horrell, *Solidarity and Difference: A Contemporary Reading of Paul's Ethics* (London: T&T Clark International, 2005), 59.
30. Gascoigne, *Public Forum*, 8.
31. Ibid., 161.
32. Ibid.
33. Ibid., 175–77.
34. Ibid., 305.
35. David Fergusson, *Community, Liberalism and Christian Ethics* (Cambridge: Cambridge University Press, 1998), 22–33.
36. Ibid., 159.
37. Ibid., 160.
38. Ibid., 165.
39. Ibid., 166.
40. Ibid., 163.
41. Ibid., 162.
42. Ibid.
43. Ibid., 166.
44. Ibid., 167.
45. Ibid., 162.
46. Gascoigne's work was published later than Fergusson's and includes an exposition of and response to Fergusson, largely in terms of the distinction between a Reformed theology of the Word and a Catholic theology of human transcendence. On this basis Gascoigne focuses on the respective accounts he and Fergusson can give of human rights. See Gascoigne, *Public Forum*, 182–88.
47. Richard Hays, *The Moral Vision of the New Testament: Community, Cross, New Creation; A Contemporary Introduction to New Testament Ethics* (New York: HarperCollins, 1996), 5.
48. See Hays's response to Luke Johnson on this issue in *Moral Vision*, 191n4.
49. Ibid., 190.
50. Ibid.
51. Ibid.
52. Ibid.
53. Stephen C. Barton, "The Epistles and Christian Ethics," in *The Cambridge Companion to Christian Ethics*, ed. Robin Gill (Cambridge: Cambridge University Press, 2001), 64. Of course, care must be exercised with such an interpretation of the processes of transformation of received practices. Even allowing for "criticism and gradual transformation" of such practices in the light of Christ, it is clear that such transformation left certain ideological blinkers in place.
54. As Rowan Williams has written: "The church does not either affirm or deny 'the state' in the abstract: it asks what kind of humanity this or that state fosters— what degree of power in its citizens, what level of mutual care, what vision that is more than local, what scepticism about claims to absolute authority and the right to absolute security." Rowan Williams, *On Christian Theology* (Malden, MA: Blackwell Publishers, 2000), 237. He goes on to make parallel comments about the church's attitude to "the nation" and "the family."
55. Hays, *Moral Vision*, 196.
56. Ibid., 197.
57. Ibid.
58. Ibid., 198.
59. Max Weber, "The Profession and Vocation of Politics," in *Weber: Political Writings*, ed. Peter Lassmann and Ronald Speirs (Cambridge: Cambridge University Press, 1994), 309–69.

60. D. Etienne de Villiers, "A Christian Ethics of Responsibility: Does It Provide an Adequate Theoretical Framework for Dealing with Issues of Public Morality?," in *Scriptura* 82 (2003): 23–38.
61. My thanks to both Robert Gascoigne and David Fergusson for their responses to earlier drafts of this chapter.

Chapter 11

1. Jeremy Rifkin with Ted Howard, *Entropy: A New World View* (New York: Viking Press, 1980), 35–36; also see a physicist's more poignant and substantial discussion about the concept of entropy and its societal and cultural ramifications in Jack Hokikian's book *The Science of Disorder: Understanding the Complexity, Uncertainty, and Pollution in Our World* (Los Angeles: Los Feliz Pub., 2002).
2. George S. Hendry, *The Westminster Confession for Today: A Contemporary Interpretation* (Atlanta: John Knox Press, 1960), 79.
3. Barry Commoner, *The Closing Circle: Nature, Man, and Technology* (New York: Alfred A. Knopf, 1974), 29–41.
4. Ivan D. Illich, *Tools for Conviviality* (New York: Harper & Row, 1973), 2.
5. Lawrence O. Richards, *An Expository Dictionary of Bible Words* (Grand Rapids: Zondervan, 1991), 158–59.
6. John Dillenberger and Claude Welch, *Protestant Christianity: Interpreted through Its Development* (New York: Charles Scribner's Sons, 1954), 313.
7. Don Postema, *Space for God: The Study and Practice of Prayer and Spirituality* (Grand Rapids: Bible Way, 1983), 70–71. Also we can readily find the circular, spiral, or helical notion in modern hermeneutical theory under the label "the hermeneutical spiral."
8. Ray L. Hart, *Unfinished Man and the Imagination: Toward an Ontology and a Rhetoric of Revelation* (New York: Herder & Herder, 1968), 250–60.
9. Van A. Harvey, *A Handbook of Theological Terms* (New York: Macmillan, 1964), 123.
10. Hendry, *Westminster Confession for Today*, 103.
11. Ibid., 106–7; cf. Phil. 2:5–11.
12. Ibid., 108.
13. Hannah Arendt, *The Human Condition* (Chicago: University of Chicago Press, 1958), 261.
14. John W. Dixon, *The Physiology of Faith: A Theory of Theological Relativity* (San Francisco: Harper & Row, 1979), 307.
15. George S. Hendry, *The Gospel of the Incarnation* (Philadelphia: Westminster Press, 1958), 143.
16. Wallace M. Alston Jr., *The Church* (Atlanta: John Knox Press, 1984), 126.
17. Charles Norris Cochrane, *Christianity and Classical Culture: A Study of Thought and Action from Augustus to Augustine* (Oxford: Oxford University Press, 1972; repr., Indianapolis: Liberty Fund, 2003), 516.

Chapter 12

1. Max Weber, *The Protestant Ethic and the Spirit of Capitalism*, trans. Talcott Parsons (New York: Charles Scribner & Sons, 1956); repr. in *The Protestant Ethic and the "Spirit" of Capitalism and Other Writings* (London: Penguin Books, 2002).
2. For volumes that specifically explore the questions in relation to the Reformed theological tradition, see Robert W. Green, ed., *Protestantism and Capitalism:*

The Weber Thesis and Its Critics (Boston: D. C. Heath & Co, 1959; repr., Whitefish: Literary Licensing, 2011); and M. J. Kitch, *Capitalism and the Reformation* (New York: Barnes & Noble, 1967).
3. Robert Wuthnow, *Poor Richard's Principle: Rediscovering the American Dream through the Moral Dimension of Work, Business, and Money* (Princeton, NJ: Princeton University Press, 1996), provides a broad account of this process in the American experience whereby all forms of moral discourse, including those grounded in biblical and theological convictions, were "eclipsed" as the political economy in the nineteenth century came to be regarded as a domain that was self-regulating for the common good.
4. William J. Bouwsma, *John Calvin: A Sixteenth-Century Portrait* (New York: Oxford University Press, 1988), 198–200.
5. Kemper Fullerton, "Calvinism and Capitalism," in Green, *Protestantism and Capitalism*, 19.
6. See Justo L. González, *Faith and Wealth: A History of Early Christian Ideas on the Origin, Significance, and Use of Money* (San Francisco: HarperCollins, 1990; repr., Eugene, OR: Wipf & Stock, 2002), 228 and passim.
7. Bouwsma, *John Calvin*, 202.
8. Ibid., 199.
9. Albert Hyma, "The Economic Views of the Protestant Reformers," in Green, *Protestantism and Capitalism*, 102–3.
10. Rodney Clapp, "The Theology of Consumption and the Consumption of Theology," in *The Consuming Passion: Christianity and the Consumer Culture*, ed. Rodney Clapp (Downers Grove, IL: Inter-Varsity Press, 1998), 183–86, discusses the movement from production-oriented capitalism to consumption-oriented capitalism, which reversed the neoclassical economic equation in which supply follows demand.
11. Wuthnow, *Poor Richard's Principle*, 60, observes that Weber is but half right with respect to the American context. "In addition to the ethic of acquisitive capitalism, there is a deep tradition of moral criticism in our culture that seeks to restrict the economic life."
12. Colin Campbell, *The Romantic Ethic and the Spirit of Consumption* (Oxford: Basil Blackwell), 1987.
13. Clapp, *Consuming Passion*, 179.
14. Ibid., 180.
15. Jackson Lears, *Fables of Abundance* (New York: Basic Books, 1994).
16. Clapp, *Consuming Passion*, 180.
17. Ibid.
18. Lears, *Fables of Abundance*, quoted in Clapp, *Consuming Passion*, 180.
19. Clapp, *Consuming Passion*, 181–82.
20. Ibid., 182.
21. See Bouwsma, *John Calvin*, 198–99.
22. Clapp, *Consuming Passion*, 199.
23. Ibid., 199–200.
24. See Keller Fullerton, "Calvinism and Capitalism," in Green, *Protestantism and Capitalism*, 19, endorsing Weber's account of the Calvinist restraint on consumption to a Protestant "asceticism."
25. Quoted in Bouwsma, *John Calvin*, 200.
26. González, *Faith and Wealth*, 228–29. See also the concurring judgment of John R. Schneider that extends the claim to cover major theologians through the Middle Ages and the Reformation. Schneider, "On New Things," in Clapp, *Consuming Passion*, 133: "The common judgment was that the proper usage was determined by order of need, so that evil lurked not in the mere having of

things but in the selfishness that came with enjoyment of that which was clearly superfluous to meeting one's own real needs. The excess of wealth must not be so *abused* but instead *used* to meet the most pressing needs of others, especially the poor." As we shall see, the agreement between these two (González and Schneider) on the historical witness masks a great divide in their respective contemporary positions.

27. The resort to secondary sources for tracing Calvin's treatment of economic issues is occasioned by the fact that he tends to treat them not in major, readily available works, but in sermons, commentaries, and occasional writings that require (for this writer) the aid of scholars who have analyzed this extensive corpus. This suggests that a Reformed practical theology will be best cultivated by thorough investigation of this kind of literature.
28. Bouwsma, *John Calvin*, 197.
29. Ibid.
30. Ibid., 197–98.
31. Ibid., 198.
32. Albert Hyma, "The Economic Views of the Protestant Reformers," in Green, *Protestantism and Capitalism*, 96. For a contrary view of Calvin's acceptance of usury, see Benjamin N. Nelson, *The Idea of Usury: From Tribal Brotherhood to Universal Otherhood* (Princeton, NJ: Princeton University Press, 1949). Nelson argues that the communal solidarity encompassed in Calvin's permission of usury was achieved by redefining solidarity: Solidarity is affirmed not in the sense that no one will take advantage of another's need, but in the sense that taking advantage is understood and agreed upon for the sake of the social utility that it promotes. Nonetheless, the explicit citations of Hyma and Bouwsma seem to bear a different witness.
33. Bouwsma, *John Calvin*, 201.
34. Ibid.
35. González, *Faith and Wealth*, 233.
36. Ibid.
37. Schneider, "On New Things," in Clapp, *Consuming Passion*, 133.
38. Schneider, "On New Things," in Clapp, *Consuming Passion*, 134. For a startlingly different account of the matter, see the UN's *Human Development Report, 1999* (New York: Oxford University Press, 1999).
39. Schneider, "On New Things," in Clapp, *Consuming Passions*, 135.
40. John R. Schneider, *The Good of Affluence: Seeking a Culture of Wealth* (Grand Rapids, Wm. B. Eerdmans Pub. Co., 2002), 26.
41. Ibid., 34. "In an economy based on the creation of wealth, the rich indeed get richer. But so do the poor. D'Souza makes the same judgment I am defending. 'It turns out that our old categories for examining the issue are largely obsolete. We need a new way of thinking about inequality. For the inequality that exists under successful modern capitalism is not at all clearly immoral in the way inequality was under ancient social economies."
42. Ibid., 41–210.
43. Ibid., 32.
44. Ibid.
45. Ibid., 34.
46. Ibid., 32.
47. Wuthnow, *Poor Richard's Principle*, 80.
48. Ibid., 74.
49. See Rodney Clapp's account in "The Theology of Consumption and the Consumption of Theology"—in Alan Ehrenhalt's *The Lost City: Discovering the Forgotten Virtues of Community in the Chicago of the 1950s* (New York: Basic

Books, 1995), 191–92—that details the way in which the deification of choice in consumer behavior led to large-scale markets that inevitably sacrificed the personal sense of human community available when "the very act of shopping was embedded in the web of long-term relationships between customer and merchant."
50. Bouwsma, *John Calvin*, 197, emphasis added.
51. Ibid., 201.
52. Schneider, *The Good of Affluence*, 32.
53. See *U.N. Human Development Report 1999* (New York: Oxford University, 1999).
54. Schneider, *The Good of Affluence*, 26, emphasis added.
55. Lizabeth Cohen, *A Consumers' Republic: The Politics of Mass Consumption in Postwar America* (New York: Vintage Books, 2003), 18–109.
56. Ibid., 111–65.
57. Ibid., 188; also see 111–91.

Chapter 13

1. John Carey et al., "The Biotech Century," *Business Week*, March 10, 1997, 79; cf. Jeremy Rifkin, *The Biotech Century: Harnessing the Gene and Remaking the World* (New York: Jeremy P. Tarcher / Putnam, 1998); Craig Venter and Daniel Cohen, "The Century of Biology," *New Perspectives Quarterly* 21, no. 4 (November 2004): 73–77, http://www.digitalnpq.org/archive/2014_winter/07_ventercohen.html.
2. Stephen Hawking, *A Brief History of Time: From the Big Bang to Black Holes* (New York: Bantam Books, 1988), 175.
3. Lawrence Fisher, "Investing: Strategies for the Genetically Disposed," *New York Times*, August 29, 1999, http://www.nytimes.com/1999/08/29/business/investing-strategies-for-the-genetically-disposed.html?pagewanted=2&src=pm. Another indicator for the importance of biotechnology is the announcement of IBM in December 1999 to spend US$100 million within the next five years to build Blue Gene, a supercomputer 500 times faster than the fastest computer today, for simulating the process of forming protein from amino acids and helping biologists observe the invisible processes of protein folding and gene development. Blue Gene will be 1,000 times faster than Deep Blue, the computer that defeated Garry Kasparov in 1997. A Blue Gene/Q system called Sequoia was ranked as the world's fastest supercomputer in June 2012. See https://www.llnl.gov/news/nnsas-sequoia-supercomputer-ranked-worlds-fastest.
4. Ian Wilmut et al., "Viable Offspring Derived from Fetal and Adult Mammalian Cells," *Nature* 385 (February 27, 1997): 810–13.
5. The title of this subheading is taken from Alan P. F. Sell's *A Reformed, Evangelical, Catholic Theology: The Contribution of the World Alliance of Reformed Churches* (Grand Rapids: W. B. Eerdmans Pub. Co., 1991).
6. David Fergusson, "Reformed Confession: Retrospect and Prospect," in *Korea Reformed Theology: The Reformed Theology of the 21st Century* (Seoul: Soongsil University, 1998), 120, 135. As examples Fergusson gave the five-point Calvinism (TULIP: http://www.reformed.org/calvinism/) and the doctrine of predestination. Both have been modified or disregarded in more recent Reformed confessions or declarations. Moreover, the doctrine of predestination, although a significant feature in Calvin's theology, can be also found in the theologies of Augustine, Aquinas, and some other medieval thinkers.

7. Fergusson, "Reformed Confession," 138. Examples of criticisms of the Westminster Confession by Scottish theologians can be found in T. F. Torrance, *Scottish Theology: From John Knox to John McLeod Campbell* (Edinburgh: T&T Clark, 1996), 125–55; also in some of the essays in *The Westminster Confession in the Church Today*, ed. Alasdair Heron (Edinburgh: St. Andrew Press, 1982).
8. R. T. Kendall, *Calvin and English Calvinism* (London: Oxford University Press., 1979; repr., Eugene: Wipf & Stock, 2011), 208, 212.
9. Thus, e.g., see the declaration "The Church of Scotland is part of the Holy Catholic or Universal Church; worshipping one God, Almighty, all-wise, and all-loving, in the Trinity of the Father, the Son, and the Holy Ghost, the same in substance, equal in power and in glory." Articles Declaratory of the Constitution of the Church of Scotland in Matters Spiritual (1926). Reproduced in Heron, *The Westminster Confession Today*, 145.
10. Leon Kass, *Toward a More Natural Science: Biology and Human Affairs* (New York: Free Press, 1985), 48. Also see Kass, ed., *Being Human: Core Readings in the Humanities* (New York: W. W. Norton, 2004); Kass, *Life, Liberty, and the Defense of Dignity: The Challenge for Bioethics* (San Francisco: Encounter Books, 2004).
11. The term "making babies" appears in the titles of many books, e.g., David Bainbridge, *Making Babies: The Science of Pregnancy* (Cambridge, MA: Harvard University Press, 2000); Cynthia B. Cohen. ed., *New Ways of Making Babies: The Case of Egg Donation* (Bloomington: Indiana University Press, 1996); Inmaculada de Melo-Martin, *Making Babies: Biomedical Technologies, Reproductive Ethics, and Public Policy* (Boston: Kluwer Academic Publishers, 1998); Mary Lyndon Shanley, *Making Babies, Making Families: What Matters Most in an Age of Reproductive Technologies, Surrogacy, Adoption, and Same-Sex and Unwed Parents* (Boston: Beacon Press, 2001); Geoffrey Sher et al., *In Vitro Fertilization: The A.R.T. of Making Babies* (New York: Facts on File, 1995; repr., New York: Skyhorse Pub., 2013); Peter Singer and Deane Wells, *Making Babies: The New Science and Ethics of Conception* (New York: Charles Scribner's Sons, 1985).
12. Gilbert Meilaender, *Bioethics: A Primer for Christians* (Grand Rapids: Wm. B. Eerdmans Pub. Co., 1996; repr., 2013), 15.
13. Oliver O'Donovan, *Begotten or Made?* (Oxford: Clarendon Press, 1984), v–vi.
14. Here the Christian church uses the word "begotten" *as an analogy* to describe the divine inner relation. It therefore does not mean that all aspects of the concept "begotten" are equally applicable to the divine being. Nor does it mean that our human temporal begetting is identical to the divine eternal begetting. Moreover, we cannot say that we humans are "begotten not made" in the same absolute sense as the eternal Son of God *is*. For we who are begotten of other humans are also "made" in the image of God and by God (ibid., 2).
15. Gilbert Meilaender, "Begetting and Cloning (Paper Presented to the National Bioethics Advisory Commission on March 13, 1997)," *First Things* 74 (June/July 1997): 42.
16. "The 'life in the shadow argument' does not rely on the false premise that we can make an inference from genotype to (psychological or personality) phenotype, but only on the true premise that *there is a strong public tendency to make such an inference*." Søen Holm, "A Life in the Shadow: One Reason Why We Should Not Clone Human," *Cambridge Quarterly of Healthcare Ethics* 7 (1998): 162, emphasis added.
17. Her success and failure will be compared to that of the donor. Her development will come under cruel pressure, and her individuality will be seriously dampened.
18. Leon R. Kass, "The Wisdom of Repugnance," *New Republic* 216, no. 22 (June 2, 1997): 24.

19. Meilaender, "Begetting and Cloning," 42.
20. Kass, "Wisdom of Repugnance," 23; cf. O'Donovan, *Begotten or Made?*, 2.
21. David M. Byers, "An Absence of Love," in *Human Cloning: Religious Responses*, ed. Ronald Cole-Turner (Louisville, KY: Westminster John Knox Press, 1997), 76.
22. Paul Ramsey, *Fabricated Man: The Ethics of Genetic Control* (New Haven, CT: Yale University Press, 1970), 88.
23. In its most developed form, the "priesthood of all believers" is central to the Reformed tradition. James Torrance argues that Calvin, in his critique of medieval theology, was concerned to reinterpret the doctrine of the church christologically as a corporate, royal priesthood "participating by grace in the Sole Priesthood of Christ." James B. Torrance, "The Vicarious Humanity and Priesthood of Christ in the Theology of John Calvin," in *Calvinus Ecclesiae doctor*, ed. Wilhelm H. Neuser (Kampen: Uitgeversmaatschappij J. H. Kok, 1980), 69.
24. Abigail Rian Evans, "Saying No to Human Cloning," in Cole-Turner, *Human Cloning*, 29.
25. Ted Peters, "Cloning Shock: A Theological Reaction," in Cole-Turner, *Human Cloning*, 22–24.
26. John O'Connor, "Human Cloning Would Be Unethical," in *Cloning*, ed. Paul A. Winters (San Diego: Greenhaven, 1998), 11. For instance, "The first human clone, if there is one, will surely be treated as a freak. . . . [She] will grow up set apart, the object of tireless scientific and public *curiosity*, exposed to unending physical and psychological testing as she ages, to some degree a laboratory subject. And why not? Obviously [her] principal value to humanity [would be] what science can learn from her." Byers, "An Absence of Love," 73.
27. John A. Robertson, *Children of Choice: Freedom and the New Reproductive Technologies* (Princeton, NJ: Princeton University Press, 1994), 149–72.
28. Philip Kitcher, *The Lives to Come: The Genetic Revolution and Human Possibilities* (New York: Simon & Schuster, 1996), 201–4.
29. Gregory E. Pence, *Who's Afraid of Human Cloning?* (New York: Rowman & Littlefield, 1997), 101–2. It is not uncommon for people to claim to do things in the interest of the child when they have their own interests in mind.
30. Singer and Wells, *Making Babies*, 145–48.
31. R. Albert Mohler Jr. "The Brave New World of Cloning: A Christian Worldview Perspective," in Cole-Turner, *Human Cloning*, 91–105.
32. Bonnie Rochman, "Family with a Risk of Cancer Tries to Change Its Destiny," *Wall Street Journal*, February 17, 2014, http://www.personalizedmedonc.com/article/family-with-a-risk-of-cancer-tries-to-change-its-destiny/.
33. Peters, "Cloning Shock," 23.
34. William Klempa, "The Concept of the Covenant in Sixteenth- and Seventeenth-Century Continental and British Reformed Theology," in *Major Themes in the Reformed Tradition*, ed. Donald K. McKim (Grand Rapids: Wm. B. Eerdmans Pub. Co., 1992), 94–107.
35. James B. Torrance, "Covenant or Contract: A Study of the Theological Background of Worship in Seventeenth-Century Scotland," *Scottish Journal of Theology* 23 (1970): 51–76.
36. Here the use of pronouns for God is in their inclusive sense, as always intended in the Christian tradition.
37. Martin Buber, *Moses: The Revelation and the Covenant* (New York: Harper & Row, 1958), 103.
38. Brent Waters, "One Flesh? Cloning, Procreation, and the Family," in Cole-Turner, *Human Cloning*, 83.
39. Paul Tillich, *A History of Christian Thought* (London: SCM Press, 1968), 262.

40. "For Calvin, the understanding of God's accommodation to the limits and needs of the human condition was a central feature of the interpretation of Scripture and of the entire range of his theological work." Ford Lewis Battles, "God Was Accommodating Himself to Human Capacity," *Interpretation* 31 (1997): 19.
41. Thomas F. Torrance, *Space, Time, and Incarnation* (Oxford: Oxford University Press, 1969; repr., Edinburgh: T&T Clark, 2005), 75.
42. John Calvin, *Institutes of the Christian Religion*, trans. Ford Lewis Battles, ed. John T. McNeill (Philadelphia: Westminster Press, 1960), 4.17.2. In another passage Calvin speaks of Christ's receiving anointing for our sakes: "'He was anointed above his fellows' [Ps. 45:7], for if such excellence were not in him, all of us would be needy and hungry. . . . He did not enrich himself for his own sake, but that he might pour out his abundance upon the hungry and the thirsty. The Father is said 'not by measure to have given the Spirit to his Son' [John 3:34]. The reason is expressed as follows: 'That from his fullness we might all receive grace upon grace' [John 1:16]. From this fountain flows that abundance of which Paul speaks: 'Grace was given to each believer according to the measure of Christ's gift' [Eph. 4:7]" (*Institutes* 2.15.5).
43. Nearly 1.7 million were discarded unused in the UK, according to recent statistics gathered by the Human Fertilisation and Embryology Authority (HFEA). Lord Howe, the Health Minister, said that embryos were being created and thrown away in "industrial" numbers. "It happens on a day-by-day basis with casual indifference. This sheer destruction of human embryos—most people would not know that it took place on such a scale." Andrew Hough, "1.7 Million Human Embryos Created for IVF Thrown Away," *The Telegraph*, December 31, 2012, http://www.telegraph.co.uk/news/health/news/9772233/1.7-million-human-embryos-created-for-IVF-thrown-away.html.
44. Ronald Cole-Turner, "Testimony of Ronald Cole-Turner," in *Ethical Issues in Human Stem Cell Research* (Rockville, MD: National Bioethics Advisory Commission, 2000), A3.
45. Here Torrance takes his cue from the second-century Greek father Irenaeus, who spoke of the saving humanity of Jesus Christ as sanctifying our infancy in his infancy and our childhood in his childhood. This is the meaning of Christ's words, "For their sakes I sanctify myself" (John 17:19). Moreover, it is important to observe that *the saving humanity of the unborn Jesus belongs to the catholic Christian tradition*, as evidenced in the Yuletide hymns: "God of God / Light of Light / Lo! he abhors not the Virgin's womb / Very God / Begotten, not created" (in "O Come, All Ye Faithful") and "Christ, by highest heaven adored / Christ, the everlasting Lord / Late in time behold him come / Offspring of a Virgin's womb / Veiled in flesh the Godhead see / Hail, the Incarnate Deity / Pleased as Man with man to dwell / Jesus, our Immanuel!" (in "Hark! The Herald Angels Sing"). Thomas F. Torrance, *Test-Tube Babies: Morals, Science and the Law* (Edinburgh: Scottish Academic Press, 1984).
46. The Reformed tradition maintains that the Son comes to us from the heart of the inner Being of God himself and is never separated from his Father; even as the incarnate Son on earth, he through his eternal and holy Spirit, "the Spirit of Sonship," maintains an unbroken filial and intimate relation to the Father and remains the *enousios hyios* (or *enousios logos*) of the Father. This is the so-called *extra-Calvinisticum*.
47. Karl Barth, *Church Dogmatics*, III/4, *The Doctrine of Creation, Part 4* (Edinburgh: T&T Clark, 1961), 424.
48. Gilbert Meilaender, "Testimony of Gilbert Meilaender," in *Ethical Issues in Human Stem Cell Research*, E3.

49. James D., Watson, "Moving toward the Clonal Man: Is This What We Want?," *Atlantic Monthly* 227, no. 5 (May 1971): 53.
50. Kass, "Wisdom of Repugnance," 20.
51. Suffice to mention here the possibility of saving a sibling's life through cloning a child. A categorical rejection of cloning would mean a total disregard for the ill child when that life could be saved by technology.
52. For various theological assessments and responses on human cloning, see Cole-Turner, *Human Cloning*.
53. From a report to the 1997 General Synod of the United Church of Christ in the United States by its Committee on Genetics. It refers, in particular, to human preembryo research, such as germline experimentation or research involving cloned preembryos.

Chapter 14

1. Calvin's view is that what is renewed in Christ—true knowledge (Col. 3:10), righteousness, and holiness (Eph. 4:24)—must be what had been originally endowed and then forfeited. John Calvin, *Institutes of the Christian Religion* (1559), trans. Ford Lewis Battles, ed. John T. McNeill (Philadelphia; Westminster Press, 1960), 1.15.3–4; 2.12. 6–7; 3.3.9.
2. Calvin, *Institutes* 3.3.8.
3. I owe this way of putting this matter, and much general enlightenment on the predicament of the depleted self, to my colleague Ronald Nydam. For a classic statement, see Donald Capps, *The Depleted Self: Sin in a Narcissistic Age* (Minneapolis: Fortress Press, 1993). Capps borrows the title from Heinz Kohut, who used it to describe the devastation of long-term shaming. See Heinz Kohut, *The Analysis of the Self: A Systematic Approach to the Pyschoanalytic Treatment of Narcissistic Personality Disorders* (New York: International Universities Press, 1971), 16-17. Cited in Capps, 97–99.
4. Or, in the case of Ephesians, as Marilyn McCord Adams once memorably put it, "Let's just call the author 'Pauline.'"
5. G. C. Berkouwer, *Man: The Image of God*, trans. Dirk W. Jellema (Grand Rapids: Wm. B. Eerdmans Pub. Co., 1962), 112.
6. Rom. 8:18–23, 29, 32; 2 Cor. 3:18; 4:10–11.
7. Abraham Heschel, *The Prophets* (New York: Harper & Row, 1962; repr., New York: HarperCollins, 2001).
8. Phil. 3:10; 1 Cor. 15:48; Rom. 6:1–11.
9. See Lewis B. Smedes, *All Things Made New: A Theology of Man's Union with Christ* (Grand Rapids: Wm. B. Eerdmans Pub. Co., 1970; repr., Eugene: Wipf & Stock, 1998), 145–46.
10. See esp. Rom. 6:1–14 and Col. 3:1–17.
11. Heidelberg Catechism, Question 88: "What is involved in genuine repentance or conversion?" Answer: "Two things: the dying-away of the old self and the coming-to-life of the new [self]." https://thereformedmind.wordpress.com/2012/02/13/heidelberg-catechism-questions-88-91/.
12. Films for the Humanities and Sciences, produced by Public Affairs Television, 1999.
13. I owe the substance of the next two paragraphs to Ronald Nydam.
14. I owe this observation to Nancy Ramsay, who made it with acknowledgment of such contemporary feminist thinkers as Judith Plaskow.
15. The language of empathy as oxygen comes from Heinz Kohut, *The Restoration of the Self* (New York: International Universities Press, 1977), 85. See Chris R.

Schlauch, "Empathy as the Essence of Pastoral Psychotherapy," *Journal of Pastoral Care* 44 (1990): 6.
16. *New York Review of Books*, February 26, 2004, 50.
17. Capps, *Depleted Self*, 98. Depleted selves come in lots of varieties, as Max Stackhouse has remarked. Burned-out preachers qualify. So do certain anxious professionals in highly competitive work environments. The same may be said even of people who resist the confession of sin, thereby robbing themselves of the assurance of forgiveness.
18. Karl Barth, *Church Dogmatics*, II/2, *The Doctrine of God, Part 2* (Edinburgh: T&T Clark, 1957), 579, 581.
19. Otto Weber, *Foundations of Dogmatics*, trans. Darrell Guder (Grand Rapids: Wm. B. Eerdmans Pub. Co., 1983), 1:342, 402, 406.

Chapter 15

1. Amos Wilder, "Electric Chimes and Ram's Horns," *Christian Century* 88, no. 4 (January 27, 1971), 105.
2. Harvey Cox, *Fire from Heaven: The Rise of Pentecostal Spirituality and the Reshaping of Religion in the Twenty-First Century* (Cambridge, MA: Da Capo Press, 2001).
3. Mark Yaconelli, *Contemplative Youth Ministry: Practicing the Presence of Jesus* (Grand Rapids: Zondervan, 2006); Yaconelli, *Growing Souls: Experiments in Contemplative Youth Ministry* (London: SPCK, 2007); Yaconelli, *Down Time: Helping Teenagers Pray* (Grand Rapids: Zondervan, 2008).
4. See http://www.faithandpolitics.org/programs.
5. Carol Lee Flinders, *At the Root of This Longing: Reconciling a Spiritual Hunger and a Feminist Thirst* (San Francisco: HarperSanFrancisco, 1998).
6. See Fred B. Craddock, *Craddock on the Craft of Preaching*, ed. Lee Sparks and Kathryn Hayes Sparks (St. Louis, Chalice Press, 2011).
7. Phyllis Tickle, *The Great Emergence: How Christianity Is Changing and Why* (Grand Rapids: Baker Books, 2012), 164n8.
8. See Cecil M. Robeck and Amos Yong, *The Cambridge Companion to Pentecostalism* (Cambridge: Cambridge University Press, 2014).
9. For a full discussion see Michael Welker, *God the Spirit* (Minneapolis: Fortress Press, 1994).
10. Ibid., 28.
11. Ibid., 28n58, citing G. H. Mead, *The Philosophy of the Present*, ed. A. E. Murphy (LaSalle: Open Court, 1958), 69, https://brocku.ca/MeadProject/Mead/pubs2/philpres/Mead_1932_04.html.
12. Welker, *God the Spirit*, 28n58, citing Mead, *Philosophy of the Present*, 69.
13. Emil Brunner, *Dogmatics*, vol. 3, *The Christian Doctrine of the Church, Faith and the Consummation*, translated by David Cairns and T. H. L. Parker (London: James Clarke Lutterworth Press, 1960, 2002; repr., Eugene, OR: Wipf & Stock, 2014), section 1:15.
14. Karl Barth, *Church Dogmatics*, IV/2, *The Doctrine of Reconciliation, Part 2* (Edinburgh: T&T Clark, 1958; repr., New York: T&T Clark, 2008).
15. George Stroup, "Reformed Identity in an Ecumenical World," in *Reformed Theology: Identity and Ecumenicity*, ed. Wallace M. Alston and Michael Welker (Grand Rapids: Wm. B. Eerdmans Pub. Co., 2003), 265.
16. Ibid., 266.
17. John H. Leith, "The Ethos of the Reformed Tradition," in *Reformed Theology: Identity and Ecumenicity*, ed. Wallace M. Alston and Michael Welker (Grand Rapids: Wm. B. Eerdmans Pub. Co., 2003), 5.

18. John de Gruchy, "Toward a Reformed Theology of Liberation: A Retrieval of Reformed Symbols in the Struggle for Justice," in *Toward the Future of Reformed Theology: Tasks, Topics, Traditions*, ed. David Willis and Michael Welker (Grand Rapids: Wm. B. Eerdmans Pub. Co., 1999), 112.
19. Hughes Oliphant Old, *Guides to the Reformed Tradition: Worship* (Atlanta: John Knox Press, 1984), 171.
20. There is wide but far from complete agreement concerning the primacy of the Word in Reformed tradition worship. See, e.g., Howard Rice, *Reformed Worship* (Louisville, KY: Geneva Press, 2001), who argues that a proper understanding of tradition places an equal value on Word and Sacrament.
21. Old, *Guides to the Reformed Tradition*, 176.
22. Paul Scott Wilson, *The Four Pages of the Sermon: A Guide to Biblical Preaching* (Nashville: Abingdon Press, 1999), 156.
23. Ibid., 159.
24. Dawn DeVries, "The Incarnation and the Sacramental Word," in *Toward the Future of Reformed Theology: Tasks, Topics, Traditions*, ed. David Willis and Michael Welker (Grand Rapids: Wm. B. Eerdmans Pub. Co., 1999), 389.
25. Old, *Guides to the Reformed Tradition*, 133–34.
26. See, T.H.L. Parker, *Calvin's Preaching*, (Edinburgh: T&T Clark, 1992),1–47.
27. In "Incarnation and the Sacramental Word," DeVries describes Schleiermacher's incarnational view of preaching as a development of Calvin's notion of the sacramental word (386–405).
28. Howard L. Rice and James C. Huffstutler, *Reformed Worship* (Louisville, KY: Geneva Press, 2001), 89.

Chapter 16

1. Ralph Kunz, *Gottesdienst evangelisch reformiert: Liturgik und Liturgie in der Kirche Zwinglis*, 2nd ed. (Zurich: Plano-Verlag, 2006).
2. Ralph Kunz, "Inszenierung (Dramaturgie) als Kategorie des Gottesdienstes und der Predigt," in *Verkündigung und Forschung* 55 (2010): 49–60; also Kunz, "Vom Schauspiel zum Sprachspiel: Ästhetische Kriterien und theologische Prinzipien der reformierten Gottesdienstreform im Zürich des 16. Jahrhunderts," in *Liturgisches Handeln als soziale Praxis: Kirchliche Rituale in der Frühen Neuzeit*, ed. Jan Brademann and Kristina Thies (Münster: Rhema, 2014), 123–39; also Kunz, *Gottesdienst evangelisch reformiert*.
3. Ruedi Heinzer, *Liturgische Erosion?*, SEK [Der Schweizerische Evangelische Kirchenbund]-Bulletin, no. 3, 2002 (Bern), 10.
4. David Plüss, "Liturgie ist Stilsache," in *Praktische Theologie* 38 (2003): 275–86.
5. Ralph Kunz, Andreas Marti Andreas, and David Plüss, eds., *Reformierte Liturgik—kontrovers* (Zurich: Theologischer Verlag, 2011).
6. Theophil Müller, "Katholische Einflüsse—'na und?' oder 'so nicht!"? Überlegung zu Frieder Schulz, Katholische Einflüsse auf die evangelischen Gottesdienstformen der Gegenwart," in *Pastoral Theologie* (Göttingen) 86 (1997): 153–62.
7. John D. Witvliet, Series Preface, in *Christian Worship in Reformed Churches Past and Present*, ed. Lukas Vischer (Grand Rapids: Wm. B. Eerdmans Pub. Co., 2003), x.
8. Ibid., 282.
9. Ibid., 283.
10. Ibid., 284.
11. Ibid., 287.

12. Ibid., 295.
13. Martha Moore-Keish, *Do This in Remembrance of Me: A Ritual Approach to Reformed Eucharistic Theology* (Grand Rapids: Wm. B. Eerdmans Pub. Co., 2008), 15–59.
14. Elsie Anne McKee, "Reformed Worship in the Sixteenth Century," in Vischer, *Christian Worship in Reformed Churches*, 3–31.
15. Alfred Ehrensperger, "Die Gottesdienstreform der evangelisch-reformierten Zürcher Kirche von 1960–1970 und ihre Wirkungsgeschichte," in *Liturgie in Bewegung*, ed. Bruno Bürki and Martin Klöckener (Freiburg, Schweiz: Universitäts-Verlag, 2000), 195–205; Andreas Marti, "Gemeinsam verantworteter Gottesdienst," in *Musik und Gottesdienst* 56 (2002): 251–58.
16. Lee Palmer Wandel, "Envisioning God: Image and Liturgy in Reformation Zurich," *Sixteenth Century Journal* 24, no. 1 (Spring 1993): 32.
17. Ibid., 39–40.
18. Kunz, "Vom Schauspiel zum Sprachspiel," 138–39.
19. Arno Schilson and Joachim Hake, *Drama "Gottesdienst": Zwischen Inszenierung und Kult* (Stuttgart: Kohlhammer, 1998).
20. Hans-Thies Lehmann, *Postdramatisches Theater* (Frankfurt am Main: Verlag der Autoren, 1999), 466; translated as *Postdramatic Theatre* (London: Routledge, 2006).
21. Erving Goffmann, *Wir alle spielen Theater: Die Selbstdarstellung im Alltag* (Munich: Piper, 1969, 2000, 2003); translated as *The Presentation of Self in Everyday Life* (New York: Anchor Doubleday, 1959).
22. Hans-Georg Soeffner, *Der Alltag der Auslegung: Zur wissenssoziologischen Konzeption einer sozialwissenschaftlichen Hermeneutik*, vol. 1 of *Die Auslegung des Alltags* (Frankfurt am Main: Suhrkamp, 1989), 142.
23. Neil Postman, *Wir amüsieren uns zu Tode: Urteilsbildung im Zeitalter der Unterhaltungsindustrie* (Frankfurt am Main: Fischer, 1985); translated as *Amusing Ourselves to Death: Public Discourse in an Age of Show Business* (New York: Penguin Books, 1985, 2005).
24. Harald Schroeter-Wittke, *Unterhaltung: Praktisch-theologische Exkursionen zum homiletischen und Kulturellen Bibelgebrauch im 19. und 20. Jahrhundert anhand der Figur Elia* (Frankfurt am Main: Peter Lang, 2000).
25. Horst Albrecht, *Die Religion der Massenmedien* (Stuttgart: Kohlhammer, 1993).
26. Claus Eurich, *Mythos Media: Über die Macht der neuen Technik* (Munich: Kösel, 1998).
27. Marcus A. Friedrich, *Liturgische Körper: Der Beitrag von Schauspieltheorien und -techniken für die Pastoralästhetik* (Stuttgart: Kohlhammer, 2001), 52.
28. Ibid., 86.
29. Ibid., 75.
30. Ibid., 99.
31. Konstantin Stanislavsky, *Die Arbeit des Schauspielers an sich selbst: Tagebuch eine Schülers*, 2nd ed. (Berlin: Henschel, 1996), 160.
32. Friedrich, *Liturgische Körper*, 156.
33. Ibid., 212.
34. Ibid., 216.
35. Kunz, "Inszenierung (Dramaturgie)," 59–60.

Chapter 17

1. This essay previously published in *The Power to Comprehend with All the Saints: The Formation and Practice of a Pastor-Theologian*, ed. Wallace M. Alston and

Cynthia Jarvis (Grand Rapids: Wm. B. Eerdmans Pub. Co., 2009), 255–71. Reprinted by permission of the publisher; all rights reserved.
2. Karl Barth, *The Word of God and the Word of Man* (Gloucester: Peter Smith, 1978), 188.
3. Robert Coles, *Harvard Diary: Reflections on the Sacred and the Secular* (New York: Crossroad, 1988), 10.
4. Ibid.
5. Ibid., 10–11.
6. Ibid., 11.
7. Karl Barth, *The Theology of the Reformed Confessions* (Louisville, KY: Westminster John Knox Press, 2002; repr., 2005), 72.
8. Ibid., 72.
9. David Cornick, "The Reformation on Crisis in Pastoral Care," in *A History of Pastoral Care*, ed. G. R. Evans (London: Cassell, 2002), 224.
10. Ibid., 227.
11. Ibid., 227–28.
12. Ibid., 236.
13. Ibid., 235.
14. Barth, *Theology of the Reformed Confessions*, 73.
15. John McNeill, *A History of the Cure of Souls* (New York: Harper & Brothers, 1951), 198.
16. Cornick, "Reformation on Crisis," 240.
17. Ibid.
18. McNeill, *Cure of Souls*, 209.
19. Ibid., 200.
20. Ibid.
21. Ibid., 198.
22. Ibid.
23. Andrew Purvis, *Pastoral Theology in the Classical Tradition* (Louisville, KY: Westminster John Knox Press, 2001), 95.
24. Ibid., 105.
25. Ibid., 102.
26. Ibid., 110.
27. Ibid.
28. Richard Baxter, *The Reformed Pastor* (Edinburgh: Banner of Truth Trust, 1974), 181.
29. Ibid., 186–87.
30. Ibid., 187.
31. Purvis, *Pastoral Theology*, 105–6.
32. Baxter, *Reformed Pastor*, 72.
33. Dietrich Bonhoeffer, *Spiritual Care* (Philadelphia, Fortress Press, 1985), 7–8.
34. Ibid., 36
35. Ibid., 42.
36. Ibid., 23.
37. Ibid.
38. Ibid.
39. Dietrich Bonhoeffer, *Letters and Papers from Prison* (New York: Macmillan Pub. Co., 1972), 369–70.
40. Bonhoeffer, *Spiritual Care*, 67.
41. Ibid., 67–68.
42. Ibid., 68.
43. Ibid., 68–69.

44. John Leith, *The Reformed Imperative: What the Church Has to Say That No One Else Can Say* (Philadelphia: Westminster Press, 1988), 23.
45. Karl Barth, *Göttingen Dogmatics: Instruction in the Christian Religion* (Grand Rapids: Wm. B. Eerdmans Pub. Co., 1990), 1:86.
46. Graham Greene, *The Power and the Glory* (New York: Bantam Books, 1967), 190.
47. George Bernanos, *The Diary of a Country Priest* (New York: Carroll & Graf Publishers, 1994).

Chapter 18

1. See Grace Davie, *Religion in Britain since 1945: Believing without Belonging* (Oxford: Blackwell, 1994); Davie, *Religion in Europe: A Memory Mutates* (Oxford: Oxford University Press, 2000); and her essay, "The Persistence of Institutional Religion in Modern Europe," in *Peter Berger and the Study of Religion*, ed. Linda Woodhead (London: Routledge, 2001), 101–11. Davie's sociological studies of this decline in all the mainline European churches provide both the empirical data and competing theoretical interpretations of this complex and multifaceted phenomenon, as well as her own thesis about the mutation of institutional religion in Europe under the impact of secularization. Also see her recent revision and further research in *Religion in Britain: A Persistent Paradox*, 2nd ed. (Hoboken, NJ: John Wiley & Sons, 2015).
2. Cited in Philip Benedict, *Christ's Churches Purely Reformed: A Social History of Calvinism* (New Haven: Yale University Press, 2002), 118n3, 568.
3. Ibid., 115–16. I am indebted to Benedict's account and analysis of the Reformed movement in these terms, drawing on the latest scholarship, in this most recent general history of the Reformed churches and theology in the sixteenth and seventeenth centuries, as a pan-European movement.
4. Alan Lewis, "Ecclesia ex Auditu: A Reformed View of the Church as the Community of the Word of God," *Scottish Journal of Theology* 35 (1982): 13–14. This Reformed notion of the asymmetry of divine and human agency is developed by Deborah van Deusen Hunsinger, *Theology and Pastoral Counseling: A New Interdisciplinary Approach* (Grand Rapids: Wm. B. Eerdmans Pub. Co., 1995).
5. Christian Link, "The Notae Ecclesiae: A Reformed Perspective," in *Toward the Future of Reformed Theology*, ed. David Willis and Michael Welker (Grand Rapids: Wm. B. Eerdmans Pub. Co., 1999), 250, referring to Calvin's *Institutes* 4.17.9 and 38.
6. See Douglas Murray, *Freedom to Reform* (Edinburgh: T&T Clark, 1993).
7. See Association of Religion Data Archives, http://www.thearda.com/Archive/Files/Descriptions/SCTCC02.asp.
8. Eight employees are in the national church offices, as reported in *The Scotsman* newspaper, April 5, 2014. For a historical analysis and practical theological critique of the role of a centralized bureaucracy in the operation of the Church of Scotland, see William Storrar, "The Elephant, the Zombie and the Poor Church Mouse: Freeing the Church of Scotland Today," unpublished lecture delivered at St Andrews and St George's West Parish Church, Edinburgh, on the 170th Anniversary of the Disruption of the Church of Scotland, May 2013.
9. William Storrar, "Civic Calvinism: Source of Scottish Reformed Vitality," in *Reformed Vitality: Continuity and Change in the Face of Modernity*, ed. Donald A. Luidens, Corwin E. Smidt, and Hijme Stoffels (Lanham, MD: University Press of America, 1998), 185–205.

10. William Storrar, "From *Braveheart* to Faint-Heart: Worship and Culture in Postmodern Scotland," in *To Glorify God: Essays on Modern Reformed Liturgy*, ed. Bryan D. Spinks and Iain R. Torrance (Edinburgh: T&T Clark, 1999), 69–84.
11. For the historical background to this account in part 1 of this chapter, see Callum Brown, *Religion and Scottish Society since 1707* (Edinburgh: Edinburgh University Press, 1997).
12. Ibid., 128.
13. Ibid., 129.
14. Ibid., 131.
15. Ibid.
16. See Tom Allan, *The Face of My Parish* (London: SCM Press, 1953); Ron Ferguson, *George MacLeod: Founder of the Iona Community* (London: Collins, 1990).
17. See William Storrar, "A Tale of Two Paradigms: Mission in Scotland, 1946–2000," in *Death or Glory: The Church's Mission in Scotland's Changing Society*, ed. D. Searle (Edinburgh: Mentor/Rutherford House, 2001), 54–71; Alexander C. Forsyth, "The Apostolate of the Laity: A Re-discovery of Holistic Post-war Missiology in Scotland, with Reference to the Ministry of Tom Allan," PhD diss., University of Edinburgh, 2014.
18. See Callum G. Brown's thesis on the sudden and rapid nature of secularization in Scotland and the rest of the UK in the 1960s due especially to changing social mores and the life experience of women in church and society, as argued in his book *The Death of Christian Britain: Understanding Secularisation 1800–2000* (New York: Routledge, 2001; 2nd ed., 2009); and the thesis of Paul Heelas and Linda Woodhead that organized religion is giving way to personal spirituality, documented in their coedited study of an English town, *The Spiritual Revolution: Why Religion Is Giving Way to Spirituality* (Oxford: Blackwell, 2005).
19. See the 2002 *Life and Work* study of stress in the ministry of the Church of Scotland (Edinburgh: Church of Scotland, *Life and Work* magazine, 2002). For an account of the state of the Church of Scotland and its congregations by a journalist, see Harry Reid, *Outside Verdict* (Edinburgh: Saint Andrew Press, 2002).
20. Richmond Church now has a beautifully redecorated sanctuary with a well-lit display of its historic communion cups and plate, recognizing its Reformed heritage amid its remodeled space for pastoral care.
21. Elizabeth Henderson, "From Monochrome to Colour," in *Scottish Life and Society: A Compendium of Scottish Ethnology*, ed. Colin MacLean and Kenneth Veitch, vol. 12, *Religion* (Edinburgh: John Donald, 2006), 560–71. Interview with Elizabeth Henderson and Jessie Douglas, Richmond Craigmillar Parish Church, Edinburgh, April 2, 2003, by Professor William Storrar, School of Divinity, University of Edinburgh.
22. Opened in 2003, Richmond's Hope continues its ministry today: http://www.richmondshope.org.uk/.
23. Recorded interview by the author with Rev. Elizabeth Henderson and Mrs. Jessie Douglas, in Richmond Church, Edinburgh, April 2, 2003; transcribed from the recording.
24. For theological reflection on the church and congregation as space and place, see John Inge, *A Christian Theology of Place* (Abingdon: Ashgate, December 2003); Richard Giles, *Re-Pitching the Tent: Reordering the Church Building for Worship and Mission* (Norwich: Canterbury Press, rev. ed., 1999, 2004); Timothy Gorringe, *A Theology of the Built Environment: Justice, Empowerment, Redemption* (Cambridge: Cambridge University Press, 2002); Mary McClintock Fulkerson, *Places of Redemption: Theology for a Worldly Church* (Oxford: Oxford University Press, 2007); and Mark R. Wynn, *Faith and Place: An Essay in Embodied Religious*

Epistemology (Oxford: Oxford University Press, 2009). For "an approach to the study of religion in the West based on a spatial analysis of religious-secular relations," see Kim Knott, *The Location of Religion: A Spatial Analysis* (London: Equinox, 2005).

25. For a revealing account of an earlier, valiant, but ultimately failed attempt to maintain the Richmond congregation as just such a membership body, written by a gifted parish minister working there in the mid-1960s, see W. J. Christman, *The Christman File* (Edinburgh: Saint Andrew Press, 1978).
26. Elizabeth Henderson, "From Monochrome to Colour," 561.
27. For my own further reflections on how this spatial approach to congregational studies might be developed, drawing on this case study, see William Storrar, "Perspectives on the Local Church: Theological Strand—Resources and People," in *Studying Local Churches: A Handbook*, ed. Helen Cameron et al. (London: SCM Press, 2005), 174–87.
28. Robert Wuthnow, *Loose Connections: Joining Together in America's Fragmented Communities* (Cambridge, MA: Harvard University Press, 1998, 2002).
29. Robert Wuthnow, *After Heaven: Spirituality in America since the 1950s* (Berkeley: University of California Press, 1998, 2000).
30. For Richmond Craigmillar Parish Church, Edinburgh, today: http://www.facebook.com/RichmCafeChurch

Chapter 19

1. See Ian Breward, *Australia: The Most Godless Place under Heaven?* (Melbourne: Beacon Hill Books, 1988).
2. Gary Bouma, *The Australian Soul: Religion and Spirituality in the Twenty-First Century* (Port Melbourne: Cambridge University Press, 2006), 2, 18–19, 27–28.
3. Gary Bouma, *Being Faithful in Diversity: Religions and Social Policy in Multifaith Societies* (Adelaide: ATF Press, 2011), 27–28.
4. Bouma, *Australian Soul*, 1.
5. Bouma, *Being Faithful in Diversity*, 13.
6. Ibid., 15.
7. Ibid., 75–105.
8. Ibid., 27–30.
9. See ibid., 6, 9. Through his use of census statistics, Bouma provides a means of comparing the percentage of those who declare themselves to have no religion in Australia (2006: 18.7%), Canada (2001: 16.2%), New Zealand (2006: 32.3%), the United Kingdom (2001: 15.1%), and the United States (2008: 16.1%). These kinds of tables should not be used in such a way that it is assumed that the practice of religion and its profile in Australia and New Zealand is similar to that which is found in North America and Europe. The "institution of religion" in Australia has not been bound at its formative stages by its being bound to an established church or the declared purpose of pilgrims seeking a more tolerant setting for the expression of their beliefs. See, Bouma, *Being Faithful in Diversity*, xiv.
10. Philip Kitcher, *Life after Faith: The Case for Secular Humanism* (New Haven, CT: Yale University Press, 2014).
11. Hans Joas, *Faith as an Option: Possible Futures for Christianity* (Stanford, CA: Stanford University Press, 2014), 117–19.
12. See David Cornick, *Letting God Be God: The Reformed Tradition* (Maryknoll, NY: Orbis Books, 2008), 11–12. The Uniting Church in Australia declares itself to be catholic, reformed, and evangelical; the Anglican tradition of the Sydney

archdiocese sees itself as being reformed. Muriel Porter observes how the mission plan of the archdiocese seeks to be inclusive of churches of a similar theological pedigree but fails to include the Uniting Church. See Muriel Porter, *Sydney Anglicans and the Threat to World Anglicanism: The Sydney Experiment* (Burlington, VT: Ashgate, 2011), 138–39.

13. Donald McKim, *Introducing the Reformed Faith: Biblical Revelation, Christian Tradition, Contemporary Significance* (Louisville, KY: Westminster John Knox Press, 2001), 177–80.

14. The relativizing of the Christian faith and the flaws in the secularization hypothesis have not led to any widespread usage of the descriptive term "postsecular." Sophie Sunderland expresses the fear that any reference to Australia now being "postsecular" and in search of an "Australian spirituality" will privilege a "coded" Christian faith and an Anglo-Celtic subjectivity. See Sophie Sunderland, "Post-Secular Nation, or How 'Australian Spirituality' Privileges a Secular, White, Judeo-Christian Culture," *Transforming Cultures E-Journal* 2, no. 1 (2007): 57–77.

15. Bouma observes that the "basic assumptions of public life may feel Christian to the non-Christian migrant (but) things are not Christian in the way they were before." *Being Faithful in Diversity*, 14.

16. For an example of such, see Aaron Ghiloni and Sylvie Shaw, "Gumboot Religion: Religious Responses to an Australian Natural Disaster," *Journal for the Study of Religion, Nature and Culture* 7, no. 1 (2013): 27–48.

17. Andrew Hamilton, "Anzac Day Celebrates Humanity, Not Nationalism," *Eureka Street* 17, no. 7 (2007); "Turning the Anzac Myth to Society's Good," *Eureka Street* 25, no. 7 (2015). For a perspective on the ambiguity of this civic religion in a multicultural society, see Fatima Measham, "Anzac Day a Jarring Experience for Migrants," *Eureka Street* 17, no. 7 (2015). For another alternative rendering of Anzac remembrance, see James Brown, *Anzac's Long Shadow: The Cost of Our National Obsession* (Melbourne: Black Inc., 2013). Brown argues that "too much, too time, too energy" is spent on the Anzac legend. It engenders a "cult of remembrance" that is no longer in tune with contemporary military and defense issues.

18. Joas believes that one of the greatest "intellectual challenges" facing the Christian faith is the "disappearance" of transcendence. *Faith as an Option*, 133–34.

19. Charles Sherlock, "From 'Mate Upstairs' to 'Spirituality Sponsor': God Images in Australian Society," in *Developing an Australian Theology*, ed. Pete Malone (Strathfield: St. Pauls, 1999), 43–64.

20. David Tacey, *Edge of the Sacred: The Transformation of Australia* (Sydney: HarperCollins Publishers, 1995); Tacey, *Re-Enchantment: The New Australian Spirituality* (Sydney: HarperCollins Publishers, 2000); Tacey, *The Spirituality Revolution* (Sydney: HarperCollins Publishers, 2003); *Edge of the Sacred: Jung, Psyche, Earth* (Einsiedeln: Daimon Verlag, 2009).

Tacey writes from a Jungian background. He is conscious of a general disillusionment/disenchantment with materialist understandings of the "good life." The present period is witnessing a burgeoning interest in spirituality that reflects a human desire for the numinous. That mode of thinking found in *Re-Enchantment* has been more recently expressed in *The Darkening Spirit: Jung, Spirituality, Religion* (New York: Routledge, 2013). Here Tacey draws upon Jung for the sake of negotiating a way through the "postsecular world."

Tacey makes frequent references to the Christian faith and its organizational form throughout his writings. His most recent publication is a study of a number of biblical stories where he argues that their purpose is to resonate within the

soul and direct us to transcendental realities. These stories can be reread as metaphors of the spirit and the interior life. See Tacey, *Religion as Metaphor: Beyond Literal Belief* (Piscataway, NJ: Transaction Publishers, 2015).
21. Rachael Kohn, *The New Believers: Re-Imagining God* (Sydney: HarperCollins Publishers, 2003, 2005). These "new believers are reimagining God to embrace the self-help movement, the Westernisation of Buddhism, and the moral agenda of environmentalism."
22. Bouma, *Australian Soul*, 34-36.
23. Steve Crittenden, "Highly Spirited," *Sydney Morning Herald*, January 3, 2001. This dislike of "brokenness," and by extension the language of sin, can be placed alongside the (admittedly) contested research done by the BBC and published in the February 2010 edition of its magazine, *Focus*, "Born to Sin: Why Nature Wants You to Be Bad." Out of a survey of thirty-five nations, Australia was reckoned to be "the world number one for sinning." Of the seven deadly sins, it topped the poll for envy and was third for lust and gluttony. The relationship between brokenness and guilt, on the one hand, and the desire for happiness and well-being is further explored by James Boyce, *Born Bad: Original Sin and the Making of the Western World* (Melbourne: Black Inc., 2014). Boyce has made a sustained description of how the idea of original sin came into being and how it has been understood by leading theologians and thinkers, beginning with Augustine. Boyce argues that its contemporary presence is "receding fast," yet its shadow can be found in one secular thinker after another, and it is responsible for the feelings of "guilt" and "inadequacy" that continue to pervade Western experience. The audience for *Born Bad* is evidently the public at large: it has attracted long reviews in *The Australian*, August 23, 2014; *The Sydney Morning Herald*, September 5, 2014; the online Australian version of *The Guardian*, July 22, 2014; *The Monthly*, September 2014; and national radio, ABC, July 21, 2014.
24. Thinking about the task of putting "Christ back into Christmas," James Murray, the religious correspondent for *The Australian*, observed that the church, "once the great communicator," is now "so inept that it cannot put its message across." In the midst of a general condemnation of preaching, Murray raised the question: "Is it that the church has failed to free itself from a religious lingo that needs initiation in order to understand it, and which, frankly, often makes no contemporary sense at all?" See "And the Word Was Boredom," *The Australian*, December 24, 2003.
25. The principal observer of what kind of language is most dominant in the public domain in Australia is Don Watson. In the course of his career, he has been an academic historian, a public speaker, a satirist, and a political adviser and speech writer. Watson coined the term "weasel words" to describe words and phrases that give the misleading impression of something very meaningful and purposeful. Those words or phrases are really "sneaky," "deceptive," mask responsibility, and can be rather manipulative under the cover of being ambiguous and vague. Watson's most sustained critique of such has been his highly praised *Death Sentence: The Decay of Public Language* (Milsons Point: Knopf, 2003). In and around the same time he published *Watson's Dictionary of Weasel Words, Clichés, Cant and Management Jargon* (Milsons Point: Random House, 2004). Watson returned to these themes in his *Bendable Learnings: The Wisdom of Modern Management* (North Sydney: Vintage Books, 2010). Here he noted that the language (and implications) of "mission statements" and "vision statements" had spread to the church "even though it has a very good language of its own to go by."
26. Of particular interest is the following observation made by Gordon Dicker in his article on "The Reformed Heritage and the Uniting Church," *Uniting Church*

Studies 9, no. 2 (August 2003): 22: "The ordering of our councils seems to be more on the basis of convenience and the imitation of the corporation than what is appropriate for the communal life of the people of God."

27. Richard Cashman, *Paradise of Sport: The Rise of Organised Sport in Australia* (South Melbourne: Oxford University Press, 1995), 205–8. See also Daryl Adair, "Paradise of Sport? The Cashman Thesis and Australian Sports History," *Sporting Traditions* 12, no. 1 (1996): 121–32.

28. Leonie Huntsman, *Sand in Our Souls: The Beach in Australian History* (Carlton South: Melbourne University Press, 2001).

29. William Joseph Baker, *If Christ Came to the Olympics*, New College Lectures (Sydney: UNSW [University of New South Wales] Press, 2000).

30. Susan Maushart, "Bearing Gifts and Guilt," *The Weekend Australian Magazine*, September 7–8, 2004, 38. Maushart's body of published writing is gender-related and focuses on the contemporary living out of the roles of mother and wife. See Maushart, *The Mask of Motherhood: How Becoming a Mother Changes Our Lives and Why We Never Talk about It* (New York: Penguin Books, 2000); Maushart, *Wifework: What Marriage Really Means for Women* (New York: Bloomsbury, 2001); Maushart, *The Winter of Our Disconnect: How Three Totally Wired Teenagers (and a Mother Who Slept with Her I-Phone) Pulled the Plug on Their Technology and Lived to Tell the Tale* (North Sydney: Random House, 2010).

31. For a description of the intersection of religious belief and government, see Marion Maddox, *For God and Country: Religious Dynamics in Australia's Parliament* (Canberra: Department of the Parliamentary Library, 2001); Maddox, *God under Howard: The Religious Right in Australian Politics* (Crow's Nest: Allen & Unwin, 2005); Maddox, *Taking God to School: The End of Australia's Egalitarian Education?* (Crow's Nest: Allen & Unwin, 2014).

32. The outstanding exception to this "rule" is the recent disclosures of sexual misconduct by several teachers at the prestigious Knox Grammar School, Sydney. Writing in *The Monthly* ("The Old Boy," March 2011), Malcolm Knox noted that the school was named after the "founder of the Church of Scotland."

33. Peter FitzSimons, "Go Tell It on the Mountain with the Volume Turned Down," *Sydney Morning Herald*, June 12, 2001. See also Clive Pearson, "Speaking of God: Ballyhooing in Public," in *Christians in Public: Aims, Methodologies and Issues in Public Theology*, ed. Len Hansen (Stellenbosch: SUN Press, 2007), 61–78.

34. Peter FitzSimons, "Move Over, God, It's Time to Make Room for a Real Power," *Sydney Morning Herald*, February 19, 2004.

35. Peter Matheson, *The Imaginative World of the Reformation* (Edinburgh: T&T Clark, 2000), 6.

36. Ibid.

37. Ibid., 1.

38. Ibid.

39. The descriptive phrase "the big little issue" is taken from Mark Bonnington and John Fyall, *Homosexuality and the Bible* (Cambridge: Grove Books, 1996).

40. Daniel Hardy, "The Future of Theology in a Complex World," in *Christ and Context: The Confrontation between Gospel and Culture*, ed. Hilary D. Regan and Alan Torrance (Edinburgh: T&T Clark, 1993), 21.

41. Matheson, *Imaginative World of the Reformation*, 7.

42. It is arguably the case that a Reformed faith is inclined toward the cerebral. The dilemma Bouma has discerned for this form of faith is that "religious meaning is provided in various ways" and not confined to the creedal, confessional, and the rational. Bouma argues that "religions work by providing action frames,

patterns of interaction and social networks that link people [and] encourage movements towards hope." That language of hope and its possibility are critical. These action frames can furnish an "experienced basis for hope" that emerges not just out of what we think and confess, but also out of our "human interaction." See Bouma, *Australian Soul*, 18–19.
43. Anthony Moran, *Australia: Nation, Belonging, and Globalization* (New York: Routledge, 2005), 87–128.
44. For a brief description of this practice, see Clive Pearson, "Christology in Context Down Under: Mapping Trans-Tasman Christologies," in *Mapping the Landscape: Essays in Australian and New Zealand Christianity*, ed. William Emilsen and Susan Emilsen (New York: Peter Lang, 2000), 303–7.
45. Douglas John Hall, *Thinking the Faith: Christian Theology in a North American Context* (Minneapolis: Fortress Press, 1991), 17.
46. Daniel Migliore, "Christology in Context: The Doctrinal and Contextual Tasks of Theology Today," *Interpretation* 49, no. 3 (1995): 244.
47. Paul Louis Metzger, *The Word of Christ and the World of Culture: Sacred and Secular through the Theology of Karl Barth* (Grand Rapids: Wm. B. Eerdmans Pub. Co., 2003), xxi, 225–34. The comparison can be made with Timothy Gorringe, *Karl Barth against Hegemony* (Oxford: Oxford University Press, 1999); and Paul S. Chung, *God's Word in Action* (Eugene: Cascade Books, 2008)—both of whom seek to show how a particular context shaped Barth's own theology and how it was directed back to that context. Geoff Lilburne draws upon Barth for the sake of a Protestant methodology in his well-thought-through "Contextualising Australian Theology: An Enquiry into Method," *Pacifica* 10 (1997): 350–64.
48. Alistair MacFadyen, *Bound to Sin: Abuse, Holocaust and the Doctrine of Sin* (Cambridge: Cambridge University Press, 2000), 5–13.
49. Ibid., 50.
50. Stephen B. Bevans, *Models of Contextual Theology* (Maryknoll, NY: Orbis Books, 1992, 2002); Robert Schreiter, *Constructing Local Theologies* (Maryknoll, NY: Orbis Books, 1985); Angie Pears, *Doing Contextual Theology* (Abingdon: Routledge, 2010).
51. Alberto Garcia and Victor Raj, *The Theology of the Cross for the 21st Century* (St. Louis: Concordia Publishing House, 2002).
52. Dicker, "The Reformed Heritage," 11–23.
53. William Dyrness, *Reformed Theology and Visual Culture: The Protestant Imagination from Calvin to Edwards* (Cambridge: Cambridge University Press, 2004), 304–8.
54. William Edgar, *Truth in All Its Glory: Commending the Reformed Faith* (Phillipsburg, NJ: P&R Pub., 2004).
55. Albert M. Wolters, *Creation Regained: Biblical Basics for a Reformational Worldview* (Grand Rapids: Wm. B. Eerdmans Pub. Co., 2005).
56. James K. A. Smith and James H. Olthuis, eds., *Radical Orthodoxy and the Reformed Tradition: Creation, Covenant, and Participation* (Grand Rapids: Baker Academic, 2005).
57. Amy Plantinga Pauw and Serene Jones, eds., *Feminist and Womanist Essays in Reformed Dogmatics* (Louisville, KY: Westminster John Knox Press, 2006).
58. Chris Budden, *Following Jesus in Invaded Space: Doing Theology on Aboriginal Land* (Eugene, OR: Wipf & Stock, 2009).
59. For writings that originate out of a Uniting Church background, see Clive Ayre, *Earth, Faith and Mission: The Theology and Practice of Earth Care* (Eugene, OR: Wipf & Stock, 2013); William Emilsen, ed., "Future Scenarios," *Uniting Church Studies* 20, no. 1 (June 2014); Jan Morgan, *Earth's Cry: Prophetic Ministry in*

a More-Than Human World (Melbourne: Uniting Academic Press, 2013); and Clive Pearson, "The Purpose and Practice of a Public Theology in a Time of Climate Change," *International Journal of Public Theology* 4, no. 3 (2010): 356–72.

60. Barney Swartz, "For God's Sake, Kids, Jesus Isn't a Profanity," *Sydney Morning Herald*, November 11, 2003.

61. Augustine, *City of God* 16.9; see also Clive Pearson, "For Christ's Sake: From Expletive to Confession," *Pacifica* 17, no. 2 (2004): 197–215.

Contributors

Denise M. Ackermann was formerly Professor of Christianity and Society at the University of the Western Cape and Extraordinary Professor of Practical Theology, University of Stellenbosch, South Africa.

Jana Childers is Dean of San Francisco Theological Seminary, California, as well as Professor of Homiletics and Speech Communication.

Susan E. Davies served as Co-Chair of the Faith and Order Commission of the National Council of Churches (USA) and was formerly Jonathan Fisher Professor of Christian Education at Bangor Theological Seminary, Maine. She is currently the Moderator of the Transformative Theology working group of Oikotree, an international movement of movements working for economic and ecological peace and justice.

Etienne de Villiers was formerly Professor of Christian Ethics in the Faculty of Theology as well as Director of the Centre for Public Theology at the University of Pretoria, South Africa.

Cynthia Jarvis is the Minister of the Presbyterian Church of Chestnut Hill, Philadelphia; she and Elizabeth Johnson are series editors for the Feasting on the Gospels volumes.

Jong-Hyuk Kim is Professor of Christian Ethics at Soong Shil University, Seoul, South Korea. Formerly he was a professor at Han Il Presbyterian University, where he was Acting President and Dean of the Graduate School.

Ralph Kunz is Professor of Liturgy, Counselling and Religion and Gerontology, University of Zurich, Switzerland.

Cameron Murchison is Professor Emeritus of Ministry, Columbia Theological Seminary, Decatur, Georgia.

Piet Naudé is Professor and Director of the University of Stellenbosch Business School, South Africa. He was formerly Professor of Ethics at the Nelson Mandela Metropolitan University in Port Elizabeth.

Clive Pearson is a Research Fellow of the Public and Contextual Theology Research Centre at Charles Sturt University, Australia; he was formerly Head of the School of Theology at Charles Sturt University and Principal of United Theological College, Sydney.

Cornelius Plantinga Jr. was formerly President of Calvin Theological Seminary, Grand Rapids, Michigan. He is Senior Research Fellow at the Calvin Institute of Christian Worship.

Nancy J. Ramsay is Professor of Pastoral Theology and Pastoral Care at Brite Divinity School, Fort Worth, Texas.

Kang Phee Seng is Vice-President and Eleanor and Wayne Chiu Professor of Systematic Theology as well as the Director of the Centre of Faith and Public Values, China Graduate School of Theology, Hong Kong.

Dirk Smit is Professor of Systematic Theology in the Faculty of Theology, Stellenbosch University, South Africa.

Max Stackhouse was the Rimmer and Ruth de Vries Professor of Reformed Theology and Public Life Emeritus at Princeton Theological Seminary, New Jersey; he was the first Director of its Abraham Kuyper Center for Public Theology.

William Storrar is Director of the Center of Theological Inquiry in Princeton, New Jersey; formerly he was Professor of Christian Ethics and Practical Theology and Director of the Centre for Theology and Public Issues at the University of Edinburgh.

Geoff Thompson is Co-ordinator of Studies–Systematic Theology at Pilgrim Theological College within the University of Divinity, Melbourne, Australia. He previously held a similar role at Trinity Theological College, Brisbane.

Hmar Vanlalauva is currently an Adjunct Professor at Aizawl Theological College in Mizoram, India. He is a former Principal of the College and was Dean of the Department of Research and the South Asia Research Institute at Serampore College.

Michael Welker is senior Professor of Systematic Theology and director of FIIT (Research Center International and Interdisciplinary Theology) at the University of Heidelberg, Germany. He is Honorary Professor at Seoul Theological University and member of the Heidelberg and the Finish Academies of Science and Letters.

Index

abortion, 167
ABRECSA (Alliance of Black Reformed Christians in Southern Africa), 131
accountability, 92, 117. *See also* responsibility
Accra Confession, 54, 303n6
Ackermann, Denise, 5, 10, 35, 50, 51
acquisition, 197
acquisitiveness, celebration of, 198
activist membership institutions, 261–62
actual sin, 112
Adams, Edward, 321n17
addiction, 179
Addy, Tony, 62
Adonis, Hannes, 40
Advaita, 74
aesthetic justice, 54, 62
affirmative action, 114, 119
Africa. *See also* South Africa
  postcolonial societies in, 142–43
  southern, Christianity in, 159
African Independent Churches, 307n80
African National Congress, 100, 107, 132
African Renaissance, 58
Afrikaans Reformed Church, 49, 130–32
Afrikaner Broederbond, 100
After Heaven (Wuthnow), 273
alienation, cloning and, 204
Alston, Wallace, 5, 7
Anabaptists, 161, 164, 320n7
ANC. *See* African National Congress
anomie, 305n39
Anthropocene epoch, 20, 30, 33
anthropocentrism, 135, 230
antipodes, 286, 289–90
antitheism, 157
Anzac Day (Australia), 279, 338n17
Aotearoa, 284, 289

apartheid, 10–11, 12, 22, 28, 35, 41, 96, 131–32
Aquinas, Thomas. *See* Thomas Aquinas
Arendt, Hannah, 188
Arminians, 77
artificial intelligence, 33
Athanasius, 78
atomic energy, 178
Augustana Confession, 250
Augustine, 73, 77, 78–79, 231, 289, 339n23
Austin, Victor Lee, 33
Australia
  ecumenism in, 163
  immigration policy in, 278
  language in, 339n25
  Reformed theology and ethic for, 286–90
  Reformed tradition in, 277, 283–84
  reinvention of, 285
  religion in, 277–82
  sin in, 339n23
  sports in, 280–81
  theologians in, 285–86
Australian Soul, The (Bouma), 277–78
Australian spirituality, 279
aversive racism, 22–24, 115–16, 294n61

Baker, William James, 280
Banaji, Mahzarin, 23
baptism, sacrament of, 215–16, 237
Barmen Declaration, 43, 300n25
Barth, Karl, 9, 41, 45, 49, 73, 79, 135, 140, 148, 153–54, 168, 209, 220, 227, 228, 250, 258, 285, 299n9, 300n25, 316n15, 320–21n8
Barua, Ankur, 26, 27, 295nn83–85
Bass, Dorothy, 17

345

Battles, Lewis, 41, 44
Bauman, Zygmunt, 57
Baxter, Richard, 253–55, 258
BCM. *See* Black Consciousness Movement
Bedford-Strohm, Heinrich, 54
begetting, 34, 204, 327n14
Belhar Confession, 43, 66, 300n25
Bellah, Robert, 141
Benedict, Philip, 262
Benoit, Jean Daniel, 252
Berger, Peter, 57
Bernanos, Georges, 259
Berry, Thomas, 57, 305n40
Berry, Wendell, 121, 122
Bevans, Stephen, 286
Beyer, Peter, 134, 140–41
Beyers, Christian Frederick, 99
Bible
  apartheid and, 41, 131–32
  authority of, 70, 71–72
  God's power in, 77
  knowing God through, 71–73
  as moral code, 138–39
  moral message of, 135–36
biblical scholarship, power of, 50
Biko, Steve, 99, 102
biotechnology, 33–34, 202, 326n3. *See also* cloning; genetic engineering
Black Consciousness Movement, 102, 107
de Blank, Joost, 100–101
Blindspot (Banaji and Greenwald), 23
Boesak, Allan, 40, 49, 131
Bohren, Rudolf, 47
Bonhoeffer, Dietrich, 249, 255–58
Bonneuil, Christoph, 30
Bons-Storm, Riet, 50–51
Born Bad (Boyce), 339n23
Bosch, David, 40, 146–47
Botman, Russel, 40, 49
Böttger, Paul, 42
Bouma, Gary, 277–78, 279, 340–41n42
Bouwsma, William J., 195
Boyce, James, 339n23
Boys' Brigade (Scotland), 265
Braden, Anne, 123
Brecht, Bertold, 243, 245
Brelsford, Theodore, 123–24
Brief Statement of Faith of the Presbyterian Church (U.S.A.), 43, 112, 300n25

Brown, Callum, 265–66
Brown, Cathy G., 336n18
Brown, Peter, 250
Brueggemann, Walter, 8–9, 292n13
Brunner, Emil, 153, 227
Buddhism
  emptiness and, 150
  metaphysics in, 157
  on nature, 158
Burger, Coenie, 40, 46, 47–48, 51, 302n47
Bushnell, Horace, 93, 95

calling, doctrine of, 198
Calvin, John, 9, 12–13, 14, 69, 96, 227, 258, 325n27
  on the Bible and the Holy Spirit, 71–72
  on calling, 32, 194
  capitalism and, 31, 192–200
  Christian life and, 43–45
  on Christ's anointing, 329n42
  on community, 195, 199
  committed to the church, 51
  on creation, 32, 194
  exclusivism and, 26, 75
  on faith, 45
  on the fall, 71, 78
  on God's majesty, 208
  on God's sovereignty, 76–81
  on grace, 94, 218
  on the Holy Spirit, 232
  Indian Christianity and, 25–27, 69–70
  on knowing God, 70–75
  on local autonomy, 262
  on natural law, 321n17
  as pastor, 44–45, 50, 51, 252–53
  political interests of, 44
  as preacher, 228, 229
  on preaching, 231–32
  realism of, 45
  scholastics disagreeing with, 73
  on social engagement, 165
  as social reformer, 44–45
  sociopolitical influence of, 146
  theology of, 18, 26–27, 41–42, 45, 46, 301n31, 329n40
  on wealth, 192, 194
  Westminster theology and, 203
  on wisdom outside the church, 164–65
  on worship, 238
  writings of, context for, 75, 77, 80, 197

Calvin, Geneva, and the Reformation (Wallace), 44–45
Calvin's Rhetoric of Piety (Jones), 42
Campbell, Colin, 193
Candler, Asa, 193
Cape Dutch Reformed Church, 101
capital accumulation, 194
capitalism, 32, 141, 324n10
   Calvinism and, 192–200
   consumption-oriented, 192–93, 196, 199
   cultures within, 199–200
   production-oriented, 192–94, 196
   Reformed theology and, 96
   varieties of, 148
Capps, Donald, 21, 218, 330n3
care. *See also* pastoral care
   ministries of, 111
   praxis of, 19, 20–21
Casanova, José, 142
categorization, 23
Catholic Church, practical theology and, 18
cell fusion technology, 178–79
Center of Theological Inquiry (Princeton), 5
charismatic movement, 318n13
Charry, Ellen, 42
chemical fertilizers, 179
Childers, Jana, 5, 7, 8, 9
children, racism of, 115
China, Christianity in, 159
Christ
   anointing of, 329n42
   body of, 262–63
   confession of, as political act, 64
   consciousness in, 65
   cosmic, 295n84
   culture and, 285
   dying and rising with, 215–16
   God's revelation in, 71, 72, 73. *See also* God, revelation of
   humanity of, 208
   liberation in, 66
   limitation of, 75
   lordship of, 289–90
   personhood of, 186, 187, 208
   presence of, outside the church, 27, 75, 173
   redemption in, 160
Christengemeinde and Bürgergemeinde (Barth), 135

Christ event
   God's revelation through, 71–75
   self-giving love of, 75
Christian church
   confession of, 44
   ethics of, 33
   history of, experimentation in, 4
   moral formation of, 172–73
   responding to globalization, 65–67
   as social ethic, 161
Christian Institute (South Africa), 101–2, 105–7, 109–10
Christianity
   and the common good, 162–63, 169
   commodification of, 193
   cultural values and, 141
   democracy and, 140, 141
   distinctiveness of, 162–63
   geographic shift of, 25
   isolation of, 168
   moral values and, 136
   policy formation and, 140, 141
   racism and, 113
   worldview of, 26
Christian life, Calvin on, 43–45
Christian Nurture (Bushnell), 93
Christians
   depleted, 213–14, 217–21
   encountering the law, 164
   identity of, 65, 166–67
   learning from non-Christians, 164–65
   responding to ecosystems' deterioration, 188–89
   responsibility of, for the world, 85, 89–93, 93
Christian social engagement, 165
Christian social ethics, 134, 136–39, 161
Christian Worship in Reformed Churches (ed. Vischer), 7
Chrysostom, John, 78, 233
Church of Scotland, 203, 261–68. *See also* Scotland
   collapse of, 263, 267–68
   operation of, 335n8
   parish model in, 263–64
   UPA Churches and Ministries, 268–69
CI. *See* Christian Institute
Circle of Concerned African Women Theologians, 91
civil government, 164
civil religion, 101
civil responsibility, 29

civil rights movement, 119
Clapp, Rodney, 193
clergy sexual abuse, 96, 281–82
Cleveland, Christena, 23
climate change, 19, 30
clinical pastoral education, 248, 249
cloning, 145–46, 178, 203–6, 209, 328n26, 330n51
Cochrane, Charles Norris, 189
Cohen, Lizbeth, 199–200
Coles, Robert, 249
Cole-Turner, Ronald, 208
commodification, 193
common good, 19, 28–29, 151
   agreement on, 169–70
   Christian commitment to, 162–63
   climate change and, 30
   implausibility of, 162
   moral formation and, 170, 173
   pursuit of, in liberal societies, 166
common grace, 29, 146, 153, 159, 160, 165
Commoner, Barry, 181
"Common Reflection on Christian Worship in Reformed Churches Today, A," 237
communal justice, 194
communal lament, 51
communication
   church identity and, 166, 167
   religion's role in, 140–41
communitarianism, 152, 162, 168, 170
community, 172–73
   egalitarian view of, 66
   identity and, 66
   moral formation of, 170–74
   responsibility to, 91
   of spirits, 150
   survival of, 58
   worship demonstrating, 245
Community, Liberalism and Christian Ethics (Fergusson), 168–69
compassion, 216, 219, 220
competition, as value, 137
competitive piety, 13, 278
Cone, James, 91
Confessing Church, 255
Confessio Belgica, 130
confession, 216, 255
Confessio Tetrapolitana, 250
Confucianism, 158–59
congregations, inclusiveness of, 124

connected criticism, 104, 108
Conradie, Ernst, 30, 296n99
conscientia, 71
consumerism, 31–32, 58, 305n42
consumption, 32, 192–93. *See also* capitalism
   expansion of, 193
   practical theology of, 197
contextualization, 6, 49–50, 285, 290
contextual theology, 25, 285, 286
conviction, ethics of, 135
Cornick, David, 9, 12, 16, 250–52
cosmology, 57
costly commitment, 307n73
costly obedience, 307n73
costly unity, 307n73
Cottesloe Consultation, 100–101
covenant, theology of, 206
Cox, Harvey, 223
Craddock, Fred, 224
creation, 165, 176
   communal nature of, 187
   doctrine of, 29–20, 145, 194, 196, 198, 205, 296n99
   estrangement of, from God, 184–86
   ethics and, 146, 154
   gift of, 185–86, 188
   God's freedom and, 319n15
   God's preservation of, 78
   by humans, 198
   intelligibility of, 155
   justice and, 146
   new, 172–73
   order of, 146–48, 159, 168
   practical theology and, 154
   protection of, 146
   purpose of, 149–50
   redemption and, 21
   restoration of, 183, 184
   salvation and, 30, 186
   stories of, 319n21
   world religions and, 156–57
creationists, 318–19n15
Crittenden, Steve, 279
Cronon, William, 157–58
cross, the, 172–73
cultural industries, 62
cultural injustice, 59–62, 65–67
cultural justice, 19, 27–28, 54, 56
cultural mandate, 154–55
cultural values, 136–37

culture
  defined, 54–55
  fluidity of, 55
  globalization of, 54–56
  negotiation of, 55
  race and, 22
  threat to, 55
  transformation of, 22
Curl, Robert F., Jr., 201–2

Darwin, Charles, 150–51
Davie, Grace, 335n1
Davies, Susan, 4, 8, 24, 35
Declaration on Racism (General Council of the World Alliance of Reformed Churches), 131
de Gruchy, John, 10, 16, 40, 45, 49, 51, 101, 228–29
democracy, Christianity and, 140, 141
depersonalization, 56
development, 58
devil, control of, 78
de Villiers, Etienne, 10–11, 13, 22, 48, 49, 51
DeVries, Dawn, 231
dharmic law, 150
Dicker, Gordon, 286–87, 339–40n26
Different Mirror, A (Takaki), 118–19
dignity, 229–30
discourse ethics, 166–68, 321–22n29
discrimination, hidden, 23
disorder, 16, 35, 112, 158, 176, 180
distributive justice, 54
Disunity in Christ (Cleveland), 23
Dollard, John, 119
dominative racism, 294n61
Do No Harm (Ray), 117
double identity, 61
double vision, 45, 48
Douglas, Jane Dempsey, 90
Dovidio, John, 22–23
Dowey, Edward E., 70
drama aesthetic, 243, 245
dramaturgical models, worship and, 243
D'Souza, Dinesh, 197, 325n41
Dube, Musa, 93
Duns Scotus, 79
Durand, Jaap, 40
Durkheim, Émile, 305n39
Dutch Reformed Church, 10, 49–50, 100
  Beyers Naudé leaving, 102
  and biblical justification for apartheid, 131
  isolation of, 105
  opposition in, to South African policies, 101
  Reformed tradition in, 40–41
  Southern Transvaal Synod, 100, 101, 110
  struggling with its history, 110
  theocratic ideal of, 315–16n4
Dykstra, Craig, 17
Dyrness, William, 15, 287

early Christianity, 64, 196, 204
ecclesia reformata semper reformanda, 44, 87–88
Eck, Diana, 27
ecological crisis. *See* environmental crises
ecological-economic model, 31
ecological justice, 54
ecology, 145–46, 181
economic inequality, 199
economics, 20, 31–32, 192
ecosystem, degradation of, 180
ecumenism, 55–56, 100–101, 106, 163, 228
Education of a WASP, The (Stalvey), 123
Edwards, Jonathan, 159
election, doctrine of, 90, 95, 147
embryos
  discarding of, 329n43
  status of, 208–9
emergence, 226–27
Emerging Worship, 224
empirical theology, 47
emptiness, 150
energy, science of, 180
entropy, 180
environment, care for, 29–30
environmental crises, 175, 319n17
  causes of, 179–80
  as revelation, 175–76
epic theater, 243, 245
eschatology, 150, 151, 152, 295n84, 296n99
ethical imagination, 24
ethics, 5, 10
  biblically based, 165
  common theological bases for, 148
  contextuality of, 49–50
  ecumenical, 165
  in South Africa, 48–52

ethics (*continued*)
  theology and, 286
  thick vs. thin, 317n25
Ethics (Bonhoeffer), 249
eugenics, 33, 119, 205–6
Eurocentric worldview, 116
Europe, Reformed tradition's decline in, 14, 261
European Americans
  language of, for racial groups, 117–18
  resources for, on racism, 123–24
Evans, James, Jr., 21
evil, divine permission of, 79
evolution, 28, 145, 157, 319n
exclusion, 59–62, 75, 162
expository preaching, 229
expressive individualism, 133
extra-Calvinisticum, 75, 329n46
extraterrestrial life, 33

Facing the Truth, with Bill Moyers (dir. Pellett), 217
faith, 193
  Calvin's perspective on, 45
  conditional nature of, 253
  gift of, 94–95, 97
  grace and, 85, 93–96, 218
  language of, 280
  living tradition of, 11–12
  pastoral care and, 254–56
  pastor's perspective on, 254–57
  politics of, 284
  seeking understanding, 95, 96–97
  theology and, 12
  traditioning of, 14, 15
Faith and Politics Institute, 223
faiths, other, 19, 24–27
Faith Seeking Understanding (Migliore), 6
Faith and Wealth (González), 196
fall, the, 77, 78, 146, 176, 180–81, 182, 184–86
  racism and, 116
  significance of, 71
family, 207
Farley, Wendy, 116
farmland, chemical fertilization of, 179
federal theology, 206
feminism, fourth turning of, 223
feminist organizations, nonchurch, 90
feminist pastoral theology, 88, 91
feminist practical theology, 50–51
feminist theology, 92–93

Fergusson, David, 166, 168–70, 173, 202
fideism, 161
Firet, Jaap, 51
Fischer, Johannes, 138, 305n41
FitzSimons, Peter, 282
Flinders, Carol Lee, 223
forgiveness, 219
formation, 5
  of Christian community, 29
  cultural upbringing and, 5
  of pastor-theologians, 7
Forrester, Duncan, 110
Fortune, Marie, 96
Fosl, Catherine, 123
Foster, Charles, 123–24
Free Church of Scotland, 264–65
freedom, 155–56, 166
  absence of, in nature, 181
  in being children of God, 182–83
  in church life, 261
  liturgical, 238
  ordered, 7
  sin and, 117
Friedrich, Marcus A., 243–44
frugality, 194
functional values, 136–37

Gaertner, Samuel, 22–23
Gannon, Maartin J., 304n12
Garcia, Alberto, 286
Gascoigne, Robert, 166–70, 173
Geertz, Clifford, 54
Gemenne, François, 30
general revelation, 153
genetic engineering, 20, 146, 202
genetic research, 33
genetic testing, 206
Geneva Catechism, 42
genuineness, in performance, 243
geoengineering, 146
Gerrish, Brian, 231
GI Bill, 119
global Christianity, 295n80
global civil society, 148, 149
globalization, 13, 19, 24, 27–28, 44, 96, 140, 147, 148
  biblical perspectives on, 63–64, 66–67
  challenges of, 56–63, 65–67
  contradictions of, 56
  cosmology of, 28, 57
  as cultural force, 54–56, 133
  defined, 53

ideological nature of, 56
interdependence and, 149
as religion, 64
skepticism about, 53–54
global values, 64
global village, 54, 65, 307n75
God
   children of, 182–83
   churches prioritizing worship of, 261, 262
   corrupted knowledge of, 72
   as Creator, 152–56
   dethroning of, 151
   divine accommodation of, 208
   estrangement from, 183–86
   fatherhood of, and human families, 207
   freedom of, 78
   glorification of, 229–30
   healing power of, 85
   Hindu knowledge of, 74
   image of, 20–22, 71, 214–15, 219–21, 245
   Islamic knowledge of, 74
   knowing, 26, 42, 70–75, 146
   as Lord of history, 129
   love of, 77–78, 188
   mediated knowledge of, 74
   names for, 80
   populist understandings of, 279
   presence of, 71, 95, 240
   providence of, 76, 78, 80
   redemptive work of, 20
   as relativizer, 87, 88–89
   revelation of, 70–71, 74, 166, 208
   sovereignty of, 22, 24, 26, 76–81, 85, 87–89, 96, 112, 185, 230
   transcendence of, 74, 80
   will of, 70, 77, 79, 135
godlikeness, characteristics of, 214
God the Spirit (Welker), 226–27
Goffman, Erving, 242
González, Justo, 196, 197
Good Samaritan, parable of, 113, 122
Grabill, Stephen J., 320–21n8
grace, 76, 185, 188, 193, 205, 206, 218, 220. *See also* common grace
   divine covenant of, 206
   existence as gift of, 153
   faith and, 85, 93–96, 218
   predestination and, 78–79
Graham, Billy, 266

Graham, Elaine, 17
Grand United Theory, 202
gratitude, 185–86, 219
Greene, Graham, 258
Greenwald, Anthony, 23
Gregory, Brad S., 297n114
Gregory of Nyssa, 310n7
Grotowski, Jerzy, 243–44, 245
Group Areas Act, 100
Gustafson, James, 48
GUT. *See* Grand United Theory

Habits of the Heart (Bellah), 141
Hall, Douglas John, 12
Hamilton, Clive, 30
Haney, Elly, 97
Hardy, Daniel, 284
Harvard Diary (Coles), 249
Harvey, Jennifer, 23–24
Hauerwas, Stanley, 57, 161–62, 167, 168, 320n7
Hawking, Stephen, 202
Hays, Richard, 29, 163, 171, 172–73
healing, 51, 85, 86. *See also* justice healing
Heelas, Paul, 336n18
Heidelberg Catechism, 43, 66, 112, 216, 300n25
Heinzer, Ruedi, 235–36, 238
Heitink, Gerben, 51, 302n47
Hendry, George S., 181
Heschel, Abraham, 215
hierarchy, challenging of, 89
Hiltner, Seward, 111
Hindu tradition, 74, 295n85
   dharmic law of, 150
   God's sovereignty in, 80
   tolerance in, 26
history
   disruptions in, 150
   theology of, 145, 156
Hollenbach, David, 104, 109
Holy Spirit
   age of, 8, 224–27
   Bible and, 71–72
   change and, 226–27
   preaching and, 232–33
   presentation of, 240
homosexuality, 145–46, 288
hope, language of, 341n
Horrell, David, 321–22n29
households, nature of, 65, 66
Houston, Fleur, 9, 24

Howard, Ted, 180
h+, 33
Hulme, Mike, 30
humans
   alienation of, 156
   commodification of, 206
   as covenantal, 156
   creation by, 198
   cultural mandate of, 154–55
   dignity of, 21
   division in, 160
   estrangement of, from God, 184–86
   family relationships of, 207
   freedom of, 78
   made in God's image, 71, 78, 112, 113, 120–21, 123, 153, 155–56, 205, 213–15
   pollution and, 175–76
   relation with God, 206
   relation with nature, 30
humility, 219
Huntsman, Leone, 280
Hurley, Denis, 100
Hutchinson, Anne, 96
hybrid membership bodies, 266–67, 271
Hyma, Albert, 192, 195

identity
   community and, 58, 66
   fluidity of, 55, 119
   journey of, 58–59
   justice and, 27–28
   language and, 60–62
   national symbols of, 28
   positioning and, 3–4
   privileging of, 114–16
   renegotiation of, 60–62
   self-awareness about, 124
   symbols and, 62
   tensions from, 55
image, cultivation of, 241–42
imaginaries, 15–16, 35
imago Dei, corruption of, 165
incarnation, doctrine of, 286
inclusivity, 105–6, 124
India
   Calvin's doctrine and, 73–75, 80–82
   Calvin's influence in, 69–70
   mainline religious traditions in, 74, 80
   social conditions in, 81
individualism, 21, 58, 133, 141
Institute of African Women in Religion and Culture, 93

Institutes of the Christian Religion (Calvin), 41–42, 44, 69, 80, 231
interconnectedness, 24, 53–54, 184
interfaith dialogue, 25
intergenerational justice, 298n119
intergroup bias, 23
Irenaeus, 329n45
Islam, 74
   God's sovereignty in, 80
   primitive paradise of, 150
isolation, 151–52

Jakes, T. D., 224
Jarvis, Cynthia, 7, 20
Jim Crow, 119
Joas, Hans, 278
John Calvin's Doctrine of the Christian Life (Leith), 43
Jones, Serene, 42
Jonker, Willie, 40, 46–49, 51, 302n47
Joseph, Helen, 99
Julian of Norwich, 219
justice, 19, 54
   communal, 194
   creation and, 146
   healing and. *See* justice healing
   intergenerational, 298n119
   responsibility and, 136
justice healing, 86–87, 89, 97
justification, 250

Kang Phee Sang, 33
Kass, Leon, 209–10
Keet, Barend Bartholomeus, 312–13n4
Keillor, Garrison, 229
Kelly, Tony, 280
Kendall, R. T., 203
Kerr, Hugh, 3–6, 10, 13
Kilner, John, 21
Kim Jong-Huk, 30–31
King, Martin Luther, Jr., 120, 122
Kinghorn, Johan, 100
Kitcher, Philip, 205, 278
Klopper, Sandra, 306n62
knowledge, 42, 94
Kobia, Samuel, 56
Kohn, Rachael, 279
Kohut, Heinz, 330n3
van der Kooi, Cornelis, 72
Koopman, Nico, 48, 103
Korea, Christianity in, 159
Kotze, Theo, 102
Kovel, Joel, 22, 294n61

kragvelde, 40
Kraus, Hans-Joachim, 42
de Kruijf, Gerrit, 140, 141
Kunz, Ralph, 7–8, 9
Kuyper, Abraham, 41, 45, 49, 146–47, 151–55, 157, 159, 318n13
Kwenda, Chirebo, 55, 59

language
  in Australia, 339n25
  human creation of, 88
  identity and, 60–62
  race and, 113, 117–18
  social sin and, 117
  trust in, 88
Laudato Si' (Francis), 18
law, 165
lay religious organizations, 265
leadership, 261, 262
Lears, Jackson, 193
Lectures on Calvinism (Kuyper), 146–47
Leith, John, 5, 11, 14, 16, 19, 20, 42, 43, 45, 87, 228, 248, 258–59, 301n31
Letters and Papers from Prison (Bonhoeffer), 256
Lévi-Strauss, Claude, 56
Lewis, Alan, 262
liberal guilt, 90
liberalism, 162, 166, 170
Liberating Faith Practices (ed. Ackermann and Bons-Storm), 50
Liberating Reformed Theology (de Gruchy), 40
liberation theology, 96, 111, 148, 154
Link, Christian, 262–63
liturgical movement, 239
liturgical pluralism, 236
liturgy
  freedom and, 238
  participation in, 244, 245
  pauper's theater and, 234, 244, 245
  structure of, 238–39
  truth in, 243
local congregations
  as activist membership institutions, 264–65
  competing with commercial leisure, 266
  as hybrid membership bodies, 266–67
  as leisure centers, 265–66
  as membership bodies, 263, 264–65
  new model for, 271–74
  secularization and, 263
  sustainability of, 263–64

Loff, Christiaan, 40
loose connections, culture of, 272–73
Lord's Supper, service for, 239–40
Lorde, Audre, 91
Louw, Daniel J., 51, 302–3n47
loyalty, 105
Luther, Martin, 14, 69, 73, 96, 195, 231, 307n75
Lutheranism, two-kingdom approach, 134
Lysaught, Therese, 33–34

MacFadyen, Alistair, 286
Macintyre, Alasdair, 41
Maluleke, Tinyiko Sam, 60
Mandela, Nelson, 99
Manifest Destiny, 96
market capitalism, 31
Marty, Martin, 104
Marvin, Ernest, 8
Marxism, 150, 159
Mashinini, Emma, 99
Matheson, Peter, 15, 16, 282–84, 286
Matsuoka, Fumitaka, 120
Maushart, Susan, 281, 340n30
McCann, Dennis P., 47
McFague, Sallie, 31, 32, 297n100, 297n109
McKee, Elise, 93, 239
McKim, Donald, 94, 278
McNeill, John T., 252
Mead, G. H., 227
media, Christian views in, 142
medialization, 241–42
mediation, 74, 187
Meilaender, Gilbert, 209
membership bodies, 263, 264–65
meritocracy, 116–17
Messer, Neil, 33, 34
metanoia, 256
Metzger, Paul Louis, 285
microaggressions, 23
Midler, Bette, 224
Migliore, Daniel, 6, 16, 285
migrants
  fear of, 24–25
  status of, 119
migration, 27
Millar, David, 27
ministry of all believers, 263
missionaries, 25–26, 69, 81, 193
Mizos, 74, 81
modernism, 147, 225

modernity, 15, 33, 57, 142
modernization, 140, 148–49
Mofokeng, Takatso, 40
Moltmann, Jürgen, 132
Moody, Dwight L., 265
moral authority, 108
moral covenants, 138
moral discourse, 48
moral formation, 64, 163, 170–74
morality, thick vs. thin, 317n25
moral realism, 169
moral values, 136–37
moral vision, images for, 172–73
Moral Vision of the New Testament, The (Hays), 171
Moran, Anthony, 285
mortification, 213–14
Mouton, A. E. J., 51
Mouw, Richard J., 165, 170, 320n2
mudsill, 119
Muers, Rachel, 33, 298n119
Muhammad, 74
Mullen, Deborah, 93
Muller, Richard A., 12–13, 41
Müller, Theophil, 236
multiculturalism, 27, 55–56, 124
Müntzer, Thomas, 96
Murchison, Cameron, 31, 32
Murray, Les, 278–79
music, in worship, 244–45

narcissism, 217–18
narrative ethics, 57
national church, 15
nationalism, 89, 106, 130–31, 147
natural law, 145, 146, 153, 164, 166, 168–70, 173, 321n17
natural order, intervention in, 158–59
natural revelation, 321n17
natural selection, 157
natural theology, 145, 153, 169
nature
  belief in, 157
  divided against itself, 159–60
  God's revelation in, 71, 74
  open system of, 29
  relationship of, with humanity, 30
  structure of, 176–77
Naudé, Beyers, 10, 311
  banning of, 102–3, 107–8
  inclusiveness of, 105–6
  life of, 99–105
  moral authority of, 108
  as public theologian, 104–10
Naudé, Ilse, 103, 107
Naudé, Piet, 24, 27–28, 40, 48, 49, 50
Nederduitsch Hervormde Kerk, 101
neighbor
  love of, 112, 113, 122–23
  two-tiered perspective on, 115, 116, 117
Nelson, Benjamin, 325n32
Neo-Calvinism, 160
Neo-Hinduism, 74
New Testament
  moral formation and, 171
  moral vision of, 163
  tension in, 171–72
NHK. *See* Nederduitsch Hervormde Kerk
Niebuhr, H. Richard, 45, 57
Niebuhr, Reinhold, 45, 318n14, 319n20
Nietzsche, Friedrich, 219
Nirguna Brahman, 74
Njoroge, Nyambura, 93
Noble, T. A., 70
noblesse oblige, 89–90
nones, 278
nontheist views, 157–58
normativity, discovery of, 149
notae ecclesiae, 263
Ntoane, Lekula, 40
nuclear transportation technology, 178–79
Nydam, Ronald, 330n3

O'Donovan, Oliver, 34, 203
Old, Hughes Oliphant, 229, 231
open system, life as, 157
oral culture, welcoming in, 3
Origen, 78
original sin, 112, 117, 120, 339n23
Other
  aesthetics of, 306n62
  attending to, 122
  categorizing, 24
  commodification of, 112
  naming of, 60–61
  prejudice and, 24–25
  subjugation of, 62
Outler, Albert, 43
Oxford Handbook of Christianity and Economics, The (ed. Oslington), 32

PAC. *See* Pan Africanist Congress
Pan-Africanist Congress, 100, 132

Panikkar, Raimondo, 75
paraenesis, 220
parish ministry, 91–92
pastoral care, 111–12, 214, 249–59
   faith and, 254–56
   globalization and, 19
   preaching and, 20, 251–52, 258
   process of, 258
   psychology and, 112, 250, 255
   Reformed understanding of, 20
   Scripture and, 258
   visitation and, 253–54
pastoral ministry, 221, 247–48
pastoral theology, 85–86, 111–12
   healing and, 87
   as interdisciplinary enterprise, 112
   public policy and, 112
   responsibility of, 86, 87, 89, 92
pastors, spiritual care of, 256–57
pastor-theologian, formation of, 7
paternalism, 295n84
patristics, Calvin and, 73, 78–79
Pattison, Stephen, 293n42
Pears, Angie, 286
Pearson, Clive, 13, 15, 30
Pelagianism, 230
Pelagius, 77
Pence, Gregory, 205
Pentecostalism, 223, 224, 225, 318n13
personhood, 21
phenomenological theology, 47
Phiri, Isabel, 93
Pieterse, Hennie, 46
Pighus, 77
Plantinga, Cornelius, Jr., 20–21
pluralism, 26, 123, 124, 133, 152, 170
   liturgical, 236
   public theology for, 154
plurality, 135
Plüss, David, 236
pneumatology, emergence in, 226
Political Economy of Transition, The (Addy and Silny), 62
political structures, 88–89
Politik als Beruf (*Politics as a Vocation*; Weber), 135
pollution, 175–76
positioning, 3–4, 13, 17, 19, 21
postapartheid memory, 10
postcolonial world, 25, 142–43
Postema, Don, 185–86
posthumanism, 33
postliberation struggles, 60

Postman, Neil, 242
postmodernism, 57, 147, 149, 225
postsecular, 338n14
post(trans)human, 20
Powell, Ruth, 289
Power to Comprehend with All the Saints, The (ed. Alston and Jarvis), 7
practical theology, 5, 10, 13, 17
   Catholic approach to, 17–18
   characteristics of, 46–47
   of consumption, 197
   concerns of, 17
   defined, 17
   feminist voices in, 50
   public, 104, 108
   Reformed theology and, 191, 194
   in South Africa, 46–48, 50–52
   zombie categories in, 19
preaching, 224
   embodied, 233–34
   globalization and, 19
   and the Holy Spirit, 232–33
   intent of, 8
   pastoral care and, 20, 251–52
   priority of, 8
   in the Reformed tradition, 227–30, 233–34
   sacramental act of, 230–32
   theology and, 19
predestination, 26, 76, 78–79. 90, 150, 326n6
preembryo research, 330n53
preimplantation genetic diagnosis, 206
Prejudice, Discrimination, and Racism (Dovidio and Gaertner), 22
premodernism, 147
Presbyterian Church (U.S.A.), 43, 112, 224
priesthood of all believers, 205, 263
primal order, restoration of, 158
primal religions, 150
privatization, 62
privilege, 114–16, 121
Pro Veritate (campus newspaper), 100
Pro Veritate (journal), 101–2, 106, 109–10
process theology, 111
Programme to Combat Racism (WCC), 108
prophetic cult critique, 242
Protestant ethic, 193, 196–97
Protestant Ethic and the Spirit of Capitalism, The (Weber), 31, 191

Protestants
  status of, 283
  suffering of, 76–77, 80
providence, 78, 165, 169
psychology, pastoral theology and, 112
Public Forum and Christian Ethics, The (Gascoigne), 166–68
public policy, pastoral theology and, 112
public theology, 29, 103–4, 108–10, 112, 149, 152, 154
Puritans, 118
Purvis, Andrew, 253, 254

race
  culture and, 22
  doctrine of, 147
  language and, 113, 117–18
  as social construction, 117
racial identity, fluidity of, 119
racial identity development theory, 124
racism, 19, 21–24, 294n61. *See also* apartheid
  aversive, 22–24, 115–16
  class interests and, 120
  deconstructing, 123
  dehumanizing effect of, 120–21
  in employment, 113–14
  European Americans' definition of, 114, 116
  falsehood of, 116–17
  health outcomes and, 23
  history of, in the US, 118–20
  interruption of, 120
  learning of, 115–16
  neighbor love and, 115–17, 122
  predestination and, 90
  as sin, 112, 113, 116, 117, 120
  systemic, 114–16
  unconscious, 23
  wound of, 121
Rahner, Karl, 231
Raiser, Konrad, 54, 55–56
Raj, Victor, 286
Ramsay, Nancy, 5, 22–23, 24, 35
Randall, Peter, 99, 101–3
Rasmussen, Larry, 57
rationalization, 116
Ray, Stephen, 117
Reader, John, 13, 19
realism, ontological, 169, 170, 173
reason, knowing God through, 73
reciprocity, 32
reconciliation, 184–86, 188, 189

Reconstruction and Development Program (African National Congress), 139
redemption, 21, 160, 176, 182–83, 187–88, 205, 213, 214–15, 219
Reformation
  effecting a shift in reality, 283
  iconopoiac energies in, 15, 16, 19
  legacy of, 297n114
  worship service changes during, 242
Reformed churches
  declining number of, 261
  reforming of, 261–62, 264
Reformed ethics, 5, 10, 16, 19–20
  responsibility of, 139–40
  in South Africa, 49
  as vocation, 129–30
Reformed faith
  characteristics of, 43
  defined, 278
  symbols of, 284
Reformed identity, liturgy and, 236–38
Reformed imaginary, 16, 18, 19, 21, 27, 34
Reformed Imperative, The (Leith), 248
Reformed mission, outcomes of, 25–26
Reformed Pastor, The (Baxter), 253–54
Reformed theology, 49, 52, 202–3
  for Australia, 286–90
  capitalism and, 96
  as liberating theology, 40
  practical theology and, 191, 194
  world religions and, 149
Reformed tradition
  apartheid and, 10–11, 12, 28, 131
  and the common good debate, 163
  cultural transformation and, 22
  decline of, in Europe, 14
  dignity and, 229–30
  diversity in, 12, 13
  emphases of, 4
  ethics and, 39–41
  healing of, 96–97
  identity and, 5, 6, 10, 52
  influence of, 160
  leadership in, 261–62
  as living tradition, 41
  openness of, 14
  other faiths and, 25, 27
  pastoral care in, 249–59
  practical theology and, 5, 10, 16, 19–20, 39–41
  preaching and, 8–9, 225, 227–30, 233–34

relevance of, 19
shared, 17
social ethics and, 146
spiritual direction and, 253
strengths of, 13–14
on the Trinity, 329n46
transformation approach of, 129–30, 132–34
trust in, 87
Reformed worship, 7–9, 14–15
characteristics of, 236–38
identity of, 235–36
reflecting image of God, 245
Word and Sacrament in, 332n20
Zurich liturgy and, 238–39
Reforming Worship (ed. Riglin, Templeton, and Tilby), 7, 9
relationality, 4, 112, 182–83
relationship, faith and, 94
religion
antisystemic role of, 140–41
consumerism and, 32
globalization and, 148
in postcolonial societies, 143
privatization of, 142–43
production of, 241
role of, 57, 140–41
religious diversity, 27
religious experiences, shift in, 273
repentance, 218–21
reproductive techniques, development in, 203
responsibility, 78, 89–93, 135–36
resurrection, 215
revelation, environmental crises as, 175–76
revivalism, 193
Rice, Howard, 234
Richmond Parish Church (Church of Scotland), 268–74
Ricoeur, Paul, 9
Rifkin, Jeremy, 180
Riglin, Keith, 7, 8, 9
Rittel, Horst, 296n94
Robertson, John A., 205
Rochelle, Jay, 255
Rodriguez, Richard, 61–62
Roman Empire, 63–64, 189
round table, theology at, 6
Russell, Letty, 6, 92

SACC. *See* South African Council of Churches

SACLA. *See* South African Christian Leadership Assembly
sacramentality, 230–31
salvation, 149–52, 165, 216, 250
Buddhist idea of, 158
children and, 93
creation and, 30, 186
doctrine of, 296n99
God's sovereignty and, 76
grace and, 79
healing and, 86
predestination and, 78
theology of, 145
varying views of, 153
Samartha, S. J., 75
Sankey, Ira D., 265
Schlebusch Commission (South Africa), 106
Schleiermacher, Friedrich, 17
Schneider, John R., 32, 197–200, 324–25n26
scholastics, 73, 78, 79
Schreiter, Robert, 286
Schweiker, William, 137
science, 155, 180, 210, 318–19n15
Scotland. *See also* Church of Scotland
churches reuniting in, 266
dissenting churches in, 264–65
evangelism in, 266
home mission in, 266
suburban churches in, 265
Scripture. *See also* Bible; New Testament
Christian ethics and, 33
divine revelation and, 74
pastoral care and, 258
preaching and, 229–30
primacy of, 74–75
reliance on, 8, 9
Second Helvetic Confession, 228
Second Vatican Council, 239, 242
sectarianism, 134, 164
secularization, 50, 142, 263, 336n18
self
depleted, 20–21, 331
emptying of, 217
and image of God, 20–21
reconstruction of, 58
self-fulfillment, 193
sensus divinitatis, 71
sermon, place of, in Reformed worship, 9
sexual orientation, and ministerial leadership, 284
Shakespeare, William, 118

Index

Sherlock, Charles, 279
Shezzi, Tandy, 217
Sider, J. Alexander, 320n7
Silny, Jiri, 62
Simons, Robert, 104
sin, 112, 146, 165. *See also* original sin; social sin
   brokenness of, 339n23
   confession of, 216
Singer, Peter, 205–6, 319n18
Sisters in the Wilderness (Williams), 93
Sisulu, Albertina, 99
Sisulu, Walter, 99
Sixty-Seven Theses (Zwingli), 251–52
slavery, 118–19
Smart, Ninian, 57
Smit, Dirk, 10–13, 18, 109, 293n
Smith-Christopher, Daniel L., 320n7
Snyder, Susanna, 24–25
social change, 226
social engineering, 146
social ethics, 11, 29, 320n
social imaginaries, 15–16
social involvement, 163
sociality, 21
social justice, 19, 27–28
social sin, 112, 117
social structures, 88–89
society
   Christianization of, 134–35
   humanization of, 135
   transformation of, 129–30, 132–34
   transitional, 57–58
solidarity, 325n32
Sölle, Dorothee, 104–5
South Africa. *See also* apartheid; Naudé, Beyers
   activists in, 99
   as African society, 142
   as Christian country, 130–31
   Christian social ethics in, 136
   Christian social vision for, 137–39
   church-state separation in, 133, 141–42
   confessing church in, 101
   Cottesloe resolutions in, 100–101
   Dutch Reformed Church in, 100. *See also* Dutch Reformed Church
   ethics in, 48–52
   identity reconstruction in, 60
   individualism in, 133
   loyalty in, in Afrikaner society, 105
   moral discourses in, 48–49
   multiethnicity of, 147
   Nationalist government of, 131
   pluralism in, 133
   practical theology in, 46–48, 50–52
   public theology in, 103–4
   reading Calvin through, 41–42
   Reformed tradition in, 10–11, 12, 39–41, 130
   religion's importance in, 141–42
   secularization in, 50
   Sharpeville massacre in, 100
   social structures modernized in, 133
   Truth and Reconciliation Commission, 132
South African Christian Leadership Assembly, 138
South African Council of Churches, 103
South African Council of Human Science Research, 46
South African Students Organization, 102
Spirit and the Forms of Love, The (Williams), 121–22
spirits, community of, 150
Spiritual Care (Bonhoeffer), 255
spiritual resources, phenomena of, 225
spontaneity, in worship, 7
Stackhouse, Max, 28–29, 32
staging, 241–42
Stalvey, Lois, 123
Stanislavsky, Konstantin, 243, 244
state
   Christian relation to, 171–72
   idealized, 151
   as institution of God, 130
   purpose of, 316n15
Stevens, William R., 321n10
Storrar, William, 5, 14–15
Strain, Charles R., 47
Strothmann, Hermann, 252
Stroup, George, 228
Subversive Southerner (Fosl), 123
Sue, Derald Wing, 23
suffering, 160
   endurance of, 189
   love and, 122
   taking on others', 216
Sullivan, Andrew, 162
superwicked problems, 30, 296n94
Swiss Federation of Protestant Churches, 7

Swiss Protestants, worship by, 235–36
symbols
   culture and, 54–55
   identity and, 62
   US government's use of, 89
systematic theology, 47

Tacey, David, 279, 338–39n20
Takaki, Ronald, 118–19
Tatum, Beverly, 124
Taylor, Charles, 15–16
Tayob, Abdulkader, 142
technology, 201
   ecosystems and, 179
   proficiency in, 155
   Reformed approach to, 19
Tell Scotland movement, 266
temperance, 194
Tempest, The (Shakespeare), 118
Templeton, Julian, 7, 8, 9
Thales of Miletus, 66
theocentrism, 112
theodicy, 296n99
theologia practica, 41, 42, 46
theological anthropology, 77
theological change, 226
theological ethics, 32–34, 48, 51
theological realism, 301n31
theological reflection, 17
theology. *See also* contextual theology; empirical theology; federal theology; feminist pastoral theology; feminist practical theology; feminist theology; liberation theology; natural theology; pastoral theology; phenomenological theology; practical theology; process theology; public theology; Reformed theology; systematic theology
   critical correlation approach to, 104
   ecological rendering of, 296n99
   economics and, 192
   ethics and, 286
   evolution and, 28
   faith and, 12
   globalization and, 53–54
   of history, 145, 156
   moral future of, 284
   new forms of, 91
   realistic, 45
   at the round table, 6
   of salvation, 145
   science and, 210
   self-conscious, 285
   self-secularization and, 51
   speculation in, 301n31
Theology of the Reformed Confessions, The (Barth), 250
Thiemann, Ronald, 104, 108
Thomas Aquinas, 79
Thompson, Geoff, 29
Tilby, Angela, 7, 8
Tillich, Paul, 208, 319n20
Timken, William, 305n42
Torrance, James, 328n23
Torrance, Thomas F., 45, 208–9
totalitarianism, 64
Townes, Emilie, 93
Tracy, David, 50, 57, 104
traditioning, 14, 15, 16
transcendence, 34, 157, 158
transconfessionalism, 13, 278
transformation approach, 129–30, 132–34, 143
transhumanism, 33
transitional society, 57–58, 305n37
Transvaal Dutch Reformed Church, 101
tribalism, 152
tribal religious traditions, in India, 81
Trinity
   language for, 88
   liturgical emphasis on, 237
   participation of, in creation, 186
   relations within, 207
Troubling in My Soul, A (Townes), 93
Truth and Reconciliation Commission (South Africa), 217
Tutu, Desmond, 99, 103
two-kingdom approach, 134

United Presbyterians (Scotland), 264–65
United States
   capitalism in, 199–200
   census forms in, 119
   Christian symbols and, 89
   ethnoconfessional communitarianism in, 152
   moral values in, 141
   multiethnicity of, 147
   neoimperialism of, 147–48
   racism in, 113–14, 117–20
Uniting Church (Australia), 163, 286–87, 337–38n12
urban priority areas (UPAs), 269

usury, 136, 138, 195
utilitarian individualism, 133, 141

values, collapse of, 57–58
Vanlalauva, Hmar, 25–27
van Ruler, A. A., 45
Verhey, Allen, 307n69
Verwoerd, H. F., 100, 101
Virginia, colony of, 118–19
Vischer, Lukas, 7, 236–37
vivification, 213–14
Volf, Miroslav, 59, 60

Waakzaam en nuchter (Vigilant and levelheaded; de Kruijf), 140
Waander, D. W., 95
Wall, Jim, 229
Wallace, Ronald S., 44–45
Walshe, Peter, 100
Walton, Heather, 17
Wandel, Lee Palmer, 239–40
Wannamaker, John, 193
Ward, Francis, 17
water, characteristics of, 177–78
Waters, Brent, 33
Watson, Don, 279–80, 339n25
Watson, James, 209
WCC. *See* World Council of Churches
wealth
    accumulation of, 194
    creation of, 197–98
    purpose of, 31–32
We Are the Church Together (Foster and Brelsford), 123
Webber, Melvin, 296n94
Weber, Max, 31, 135–36, 191–94, 196
Weber, Otto, 220
Weinrich, Michael, 87–88
welcoming, practice of, 3, 5
Welker, Michael, 5, 6, 17, 45, 51, 53–54, 57, 64, 226–27
Well, Deane, 205–6
Westminster Confession, 202–3
White, Lynn, Jr., 319n16
Whitehead, Alfred North, 226, 227
whiteness, 117, 118
"Why Are All the Black Kids Sitting Together in the Cafeteria?" And

Other Conversations about Race (Tatum), 124
wicked problems, 30, 296n94
van Wijk-Bos, Johanna, 97
Wilcox, Cathy, 281
Wilder, Amos, 223, 224
William of Ockham, 79
Williams, Daniel Day, 121–22, 124–25
Williams, Delores, 93
Williams, Rowan, 322n54
Wilmut, Ian, 209
Wilson, Paul Scott, 230
Wolfteich, Claire, 17–18
Wolters, Albert, 287
Woman's Guild (Scotland), 265
Woodhead, Linda, 25, 336n18
Woodward, James, 293n42
work, fundamental nature of, 194
World Alliance of Reformed Churches, 43, 131, 300n25
World Council of Churches, 100–101, 108
world religions
    creation and, 156–57
    Reformed theology and, 149
worship
    aesthetics and, 235, 239
    critical interest in, 242
    demonstrating community, 245
    dramaturgical models for, 243
    practice of, 224
    primacy of, 14–15
    as production, 239–41
    reform of, 242
    spontaneity in, 7
    theatricality of, 7
    theology of, 239
    Zwinglian approach to, 235
Wuthnow, Robert, 198, 270, 272–73

Yaconelli, Mark, 223
Yoido Full Gospel Church (Seoul), 224

Zihlangu, Mama, 99
Zurich liturgy, 238–39
Zwingli, Ulrich, 7, 96, 235, 239, 242, 244, 251–52, 258
Zwinglian worship, 235, 239–40

p. 119-120 60p
122   Roy B
"if could ab T - what would happen
                        to him
your humanity in pail

CPSIA information can be obtained
at www.ICGtesting.com
Printed in the USA
FFOW03n2343220917
40171FF